Advances in Information and Communication Research

Volume 2

Series Editor

Hitoshi Mitomo, Graduate School of Asia-Pacific Studies, Waseda University, Tokyo, Japan

This book series focuses on socioeconomic aspects of information and communication. Information and communication technology (ICT) is now indispensable as an infrastructure supporting the advancement of society. ICT has benefited modern civilization, and its influence has spread over numerous aspects of our life and economy. Along with technological progress, much has happened in this arena, with new developments continuing at a rapid pace.

Constructive use of ICT makes our society more efficient. On the other hand, however, inappropriate use of ICT causes serious social problems that have not been experienced until now. In such a rapidly changing area, our attention tends to be drawn to superficial phenomena rather than gaining deep insight into them. In order to understand the role of ICT in modern life, social science is essential for capturing the impact of the development of networks and the advancement of information and communication services and applications. Social sciences shed light on a variety of issues and provide a framework for promoting the utilization of ICT while avoiding the potential drawbacks.

The series Advances in Information and Communication Research helps to provide academics, government officials, and practitioners with the information and expertise necessary for understanding social phenomena and making policies appropriate for those new trends. Many ideas and suggestions are offered that are practical not only in the developed world but that can be applied in developing nations as well. In emerging countries ICT is highly anticipated as a means of improving the quality of life, promoting economic growth, and bridging the gaps among people and regions.

Readers will gain deep insight into the impacts of utilizing ICT in diverse societies. Interdisciplinary approaches help in understanding how those influences can be captured both qualitatively and quantitatively through studies stemming from various social sciences — economics, sociology, legal studies, media studies, marketing, regional studies, socioeconomic planning, and other relevant disciplines.

More information about this series at http://www.springer.com/series/16002

Minoru Sugaya
Editor

Perspectives on the Japanese Media and Content Policies

Springer

Editor
Minoru Sugaya
Keio University
Tokyo, Japan

ISSN 2524-3322 ISSN 2524-3330 (electronic)
Advances in Information and Communication Research
ISBN 978-981-15-4703-4 ISBN 978-981-15-4704-1 (eBook)
https://doi.org/10.1007/978-981-15-4704-1

This Springer imprint is published by the registered company Springer Nature Singapore Pte Ltd.
The registered company address is: 152 Beach Road, #21-01/04 Gateway East, Singapore 189721, Singapore

Preface

Media and media contents have had a dynamic influence on human affairs around the globe politically, economically, and socially. In this era of globalization and atmosphere of societal uncertainties, the roles played by media, the functions of media and the contents of media rather than decrease should increase. Technologically speaking, the penetration of digitalization in daily-life matters and the pronounced impacts of the Internet, continue to rapidly restructure the environment in and around media, a notable facet of this is the almost complete disappearance of the difference in penetrating power between broadcasting and other forms of contents distribution. Moreover, amateurs now are empowered to create their own digital contents and can easily access distribution windows using tools more powerful than those in the hands of professional broadcasters. From an industrial perspective, online-platforms are surpassing the platforms of historic media companies and are actively promoting mergers and acquisitions as well as global deployment. This situation is not endemic to other peoples and other lands; it is equally applicable to Japan. With the changes and uncertainties we are facing today induced by 'borderless media,' policies must by necessity change and become very much the objects of everyone's sharply focused attention.

The appropriate and adequate policies cannot be neither considered nor realized without discussion of a global perspective in the digital and Internet era. In order to do this in Japan, a global awareness of Japan's policies as well as intensive communication with global scholars and researchers is necessary.

In this context, on the occasion of the 35th anniversary of The Japan Society of Information and Communication Research, we have the ambitious intention to review industries and the policies and contents of Japanese media in a structured manner. Because the interests and scope of media and contents are extremely broad, this challenging objective is a difficult one to achieve. Still, we hope that our efforts will contribute to a keener insight into the situations and policies of media and contents in Japan.

This book is not simply a presentation of a history of policies. Based on the findings of the comprehensive survey of situations and trends applying to Japanese industries and associated policies applying to media and contents, we discuss the future development of topics from a global perspective. In concrete terms, we have focused sharply on broadcasting and content policies in this work, which consists of 13 chapters: Chapters "Terrestrial Broadcasting" through "Community Radio Broadcasting" are devoted to broadcasting issues, Chapters "Film and the Other Video Contents (TV program and Internet Video)" through "Copyright Clearance" to content issues, and Chapters "Over-the-Top (OTT) Video Service" and "Assistance for International Coproductions and Overseas Broadcasts of Japanese Broadcast Content" to OTT (over-the-top) and global promotion of Japanese broadcast contents as horizontal issues.

Regarding broadcasting, Chapter "Terrestrial Broadcasting" (Jun Inoue) gives a general view of terrestrial broadcasting policy. As highlighted in this chapter, the dual system of public and commercial broadcasting is characteristic in Japan. Knowledge of public and commercial broadcasting is essential to an understanding of Japanese policies. Chapter "The Japanese Public Broadcaster NHK and Its Related Policy: The Origin of Public Broadcasting and Changing Policy Environment in the Digital Transformation" (Tsutomu Kanayama) discusses public broadcasting, NHK (Nippon Hoso Kyokai), and provides an in-depth historic overview and current trends. Chapter "The Developmental Process of Commercial Television Broadcasting Industry" (Minoru Sugaya) analyzes commercial broadcasting by presenting its development in five stages and collaborations with online businesses. In addition to terrestrial broadcasting, satellite broadcasting is a basic and essential medium in Japan with a 30-year service history; in 2018, the industry introduced new-technology 4K/8K broadcasting. Chapter "Policy on Satellite Broadcasting" (Yuichiro Ogawa) discusses satellite broadcasting policy. Broadcasting under the policy delivers not only national contents but also local contents. Cable Television and community FM broadcasting play a crucial role airing local information, including sharing news common to regional areas. Chapter "Cable Television" (Nami Yonetani) discusses Cable Television and its role in Japan as a local-oriented service. And Chapter "Community Radio Broadcasting" (Tomoko Kanayama) focuses on community FM broadcasting and its significant public-safety roles in times of natural disasters.

Regarding contents, we present four areas—film, animation and pop culture, games and music—that are strategically indispensable for the Japanese contents industry. An activity indicating the importance of the selected areas is their promotion by the Visual Industry Promotion Organization (VIPO), a nonprofit organization for public and private partnerships promoting the global competitiveness of such creations. Regarding film, Chapter "Film and the Other Video Contents (TV program and Internet Video)" (Takashi Uchiyama) analyzes Japanese policies for film, presents comparisons with European policies, and points out the weakness of the Japanese system. Regarding animation, Chapter "Anime's Economic Value: the Government's Response to a Changing Environment" (Mariko Koizumi) reviews the history of policies for animation and stresses the need to create animations that mirror a global perspective and vision. Regarding games, Chapter "Video Games: the Once Sustainable Industry is in Need of Policy" (Mariko Koizumi) details how policy resources have been less spent on games compared with animation while the Japanese game industry was internationally competitive by itself; the chapter alerts that with the emergence of online games, the competitiveness of the Japanese game industry is shrinking, making policy revitalization a high-priority in this sector. Concerning music, Chapter "Music" (Stevie Yoshida) overviews the transitions of business models and practices as well as the education, cultural and competition policies and profiles how the transitions are influenced by technological change. As a common issue for contents, Chapter "Copyright Clearance" (Yu Terada) considers the state of real-life copyright clearance from a business perspective and lessons learned through experience; further, it reveals the "walls" as practical obstructions and presents realistic solutions with categorized content types

Last but certainly not least, we must look at the global perspective from a horizontal point of view. Chapter "Over-the-Top (OTT) Video Service" (Yoko Nishioka) analyzes the current situation of OTT services, a key platform delivering content, and reviews policies that look to the future. Chapter "Assistance for International Coproductions and Overseas Broadcasts of Japanese Broadcast Content" (Masahiko Komiya) introduces the policies promoting joint international production of the contents of broadcasting and airing them abroad.

While this work is primarily aimed at academic scholars and researchers, it also presents useful data and information that will be interesting to people who have a general interest in the media and media contents of Japan. Finally, as a project editor, I wish to thank the authors of the chapters for their penetrating insights, and Jun Inoue who contributed greatly to this works not only as a chapter author but also as a co-editor.

Tokyo, Japan Minoru Sugaya

Acknowledgements

This book is published as the first volume in the book series of the Japan Society of Information and Communication Research (JSICR). JSICR, as an academic organization focusing on Japanese media and content policies, is making an international contribution to the enhancement of ICT. This volume, together with the previous volume focusing on policies and socio-economic aspects of ICT, is commemorating the publication of this series. Publication of this book would not have been possible without the cooperation of MIC.

The editor is also indebted to KDDI Research, Inc. for their assistance to the publication of this book.

Contents

Editor and Contributors

About the Editor

Minoru Sugaya is a Visiting Professor of Media Policy and Economics at Hakuoh University, Oyama, Japan and also an Emeritus Professor at Keio University, Tokyo, Japan. B. A. at Keio University, M.A. at International Christian University, M.A. at Michigan State University, and Ph.D. at International Christian University in 1988. He was visiting researcher at the Kennedy School at Harvard University in 1991 and at Michigan State University in 1992. In 1998, he was in the department of communication at the University of Hawaii as a Fulbright senior researcher. He has published and edited number of books including Pacific Island Regional and International Cooperation: ICT Policy and Development (2013 in Japanese and 2015 in English), The Transformation of Telecommunication Regulatory Structure in Japan, Keio Communications Review (2009), Video Content Industry and Film Policy (2009 in Japanese), Digital Content in the age of Transnational (2007 in Japanese), the Media Content Distribution in the East Asia (2005 in Japanese and Korean), Economics of Broadcasting Media (2000 in Japanese and Korean), and Media Industry Policy in the United States (1997 in Japanese). He has served as several government committee members and chairpersons in the area of universal service, cable television, and media convergence policies. In 2006, Former Minister of Ministry of Internal Affairs and Communications, Mr. Takenaka, designated him as a member of his study group on the future of telecommunication and broadcasting. He is also former President of the Japan Association of Information and Communication Research.

Contributors

Jun Inoue is an Associate Professor (Visiting Researcher) at the Institute of Journalism, Media and Communications, Keio University, Tokyo, Japan. He earned a Master of Public Policy Analysis from University of Rochester, U.S. in 1999. In

1996 he joined the Ministry of Posts and Telecommunications (former Ministry of Internal affairs and Communications). He has served as Director of International ICT R&D collaboration, Director of ICT global strategy, etc. He has published several articles in The Japan Society of Information and Communication Research Journal.

Masahiko Kamiya has been Deputy Director to the Counselor in the Cabinet Secretariat's National Strategy Office of Information and Communication Technology since July 2019. In his current position, he is charged with stipulation of the national ICT strategy and the basic plan for data utilization, which is approved by the cabinet. In his previous role as Deputy Director in the Promotion for Content Distribution Division of the Ministry of Internal Affairs and Communications (MIC), he advanced global deployment of Japanese broadcasting content and its industry.

Tomoko Kanayama is a Professor of Institute of Advanced Media Arts and Sciences [IAMAS] and Director of Research Center for Industrial Culture of IAMAS. B.A. at Keio University, M.A. at Ohio University, M.S. Syracuse University, and Ph. D. at Ohio University in Mass Communication. Her research mainly focuses on community and communication, and the citizen empowerment and media. She has published 12 authored/co-authored books including Media Strategy for Nonprofit Organizations (2005), Community Media (2007), Social Capital Formation and Citizenship in Net Era (2007), Small Radio Stations and Community Revitalization (2014), and Community Broadcasting in Japan (2017).

Tsutomu Kanayama is a Professor of the College of Global Liberal Arts at Ritsumeikan University. After obtaining bachelor's degree specialized in Occidental History at Yamaguchi University, he became a broadcast journalist and announcer. Followed by his professional experience, he shifted to study media and communication and obtained M.A. (Western Michigan University) and Ph.D. from Ohio University in 1998. In 2004–2005, he was a Fulbright Visiting Researcher at George Washington University. He has published articles and chapters, and edited books, such as Public Access in the age of Internet (2010) and Encyclopedia of Media & Communication Studies (2019).

Mariko Koizumi is an Associate Professor of Cultural Economics at Kyoto Seika University. Graduated from the University of Tokyo with a Ph.D. in media environmental studies. Has worked for Mitsubishi Corporation in new business development for the Internet, Keio University as research associate in media business and University of California, San Diego as visiting scholar.

Wrote (Coauthor) books about media industries: "Video Games in East Asia (2016)," "White Paper on Animators' Labor Conditions 2009," and others. Served as a government committee member in the area of overseas content distribution and lectured in several countries.

https://www.kyoto-seika.ac.jp/edu/faculty/koizumi-mariko/.

Yoko Nishioka is Professor of Faulty of Global Media Studies at Komazawa University, has an extensive range of experiences in international business and policy research over communications industries including telecommunication, broadcasting, and related creative industries. Her primary interest in research is the institutional change in communication industries because of new technologies and its possible influence on the flow of communication. She received her Ph.D. in Media and Governance from Keio University in Tokyo, Japan, and Master in Communications from Annenberg School for communication, University of Pennsylvania, in Philadelphia, U.S.A. She visited UC Berkeley in 2018 as a visiting scholar.

Yuichiro Ogawa is Deputy Director of Satellite, International and Regional Broadcasting Division, Information and Communications Bureau at the Ministry of Internal Affairs and Communications, Japan. In 2012, he joined the Ministry of Internal Affairs and Communications. He has served as Official of Broadcasting Policy Division, Official of Advanced Information Systems and Software Division, Unit Chief of Planning Division in the Postal Services Policy Department, etc.

Yu Terada is President of Schwan, Inc. (Copyright Agent) in Tokyo, Japan. B.A. and M.A. at Keio University in 1998, studied in Paris 3 University-New Sorbonne in 1993 on an exchange program. Translator and interpreter in French before joining Schwan, Inc. in 2003. She served as an external researcher at Media Communication Research Institute, Keio University 2007–2008. In 2008 she succeeded her father and became President of Schwan, Inc. She is the author of the chapter "Copyright processing", in the Material Foundation of Digital Archives (2016 in Japanese), and in the Construction and Techniques of Digital Archives (2014 in Japanese).

Takashi Uchiyama is Professor in Aoyama Gakuin University, majoring in economics (government policy, managerial economics and public utility economics) and business administration of motion picture and broadcasting industry. After finishing Ph.D course in graduate school of business administration in Gakushuin University in 1994, I got the job as an assistant professor in Chiba University of Commerce in 1994, promoted associate professor in 1997 and professor in 2003 and professor in Aoyama Gakuin University since 2008.

Nami Yonetani is a researcher at the Foundation for Multimedia Communications in Tokyo, Japan. Her research interests focus on broadcasting policy and local media. After receiving her Ph.D. in Media and Governance at Keio University in 2017, she has published her dissertation as a book entitled Cable TV in East Asia: Social Role Development and Business-Government Relationship in March 2019. Most recently she wrote a chapter, "Online Local Media in Canada: Effort to Alleviate Local News Poverty" in Media Localism: The Public Mission of Local Information & News which is scheduled for publication in September 2019.

Stevie Yoshida is Founder & CEO of The Glendon Partners, a seed investment and management consulting company for entertainment companies, and Co-Founder at Russell Mindfulness Entertainment, a mindfulness-focused entertainment company backed by Glendon. Prior to his current positions, Stevie served as Corporate Executive at Avex, CEO at Avex Asia, SVP at Avex International, Board Member at Irresistible Film Fund, and Business Development Manager at The Walt Disney Company. He received MBA from MIT Sloan School of Management, Bachelor of Arts from Kyoto University of Art and Design, and Bachelor of Laws and Certificate in Journalism from Keio University.

Broadcasting Policies

Terrestrial Broadcasting

Jun Inoue

1 Introduction

"Broadcasting," especially television, is the most familiar medium in our lives. According to the Institute for Information and Communications Policy of the Ministry of Internal Affairs and Communications (hereinafter referred to as MIC) (2018), the television (real time) viewing time of Japanese people is 159.4 min on weekdays and 214.0 min on weekends and holidays, as shown in Fig. 1. On the other hand, the internet usage time is 100.4 min on weekdays and 123.0 min on weekends and holidays. The television viewing time is tending to decrease and the internet usage time is tending to increase; however, as of 2018, television is still the most familiar medium to the people in Japan. Also, given the many disasters that occur in Japan, television is a significant means of information transmission.

Because television broadcasting is so familiar to us, it has a significant impact on our lives. The broadcaster not only aims at making a profit, but also serves a public role in the distribution of basic information necessary for daily life. With the emergence of various media and platforms as well as the distribution of information, whether it is factual or fake, the role of broadcasting is growing with more considerable attention.

This chapter outlines the history, market, and rules of terrestrial television in Japan and describes the recent efforts made toward complete digitization of terrestrial television as major policy issues in 2011.

J. Inoue (✉)
Institute of Journalism, Media and Communications, Keio University, Tokyo, Japan
e-mail: j.inoue@keio.jp

M. Sugaya (ed.), *Perspectives on the Japanese Media and Content Policies*, Advances in Information and Communication Research 2,
https://doi.org/10.1007/978-981-15-4704-1_1

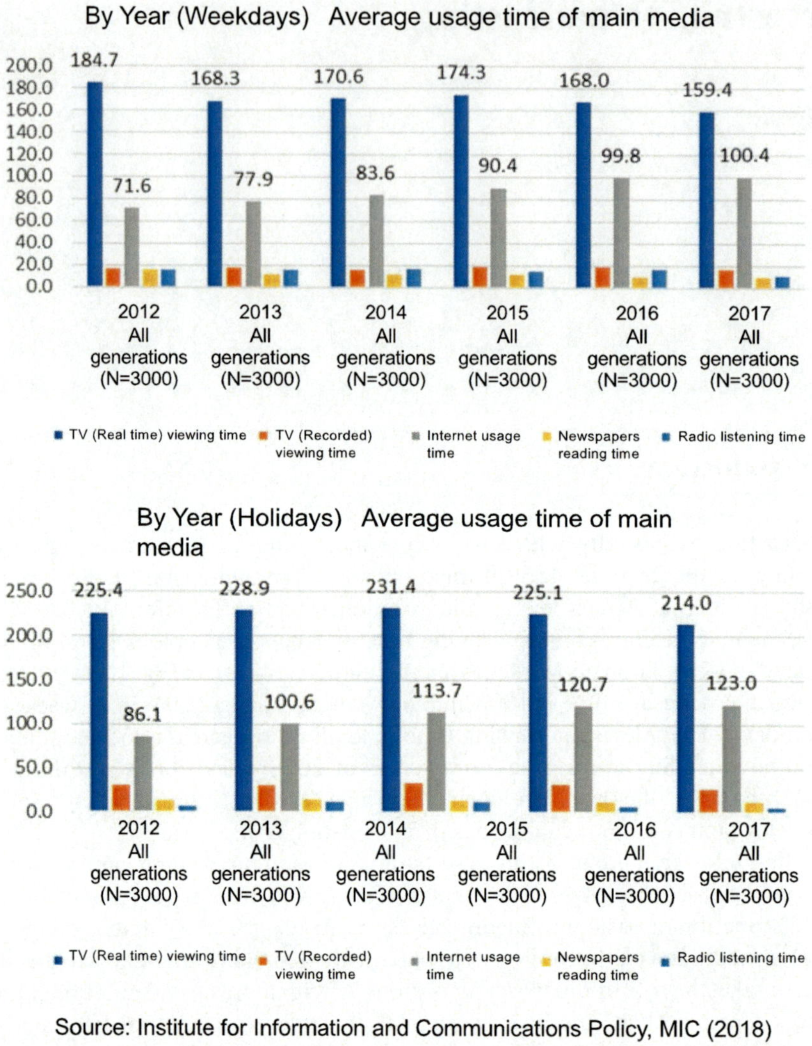

Fig. 1 Average viewing time of media on weekdays, and weekends and holidays (All generations)

2 Development of Broadcasting

2.1 Development of Broadcasting Media

The development of Japanese broadcasting media is described based on Fig. 2. Broadcasting (AM radio) began in 1925 with the broadcasting stations of a nonprofit organization serving the cities of Tokyo, Nagoya, and Osaka, respectively. The following year (1926), the three stations were integrated to promote nationwide broadcasting,

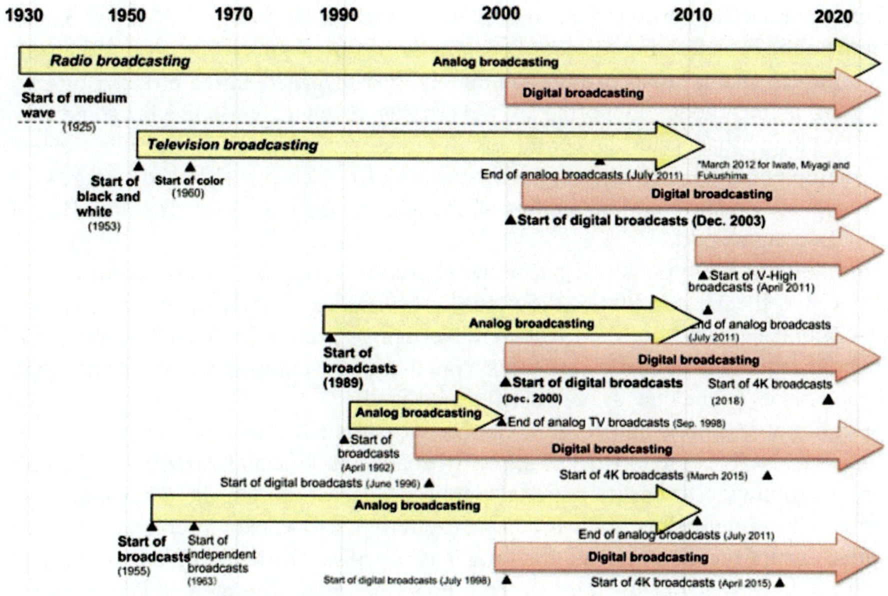

Reference: Prepared based on the Ministry of Internal Affairs and Communications (2015)

Fig. 2 Progress of broadcasting media

and the Japan Broadcasting Corporation (hereinafter referred to as NHK which stands for "Nippon Hoso Kyokai") was established.[1] Until the end of August 1951, NHK was the only company providing AM broadcasting; however, on Sept. 1 of the same year, two commercial companies, Chubu Nippon Broadcasting (currently CBC radio) in Aichi Prefecture and New Japan Broadcasting (currently Mainichi Broadcasting System) in Osaka, also started broadcasting. On Feb. 1, 1953, NHK started television broadcasting, and on Aug. 28 of the same year, Nippon Television Network Corporation (NTV), a commercial company, also began television broadcasting.

The first television broadcasts were in black and white, and color broadcasts were introduced in the1960s. Then, multichannel broadcasting progressed through broadcast satellites in 1989 and communications satellites in 1992. In 2011, analog wave transmission, which had been used for 60 years, was discontinued for terrestrial television broadcasting and was switched completely to digital broadcasting. The transition to digital broadcasting for terrestrial television is described in Sect. 5.

Before seeing the development into details, we would like to touch upon the dual system of public and commercial broadcasting in Japan, which began in 1950 with the introduction of the Broadcasting Act. This was earlier than in continental Europe

[1] NHK was established as an incorporated association. After entering the Broadcasting Act into force, NHK restarted as a special corporation (meaning a corporation which was directly established by law or by special act of incorporation pursuant to a special law, which is subject to the provisions of Article 4, para. (1), item (ix) of the Act for Establishment of MIC (Act No. 91 of 1999)).

where commercial participation took place in the 1980s and in the United States where public broadcasting services began in the 1970s. At the same time as the start of public television broadcasting, commercial broadcasters started broadcasting by adopting a free model supported by advertising revenue. It should be noted that "while public broadcasters and commercial broadcasters exercised their advantages, they complemented each other by compensating for each other's disadvantages, so that Japanese people could fully enjoy all the benefits from broadcasting (Full Bench of the Supreme Court 2017)".

In addition, the broadcasting revenue source in Japan is different from that in Europe and the United States. As a public broadcaster, NHK operates solely on subscription fees and does not receive advertising revenue or donations. By clarifying the difference in financial sources from that of the commercial broadcaster, the characteristics of the dual system are fully utilized.

Furthermore, public and commercial broadcasters have different target areas for broadcasts. NHK is established as the only broadcaster in which broadcasting target area is nationwide to ensure national public broadcasting. On the other hand, for commercial broadcasters, their broadcasting target area is each prefecture in principle to ensure regional information broadcasting, also, while multiple broadcasters coexist in one broadcasting area.[2] According to the Japan Commercial Broadcasters Association (2018), the number of commercial broadcasters as of Aug. 2018 was 195 (95 television broadcasters, 32 AM and television broadcasters, and 68 other sole operation broadcasters which are AM, shortwave radio broadcasting, and FM).

Cable television broadcasting began in 1955, almost the same time as the start of television broadcasting. It was initially introduced as a measure against poor reception in terrestrial television broadcasting. Original broadcasting channels in cable television began in 1963, and currently, multichannel broadcasting services provide over 100 channels.

2.2 *Market Size of Broadcasting Media*

Figure 3 shows that the market size (income base) of broadcasting media has remained flat at about 4 trillion JPY in the last 10 years. The income details show that the income of commercial terrestrial broadcasters was the largest at 60.3% in fiscal 2016.

Figure 4 shows that the advertising expenditure per Japanese medium, including media, other than broadcasting, is the largest for terrestrial television broadcasting at over 1.8 trillion JPY, followed by 1.05 trillion JPY for the internet. The growth in internet advertising expenditure is significant. According to Dentsu inc. (2018a), the relative change in internet advertising expenditure compared with the previous year is 115.2%. On the other hand, the relative change in television media advertising expenditure for both terrestrial and satellite broadcasters compared with the previous

[2]For terrestrial broadcasting by commercial base broadcasters at each target area, the goal is to have four comprehensive broadcasting systems.

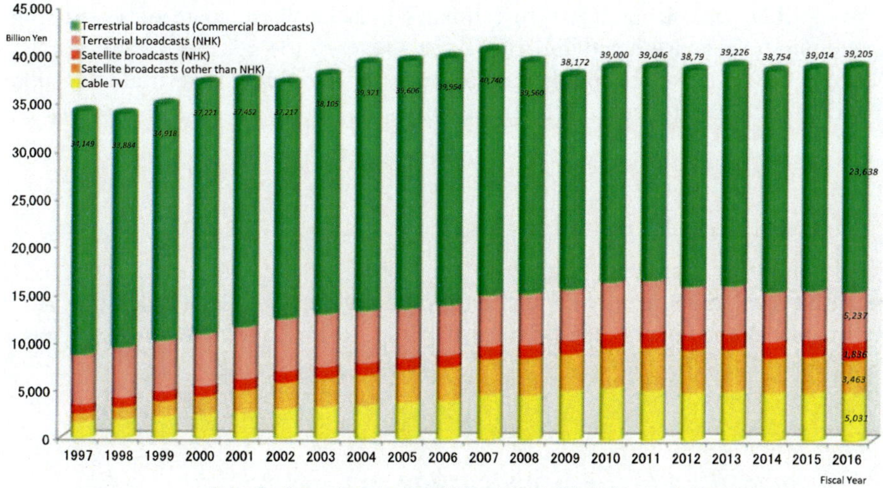

Reference: Prepared based on the Ministry of Internal Affairs and Communications (2015)

Fig. 3 Market size of broadcasting media

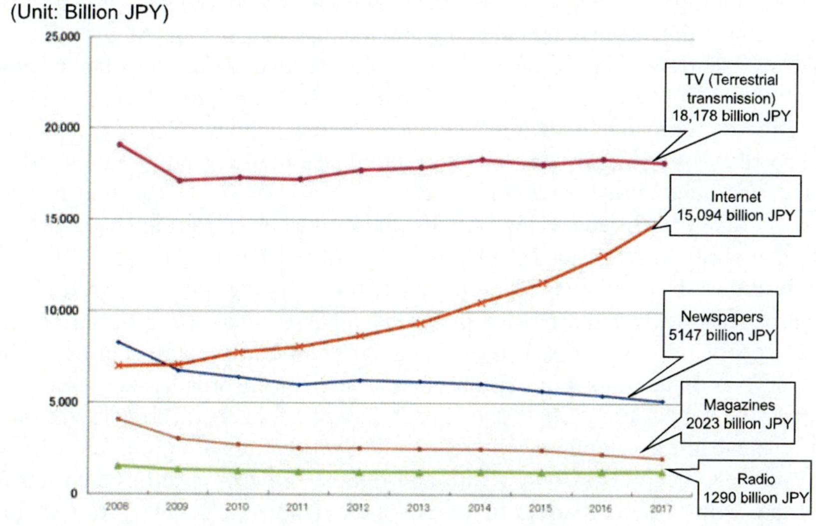

Reference: Prepared by the author based on the Ministry of Internal Affairs and Communications (2015); Values used in the graph and table are from Dentsu (2018a).

Fig. 4 Change of advertisement market

year is 99.1%. Dentsu inc. (2018b) estimates that the world share of advertising expenditure for television and digital will see a reversal (35.5% and 38.4%, respectively); however, in Japan, commercial broadcasters providing terrestrial television broadcasting remain to have a greater presence.

3 Regulations of "Broadcasting"

Broadcast regulations mainly depend on the Radio Act and the Broadcasting Act. This chapter discusses only the Broadcasting Act. Regarding the Radio Act, please see Mitomo (2020).

3.1 Composition of the Broadcasting Act

The Broadcasting Act was established in 1950 under the indirect governance of GHQ. Since then, it has been revised to reflect the changing times to reach its present form.

The composition of the Broadcasting Act as of the end of August 2018 is as follows.[3] Current chapter describes its purpose and definition, and Chapter "The Japanese Public Broadcaster NHK and Its Related Policy: The Origin of Public Broadcasting and Changing Policy Environment in the Digital Transformation" describes the general rules on the editing of broadcast programs. Chapters "The Developmental Process of Commercial Television Broadcasting Industry" and "Policy on Satellite Broadcasting" specify the provisions regarding Japan Broadcasting Corporation (NHK) and the Open University of Japan. Chapter Cable Television describes the provisions regarding basic broadcasting such as terrestrial television broadcasting, where provision of "Plans to Disseminate Basic Broadcasting," and the specific discipline of broadcasting programs only for the basic broadcasters, such as maintaining mutual consistency between the broadcast programs, are provided. Chapter "Community Radio Broadcasting" is for general broadcasting such as cable television in which and the registration procedures are provided. Chapter "Film and the Other Video Content (TV and Internet Video)" specifies the rules for paid broadcasting where, in order to protect of the recipients, the obligation of notification and public announcement of agreement clauses as well as of explanation of the provision conditions are provided. Chapter "Anime Policy: Various Aspects and the Importance of Industry" specifies the provisions for Certified Broadcasting Holding Companies. To ensure plurality of broadcasting, broadcasters subject to the provisions for preventing mass media concentration, and broadcasting opportunities

[3]For the English version of the Broadcasting Act, it is available on the Japanese Law Translation website (https://www.japaneselawtranslation.go.jp/law/detail/?id=2954&vm=04&re=01) [Accessed on January 15, 2019]. However, please be noted that it is not official texts and the original Japanese texts have legal effects.

are provided to as many people as possible. As one of the special cases, the system of Certified Broadcasting Holding Companies is established. Chapter "Video Game Policy: Its Background and Its Role in the Industry's Development" specifies the provisions for Broadcasting Program Centers. Chapters "Music" and "Copyright Clearance" cover other provisions.

This chapter focuses on the common purposes, definitions, rules for editing broadcast programs, and topics largely associated with terrestrial television broadcasting.

Much of the contents in this chapter based on Kanazawa (2012) are described by individuals involved in the broadcasting administration in MIC.[4]

3.2 *Purpose of the Broadcasting Act*

Article 1 of the Broadcasting Act stipulates the purpose of the act.

Article 1 The purpose of this act is to regulate broadcasting, so as to conform to standards for public welfare and to facilitate the sound development of broadcasting in accordance with the following principles:

(i) Guaranteeing that broadcasts reach as much of the general public as possible and that the benefits derived from broadcasts are fully realized.
(ii) Ensuring freedom of expression in broadcasting by guaranteeing impartiality, truth, and autonomy.
(iii) Enabling broadcasting to contribute to the development of a healthy democracy by clarifying the responsibilities of persons involved in broadcasting.

Item (i) specifies that broadcasts reach as much of the general public as possible. Kanazawa (2012) states the significance of the spread of broadcasting is "to include geographical implications and means that broadcasting can be received in any region in Japan." In the Broadcasting Act, NHK is thus established as a special corporation having an obligation to provide broadcasting throughout Japan and the commercial basic broadcasters are to endeavor to ensure that the basic broadcasting may be received in their regions. Regarding the concept of "reach as much of the general public as possible," the significance of bridging the digital divide besides geographical coverage is considered to be contained, and according to Kanazawa (2012), its concept "also includes environment development so that audiovisual handicapped people can enjoy the effects of broadcasting since the benefit of the recipients is duly considered."

Item (ii) specifies "ensuring freedom of expression in broadcasting by guaranteeing impartiality, truth, and autonomy." Broadcasting uses limited, low-frequency radio waves. This might lead to an oligopolistic market situation and could cause a bottleneck that hinders the diversity and plurality of information that the public has a right to know. Also, the significant penetration powers of television broadcasting with its images and sounds gives it considerable social influence, especially as it

---

[4]For other perspectives, refer to Suzuki and Yamada (2017).

breaks directly into the family room where the viewers include both adults and children. Therefore, the minimum requirements assuring impartiality and truthfulness of the broadcasters are necessary. Having said that, the basic principle is to rely on the autonomy and independence of broadcasters as much as possible as we see below, thereby trying to secure the freedom of expression of broadcasters.

Item (iii) specifies "enabling broadcasting to contribute to the development of a healthy democracy by clarifying the responsibilities of persons involved in broadcasting." Those engaged in broadcasting include not only NHK, broadcasters, and the Open University of Japan, but also the administration. Each undertaking and organization should deeply consider his job responsibility and regard the development of democracy as the provision principle.

Article 1 stipulates the purpose of the Broadcasting Act as the popularization of broadcasting, securing freedom of expression by broadcasting, and contributing to the development of a healthy democracy through broadcasting. This provision has remained without substantial revision since the Broadcasting Act was established in 1950. For the provisions in Article 2 and onward, various revisions have been made, within the scope of the purpose specified in Article 1. The Broadcasting Act is operated based on the purpose specified in Article 1, which shows the consistent attitude toward broadcasting from the end of World War II.

3.3 Definition of "Broadcasting"

Here, the definition of "broadcasting" in the Broadcasting Act is explained.

(Definition)

Article 2

(i) The term "broadcasting" means the act of transmitting (including transmitting using the telecommunications equipment of other persons (meaning the telecommunications equipment provided for in Article 2, item (ii) of the Telecommunications Business Act (Act No. 86 of 1984); the same applies hereinafter)) through telecommunications (meaning telecommunications as provided for in Article 2, item (i) of the Telecommunications Business Act) content intended to be received by the public;

(ii) The term "basic broadcasting" means broadcasting using radio waves of frequencies allocated either exclusively or preferentially to radio stations broadcasting pursuant to the provisions of the Radio Act (Act No. 131 of 1950);

(iii) The term "general broadcasting" means broadcasting that does not fall under basic broadcasting;

According to Article 2(i), "broadcasting" is a part of telecommunications and is unilaterally sent with the purpose of being received by an unspecified number of the public.[5] Radio waves of televisions are unilaterally sent from a broadcasting station without specifying the recipients, so that they fall into "broadcasting" as defined in the Broadcasting Act. Regarding streaming video and audio via the internet, each packet has the specified recipient's address based on the recipient's request (unicast is assumed), so that they are not sent without specifying the recipients then not defined as "broadcasting." When the Broadcasting Act was being revised in 2010, discussions were held on whether to include live streaming services via the internet as a subject of the provisions by referring to the regime used in the European Union; however, due to the many critical and deliberate opinions received, it was determined not to include this service in the provisions of the Broadcasting Act. For the time being, the content of video distribution through the internet (unicast) retains unregulated in the Broadcasting Act and other acts regarding the contents. In Japan, the services regulated as broadcasting are to target.

Items (ii) and (iii) under the same Article define "basic broadcasting" and "general broadcasting." Basic broadcasting is broadcasting by radio to fulfill appropriately and certainly the social role of broadcasting, and general broadcasting is broadcasting other than basic broadcasting, which is expected to realize their social roles by the market principles by enabling flexible frequency usage, etc. Concretely, "basic broadcasting" is AM and FM radio broadcasting, television broadcasting within terrestrial broadcasting, BS broadcasting, and 110° east longitude CS broadcasting within satellite broadcasting. Any other broadcasting is "general broadcasting." These classifications were introduced at the revision of the Act in 2010. In recent broadcasting, various transmission media have emerged and multi-channelization is progressing; therefore, there is a difference in social roles among the channels. Under these circumstances, if regulations are uniformly imposed, they could become inversely proportional regulations. For this reason, a difference is provided in the regulations for "general broadcasting" by relaxing the regulation contents that were imposed on broadcasting before 2010.

3.4 *General Rules on Editing of Broadcast Programs*

This section describes the rules for broadcasters when editing broadcast programs.

(Editorial Freedom of Broadcast Programs)

Article 3 Broadcast programs must not be interfered with or regulated by any person, except in cases pursuant to the authority provided for in-laws.

(Editing and Other Matters Related to the Broadcast Programs in Domestic Broadcasting)

[5]"Public" is an unspecified number of people, and "Unspecified" and "Specified" are determined by the degree of strength of the linkage between the sender and the receiver, the manner of communication, confidentiality, etc.

Article 4(1) A broadcaster must comply with the following when editing domestic broadcast programs or domestic and international broadcast programs (hereinafter referred to as "domestic broadcasts, etc."):

(i) It must not negatively influence public safety or good morals;
(ii) It must be politically fair;
(iii) Reporting must not distort the facts; and
(iv) It must clarify the points at issue from as many angles as possible where there are conflicting opinions concerning an issue.

In principle, the Broadcasting Act allows the autonomy of broadcasters regarding regulations. Article 3 clearly stipulates that no interference will be imposed excluding a case that is based on the authority determined by the law. In addition to the Broadcasting Act, Radio Act, Public Office Election Law, and the laws corresponding to natural disasters such as the Meteorological Service Act can be considered as the authority determined by law, which is fairly limited.

Article 4 specifies four principles: "Not to negatively influence public safety or good morals," "Be politically fair," "Not to distort the facts," and "To clarify the points from many angles where there are conflicting opinions concerning an issue." The purpose of these rules is to maintain a balance between the expression of freedom and public welfare by considering the magnitude of the social influence of broadcasting. Basically, compliance with these rules depends on broadcasters themselves. Although a violation of the act including this article can result in the termination of operation of a broadcasting station under Article 76 of the Radio Act, its application is very strict. In the nearly 70 years since the Broadcasting Act was established, the suspension of operation has never been ordered. In the case of a violation of the act voluntarily confirmed by a broadcaster, administrative guidance may be given to prevent the problem from recurring,[6] but this guidance is given carefully. According to Suzuki and Yamada (2017), during the period from 1985, when administrative guidance was first provided, to the end of April 2015, guidance was provided on average one time per year. In Article 5 and onward, the principle of autonomy of broadcasters is also specified.

(Program standards)

Article 5 (1) A broadcaster must stipulate standards for editing the broadcast programs (hereinafter referred to as "program standards") in accordance with the classification of the broadcast program (meaning categories such as cultural programs, educational programs, news programs, entertainment programs, etc.; the same applies hereinafter) and the target audience of the broadcasts and must edit the broadcast programs in compliance with those standards.

(Deliberative body for broadcast programs)

---

[6]Administrative guidance means "an administrative body to provide guidance, recommendations, advice, and other actions that do not apply to disposition seeking specific acts and omissions on specific persons to realize certain administrative purposes within the scope of their duties or affairs." (Administrative Procedures Act (Law No. 88 1993) Article 2, No. 6).

Article 6 (1) A broadcaster is to establish a deliberative body for broadcast programs (hereinafter referred to as a "deliberative body") in order to ensure that those programs *are* appropriate.

Article 5 clarifies that the broadcaster decides the editing criteria of broadcast programs. Article 6 stipulates that a broadcaster appoints the members of the deliberative body for the broadcast programs and the applicable body should evaluate the conformity of program standards. Program standards are not determined by the government or an independent administrative agency but by the broadcaster. Supervision is also basically conducted by the broadcaster by establishing its own deliberative body for broadcast programs. This is referred to by Sogabe (2012) as the "Japan model," a model emphasizing the autonomy of broadcasters. Also, the correction of broadcasts in Article 9 is not ordered by the administrative agency; the broadcaster decides the need for correction broadcasting on its own initiative.

In addition, the other examples in which the autonomy of a broadcaster is primarily considered are followed. Audiovisual media services in the European Union place specific restrictions on alcohol and medications, including an upper limit for broadcasting these products in advertisements. The regulations for advertisements in the Broadcasting Act in Japan is only for broadcasting educational programs for schools (Article 109).[7] The type and number of advertisements were decided by the broadcasters themselves.

Moreover, commercial broadcasters and NHK have established a third-party agency called the Broadcast Ethics and Program Improvement Organization (hereinafter referred to as BPO), which independently investigates and evaluates such problems as ethical issues of broadcast programs, privacy, and defamation, and also provides recommendations, etc. for broadcasters. The BPO was not established based on the Broadcasting Act, but rather on the initiative of the broadcasters themselves. It should be stressed again that the Broadcasting Act clarifies, in principle, the independence and autonomy of broadcasters in Japan.

3.5 Structural Regulations

In addition to the rules for program editing discussed in Sect. 3.4, the Broadcasting Act also attempts to secure multidimensional and diverse broadcasting in regions with structural restrictions. Specifically, Article 91 specifies Plans to Disseminate Basic Broadcasting to achieve systematic spread and sound development of basic broadcasting. In the plan, guidelines for the purpose of enabling as many people as possible to enjoy the freedom of expression through basic broadcasting (mass media concentrated exclusion principle) as well as goals for the numbers of broadcasters for each region for broadcasts are determined.

[7]Public broadcaster NHK's prohibition on advertisement broadcasting to maintain the dual system is specified in Article 83.

The number of each region is to be determined by the possible number of radio allocations, the development of broadcasting technology, and the trend in demands, but the number must be limited. Then, the guideline for enjoying the freedom of expression provides an upper limit on the number of voting rights, concurrent executives, and broadcast stations that one person can control, so that as many persons as possible can have the opportunities to engage in broadcasting.

In 2010, to strengthen the economic operating foundations of broadcasters, a certified system for broadcasting holding companies was implemented with some relaxation of the principles to prevent mass media concentration. However, the certification needs clarifying some conditions, so that the principles of "pluralism," "diversity," and "regionality" of broadcasting remains unchanged.

3.6 Summary

Since its introduction in 1950, the Broadcasting Act has been revised as required by the changes in the economic and social environment; however, the principle of the regulatory regime remains consistent: the independence and autonomy of the broadcasters regarding programming. At the same time, the regime endeavors to secure "pluralism," "diversity," and "regionality" of broadcasting and to support the Japanese people's right to know.

During these 70 years, technology has made huge advances. In particular, the emergence of the internet and the progress in digital technology have resulted in the broadcasting environment changing with overwhelming speed and power. It was necessary to promote digitization of broadcasting for terrestrial television broadcasting to continue providing basic information and secure the Japanese people's right to know. In Japan, approximately 20 years were spent on the digitization of terrestrial television broadcasting for termination of analog and complete transition to digital, which was a national project in the sense that the cooperation of industry, academia, and government, as well as the citizens of Japan, was essential. The trajectory of this effort is introduced in the next section.[8]

4 Outline on Digitization of Terrestrial Broadcasting

Television broadcasts reach approximately 50 million households in Japan, and people acquire not only disaster information but also basic information for daily life. To make the transition from analog to digital broadcasting, significant efforts by the public and private sectors were necessary. Broadcasters that transmitted information needed to invest additional capital, and Japanese people generally needed to

[8]Much of the contents of "4" refer to the Editorial Committee (2013) of the "Transition to Digital Terrestrial Broadcasting in Japan," the Japanese Commercial Broadcasters Association.

replace their TVs to receive digital broadcasting. On July 24, 2011, 115 commercial broadcasters, NHK, and the Open University of Japan in 44 prefectures terminated analog broadcasting, and on March 31, 2012, 12 commercial broadcasters and NHK in Iwate, Miyagi, and Fukushima prefectures where the East Japan Great Earthquake hit terminated.[9] The following summarizes the path and efforts from the start of examination to the completion of digital broadcasting.

4.1 First Step

In the final report in March 1995 by the discussion group regarding broadcasting in the era of multimedia (held from May 1994), the policy on the digitization of terrestrial television broadcasting was indicated in the administrative agency for the first time. It was mentioned that efforts should be made to enable digitization of terrestrial broadcasting from the first half of the 2000s. In May 1997, specific discussions were carried out in the terrestrial digital broadcasting discussion group. In October 1998, its report concluded that digital broadcasting should start in the wide area of Kanto, Kinki, and Chukyo by the end of 2003, and analog broadcasting should end sometime in 2010. Based on this report, the draft of the frequency assignment plan for the digital terrestrial television broadcasting was presented in December 1998. In the draft, a framework was presented, such as that 6 MHz per channel (HDTV: High-Definition Television) would be allocated with giving priority to existing broadcasters.

4.2 Efforts and Measures by Broadcasters

To realize the plan, a number of problems needed to be solved. According to the survey conducted in 2007 by the National Association of Commercial Broadcasters, the investment required for commercial broadcasters to transit to digital broadcasting exceeded 1 trillion yen. It was different if the advertising revenue had been likely to increase in digital broadcasting, but in reality, it was a burden and a major problem.

Also, the transition to digital broadcasting required measures for changes in analog frequency to another analog frequency, which involves switching the frequency band of analog broadcasting that may interfere with other frequency bands during simultaneous analog and digital broadcasting. This task also involved expenses; the number of households affected by antenna arrangement for receiving the changed analog frequency was 4 million and the cost was estimated at about 180 billion JPY by the National Terrestrial Digital Broadcasting Promotion Committee structured by MIC and the broadcasters.

[9]Terrestrial digital broadcasting in Japan adopts the ISDB-T method in which the characteristics are high-quality broadcasting, efficiency in actualizing broadcasting for fixed terminals and mobile terminals with one transmitter, and disaster tolerance that enables emergency warning broadcasting.

It was agreed that investment in digital broadcasting was related to the original business of broadcasters, and therefore should, in principle, be paid by the broadcasters.[10] However, the analog frequency change measure was temporary and no benefit to the business of broadcasters. In the end, it was concluded that the analog frequency change measure was unavoidable to improve the environment for transitioning to digital broadcasting, so it was paid as a government expense for a source of radio usage fees. Even though, in addition to government expenses, cooperation between the public and private sectors was also necessary such as for antenna adjustment in each household.

4.3 *Efforts and Measures by Viewers*

Television is an essential information means for viewers to gain information including emergency information during a natural disaster. It would not be unacceptable if what was available in analog broadcasting would not be available in digital broadcasting. When analog broadcasting ended and they suddenly were unable to watch TV, there would have been so-called chaos. In 2008, the Minister of Internal Affairs and Communications, Mr. Masuda, said, "We need to do our best to respond to each one of our citizens. We would like to hear suggestions and opinions. Meanwhile, we will pay attention to covering all regions and families, and not leave out a single area or family. We continue to make our best effort."[11] Both public and private sectors carried out activities to raise awareness on the digitization of broadcasting.

To receive digital broadcasting, the receiving parties needed to switch to digital television and adjust their antenna accordingly. While there was no comprehensive database showing where TVs were located and how many there were, or the status of antenna adjustment, receiving parties themselves should aware of digital switching and do actions such as switching the TV and adjusting the antenna. For this reason, the government conducted a wide range of support measures and tasks such as raising awareness, accepting consultation by phone, field investigation, briefing sessions, door to door visits, measures for reception problems, and the promotion of digitization in collective housing as part of the work of the Television Recipient Support Center (nickname: Digi-Suppo) established throughout Japan and operated by MIC. At maximum, 25,000 people nationwide conducted briefing sessions and door to door visits.

[10]A part of public support was utilized for digitization investment. In 2007 fiscal year, 18.29 billion yen was used to correct the geographical digital divide, and in 2008 fiscal year, 5.97 billion yen was used as the transmission/reception environment improvement to complete migration to digital broadcasting.

[11]May 21, 2008 Response to the House of Councilors and the Settlement Committee. (https://kokkai.ndl.go.jp/#/detail?minId=116914103X00920080521&spkNum=135&current=11)[Retrieved on 27 Dec. 2019].

The government also promoted the replacement of TVs by utilizing related measures. "Eco-point" was one of the measures to overcome the economic downturn after the Lehman Shock in 2008. Those who purchased energy-efficient products could earn eco-points that could be exchanged for gift certificates. Eco-points could be earned when buying an energy-efficient digital television. For example, someone buying a 46-inch or larger TV would earn 36,000 eco-points (1 point equals 1 JPY). The system was introduced in May 2009 and continued to the end of March 2011, during which time it was revised to decrease the number of redeemable points. By the end of December 2010, the system was utilized to replace 100 million TVs.

Support was provided for economically vulnerable who had difficulty to buy a digital TV by providing a simple tuner free of charge. Households under welfare (approximately 1.2 million households) as well as city tax-exempt households (maximum 9.3 million households) were also given free tuners. It was the common understanding that the TV reception environment was maintained as a lifeline.

4.4 Last Efforts

As of March 2010, less than a year and a half to the termination of analog broadcasting, the installation of relay stations by the broadcasters (the senders) was on schedule, but problems on the viewers' side such as replacing televisions and common antenna facilities still remained. According to the Editorial Board for "Transition to Digital Terrestrial Broadcasting in Japan" (2013), the household rate for the spread of digital televisions was 83.8% in total, but the rate was 67.5% for households with an annual income of less than 2 million JPY. The digitization rate of common antenna facilities for reception failure measures was also approximately 30,000 (47.8%) in terms of facilities and 3,320,000 (51%) in terms of households. In addition, the digitization rate of collective housing common communication facilities was approximately 1,650,000 (77.3%) in terms of facilities and 16,770,000 in terms of households. Therefore, further efforts were necessary. Especially in the south Kanto area, there were many households that did not have a UHF antenna installed and door to door visits were conducted intensively in the area.

In March 2011, the Great East Japan Earthquake struck Japan, causing devastating damage, especially in the Tohoku prefectures of Iwate, Miyagi, and Fukushima. Part of the relay stations on the transmitting side suffered damage as well as power and transmission outages. Broadcasting functions were quickly recovered due to hard work mainly by the local broadcasting stations. In the meantime, the prefectures proposed that the termination of analog broadcasting planned for July of the same year be extended as about 60,000 households still needed to prepare for the switch. On April 20, the government decided to extend the deadline for terminating analog broadcasting in the three prefectures for a maximum of 1 year. In July, after hearing the opinions of broadcasters and the prefectures, it was determined that the termination date of analog broadcasting in the three prefectures would be March 31, 2012.

On July 24, 2011, the planned day for termination of analog broadcasting in 44 prefectures (excluding the above three prefectures) successfully terminated analog broadcasting. On that day, the digital broadcasting call center received approximately 120,000 inquiries, which decreased to 70,000 on the next day and to less than 10,000 by the end of July. It is concluded that termination of analog broadcasting was stably conducted without major confusion. On March 31, 2012, analog broadcasting was terminated for the three prefectures affected by the earthquake, and digitization of terrestrial television broadcasting was completed as planned.

Even after the termination of analog broadcasting, some problems occurred and remained (e.g., new poor reception in digital,[12] delayed replacement of common antenna, and digital interference). The households suffering from these problems were about 280,000 households, but by providing "safety net" via satellite and changing digital signals to analog ones in cable TV,[13] measures were taken as temporary solutions up to the end of March 2015. During this time, such measures as the installation of additional stations and improvement construction were implemented. These temporary measures were also completed by the end of March 2015 as scheduled.

4.5 Summary

Television is an essential medium in everyday life. If everyone's TV suddenly stopped displaying, it could even cause social anxiety. Digitization of terrestrial television broadcasting was required to replace analog television serving as the lifeline in households, which had never been done before. Detailed, careful planning helped actualize the termination of analog broadcasting and the transition to digital broadcasting. The investment by broadcasting companies exceeded 1 trillion JPY, and the support by the government exceeded 240 billion JPY.[14] The project, which involved both public and private entities, took approximately 20 years but was smoothly completed in general.

Digitization of terrestrial television broadcasting not only made it possible to view high definition video on television, but it also enabled efficient radio usage by using the VHF band (90–108 and 170–220 MHz) and the UHF band (710–770 MHz). Thus,

[12]A problem whereby analog broadcasting could be received, but not digital broadcasting.

[13]The satellite safety net refers to temporarily broadcast NHK general programs, NHK educational programs, and broadcast programs of Tokyo key stations via the broadcast satellite in the area where relay stations cannot be constructed by the termination of analog broadcasting. At maximum, approximately 110,000 households used the safety net. DA conversion of cable TV refers to the conversion of digital broadcasting to analog signals at the head end of cable TV stations, which is sent to each household, and 331 businesses adopted this method (discontinued by the end of April 2015).

[14]Total budget related to terrestrial digital broadcasting from fiscal years 2009 to 2012 by the Ministry of Internal Affairs. Excluding the expenses for the analog frequency change measure.

new frequency resources contribute to respond to imminent high demand of wireless communication, which is served as the foundation to support the future IoT/AI era.

For the international point of view, overseas deployment of Japan's terrestrial television broadcasting system (ISDB-T system) is also in progress, and it has been adopted in 19 countries as of January 2017. As a result, it has helped expand the opportunities for exporting transmitters and receivers with the Japanese television system as well as raise the potential for overseas development of Japanese broadcast programs.

5 Conclusion

This chapter provided an overview of the market regulations of broadcasting in Japan and described the efforts made toward the digitization of terrestrial television broadcasting. As part of the summary, the following describes one of the issues facing the broadcasting business in Japan.

The convergence of telecommunications and broadcasting is progressing rapidly. Various movements can be seen such as the establishment of terrestrial broadcasters and the purchase of SVOD (Subscription Video on Demand) companies. Looking at other countries, it is not surprising that in the USA, the media industry is actively consolidating. Broadcasting, cable television, movies, SVOD, and entertainment industries are repeatedly undergoing mergers and acquisitions aiming to increase their market hegemony. The current competition among media is quite different from that in the past. The competition up to now was domestic, and fluctuations in companies were a domestic problem. From a macroeconomic perspective, it was the metabolism of the media. However, the current competition is global.

The advertising expenses paid by Japanese companies and the subscription fees paid by the Japanese people are transferred to foreign conglomerates. It will not only cause the metabolism of domestic media, but also reduce the ability to produce domestic contents. So far, the Japanese language was a natural barrier to entry into the Japanese market. However, with the development of artificial intelligence including language processing by machine, the language barrier for entry into Japan will quickly disappear. Now is the time to act.

The following is an item for broadcasting in Growth Strategy 2018 of the Japanese government in 2018.

> II Creating a foundation for economic innovation.
>
> [1] Improvement of the common infrastructure of a data-driven society.
>
> 1. Promoting investment in infrastructure system and technology.
>
> ⑦ Promotion of measures aiming at the future image of broadcasting and contents business.
>
> With the further integration of technological innovation and telecommunications and broadcasting, based on the current situation, where international competition beyond the framework of conventional telecommunications, broadcasting, and contents have already begun, taking into account the future in which the broadcasters provide more diversified and high-quality contents and fulfill all their social roles, construction of a business model exceeding

the framework of telecommunications, and broadcasting like the promotion of internet distribution of broadcast contents, global deployment, and effective utilization of broadcast contents; improvements of business and working practices relating to production and facilitation of distributing contents will be promoted.

As seen in Sect. 2, from a global perspective, the internet has become to overtake broadcasting; however, in Japan, terrestrial broadcasting still has the highest advertising revenue as well as strength. As specified in Growth Strategy 2018 mentioned above, it is essential to take proactive measures while still having the strength.

References

Dentsu Inc. (2018a) Advertisement expense of Japan in 2017. https://www.dentsu.co.jp/news/release/2018/0222-009476.html. Accessed 17 Sept 2018

Dentsu Inc. (2018b) Presentation of "Prediction of World Advertisement Expense Growth Rate". https://www.dentsu.co.jp/news/release/2018/0614-009553.html. Accessed 17 Sept 2018

Editorial Board for "Transition to Digital Terrestrial Broadcasting in Japan", Japan Commercial Broadcasters Association (2013) Record of digital terrestrial broadcasting (in Japanese). The Japanese Commercial Broadcasters Association, Tokyo

Full Bench of the Supreme Court (2017) Minshu, vol 71, no 10, p 1817

Institute for Information and Communications Policy, Ministry of Internal Affairs and Communications (2018) 2017 investigation on usage time and information behavior of information communication media. https://www.soumu.go.jp/menu_news/s-news/01iicp01_02000073.html. Accessed 17 Sept 2018

Kanazawa K (2012) Broadcasting legislative commentary revised version (in Japanese). DSK, Tokyo

Mitomo H (ed) (2020) Telecomunications policies of Japan, vol 1. Springer, Singapore

Sogabe M (2012) Formation and development of the Japanese model in broadcast program regulations (in Japanese). In: Sogabe M, Akasaka K (eds) Principle and development of constitution reform last volume. Shinzansha, Tokyo

Suzuki H, Yamada K (eds) (2017) Outline of broadcast system—understanding the new broadcasting act. Shojihomu, Tokyo

The Japan Commercial Broadcasters Association (2018) What is JBA? (in Japanese). https://www.j-ba.or.jp/mlist/. Accessed 18 Sept 2018

The Japanese Public Broadcaster NHK and Its Related Policy: The Origin of Public Broadcasting and Changing Policy Environment in the Digital Transformation

Check for updates

Tsutomu Kanayama

Abstract Japanese Broadcasting is understood to be a well-blended and balanced system and has been referred to as a dual structure comprised of public and commercial radio and television stations. This chapter will focus on the public broadcasting system of Japan, by mainly dealing with its fundamental philosophy and historical context as a unique public entity in broadcasting and the changing broadcasting environment related to broadcast policy implications, especially for the public broadcaster NHK.

1 Introduction

Japanese Broadcasting is understood to be a well-blended and balanced system and has been referred to as a dual structure comprised of public and commercial radio and television stations.

Notably, the Public Broadcasting System and its related operations have been well recognized since the British Broadcasting Corporation (hereinafter referred to as BBC) was established in 1927, followed by the wireless airwave industry, the British Broadcasting Company, under the leadership of Sir John Reith, then Secretary General of the BBC.

After World War II and as a result of the democratization guided by the Supreme Commander of the General Headquarters, Douglas MacArthur, Japan learned a tremendous amount from the UK in regard to public broadcasting service philosophy and its operations, as well as from the USA regarding commercial broadcasting.

Based on Japan's dual structure of broadcasting, regarding basic or conventional terrestrial broadcasters utilizing over-the-airwaves, such as what is called "Chijo Ha Hoso" in Japanese, the Japan Broadcasting Corporation, which is named Nippon Hoso Kyokai (hereinafter referred to as NHK) in Japanese, has existed as the public

T. Kanayama (✉)
The College of Global Liberal Arts, Ritsumeikan University, Ibaraki, Osaka, Japan
e-mail: kanayama@fc.ritsumei.ac.jp

M. Sugaya (ed.), *Perspectives on the Japanese Media and Content Policies*, Advances in Information and Communication Research 2,
https://doi.org/10.1007/978-981-15-4704-1_2

broadcaster, and commercial broadcasters, comprised of 127 terrestrial commercial broadcasting television stations and 101 radio stations.

Japan's public broadcasting is unique and has long maintained a fee-based system from the very beginning of its establishment. One of the unique aspects of Japan's public broadcasting system is that, on the surface, it seems to be a paid service from the eyes of outside countries and regions. However, the overall general audience in Japan since the very beginning of its public broadcasting service back on June 1, 1950 when the Article 64 of Broadcast Act[1] was enacted has supported and nobly sustained the public broadcasting system.

In particular, Krisher (1974) emphasized that virtually the entire nation's TV set owners with a 99% acceptance rate diligently paid NHK viewing fees without any complaints. At the same time, the public broadcasting service provided by NHK could be called a utility-based service, such as electricity, gas, and water. In this regard, the article of Broadcast Act 15 indicates the purpose of the statement that the designated obligation of NHK is to transmit essential broadcasts all over Japan.

The primary broadcasting operation of NHK is to engage in broadcasting as written in Article 15 as follows:

> NHK aims to transmit domestic basic broadcasts (meaning basic broadcasts which are domestic in nature; hereinafter the same applies) through broadcasting high-quality, rich programs, which can be received throughout the whole of Japan, to conduct operations in connection with broadcasting and the advancement and development of reception thereof as well as to transmit international and international satellite broadcasts for the purpose of public welfare.[2]

This chapter will focus on the public broadcasting system of Japan, by mainly dealing with its fundamental philosophy and historical context as a unique public entity in broadcasting and the changing broadcasting environment related to broadcast policy implications, especially for the public broadcaster NHK.

Particularly in the context of broadcasting policy and its implications, it mainly focuses on the new policy implications during three main periods. The first was (1) technological advancement and changes in NHK's public status under the satellite broadcasting advancements of the 1980s, which gave NHK credit to expand any additional revenue source of its public broadcasting operation. The next was (2) digitization of broadcasting in the use of satellite broadcasting synchronized with the deregulatory movement in policy-making between the 1990s and 2000s. Finally, was the period (3) when further development of digital broadcasting for terrestrial

---

[1] Article 64(1) Persons installing reception equipment capable of receiving NHK broadcasts shall conclude a contract with NHK for the reception of those broadcasts; provided, however, that this does not apply to those persons who have installed reception equipment not intended for the reception of broadcasts or reception equipment only capable of receiving radio broadcasts (meaning broadcasts comprising of voices and other sounds that do not come under television broadcasting or multiple broadcasting; the same applies in Article 126, para. (1) or multiple broadcasting (Broadcasting Act—Japaneselawtranslation.go.jp. (n.d.). Retrieved from https://www.japaneselawtranslation.go.jp/law/detail_main?vm=02&id=2954).

[2] Broadcasting Act—Japaneselawtranslation.go.jp. (n.d.). Retrieved from https://www.japaneselawtranslation.go.jp/law/detail_main?vm=02&id=2954.

broadcasting and its integration with the broadband networks happened, between 2000 and 2010.

2 A History of the Prewar and Postwar Period of the Public Broadcaster NHK

Previously, in the prewar period between the end of the Taisho-era and the beginning of the Showa-era, Tokyo Broadcasting Station signed the first radio program off the air in March 1925. Then as a unified entity, in 1926, NHK was reestablished through the merger of three broadcasting stations, including Tokyo Broadcasting Station, Nagoya Broadcasting Station, and Osaka Broadcasting Station (NHK-a 2002, p. 4), which was located in Japan's top three major broadcasting markets. Moreover, NHK declared its entity as an incorporated association, called the Nippon Hoso Kyokai, the predecessor of today's current NHK.

In 1931, NHK started dual broadcasting with NHK Radio 1 and 2, and in its 10th anniversary year in 1935, nationwide school broadcasting and international short-wave broadcasting was put into operation, broadcasting to the western part of North America. In December 1941, it aired the news of the outbreak of the Pacific War. Furthermore, during the war, radio became a tool of propaganda by the Japanese government and military authorities to disseminate government policy. Finally, NHK broadcasted the moment of the Imperial Rescript on the Termination of the War on August 15, 1945.

When reestablishing NHK under the occupation control period by the General Headquarters (GHQ) of the Supreme Commander for the Allied Powers, the standardized broadcasting utilized only amplified modulation (AM) radio broadcasting. At the very beginning for writing up the Broadcast Act, which has been the lighted buoy of Japanese broadcasting, it prescribed that "persons installing reception equipment capable of receiving standard NHK broadcasts conclude a contract with NHK for the reception of those broadcasts" (Amishima et al. 1993, p. 54).

From the aspect of policy-making, the public broadcaster NHK was reestablished in 1950 under the auspices of the Three Radio Laws—The Radio Law, the Broadcast Law, and the Law for the Establishment of Rdio Regulatory Commission. The Three Laws were put into effect in June 1950 and NHK was Japan's public broadcaster for the democratic society in transition after World War II, together with the commercial broadcast stations including Chubu Nippon Hoso (Chubu-Nippon Broadcasting Corporation Limited, called CBC) in Nagoya, Shin Nihon Hoso (New Japan Broadcasting System, Inc., called NJB) in Osaka.

At that time, the real intention of all related personnel was to realize a broadcast system somewhat different from genuine public corporations, like the Japan National Railways, which was privatized in 1987. As a result, NHK sought its direction as a quasi-public corporation to enlist government understanding, while making a distinction from a genuine public corporation's style in that the Cabinet shall appoint the executive management committee members (Amishima et al. 1993, p. 55).

NHK, in particular, started covering the whole nation with radio broadcasting by rebuilding its radio network in the immediate postwar years and tried to contribute to restructuring the Japanese society by transmitting the necessary information for the reconstruction of society and its related system in Japan.

Therefore, by the fact that the Prime Minister shall appoint the executive management committee members of NHK after approval of the House of Councilors and the House of Representatives, NHK was able to become the entity of a quasi-public corporation. On the other hand, all other public corporations would have to follow the appointment system in finalizing the management committee members by both the House of Councilors and Representatives (Amishima et al. 1993, p. 55).

3 A Uniqueness of NHK's Public Broadcasting in Terms of Regulation

Unlike the BBC system, NHK's public broadcasting status was so unique because, historically, from the very beginning back in the prewar period, the then-government-authority, the Ministry of Communication, took the two-step flow to realize the well-organized receiving fees from the households. At that time, equipping a radio receiver at home needed permission by a government authority under the Wireless Telegraphy Law, and at the same time, the reception contract and application sheet was distributed to each household (Amishima et al. 1993, p. 54).

Therefore, all radio households were supposed to get permission from the government authority and were automatically obliged to sign the contract with NHK. However, in the reestablished public broadcasting system after the War in 1950, the Broadcasting Act does not clearly define the enforcement of the receiving fee contract without any legal penalty from NHK. According to Amishima et al. (1993), it instead emphasized the noble spirit of public broadcasting in Article 64 of the Broadcasting Act. Additionally, the method in which each household is charged depends on the Diet's approval for each fiscal year's budget proposal.

When approving the NHK budget proposal at the Diet, there is a tendency that supplementary resolution would be attached to get special attention for NHK's operation throughout the whole fiscal year. For example, when the Great Tohoku Earthquake happened in 2011, the Diet requested NHK to designate broadcasting programs to be produced, and NHK has, since then, routinely produced programs, especially on Sundays to introduce and remind the audience of the reconstruction status in regions suffered by the Tohoku Earthquake.

In this regard, the Broadcasting Act mainly aims at how the NHK operates broadcasting activities in terms of the public interests and social welfare aspects. At the same time, it defines the broadcasting operations of NHK, as a public broadcaster playing a significant role in serving the local community. Moreover, commercial broadcasting companies are under the same umbrella as the Broadcasting Act of Japan, meaning even commercial broadcasting is to oblige general public responsibility in daily broadcasting operations.

Figure 1, shown below, describes all of the television broadcasting stations operating in Japan. Public broadcaster NHK allocates its budget not only focusing on producing national and international related news, documentaries, sports, and entertainment programs but also essential regional news and information to be disseminated and shared. NHK has placed at least one local branch station in each prefecture and also, if needed, as in the case of the northern island of Hokkaido, there are six additional subbranches based on the center core station of NHK Sapporo.

Currently, NHK has provided broadcasting programs as follows: (1) General terrestrial channels, terrestrial education channels; (2) BS-1 channel for satellite broadcasting, BS-premium for satellite broadcasting; (3) NHK Radio 1, NHK Radio 2, and NHK FM; (4) NHK on-demand, data broadcasting, one-segment original service; (5) NHK online, NHK keitai (mobile phone), NHK internet radio "RAJIRU RAJIRU (live streaming of NHK Radio 1, NHK Radio 2, NHK FM), and international broadcasting; and (6) NHK world Japan (radio, television). Initially starting out only as a radio broadcaster, NHK has become a complete broadcasting house representing Japan to the world.

On the other hand, commercial broadcasters consist of network stations (Tokyo Broadcasting Systems, Nippon Television Network, Fuji Television Network, TV Asahi, TV Tokyo) headquartered in Tokyo and five network-affiliated stations regionally or locally located all over Japan. Additionally, there are also independent stations mainly placed in Japan's three major broadcasting market regions, such as greater Tokyo (six stations), greater Kansai (five stations), and greater Chubu (two stations).

This indicates that the number of broadcasting stations in each prefecture is different in the case of commercial broadcasting. For example, there is only one commercial station in Tokushima prefecture, while Hokkaido has five. In this sense, it might be pointed out that Japanese television broadcasting explicitly needs to overcome the issue of diversifying local or regional voices to some extent from the commercial broadcasting point of view.

In this sense, NHK's thoughtfully placed regional and local branch broadcasting stations have contributed to avoiding information gaps wherever the general public seek the information they need. As a result, as far as NHK's broadcasting operation is concerned, wherever people live they are able to get important and essential information in Japan. A requirement by law is for NHK to cover 100% of the Japanese television and radio households. The critical function for NHK as a public broadcaster termed the concept of universal, or "Amaneku" in Japanese means serving the general public of Japan by equipping television and radio broadcasting receiver(s) 100% of the time.

No exception is to be allowed for NHK when transmitting to achieve the purpose of public welfare by law. According to the Article 15 of the Broadcast Act by stating that "NHK aims to transmit domestic basic broadcasts (meaning basic broadcasts which are domestic in nature; hereinafter the same applies) through broadcasting

NHK and Commercial Television Networks (as of Oct. 2018)

<table>
<tr><th></th><th colspan="5">Commercial Television</th><th></th><th colspan="2">NHK</th></tr>
<tr><th>Prefecture</th><th>JNN (28 stations)</th><th>NNN (30 stations)</th><th>FNN (28 stations)</th><th>ANN (26 stations)</th><th>TXN (6 stations)</th><th>Independent stations</th><th>regional hub stations (7 stations)</th><th>local stations (46 stations)</th></tr>
<tr><td>Hokkaido</td><td>HBC</td><td>STV</td><td>UHB</td><td>HTB</td><td>TVH</td><td></td><td>Sapporo</td><td>Hakodte + 5 branch station</td></tr>
<tr><td>Aomori</td><td>ATV</td><td>RAB</td><td></td><td>ABA</td><td></td><td></td><td></td><td>Aomori</td></tr>
<tr><td>Iwate</td><td>IBC</td><td>TVI</td><td>MIT</td><td>IAT</td><td></td><td></td><td></td><td>Morioka</td></tr>
<tr><td>Miyagi</td><td>TBC</td><td>MMT</td><td>OX</td><td>KHB</td><td></td><td></td><td>Sendai</td><td></td></tr>
<tr><td>Akita</td><td></td><td>ABS</td><td>AKT</td><td>AAB</td><td></td><td></td><td></td><td>Akita</td></tr>
<tr><td>Yamagata</td><td>TUY</td><td>YBC</td><td>SAY</td><td>YTS</td><td></td><td></td><td></td><td>Yamagata</td></tr>
<tr><td>Fukushima</td><td>TUF</td><td>FCT</td><td>FTV</td><td>KFB</td><td></td><td></td><td></td><td>Fukushima</td></tr>
<tr><td>Tokyo</td><td rowspan="7">TBS</td><td rowspan="7">NTV</td><td rowspan="7">CX</td><td rowspan="7">ANB</td><td rowspan="7">TX</td><td>MX</td><td colspan="2">Headquarters Tokyo</td></tr>
<tr><td>Gunma</td><td>GTV</td><td></td><td>Maebashi</td></tr>
<tr><td>Tochigi</td><td>TTV</td><td></td><td>Utsunomiya</td></tr>
<tr><td>Ibaraki</td><td></td><td></td><td>Mito</td></tr>
<tr><td>Saitama</td><td>TVS</td><td></td><td>Saitama</td></tr>
<tr><td>Chiba</td><td>CTC</td><td></td><td>Chiba</td></tr>
<tr><td>Kanagawa</td><td>TVK</td><td></td><td>Yokohama</td></tr>
<tr><td>Niigata</td><td>BSN</td><td>TeNY</td><td>NST</td><td>NT21</td><td></td><td></td><td></td><td>Niigata</td></tr>
<tr><td>Nagano</td><td>SBC</td><td>TSB</td><td>NBS</td><td>ABN</td><td></td><td></td><td></td><td>Nagano</td></tr>
<tr><td>Yamanashi</td><td>UTY</td><td>YBS</td><td></td><td></td><td></td><td></td><td></td><td>Kofu</td></tr>
<tr><td>Shizuoka</td><td>SBS</td><td>SDT</td><td>SUT</td><td>SATV</td><td></td><td></td><td></td><td>Shizuoka</td></tr>
<tr><td>Toyama</td><td>TUT</td><td>KNB</td><td>BBT</td><td></td><td></td><td></td><td></td><td>Toyama</td></tr>
<tr><td>Ishikawa</td><td>MRO</td><td>KTK</td><td>ITC</td><td>HAB</td><td></td><td></td><td></td><td>Kanazawa</td></tr>
<tr><td>Fukui</td><td></td><td>FBC</td><td>FTB</td><td>FBC</td><td></td><td></td><td></td><td>Fukui</td></tr>
<tr><td>Aichi</td><td rowspan="3">CBC</td><td rowspan="3">CTB</td><td rowspan="3">THK</td><td rowspan="3">NBN</td><td>TVA</td><td></td><td>Nagoya</td><td></td></tr>
<tr><td>Gifu</td><td></td><td>GBS</td><td></td><td>Gifu</td></tr>
<tr><td>Mie</td><td></td><td>MTV</td><td></td><td>Tsu</td></tr>
<tr><td>Osaka</td><td rowspan="6">MBS</td><td rowspan="6">YTV</td><td rowspan="6">KTV</td><td rowspan="6">ABC</td><td>TVO</td><td></td><td>Osaka</td><td></td></tr>
<tr><td>Shiga</td><td></td><td>BBC</td><td></td><td>Otsu</td></tr>
<tr><td>Kyoto</td><td></td><td>KBS</td><td></td><td>Kyoto</td></tr>
<tr><td>Nara</td><td></td><td>TVN</td><td></td><td>Nara</td></tr>
<tr><td>Hyogo</td><td></td><td>SUN</td><td></td><td>Kobe</td></tr>
<tr><td>Wakayama</td><td></td><td>WTV</td><td></td><td>Wakayama</td></tr>
<tr><td>Tottori</td><td rowspan="2">BSS</td><td rowspan="2">NKT</td><td rowspan="2">TSK</td><td></td><td></td><td></td><td></td><td>Tottori</td></tr>
<tr><td>Shimane</td><td></td><td></td><td></td><td></td><td>Matsue</td></tr>
<tr><td>Okayama</td><td rowspan="2">RSK</td><td rowspan="2">RNC</td><td rowspan="2">OHK</td><td rowspan="2">KSB</td><td rowspan="2">TSC</td><td></td><td></td><td>Okayama</td></tr>
<tr><td>Kagawa</td><td></td><td></td><td>Takamatsu</td></tr>
<tr><td>Tokushima</td><td></td><td>JRT</td><td></td><td></td><td></td><td></td><td></td><td>Tokushima</td></tr>
<tr><td>Ehime</td><td>ITV</td><td>RNB</td><td>EBC</td><td>EAT</td><td></td><td></td><td>Matsuyama</td><td></td></tr>
<tr><td>Kochi</td><td>KUTV</td><td>RKC</td><td>KSS</td><td></td><td></td><td></td><td></td><td>Kochi</td></tr>
<tr><td>Hiroshima</td><td>RCC</td><td>HTV</td><td>TSS</td><td>HOME</td><td></td><td></td><td>Hiroshima</td><td></td></tr>
<tr><td>Yamaguchi</td><td>TYS</td><td>KRY</td><td></td><td>YAB</td><td></td><td></td><td></td><td>Yamaguchi</td></tr>
<tr><td>Fukuoka</td><td>RKB</td><td>FBS</td><td>TNC</td><td>KBC</td><td>TVQ</td><td></td><td>Fukuoka</td><td>Kitakyushu</td></tr>
<tr><td>Saga</td><td></td><td></td><td>STS</td><td></td><td></td><td></td><td></td><td>Saga</td></tr>
<tr><td>Nagasaki</td><td>NBC</td><td>NIB</td><td>KTN</td><td>NCC</td><td></td><td></td><td></td><td>Nagasaki</td></tr>
<tr><td>Kumamoto</td><td>RKK</td><td>KKT</td><td>KTU</td><td>KAB</td><td></td><td></td><td></td><td>Kumamoto</td></tr>
<tr><td>Oita</td><td>OBS</td><td>TOS</td><td>TOS</td><td>OAB</td><td></td><td></td><td></td><td>Oita</td></tr>
<tr><td>Miyazaki</td><td>MRT</td><td>UMK</td><td>UMK</td><td>UMK</td><td></td><td></td><td></td><td>Miyazaki</td></tr>
<tr><td>Kagoshima</td><td>MBC</td><td>KYT</td><td>KTS</td><td>KKB</td><td></td><td></td><td></td><td>Kagoshima</td></tr>
<tr><td>Okinawa</td><td>RBC</td><td></td><td>OTV</td><td>OAB</td><td></td><td></td><td></td><td>Okinawa</td></tr>
</table>

[dashed box] Cross-network stations (broadcasting programs from two or more key broadcasters)

Fig. 1 NHK and commercial TV networks (*Source* NHK-b, and JBA (2019)) good-quality, rich programs, which can be received throughout the whole of Japan, to conduct operations in connection with broadcasting and the advancement and development of reception thereof as well as to transmit international and international satellite broadcasts for the purpose of public welfare."

It is evident that NHK has taken the initiative to fulfill the purpose of the broadcast law, fundamentally realized as the concept of public welfare, and to lead the Japanese broadcasting scene from the cultural and technological field all the time in the democratic society of Japan after World War II under the Broadcasting Act.

Another aspect of NHK naturally is its concern for the broadcasting policy and its policy-making processes because NHK has to overcome the hurdle for the proposed budget approved by the Diet for each fiscal year.

In summary, NHK is a uniquely positioned entity in considered among numerous public broadcasters around the world, and yet it expects to be a public corporation to contribute to the whole social welfare and public interest of Japan. When delivering its programs, NHK does not make any exceptions for serving television households throughout all regions of Japan, including isolated mountainous areas and tiny islands which may have difficulty in transmitting airwaves to their television households by airing broadcast programs such as national and local news, documentaries, and entertainment.

4 The NHK Initiative for the Development of Broadcasting During the Postwar Restoration and High Economic Growth Until the 1970s

During the postwar restoration period, the number of radio signals receiving contract homes reached 10 million in August 1952 since its initial broadcast back on March 22, 1925 (Shimada 2015, p. 69).

The conventional analog television broadcasting operations, which adopted the NTSC (National Television Standard Committee) standard of the USA for its television signal reception with TV sets at home, it launched its service four hours per day with 5 kW output power on February 1, 1953.

It counted only 866 contracts in 1953 (including 303 for consumer electronics retailer for shop exhibition and collective viewing, 249 for intellectual workers, 76 with consumer retailing shops, 61 government and commercial company offices) on the first day in the Tokyo Metropolitan Area. At that time television households paid a monthly reception fee of 200 JPY to receive NHK broadcasts (NHK-a 2002, p. 127; NHK-b 1983, p. 5).

Diffusion of television broadcasting contracts marked 100,000 in October 1955, 500,000 in June 1957, 1 million in May 1958, 5 million in August 1960, 10 million in March 1962, 15 million in December 1963, 20 million in December 1967, 25 million in July 1974, and 30 million in September 1982 (NHK-b 1983, p. 5).

On the other hand, the founding broadcasting operation, radio broadcasting started with only 5,455 in the first year of 1924 and reached the 10 million users mark by 1952. The radio contracts recorded the peak as 14,605,745 in 1958, but assumingly because the advent of television eroded the number of radio contracts only households. Furthermore, when NHK introduced the color TV reception contracts in 1968, radio contracts were abolished (NHK-a 2002, p. 342).

Operating revenue marked 2.67 million JPY when the NHK radio broadcasting launched its service in 1926 of 6.869 billion JPY for the first year of television broadcasting service. In 1953, it passed the line of 50 billion JPY coming from 5,104,081 radio contracts and 13,378,973 television contracts when the new reception fee system including radio and television only reception categories were established in 1962. Finally, 287.746 billion JPY was reached from television contracts which exceeded over 30 million users in 1982 (NHK-a 2002, p. 342).

From the period of rebirth of NHK after World War II, NHK has culturally and technologically led Japan's broadcasting by itself. In fact, when a new technological innovation in broadcasting has occurred, NHK has always occupied the center role by showing its national pride in public broadcasting to the world.

In the phase of social and economic development of Japan after World War II, public broadcaster NHK played a vital role and even took the initiative to inform publicly what the general public should be aware of such as social issues to be solved from a social welfare's point of view.

During this period almost all issues, including topics such as air and water pollution, which were caused by the profit seeking and cost-effectiveness in producing consumer goods. NHK had taken an initiative that all society-centric issues and items to be considered would be covered as documentary programs and thus put them on the air from the aspect of public interest value.

In other words, the social interest and value-added approach through documentary programs produced by the public broadcaster NHK stimulated the social impact of the media to create a better society for Japan along the line of rapid economic growth from the postwar recovery period to the 1970s.

Hamada (1997, p. 37) in Studies of Broadcasting stated that public broadcasting is the product of history rather than theory when thinking about Japan's spirit of public broadcasting. More precisely, it has a unique dual structure balanced between public and commercial broadcasting systems that are crucially different from the model of typical public broadcasting developed in Europe.

It may be said that Japan developed its unique public broadcasting system while learning some useful lessons from all over the world. Therefore, Japan's broadcasting system has been growing with the Japanese historical context and cultural flow and overlapping with one another. Corresponding authors, Hamada (1997) and Browne (1999), also indicated from the aspect of comparing media systems in the world that each country and region's media system is unique and is a reflection of the country's history, society, economics, and culture.

5 The New Development Stage for NHK in Transition: For the Firm Foundation Building of Public Status

In Japan, public broadcaster NHK has always been in a central position developing advanced technologies in broadcasting and related fields and has contributed to diffusing new types of broadcasting technologies and services. Public broadcaster NHK is obliged to lead the first stage of new developments in broadcasting based on the fact that NHK is expected to serve the whole society of Japan. One of the most reliable indications is that NHK has accepted to act in line with the intent of the supplementary resolution adopted by the Diet approval for the budget proposal of NHK.

As a public entity that is allowed to collect viewer fees, NHK has faced expectations, such as providing trustworthy information and leading to the opening of a new phase of broadcasting operations as a public broadcaster. This is one of the most distinctive characteristics of NHK as a public broadcaster and at the same time differentiating it from other commercial broadcasters in Japan which rely heavily on advertising revenues.

From the aspect of media and social change, NHK's other contribution would be the establishment of shared values in society to realize rapid economic growth after World War II. In this context, NHK has tried very hard to realize the concept of "universality" enabling it to provide anyone who would be willing to receive a public broadcasting signal anywhere in Japan under which any circumstances might occur. Although it has taken a significant amount of time for NHK to accomplish this goal, the universal service philosophy of NHK is the cause of the regulatory mandate in the Broadcast Act of Japan.

In particular, media events, such as the Tokyo Olympic Games of 1964 gave significant revitalization to NHK broadcasting operations and as a result, led to rapid growth in the collection of receiving fees for NHK revenues. Behind the scenes of this, rapid growth in annual revenues was based on a steady collection of NHK receiving fees.

A strong rationale for the general public to pay NHK's receiving fees came from the professional concept of broadcasting content produced and the perfection of operations by acting as a role model of broadcasting through NHK's daily operations. Up until the 1980s, people came to believe that what NHK broadcasted was the general measurement in judging things to be considered as a professional model. Therefore an extreme belief for a specific audience was that NHK would not make any mistakes in broadcasting operations and announcing scripts.

According to Burns (1977, p. 126), the notion of professionalism for the British Broadcasting Corporation is frequently used in the context of implying the invocations of moral order leading to the professional judgments, decisions, and actions. Like the BBC, from the public broadcaster's point of view, NHK also has sought to be a professional in the broadcasting field, and this is one of the significant reasons when collecting receiving fees, which supplanted the idea of public service.

Operationally, NHK as an entity of public broadcaster has been required to be professional in all sorts of broadcasting activities and operations including technology and innovation, announcing scripts in common accent through everyday use of Japanese in society, and producing high-quality programs expected to be distinguished from other commercial broadcasters. By doing so, NHK could obtain the notion of trustworthiness from the general public as well as receive the annual budget approval for each fiscal year from the Diet. NHK would then be able to collect program receiving fees to work on the proposed fiscal year's operations.

Around the early 1980s, commercial broadcasters started complaining or even condemning NHK as being too privileged because NHK could rely on a stable annual income to produce quality programs based on the professionalism of its service. Commercial broadcasters thought NHK's broadcasting operation was so skilled and well financed that commercial broadcasters of Japan seemed to be less attractive and eventually audience viewer rates, which were the primary data source for setting up the advertising fees influenced the total amount of annual revenues for commercial broadcasters of Japan. This situation might have caused an argument regarding NHK's expansionism when entering into the age of new media leading the historical launch of satellite broadcasting service and a new type of multichannel service, the cable television.

In spite of commercial broadcasters way of viewing public broadcaster NHK, it faced financial concerns due to lacking production budget caused by the oil crisis-based inflation in the middle of the 1970s due to the high rise of production costs. This situation eventually triggered a 24% receiving fee increase proposal by NHK to a fee of 880 JPY for color television services as well as 520 JPY for ordinal black-and-white reception televisions. In 1979, the diffusion rate of television in Japan reached 90%. At that time, the total annual revenues of NHK was 28.93 million with 28.93 million coming from television home contracts (NHK-b 1980, pp. 8, 13).

The overall issue was the reflection of the media and social change, in which Japan was about to direct for the age of new media. In order for NHK to proceed in this direction, it would be forced to choose between dramatic increasing receiving fees or setting up new services to find new sources of income to contribute to NHK's steady increase of operating revenues in the future. By 1980, Japan was making a plan for an advanced direct broadcast satellite (hereinafter referred to as DBS) system. The plan was to establish and dominate the next generation of the television standard by utilizing Multiple Sub-Nyquist Sampling Encoding (hereinafter referred to as MUSE) based system.

6 Preparation Period of Satellite Broadcasting to Expand Public Broadcasting Status

Japan's highly advanced development of the DBS system had a significant impact on the Japanese broadcasting industry. Eventually, the Japanese government made an additional satellite broadcasting policy and operational uses including satellite channel allocations not only for the public broadcaster NHK but also for a possible commercial broadcaster by the end of the 1980s.

During the Cold War, the USA and the USSR competitively explored outer space development by utilizing rocket launching and satellite communication technologies. However, the period during the 1980s and 1990s encouraged the freeze and eventually the end of the Cold War. At the same time, more deregulation and commercialization of space communication industries were devitalized as a result of the end of the Cold War.

This period was crucial for NHK as well as Japan to realize the industrial policy-making to disseminate the next television standard competition in the world. At the same time, the age of cable television arrived from the USA.

One of the symbolic phenomena was the advent of the Cable News Network starting on June 1, 1980 (Flournoy and Stewart 1997). Each cable television system in Japan was about to move its basic service of retransmitting terrestrial television channel signals to the cable home to a multichannel cable television service by utilizing a satellite transmission route.

In sum, under the deregulatory policy-making atmosphere in Japan, the zeitgeist of the 1980s in media and journalism wanted to have more choice and diversification, which led the multichannel cable service to offer each subscriber a variety of channels from content providers. This type of service has been maintained based on the utilization of communication satellite (CS) from content providers to the cable operator's headend. In the 1980s, the deregulatory movement even encouraged the utilization of the communication satellite for individual program reception use, calling it the direct-to-the-home, (DDTH) service. NHK later launched this service as DBS or in Japanese as "Eisei Hoso."

In fact, under the circumstances faced in the 1980s, Japan was influenced by the deregulatory movement of the USA, and the UK and the then-Ministry of Posts and Telecommunications (hereinafter referred to as MPT) started considering the next stage of its advanced broadcasting system after diffusing color televisions followed by black-and-white television services terrestrially. MPT thought that the new broadcasting service would not only be for broadcasting use but also the alternative program delivery route directly to the subscribers. This might be imagined as a representative government and business partnership approach which could move Japan to the second largest economy of the world in the 1980s (Gershon and Kanayama 1995).

All these arguments relating to the development of new media, such as cable television and satellite television, as well as the policy-making for new media were intensely discussed among communication scholars in the 1980s.

One argument was that Japan would naturally seek the direction of direct-to-the-home program transmission, rather than cable television networks because unlike the USA, the cable network system had not developed sufficiently enough to provide a wide variety of programs throughout any region of Japan. Therefore, the critical argument was whether Japan should step forward as a cable television society or as a satellite broadcasting society (Ashibe 1986, p. 103).

7 NHK's Brave New World and Direct Broadcasting Satellite in the 1980s

Public broadcaster NHK already had started developing the direct-to-the-home program delivery service system back in the 1960s. However, in the age of new media, NHK should have been ready for handling the development of satellite broadcasting systems as a national project and yet should also have been ready for the cable carry issues when the satellite broadcasting system was implemented for general use.

Initially, the broadcast satellite operation was encouraged to plan in the 1960s by the 10th President of NHK, Yoshinori Maeda (term period: 1964–1973). President Maeda seemed to be stimulated by the idea scientifically announced by Arthur Charles Clarke (1917–2008) that the entire globe could be covered by the three communication satellites parked 22,300 miles above in space on the geosynchronous orbit. NHK Science & Technology Research Laboratories (hereinafter referred to as NHK STRL) had worked hard toward realizing the daily use of satellite broadcasting as an ordinal public broadcasting activity (NHK-c 2010).

In 1965, NHK President Maeda announced that NHK's research and development would enable Japan to provide all television households with NHK programs (NHK-a 2002, p. 249), rather than costly terrestrial transmissions and to relay of program signals. Under the Broadcast Law, NHK was mandated to cover all television households in Japan. To accomplish this goal, it was necessary for NHK to build several small relay stations terrestrially for isolated areas.

In 1978, NHK successfully launched a middle-sized experimental broadcast satellite (BS-Yuri, named Lily in English). At that time, the National Aeronautics and Space Administration (NASA) as consignee launched a 350 kg satellite up to the geosynchronous satellite orbit above the equator at 110 degrees east longitude with 100 W output power of the transmitter in the space (NHK-b 1981, p. 3).

The original purpose of satellite broadcasting, in this case, the DBS system was (1) to overcome poor signal reception situations in any point in Japan, (2) to ensure the broadcast network under the urgent occasion, such as under the natural disaster, and (3) to profoundly advance the quality broadcasting service. In Japan's broadcasting history, this was one of the most expensive projects ever completed in tandem with the Japanese government. The total cost of this experimental satellite launch project reached 60 billion JPY (equivalent to 545 million USD. Dollars in the exchange rate at 110 JPY per dollar), whose amount was cooperatively shared by NHK and the Japanese government (NHK-b 1981, p. 3).

In the 1980s, when NHK revealed its new broadcast policy-making in developing new media, called the DBS operation, this became the national project with government and at the same time this project was intended to explore outer space by involving all related industries and the agency, such as broadcasting, consumer electronics, and Japan's National Space Agency (NASDA).

It seemed that during the Cold War, the USA and the USSR had competitively launched experimental satellites in space by fully utilizing the missile launch technologies highly valued in the process. Japan was geopolitically located between the two superpower pillars and yet as the public broadcaster NHK sought an alternative way to contribute and serve the general public to utilize the highly advanced broadcasting technologies for a more democratic and peaceful manner as a part of the representative national project. This would be a typical approach as the government and business partnerships, sometimes called symbolically as "Japan Inc." (Okimoto 1989).

8 Seeking a Harmonization in Dual Structure: Overcoming the Tension Between Public and Commercial Broadcasters

After the experimental satellite launch and operation phase, NHK finally launched two broadcast satellites, called BS-2a and BS-2b for practical broadcasting operation. The first BS-2a satellite was successfully launched in January 1984 and the second BS-2b was completed in February 1986. When Japan's Space Committee under the Prime Minister's office announced launching the plan for the BS-2a and BS-2b satellites nothing was explained about how to utilize these and government was expected to make a clear communication policy, in case of the new type of broadcasting media, about how the Japanese broadcasting industry would keep a harmonized balance between the terrestrial broadcasting route and the satellite broadcasting route.

Commercial broadcasters association, known as the Japan Commercial Broadcasters Association (hereinafter referred to as JCBA) pointed out that massive broadcast operations would be realized by NHK and that these would possibly threaten commercial broadcasters status in the age of new media.

For NHK, the age of new media was the only window to seek additional revenue income to fill in the lack of budget influenced by the oil crisis of the 1970s and expand the operation of its newly developed satellite broadcasting service. Automatically, NHK distinguished the policy when developing the satellite broadcasting system by expressing a definitive statement as a public broadcasting point of view.

In this sense, NHK was released from a one-way broadcasting service by merely relying on the terrestrial program transmission to serve all television households throughout Japan. The age of new media in the 1980s gave NHK the seed of promising future operations by utilizing advanced broadcasting technologies and highly significant professional program production with stable financial resources.

NHK, in fact, internally discussed the way to realize more advanced broadcasting service policy and the pivotal issue was how public and commercial broadcasters could play a role based on the notion of public interest to be realized by the broadcasters in every corner of Japanese society. In 1980, the USA paid multichannel cable television service which had already started disseminating to society, while the MPT, the principal policy-making house in telecommunications, took the US multichannel cable service trends into consideration for Japan's future policy-making. Japan had never experienced paid multiple channel services for cable, but when adopting the DBS service in society, this might cause another fee receiving system or a subscription fee system separate from the K receiving fee system (NHK-b 1981, p. 5).

In 1982, a report on the Diversification of Broadcasting was submitted to the Minister of Posts and Telecommunications, by emphasizing that there needed to be harmonization with the terrestrial broadcasting operation when adopting the satellite broadcasting system in Japan. In addition to this basic notion, the report indicated that there could be another paid or advertising-supported broadcasting system available (NHK-b 1982, p. 6). It might be pointed out that this was a crucial moment for NHK to seek the possibility of additional receiving fees, considering those such as (1) terrestrial television receiving fees and (2) satellite television receiving fees in the future.

Thinking about the NHK obligation to cover all television households in Japan via terrestrial signals, it was a significantly tricky task to complete. However, if the satellite broadcasting system was established, it would solve the problem all at once due to the satellite coverage over footprint area households, meaning all television households would be able to receive the satellite signals. By the end of March 1982, there were 44,000 television households which were not able to receive NHK programs or poor signal reception of NHK terrestrial television programs (NHK-b 1982, p. 12). A year later, by the end of March 1983, there were 43,000 television households able to receive NHK signals (NHK-b 1983, p. 56).

It took a year to improve the signal reception for the 10,000 television households using newly created signal transmission sites, but at this pace of improvement, it would have taken over 40 years, such as until around the year 2025 to deliver NHK signals to all areas. The concept of universal, or "Amaneku" in Japanese requires NHK to serve the general public of Japan by equipping television and radio broadcasting receiver(s) 100% of the time according to Article 15 of Broadcast Act of Japan. As a result, the advent of satellite broadcasting was a highly popular way of accomplishing this task.

However, considering the start-up costs to realize a satellite broadcasting system in Japan, NHK had to face the question of how to finance the satellite system separately from the conventional terrestrial transmission system. The one significant fundamental financial indication was how to manage the startup capital of 60 billion JPY to launch and control the broadcast satellite in space. This would be a risk-taking opportunity and testing whether the country of Japan did achieve the goal regarding inaugurating the direct-to-the-home delivery of NHK' broadcasting programs.

Figure 2 shows NHK operating revenues from 1926 to 2017. The amount of total operating revenues of NHK in 1980 was recorded at 272 billion JPY, and expenditures totaled 251.3 billion JPY; in 1981 there was 282.3 billion JPY in revenue and 267.1 billion JPY in expenditure, and in 1982 there was 288.2 billion JPY in revenue and 281.1 billion JPY in expenditure (NHK-b 1983, p. 58). By merely looking at operating revenues in the 1980s, it seemed to be impossible for NHK to launch the satellite broadcasting without public aid, such as from the government. The period for launching the satellite broadcasting in Japan was synchronized with the acceleration period of the national space development of Japan.

NHK Operating Revenues (1926 - 2017 business years)

Year Amount (unit: million yen)

Year	Amount	Year	Amount	Year	Amount
1926	2.67	1957	13,719	1988	356,520
1927	4.04	1958	16,629	1989	379,750
1928	5.19	1959	25,157	1990	488,466
1929	6.58	1960	32,436	1991	523,040
1930	7.68	1961	40,864	1992	539,824
1931	9.75	1962	50,422	1993	556,280
1932	10.53	1963	60,124	1994	568,152
1933	13.48	1964	66,636	1995	578,384
1934	15.87	1965	71,301	1996	596,192
1935	13.45	1966	75,230	1997	621,797
1936	16.05	1967	78,802	1998	633,712
1937	19.93	1968	79,154	1999	645,042
1938	22.29	1969	84,800	2000	655,857
1939	26.05	1970	92,063	2001	667,626
1940	30.00	1971	100,986	2002	674,999
1941	35.54	1972	109,979	2003	680,257
1942	38.41	1973	118,723	2004	685,493
1943	40.78	1974	125,786	2005	674,946
1944	46.29	1975	131,374	2006	675,667
1945	58.84	1976	191,505	2007	684,795
1946	224.28	1977	209,124	2008	662,428
1947	945.11	1978	214,136	2009	665,866
1948	2,742.04	1979	219,107	2010	681,210
1949	3,728.14	1980	271,432	2011	694,576
1950	3,230	1981	281,576	2012	660,447
1951	5,886	1982	287,746	2013	657,018
1952	6,372	1983	292,623	2014	674,823
1953	6,869	1984	336,114	2015	687,944
1954	9,753	1985	340,763	2016	704,548
1955	10,624	1986	346,067	2017	717,732
1956	11,821	1987	351,508		

*lower receiving fees by 8.9 % in 2012

*plan to lower receiving fees by 2.5 % in 2020

Note : Statistics for 1926 - 49 are given in millions of yen in order to be of the samedenomination as those for 1950 onward.

Source : NHK *nenkan* (NHK Yearbook)

Fig. 2 NHK operating revenues (1926–2017 Business Years) (*Source* NHK-a (2002), and NHK-b)

JCBA sought to set up its own broadcasting policy-making with regard to the emerging new media environment and the new phase of commercial broadcasting operations. JCBA set three themes as follows: (1) lower growth rate trend, (2) new entrants to the current commercial broadcasting stations that would share the same advertising pie, and (3) an offensive and/or defensive strategy in case of new media entrance into the broadcasting market, imagined for the DBS industry as well as multichannel cable operations. The year 1983 was the 30th anniversary of television broadcasting in Japan. In September 1982, the JCBA executive board unanimously decided to commit to DBS development and set up the development committee in November 1982 (NHK-b 1983, p. 58).

It can be said that the 1980s decided the direction of Japanese broadcasting. Public broadcaster NHK and other commercial broadcasters eventually shared the notion that NHK's expansionism, though from the JCBA's point of view, would be a real danger for commercial broadcasters. There was a saying that small-sized local commercial stations would be in danger once the DBS system was introduced from the aspect of nationwide coverage of Japan since the satellite system could realize the cost-effectiveness and NHK was obliged to embrace the concept of universal, or "Amaneku" all at once.

9 The Age of Satellite Broadcasting and the Road to Introducing New Receiving Fees

In 1987, NHK operated two channels. BS-1 with 24-h broadcasting started on July 4, 1987, and BS-2 with supplemental programs was imported from NHK general terrestrial television channel in order for NHK to cover unserviced television households located all over Japan based on the universal service philosophy (NHK-b 1988, p. 1).

The rationale of NHK's satellite broadcasting operation was (1) solving unserviced poor reception signal households hopefully by launching a broadcasting satellite in 1984 and (2) preparing for the age of new media, such as introducing the experiment satellite broadcasting channels. However, NHK had difficulty covering all of the additional operational expenses. In 1984, NHK raised the receiving fees for a color television service from 880 JPY to 1,040 JPY and black-and-white based standard service fees from 520 to 680 JPY (NHK-b 1985, pp. 34–35).

However, satellite broadcasting was costly, even though it was positioned as a national project to compete with other countries' advanced systems. Particularly launching satellites into space required a vast amount of money NHK had to seek an additional income source by serving the television households equipped with a receiving tuner and parabolic antennae for satellite signal reception. In fact, in 1987, NHK recorded a financial loss to the amount of 12.4 billion JPY (NHK-b 1988, p. 44) and in 1988 it did even worse, ending 22.7 billion JPY in the red (NHK-b 1989, p. 10).

In order to fulfill the goal explained above, the newly emerging analog Hi-Vision service provided high-quality video and sound with satellite broadcasting. This could give the general public a greater incentive, and the then Ministry of Posts and Telecommunications of Japan announced that Hi-Vision experimental broadcasting would occur during the same time as the Seoul Olympic Games in 1988.

In October 1988, it marked a presence in 1 million satellite broadcasting television households (NHK-b 1988, p. 8; 1989, p. 2).

In 1988, the President of NHK, Masato Kawahara (term period: 1982–1988) at a press conference stated that the 100 million mark for satellite television households was one of the organization's milestones, but this did not mean NHK could start charging for the satellite broadcasting service because NHK needed to get approval from the Diet based on the judgment of the Ministry of Posts and Telecommunications. However, President Kawahara left the connotative nuance that NHK would consider the possibility of the new satellite receiving fees based on a holistic assessment (NHK-b 1988, p. 32).

Finally, in 1989, NHK satellite broadcasting started receiving the fee-based system after an announcement from the MPT that officially announced setting of the official rate (NHK-b 1989, pp. 8, 30).

NHK followed the announcement of the MPT and stated that relying on receiving the fees only from the terrestrial television service would put the public broadcasting system in danger. NHK's serious concern during that time was whether NHK was to play its obliged role for the public interest in the Broadcasting Act because NHK calculated the lack of operational expenditures at about 500 billion JPY accumulatively by 1994. In summary, NHK honestly expressed serious budget-related concerns of there being a burdensome operating expense increase and found difficulty in maintaining the quality service of public broadcasting.

Introducing the newly established satellite broadcasting service fee had a tremendous impact on the whole Japanese broadcasting industry and gave NHK a tremendous opportunity to maintain the sustainable development of the public broadcasting system as it moved toward the twenty-first century.

Moreover, the country of Japan, based on the government-industry partnership, sought an original HDTV studio standard together with the USA by utilizing the analog-based MUSE Hi-Vision technology originating from NHK STRL.

NHK and the Japanese government particularly desired that MUSE Hi-Vision technology become the analog-based advanced television (ATV) standard in the USA. However, the USA instead combined the government and industry members together, so that Japan could not continue taking steps to maintain the initiative and realize the cooperative MUSE Hi-Vision analog-based HDTV standard with the U.S. (NHK-b 1989, pp. 8–9).

In fact, the USA eventually developed the digital-based ATV with the firm digital compression technology led by Advanced Television Systems Committee (ATSC) standard, and later it was generally called digital television (DTV) for the US terrestrial transmission standard in 1990. It was a dramatic comeback to develop the made-in-the-USA advanced television in digital originated by General Instruments (Kurz 2018). It was a fact that Japan Inc.'s dream stopped in 1990, and NHK, the leading broadcaster of analog-based high definition quality broadcasting, that was called the MUSE standard, was then forced to focus on the domestic market.

One of the aspects was that because the nationally developed analog HD standard was taken into consideration worldwide and NHK was a robust prime mover of the satellite broadcasting by utilizing MUSE oriented Hi-Vision, NHK had the possibility of setting up actual satellite receiving fees approved by the Diet based on the recommendation of the policy-making entity, MPT. Newly emerging viewing fees in 1990 were set at 2,300 JPY including terrestrial and satellite color television program viewing while receiving fees for terrestrial color television only cost 1,370 JPY (NHK-b 1990, p. 40). This meant an increase in NHK satellite broadcasting viewers; and the effective increase in higher NHK operating income. As the following Fig. 2 shows, there was a big revenue jump in 1990 (488,466 million JPY) from 1989 (379,750 million JPY), and following that NHK's firm and steady financial increase took off, up until 2017.

After the USA started moving to the fully digitized advanced television (ATV), Japan shifted its focus to domestic satellite broadcasting service. Since the deregulatory movement had less strict regulatory constraints, another satellite program delivery path via a communication satellite, other than regulatory strict broadcasting satellites, started providing some unique channels including MTV and CNN like cable program delivery in the USA in 1992. There emerged a system in which the roles were divided between the co-signer of the program provider and the cosignee of the system operator to deliver such programs (NHK-b 1992, p. 9).

Thus, NHK had a narrow escape from losing ground financially to maintain its professional quality and quantity in broadcasting operations to serve the general public of Japan from the public broadcaster's point of view. In the middle of the 1990s, Japan followed the changing media environment of the digitally integrated society among advanced countries.

10 Changing Environment in NHK's Management of Finance and Deregulation in the Early 1990s

After introducing the satellite broadcasting receiving fees in 1989, public broadcaster NHK performed well by mainly providing BS-1 for 24-h broadcasting operations with timely world news event coverage, sports and entertainment, and BS-2 for the supplemental broadcast programs to realize universal coverage toward the television households left out in Japan. However, all satellite services were analog based and in terms of developing advanced television, Japan was no longer the leader nor a front-runner in the world.

The digitization of broadcasting, the world trend initiated by the USA came into effect in Japan in 1997 after having taken initiatives from the USA and the UK since 1996. On the other hand, the strict operation of the broadcasting satellite including NHK BS-1 and BS-2, and in addition WOWOW, the commercial satellite broadcaster in 1990 under the Broadcasting Act had to wait for digitization until December 1, 2000. And yet, terrestrial digitization of Japan had to wait for the initial stage for transition from analog until December 1, 2003 in Japan's three major markets, including the Greater Kanto area comprising of Tokyo and six other prefectures, the

Greater Kinki area with Osaka and five prefectures, and the Greater Chukyo area embracing Aichi, Gifu, and Mie prefectures.

Due to the broadcast policy deregulations in the 1990s, the rule of strictly enforcing concentrated responsibility in broadcasting operations by law eventually invited the revised Broadcasting Act in 1992, which enabled a new concept of the co-signer (content providers) and co-signee (system operator to deliver contents) relationship to deliver audio and video program delivery via communication satellites as an alternative method. However, 1992 was also the year which community broadcasting was established. These were mainly community FM radio stations. It was a symbolic year for media deregulation which somewhat looked forward to the citizen or consumer-centered news media environment of Japan.

As clearly noted, there were two separate satellite program delivery routes, such as via broadcast satellite and communication satellite and public broadcasters. NHK belonged to the broadcast satellite group. Thanks to the additional revenue source added on to the conventional terrestrial television receiving fees, the satellite service contract category as labeled, after 3 years of introducing the fee system, NHK increased revenue from 356.5 billion JPY in 1989 to 523 billion JPY in 1991 (NHK-b 1992, p. 9). In a sense, NHK was in a position to look for the future broadcasting policy by fully utilizing the best of the economies of scale concept. This was a critical moment for NHK even as a public broadcaster to plan and act based on its broadcasting policy proactively, rather than reactively.

In 1991, NHK announced a 5-year management plan by emphasizing (1) creativity and (2) effectiveness in management based on the firm receiving a fee-based income with the public trust. In 1991, NHK provided satellite broadcasting 24 h a day with international news and live national sports broadcasting coverage, as well as international events including the Olympic Games and the World Cup Soccer championship on BS-1. Poor reception supplemental service imported from the terrestrial General Channel and Educational Channel and especially newly added the analog Hi-Vision Channel on November 24 with the consortium project among NHK and commercial satellite broadcaster WOWOW, and commercial terrestrial broadcasters. 1993 was the turning point as the 40th anniversary of NHK, and the total number of receiving fees contract reached over 34 million including 5 million satellite receiving fees contracts (NHK-b 1993, p. 21).

In April 1993, the Ministry of Posts and Telecommunications made an inquiry for the future use of the fourth generation of the broadcasting satellite, called BS-4 to the Radio Regulatory Council of Japan. At that time, all the commercial network stations, including Tokyo Broadcasting Systems, Nippon Television Network, Fuji Television Network, TV Asahi, and TV Tokyo showed their strong willingness to be a part of a satellite broadcasting operation (NHK-b 1993, p. 28).

On the other hand, in 1993, NHK showed stable and calm attitude while seeking the twenty-first century Vision by pointing out that (1) the importance of the existence of NHK could be realized under the age of multimedia and multichannel through the notion of a well-balanced public and commercial based dual structure in broadcasting; (2) technological development of broadcasting should be accelerated along the lines of international information in dissemination internationally; and (3) stabilizing financial management of NHK would be the key in realizing open and effective public broadcasting operation (NHK-b 1993, p. 57). All these themes when looked at from the twenty-first century of NHK broadcasting operation from a policy-making point of view were unchanged except for the fact that the Japanese broadcasting operation shifted wholly from analog to a fully digital operation after 2012.

11 Political Impact on the Public Broadcasting Policy and NHK's Operation Until the MPT Announcement of Digital Transition of Satellite and Terrestrial Broadcasting

The year 1993 was significantly essential for the broadcasters' independent policy-making. One of the commercial network stations, Television Asahi, was accused of conducting a spin control favorable to the challenging new party, the Japan New Party under the environment of the dominant Liberal Democratic Party of Japan at the general election campaign coverage of the Diet. This was a moment when the independent circumstances of broadcasting journalism were put in danger, and it automatically seemed to be extended to the general management of commercial broadcasters as well as a public broadcaster, NHK. At the same time among broadcasters, commercial broadcasters started accusing NHK of accelerating commercialization by establishing affiliated or subsidiary business entities.

In 1994, instead, NHK started considering the retransmission of broadcasting channels BS-1 and BS-2 via cable channels and the agreement of the cable industry to assist in collecting satellite receiving fees for NHK. The growth of cable television households reached over 3 million multichannel cable household contracts by March 1996 (NHK-b 1994, pp. 8, 36; 1996, p. 5). And yet, because of the importance of internationalization of Japan and sending Japanese information abroad to maintain the feeling of belonging to Japan among Japanese citizens living abroad, the operation through a co-signee to send NHK programs became possible on behalf of the co-signer NHK by the revised Broadcasting Act of 1994 (NHK-b 1995, p. 73).

In March 1996, the broadcast satellite contracts reached 10.14 million with the analog-based service. At the same time, NHK had to think about the world trend of broadcast digitization from the satellite route as a project for the whole country. NHK synchronized with the national broadcasting policy, started digitization on December 1, 2000, and synchronized with the other commercial satellite broadcasting channels by utilizing BS-4 satellites.

In 1997, the Ministry of Posts and Telecommunications announced that digitization of broadcasting satellite operations, as well as terrestrial broadcasting operation, would start transitioning in 2000. At the same time, NHK announced in 1997 a dedicated opinion aimed at the Ministry of Posts and Telecommunications that NHK should play a significant role in realizing broadcasting digitization for the further development of broadcasting in Japan (NHK-b 1997, pp. 9, 15).

12 Playing a Central Role Before and After Broadcast Digitization and Some Ethical Stumbling Blocks

Thanks to the broadcasting receiving fees and increase in the number of receiving fees contracts, NHK's operating revenues reached over 62.46 billion JPY in March 1999 (NHK-b 1998, p. 23). NHK started making the transition to digital from analog satellite broadcasting in December 2000 and finished transitioning in July 2011. NHK also started its transition to the digitization of terrestrial television from December 2003 and completed it in March 2012.

In the process of making the transition from analog to digital, NHK played an essential role in every broadcasting market in Japan. Sometimes, to realize cost-effectiveness when building transmission sites on top of mountains, NHK had to work based on carefully coordinated discussions with regional commercial broadcasters.

In responding to the revision of the Broadcasting Act, NHK developed proactive broadcasting operations by taking a strong initiative in creating public interest-oriented services, such as the primary natural disaster coverage in the news, broadcasting ancillary information insertions on a television screen in the name of L Alert. It even developed an integrated broadcasting system with social media, called "Hybridcast" and started working closely with cable and communication satellite program delivery services.

In spite of a leading image as a nationally represented public broadcaster, NHK regretfully held two internal misconduct cases. These involved the unethical use of production budgets by the NHK producer in 2004 (NHK-b 2005, p. 25) and the trading of stocks by an NHK professional journalist during working hours back in 2007 (NHK-b 2008, p. 54). This triggered the intentional abstinence movement in regard to the paying of receiving fees by the contractors and the following year the misconduct case reported that operating revenues of NHK had decreased dramatically. Especially in the year of 2005, a 4.5 billion JPY decrease in receiving fees was recorded, and NHK announced a 1,200 human resources personnel cut over three years to maintain quality operations within a tight budget in 2006. As a total, the intentional abstinence movement concerning the paying of NHK receiving fees reached approximately 1.12 million contractors (NHK-b 2006, pp. 7, 9).

In 2006, NHK President Genichi Hashimoto promised the achievement of a Three Year Management Plan (2006–2008) subtitled as "NHK's Rebirth and Seeking of the Public Interest in the Digital Age." NHK contributed to widening coverage in transmitting signals all over Japan for 60% coverage in December 2005 via terrestrial digital broadcasting and achieving the goal that all of the prefectures started terrestrial digital broadcasting in December 2006 (NHK-b 2006, p. 437).

NHK thankfully worked and marketed cooperatively with commercial broadcasters in making the transition to digital terrestrial broadcasting and satellite broadcasting to make synergy in increasing satellite receiving television sets over 20 million in 2006 and reached 50 million sets in March 2009 (NHK-b 2007, p. 436; 2009, p. 477).

In December 2007, Shigeo Fukuchi became President of NHK. Previously, President Fukuchi was a senior advisor of Asahi Breweries, LTD. and he was selected externally to NHK to achieve drastic reform. He faced hardships from the very beginning in lowering receiving fees, regaining NHK's public trust, and achieving the ratio of accessing NHK contents to reach over 80% of its viewers, and finally increase the payment percentage of receiving fees to 76% as a whole (NHK-b 2008, pp. 49, 60).

Especially the quota of receiving fees payment with 76% was accomplished in 2014 as 77% with 39.73 million contracts, whose satellite broadcasting contracts counted for 43% as 19.23 million (NHK-b 2015, p. 11).

13 Continuation of the NHK's Leadership as Public Broadcaster and Toward the Future Policy-Making

In 2011, the Japanese government overhauled the related laws mainly relating to the Broadcasting Act and Radio Act for a 60-year time period. It was like the large-scale revision of the Communication Act of 1934 for the Telecommunication Act of 1996 in the USA. The Revised Act had unique characteristics like a layered shape in understanding broadcasting and communication operation on the same platform, but the core broadcasting entities still played a conventional and mainstream role with a more flexible manner (NHK-b 2011, p. 25). Yet NHK in October 2012 discounted the receiving fees by 8.9% (120 JPY) of the original charge for the terrestrial fees (NHK-b 2013, p. 459). This seemed to be accepted by the general public after the series of incidents causing damage in public trust toward NHK as an act repayment, so it recorded a decrease in operating income of about 30–40 billion JPY, respectively.

Based on the new policy-making environment set up, NHK has contributed to leading broadcasting in Japan in terms of developing new technologies in the age of the internet. Currently, another government/business partnership-oriented project has focused on the diffusion of (1) "Hybridcast" as integrated services between broadcasting and social media, (2) Radio program transmission via the Internet, Rajiru★Rajiru, (3) on-demand service, called NHK On-demand, (4) NHK developed smart-TV, Teleda possibly integrated into "Hybridcast" in the future, (5) improving quality service of international broadcasting via NHK World Television, and finally (6) Super Hi-Vision in digital form, as 4K and 8K broadcasting. At the same time from the public interest's point of view, NHK has always been and is always ready to provide urgent or breaking news on natural disasters.

14 Conclusion

NHK's recent concern is whether NHK could get into simultaneous programs transmitted via the internet. NHK is concerned about the younger generation of television viewers. In order to maintain sustainable trust in its public broadcasting operations, subscription fees would be requested in any imaginable media environment for anyone available to access NHK's programs and sometimes lifeline information is provided in urgent disaster situations.

Keeping operating revenues stable is closely connected to NHK playing its unique and mandated role in the Broadcasting Act of Japan. In 2017, NHK's operating revenues reached over the 700-billion-JPY level, and by utilizing financial resources, NHK together with government and business partners has again been dreaming of a digital-based Super Hi-Vision that could be the world standard when aggressively introduced at the 2020 Tokyo Olympic Games as a globalized marketing opportunity by utilizing satellite, cable, and broadband network routes (NHK-b 2017, p. 17).

NHK's decision-making as a public broadcaster to set up additional satellite broadcasting fees in 1989 was significant and essential to maintain its critical financial resources by fulfilling and maintaining public interest expectations from the Japanese public and by keeping technological advancements in broadcasting operations as we move toward the twenty-first century. The newly emerged unique media environment has forced NHK to move to the next phase of public broadcasting under the serious issue of whether NHK could integrate broadcasting into the Internet as well as cable and wireless broadband networks by employing NHK original "Hybridcast."

References

Amishima T, Suzuki T, Yano I, Sakai S (1993) Testimony for the broadcast history I (in Japanese). Japan Broadcast Education Association, Tokyo

Ashibe N (ed) (1986) The new scope of broadcast system in the new media era: joint discussion (in Japanese). NHK, Tokyo

Browne RD (1999) Electronic media and industrialized nations: a comparative study. Iowa State University Press, Ames, Iowa

Burns T (1977) The BBC: public institution and private world. The Macmillan Press Ltd., London

Flournoy MD, Stewart KR (1997) CNN: making news in the global market. University of Luton Press, London, U.K.

Gershon R, Kanayama T (1995) Direct broadcast satellites in Japan: a case study in government-business partnerships. Telecommun Policy 19(3):217–231

Hamada J (1997) Advanced "Public" and public broadcasting: toward a theory of "Public Subjectivity" in broadcasting. Stud Broadcast 33:37–53

JBA (The Japan Commercial Broadcasters Association) (2019) Japan commercial broadcasting yearbook 2019 (in Japanese). JBA, Tokyo

Krisher B (1974) What public television can be: Japan's NHK. In: Mass communications: a world view. National Press Books, Palo Alto, California

Kurz P (2018) Richard Wiley recalls the grand alliance on Its 25th anniversary. TV Technology. https://www.tvtechnology.com/news/richard-wiley-recalls-the-grand-alliance-on-its-25th-anniversary. Accessed 14 Dec 2018

NHK-a (2002) Broadcasting in Japan: the twentieth century journey from radio to multimedia. NHK Broadcasting Culture Research Institute, Tokyo

NHK-b (1980–2017) NHK yearbook 1980–2017 (in Japanese). NHK, Tokyo

NHK-c (2010) The evolution of TV: a brief history of TV technology in Japan (in Japanese). NHK, Tokyo. https://www.nhk.or.jp/strl/aboutstrl/evolution-of-tv/p16.html. Accessed 6 Dec 2018

Okimoto D (1989) Between MITI and the market: Japanese industrial policy for high technology. Stanford University Press, Redwood City

Shimada S (2015) A collective gathering for radio listening: document summary (in Japanese). NHK Monthly Report on Broadcast Research, November 2015, 68–69

The Developmental Process of Commercial Television Broadcasting Industry

Minoru Sugaya

1 Introduction

Television broadcasting began in 1953, more than half a century ago. Tracking the developmental process of the TV broadcasting industry since its inception, the industry structure has transformed beyond the scope of the initial assumptions, with the evolution of IT technologies. There are two kinds of players in the Japanese terrestrial broadcasting industry: a public broadcaster (NHK) and private broadcasters. This chapter examines the developmental process of the commercial broadcasters in Japan, based on the principle of maximizing the number of viewers (Owen 1975).[1] The chapter occasionally mentions NHK where necessary.

This chapter is composed of three sections: (1) clarifying the principles governing behavior in the broadcasting industry, (2) categorizing the developmental process of private broadcasters into five periods, and (3) examining the key strategy at work within the five periods of the developmental process. In conclusion, based on the considerations named above, the article aims to analyze what kind of direction the Japanese terrestrial TV will take in the future.

[1]This chapter is based on the following article in Japanese: Sugaya (2015).

M. Sugaya (✉)
Keio University, Tokyo, Japan
e-mail: sugaya@keio.jp

M. Sugaya (ed.), *Perspectives on the Japanese Media and Content Policies*, Advances in Information and Communication Research 2,
https://doi.org/10.1007/978-981-15-4704-1_3

2 The Developmental Process of the Broadcasting Industry

Looking back on the history of terrestrial broadcast's evolution, the developmental process of the Japanese broadcasting industry can be categorized into the following five stages:

The first stage: the one station-per-prefecture era (1953–1967).
The second stage: the 3+2 cross-net era (1968–1973).
The third stage: the transitional period of 4 + 1 affiliated stations (1974–1996).
The fourth stage: the transitional period to digital broadcasting (1997–2012).
The fifth stage: the digital broadcasting era (starting in 2013).

2.1 The First Stage: The One Station-per-Prefecture Era

In 1953, the first private broadcaster was founded in Japan—Nippon TV (NTV) in the Kanto region. Table 1 shows the founding year of each broadcaster thereafter. Two years later in 1955, the Tokyo Broadcasting System (TBS) was launched, following its radio broadcasting business in Tokyo.

Following that, the first TV broadcaster was launched in the Chukyo region, Kansai region as well as prefectures like Hokkaido, Okayama, Kagawa, Fukuoka, Nagano, Shizuoka, Ishikawa, Ehime, and Nigata. As seen in Table 1, the TV stations launched in each prefecture have become the first broadcasters in the area, excluding those in widespread areas.

Until 1969, UHF (Ultra High Frequency) was not used on a full scale for wireless television; most broadcasters were VHF (Very High Frequency) stations until then. They were the first broadcasters in each area, except for the ones operating in the three widespread areas. They are Kanto including Tokyo, Kanagawa, Saitama, Chiba. Gunma, Tochigi, and Ibaraki; Kansai including Osaka, Kyoto, Hyogo, Wakayama, Shiga, and Nara; and finally Chukyo including Aichi, Mie, and Gifu.

The five broadcasters, called key stations in the Kanto region, which broadcast TV programs nationwide, had launched their stations by 1959. In addition, TX (TV Tokyo) launched its business in 1964. However, it was challenging for them to form a television network with five business affiliations as seen today. This is because there was only one TV broadcaster in each prefecture, except for those across the two widespread areas: Chukyo and Kansai regions.

2.2 The Second Stage: The 3+2 Cross-Net Era

As mentioned above, most of the TV stations launched during the first stage were VHF stations, with a few UHF stations. Since 1969, however, more UHF stations were launched: 19 stations in 1969, the second largest number of stations launched

Table 1 Development of commercial broadcast stations and networks

Opening Year		Broadcasting Satation	Broadcasting Area	News Network
1953	Aug.	NTV	Kanto V1	NNN (key)
1955	Apr.	TBS	Kanto V2	JNN(key)
1956	Dec.	CBC	Tyukyo V1	JNN
	Dec.	ABC	Kansai V1	ANN
1957	Apr.	HBC	Hokkaido V1	JNN
1958	Mar.	RKB	Fukuoka V1	JNN
	Jun.	RSK	Okayama/kagawa V1	JNN
	July	RNC	Okayama/kagawa V2	NNN
	Aug.	YTV	Kansai V2	NNN
	Aug.	TNC	Fukuoka V2	FNN
	Oct.	SBC	Nagano V1	JNN
	Nov.	SBS	Shizuoka V1	JNN
	Nov.	KTV	Kansai V3	FNN
	Dec.	MRO	Ishikawa V1	JNN
	Dec.	RNB	Ehime V1	NNN
	Dec.	BSN	Niigata V1	JNN
	Dec.	THK	Tyukyo V2	FNN
1959	Jan.	NBC	Nagasaki V1	JNN
	Feb.	ANB	Kanto V3	ANN(Key)
	Mar.	CX	Kanto V4	FNN(Key)
	Mar.	MES	Kansai V4	JNN
	Mar.	KBC	Fukuoka V3	ANN
	Mar.	NKT	Shimane/Tottori V1	NNN
	Apr.	STV	Hokkaido V2	NNN
	Apr.	TBC	Miyagi V1	JNN
	Apr.	KNB	Toyama V1	NNN
	Apr.	RCC	Firoshima V1	JNN
	Apr.	JRT	Tokushima V1	NNN
	Apr.	RKC	Kouchi V1	NNN
	Apr.	RKK	Kumamoto V1	JNN
	Apr.	MBS	Kagoshima V1	JNN
	Sep.	IBC	Iwate V1	JNN
	Oct.	RAB	Aomori V1	NNN
	Oct.	KRY	Yamaguchi V1	NNN
	Oct.	OBS	Ooita V1	JNN
	Nov.	OTV	Okinawa V1	FNN

(continued)

Table 1 (continued)

Opening Year		Broadcasting Satation	Broadcasting Area	News Network
	Dec.	BSS	Shimane/Tottori V2	JNN
	Dec.	YBS	Yamanashi V1	NNN
1960	Mar.	YBC	Yamagata V1	NNN
	Apr.	ABS	Akita V1	NNN
	Jun.	FBC	Fukui V1	NNN/ANN
	Jun.	RBC	Okinawa V2	JNN
	Oct.	MRT	Miyazaki V1	JNN
1962	Apr.	NBN	Tyukyo V3	ANN
	Sep.	HTV	Hiroshima V2	NNN
	Oct.	OX	Miyazaki V2	FNN
1963	Apr.	FTV	Fukushima V1	FNN
1964	Apr.	TX	Kanto V5	TXN(Key)
1965	Sep.	GBS	Gihu U1	Ind.Sta.UHF
	Nov.	SUT	Shizuoka U2	FNN
	Nov.	HTB	Hokkaido U3	ANN
	Dec.	NST	Niigata U2	FNN
1969	Apr.	NBS	Nagano U2	FNN
	Apr.	BBT	Toyama U2	FNN
	Apr.	ITC	Ishikawa U2	FNN
	Apr.	CTV	Tyukyo U4	NNN
	Apr.	KBS	Kyoto U1	Ind.Sta.UHF
	Apr.	OHK	Okayama/Kagawa U3	FNN
	Apr.	KSB	Okayama/Kagawa U4	ANN
	Apr.	FBS	Fukuoka U4	NNN
	Apr.	STS	Saga U1	FNN
	Apr.	KTN	Nagasaki U2	FNN
	Apr.	TKU	Kumamoto U2	FNN
	Apr.	KTS	Kagoshima U2	FNN
	May	SUN	Hyogo U1	Ind.Sta.UHF
	Oct.	AKT	Akita U2	FNN
	Oct.	FTB	Fukui U2	FNN
	Dec.	ATV	Aomori U2	JNN
	Dec.	TVI	Iwate U2	NNN
	Dec.	MTV	Mie U2	Ind.Sta.UHF
	Dec.	EBC	Ehime U2	FNN
1970	Apr.	YTS	Yamagata U2	ANN
	Apr.	FCT	Fukushima U1	NNN

(continued)

Table 1 (continued)

Opening Year		Broadcasting Satation	Broadcasting Area	News Network
	Apr.	UTY	Yamanashi U2	JNN
	Apr.	TSK	Shimane/Tottori U3	FNN
	Apr.	TYS	Yamguchi U2	JNN
	Apr.	KUTV	Kouchi U2	JNN
	Apr.	TOS	Ooita U2	NNN/FNN
	Apr.	UMK	Miyazaki U2	NNN/FNN/ANN
	Oct.	MMT	Miyazaki U3	NNN
	Dec.	HOME	Hiroshima U3	ANN
1971	Apr.	GTV	Gunma U1	Ind.Sta.UHF
	May	CTC	Chiba U1	Ind.Sta.UHF
1972	Apr.	UHB	Hokkaido U4	FNN
	Apr.	TVK	Kanagawa U1	Ind.Sta.UHF
	Apr.	BBC	Shiga U1	Ind.Sta.UHF
1973	Apr.	TVN	Nara U1	Ind.Sta.UHF
1974	Apr.	WTV	Wakayama U1	Ind.Sta.UHF
1975	Oct.	KHB	Miyazaki U4	ANN
	Oct.	TSS	Hiroshima U4	FNN
1978	Jul.	SATV	Shizuoka U3	ANN
1979	Apr.	TVS	Saitama U1	Ind.Sta.UHF
	Jul.	SDT	Shizuoka U4	NNN
1980	Oct.	TSB	Nagano U3	NNN
1981	Apr.	TNN	Niigata U3	NNN
	Oct.	KFB	Fukushima U3	ANN
1982	Mar.	TVO	Oosaka U5	TXN
	Apr.	KKT	Kumamoto U3	NNN
	Oct.	KKB	Kagoshima U3	ANN
1983	Sep.	TVA	Aichi U5	TXN
	Oct.	NT21	Niigata U4	ANN
	Dec.	TUF	Fukushima U4	JNN
1985	Oct.	TSC	Okayama/Kagawa U5	TXN
1989	Oct.	TVH	Hokkaido U5	TXN
	Oct.	TUV	Yamagata U3	JNN
	Oct.	KAB	Kumamoto U4	ANN
1990	Apr.	KTK	Ishikawa U3	NNN
	Apr.	NCC	Nagasaki U3	ANN
	Oct.	TUT	Toyama U3	JNN
1991	Apr.	MIT	Iwate U3	FNN
	Apr.	ABN	Nagano U4	ANN

(continued)

Table 1 (continued)

Opening Year		Broadcasting Satation	Broadcasting Area	News Network
	Apr.	TVQ	Hukuoka U5	TXN
	Apr.	NIB	Nagasaki U4	NNN
	Oct.	ABA	Aomori U3	ANN
	Oct.	HAB	Ishikawa U4	ANN
1992	Oct.	AAB	Akita U3	ANN
	Oct.	ITV	Ehime U3	JNN
1993	Oct.	YAB	Yamagata V3	ANN
	Oct.	OAB	Ooita U3	ANN
1994	Apr.	KYT	Kagoshima U4	NNN
1995	Apr.	EAT	Ehime U4	ANN
	Oct.	QAB	Okinawa U3	ANN
	Nov.	MXTV	Tokyo U6	Ind.Sta.UHF
1996	Oct.	QAB	Iwate U4	ANN
1997	Apr.	SAY	Yamagata U3	FNN
	Apr.	KSS	Kouchi U3	FNN
1999	Apr.	GYT	Tochigi U1	Ind.Sta.UHF

*Broadcasting Area: Kanto has Tokyo, Kanagawa, Saitama, Ibaraki, Tochigi, Gunma
Chukyo has Aichi, Mie, Gifu. Kansai has Osaka, Kyoto, Nara, Hyogo
V stands for VHF station.U stands for UHF station
The numbers after V, U indicate the order in which they were opened in the area
**News, network member stations now. Ind.Sta is a non-member station
Souuce Sugaya (2015)

in a year, after the 21 VHF stations began broadcasting in 1959. The modification of the channel planning in 1967, with an aim to fully utilize the UHF broadcaster of the Ministry of Posts and Telecommunications—in charge of managing radio spectrum—helped open the market for more stations. In each prefecture, the second and third stations have launched, and in the widespread area, new prefectural stations that utilized UHF were launched.

Until then, two key stations—the NTV and the TBS—had expanded nationwide. Around this time, many UHF stations affiliated with Fuji Television launched one after another. As seen in Table 1, 11 stations, more than half of the 19 UHF stations going on air in 1969, were in this affiliated group.

We call this second stage "the 3+2 cross-net era," as "3" includes the CX that developed its national network, in addition to NTV and TBS. As of 1971, NTV had 17 NNN-affiliated stations, TBS had 24 JNN-affiliated stations, and CX (TV Fuji) had 22 FNN-affiliated stations. In contrast, EX (TV Asahi), specialized in education—which was then called NET—had 10 affiliated stations, while TX, which specialized in science and technology, had not established a national network yet.

2.3 The Third Stage: The Transitional Period of 4+1 Affiliated Stations

EX constructed a nationwide network during this stage. As mentioned above, EX was founded with a license specializing in education, with such stockholders as Toei, Obunsha, and Asahi Shimbun. It was then called NET. Since EX specialized in education, the license required having at least 53% of programming devoted to educational content and a minimum of 30% total airtime focused on cultural programs. In 1973, commercial stations specializing in educational programming were abolished, leading NET and other educational stations to become general-purpose broadcasters.

In 1975, the Mainichi Broadcaster (also founded as an educational station), which had been affiliated with NET in the Kansai region, left the affiliated network. In addition, ABC operating in the same region became an affiliated station of NET. At the time, ABC owned both a TV station and a radio station, as did TBS. Therefore, the following combinations took shape: NET, an Asahi Shimbun affiliate, with ABC, as well as TBS, a Mainichi Shimbun affiliate, with MBS.

In 1977, NET changed its company name to ANB; in 2003, EX officially changed its name to TV Asahi.

It was in this third stage when EX established a nationwide network of its affiliated stations. Until 1989, EX had only 12 affiliated stations. With the aid of the policy of creating four-wave prefectural stations led by the Ministry of Posts and Communications, EX included newly opened stations in their affiliated network. By 1996, EX had created a 26 station national network with its affiliated stations and two cross-net stations. This established the current network system, with the three precedent national network affiliates.

TX, which specializes in science and technology programming, is owned and operated by the Science and Technology Foundation. In 1964, it launched as the fifth VHF station in the Kanto region. The license required the station to devote 60% of its air time to science and technology educational programs. Such requirements were challenging for the management of commercial stations that relied on advertisements as their sole source of income. As a result, TX found itself in financial trouble; therefore, in 1973, it changed its license to that of a general broadcaster, and the station became incorporated. Since then, the Nihon Keizai Shimbun has joined the station's management; the station is now called TV Tokyo (TX).

TX did not establish a national network like the one created by EX; rather, it created a network with six stations, including TX.

During this third stage, a system of "4+1 national networks" has been established, creating the terrestrial TV station networks we see today. "4" refers to the four key stations, including the three aforementioned stations, plus EX, while "1" indicates TX.

Why do broadcasters aim to create networks? It can be explained through the principle of maximizing the number of viewers. Since broadcasters are a licensed business, once they receive a license for a certain area, they cannot move. The only way to increase their viewership and increase their income is to share the same programs in several areas. While this is a rational action from a management perspective, such concentration could lack "a variety of opinions" from the viewpoint of mass media's function in providing information. To that end, an ownership policy has been imposed from the political and social perspectives, rather than that of the economically optimal structure regarding the policy of owning multiple TV stations. Therefore, it took about 40 years for the current terrestrial TV network to be established.

2.4 *The Fourth Stage: The Transitional Period to Digital Broadcasting*

Terrestrial TV broadcasting between the first and third stages during the formation process of the terrestrial broadcaster network saw the technological change from the black and white TV to the color one. However, the method of transmitting programs was consistently analog. In contrast, in the 1960s, the telecommunication industry saw the advent of data communication services that connected computers. In the late twentieth century, however, terrestrial broadcasting faced a new issue: the transition from analog to digital broadcasting.

Satellite broadcasting introduced digital signal transmission to Japan in 2000. Terrestrial digital broadcasting began in three widespread areas including Kanto, Kansai, and Chukyo during 2003; until March 2012, analog and digital broadcastings had coexisted for 9 years.

During the analog era, parenting stations used both VHF and UHF. Relay stations, located in the areas that the parenting stations' airwaves found difficulty reaching, used UHF to provide broadcasting services. When the emergence of digital broadcasting occurred, the restructuring of airwave band frequency, which made terrestrial broadcasting, utilizes only UHF. During the transition to digitalization, the relay stations were relocated, which brought so-called "transition from analog to analog."

In the USA, the digitalization of terrestrial broadcasting had already taken place. However, the service areas of the metropolitan broadcasters were limited with very few relay stations, based on the principle of localism as the basic policy, meaning that "at least one broadcaster is placed in a community." In Japan, in contrast, NHK, a public broadcaster, is required to transmit airwaves, as seen in Chapter 15 of the Broadcast Act, "to be received all over Japan nationwide." In addition, to solve the viewing difficulties, relay stations have been placed. As for private broadcasters, they are also required for "universal receiving" in the target broadcasting areas.

Under these circumstances, the transitional period to digital broadcasting required the cooperation of analog broadcasters. To make the transition proceed smoothly, an incorporated body was founded, called the Association for Promotion of Digital Broadcasting. Public and private sectors worked together for the transition.

The initial plan was to complete the transition to digital broadcasting by July 23, 2011. However, the Tohoku earthquake and tsunami on March 11, 2011 caused the three prefectures suffering the most severe damage, Iwate, Miyagi, and Fukushima, to postpone the completion of their transition until the end of March 2012.

During the transition period to digital terrestrial broadcasting, several new services were implemented. First, TV displays became of higher quality. While the previous TV displays had 350,000 pixels displayed across a 4:3 aspect ratio, the digital displays increased to about 2 million pixels, using a 16:9 aspect ratio. The previous type of display is called standard-definition television (SDTV); the new digital displays are called high definition television (HDTV).

In addition to HDTV, 1 channel going on air, mobile terrestrial digital broadcasting service, so-called "one segment broadcasting (One Seg)," began in Japan. Many developed countries implemented one of the four methods of digitization. The "One Seg" service is one of the unique characteristics of Japan's digitization method.

Making the transition to digital broadcasting requires the reallocation of the terrestrial spectrum. In Japan, terrestrial broadcasters using analog transmission have been moved to frequencies capable of transmitting HDTV. In contrast, other countries allowed new entrants into terrestrial broadcasting as part of the transition to digital broadcasting. It is also theoretically possible to allocate spectrum through auctions, rather than contests.

Along with this viewpoint, emerged an opposite perspective of "imposing digitalization" in the broadcasting industry. As mentioned above, the Japanese terrestrial broadcasters had a "transmitting duty," which imposed the placement of more than 100 relay stations to implement the "universal broadcasting service" to the area, in addition to the service provided by their parenting stations. With digitalization, all broadcasters, including relay stations, had to invest substantial costs in shifting to digital broadcasting.

It was challenging for prefectural stations with financial difficulties to incur the cost for digitalization investment when they could not foresee if the new services brought by digital broadcasting would yield new income. The perspective of "imposing digitalization" stemmed from those terrestrial broadcasters with financial issues. In the end, the government provided direct aid to cover these investments with these broadcasters. To date, no terrestrial broadcaster was forced to quit broadcasting due to financial difficulties caused by the digitization process.

Furthermore, around this period, a certain change to the broadcasting system was made, which was crucial to the formation of the Japanese broadcasting industry. In 2008, a Policy for Certified Broadcasting Holding Companies was enacted. The objective of this policy is to include prefectural broadcasters with financial difficulties caused by the digitalization into holding companies led by the key stations. To stabilize the operation of those prefectural broadcasters, the policy enables the maximum number of nine terrestrial broadcasters to join the holding companies. In April 2014, EX finally created its holding company, the TV Asahi Holdings Corporation; with this formation, all key stations launched their holding companies. Each holding company, however, added only the affiliated companies to the key stations under their umbrella. The affiliated satellite broadcasters could join but prefectural stations affiliated to the network could not.

2.5 The Fifth Stage: The Digital Broadcasting Era

Since April 2012, with the completion of terrestrial broadcasting's digitization, new developments have been observed: the convergence of telecommunication and broadcasting.

Convergence can be found in the following three business developments. First, as mentioned before, all terrestrial broadcasters made the shift from VHF to UHF. At the same time, the highly developed transmission method has created a new empty band frequency in UHF. A portion of this spectrum was allocated to telecommunications—specifically wireless mobile phone services. Some VHF frequency was utilized for a new broadcasting service: mobile TV broadcasting. Two service operators entered this market: NTT DoCoMo, the largest mobile phone company, and mmbi, which were founded using the joint capital investment from such terrestrial TV broadcasters as Fuji Television and NTV. This type of joint venture development beyond the boundary of broadcasting and telecommunication had never been seen before. The mobile TV broadcasting service called mmdi, was, however, terminated in June 2016.

Second, the digitalization of terrestrial broadcasting made it possible to transmit broadcasting programs via telecommunication lines. Internet TV provided through the telecommunication line was called IPTV (Internet Protocol Television). During the fourth stage in 2008, the NTT Plala, an affiliate company of the NTT Communications, began the IPTV service in Tokyo, and in turn, the company has expanded its coverage area. This service provides broadcasting programming by utilizing the telecommunication network, which makes it a typical converging type of service. In the real market, however, its nearest competitor is cable television, rather than terrestrial broadcasting.

Cable television, originally started as a community reception facility, offered as a solution to difficulties experienced in viewing terrestrial broadcasting. With the emergence of the satellite broadcasting service and the development of broadband cable television networks, cable television began to provide multichannel services. In addition, it launched internet service provisioning by allocating otherwise unused bandwidth. Furthermore, the voice call service was added, which made cable television a "triple play enterprise" with three different services of broadcasting, telecommunications, and internet. IPTV, on the other hand, is also a "triple play enterprise," making them competitors in the industry. In Japan, competition between cable television companies and IPTV companies has not got into full swing yet, but it is worth paying attention to competition between such operators in Korea, where this form of direct competition is well underway.

Third, convergence can be seen at the terminal level, shown in Fig. 1. The "smart equipment" named in Fig. 1 indicates smart TVs, terminals for broadcasting service, smartphones, and tablet PCs as well as telecommunication service terminals. With the advent of innovations triggered by smart equipment, a new collaborative service has emerged, not a competitive service between telecommunication and broadcasting. Moreover, platform players, who operate in the upper level layer in the network business, have been exploring new business opportunities.

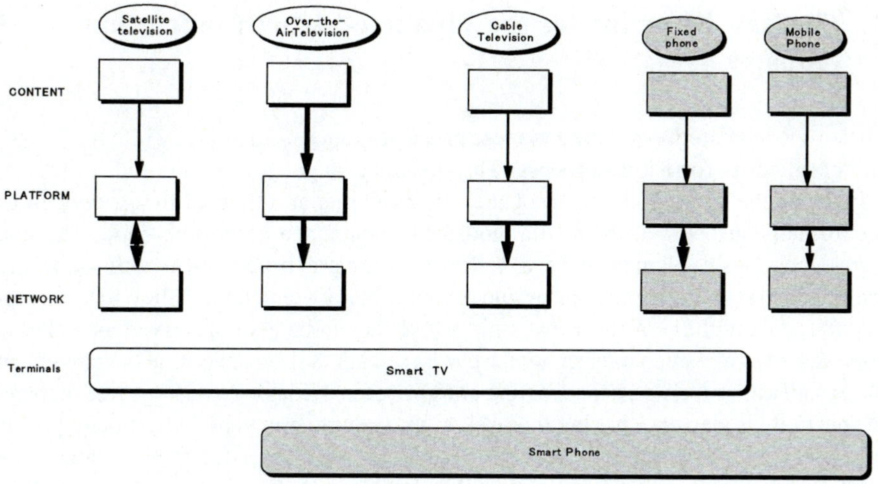

Fig. 1 Network structure. *Source* Sugaya (2015)

The following three developments have been observed in this arena:

- Multiscreen service
  Multiscreen service provides the same contents to two different terminals—smart TVs (broadcasting terminals) and smartphones and tablet PCs (telecommunication terminals). The service includes simultaneous retransmission and intertemporal transmission, which enables time-shift viewing.
- Second-screen service
  Second-screen service is provided for smartphones, with the first screen designated for smart TVs.
- Big data business
  With two screens connected to the internet, viewer activity records can be obtained through the platform layer in Fig. 1. This information belongs to personal data; as part of big data, it brings a new business development.

Until the fourth stage, the basic business model had been developed in a vertical direction—with limited convergence among the five media, terrestrial broadcasting, cable television, satellite broadcasting, fixed telecommunication, and mobile telecommunication, shown in Chart 1—while the horizontal movement of sharing contents provided by the media had been observed. However, during the fifth stage, new collaborative businesses have emerged. Cable television and IPTV developed the multiscreen service; terrestrial broadcasters started the second-screen service; and although the big data business has not fully taken off in Japan, IT ventures located in the Bay Area in America have been involved in the big data business.

3 The New Direction for the Japanese-Style Broadcasting Industry

The article has categorized the Japanese private broadcasting industry into five stages and clarified its formation process. The first four stages are considered formative: it includes the formation period of the five networks and their affiliates as well as the formative process of the media industry in Japan, centering on broadcasters and newspapers. As explained in Sect. 1 above, as long as broadcasters aim to expand their businesses through the "principle of maximizing viewership," they will attempt to enlarge their share of the viewership pie. This can be also preserved as a classic approach of a two-sided market, which can be seen in the current online businesses. In the broadcasting market, broadcasting enterprises provide programs for free, expand the pie of their viewers, making themselves into advertising vehicles to obtain profits by selling advertisements to advertising clients. No model for paid broadcasting existed. Later, such set-top boxes, as cable television, satellite broadcasting, or IPTV, have emerged, linking information between senders and recipients. Nevertheless, the free broadcasting model has not disappeared.

In the fifth stage—that is, during the era of digital broadcasting—the circumstances surrounding terrestrial broadcasting have changed drastically, making it impossible for broadcasters to maintain and develop their businesses within the free model. In reality, advertising revenue for television has already hit the wall in the fourth stage; therefore, broadcasters now invest substantial time and manpower on strategies to increase revenues outside broadcasting, since they must look beyond their advertising-based revenue in order to increase revenue. This condition will persist in the future.

Japanese broadcasters have side businesses, such as real estate and property rental businesses, which were acquired during the golden age of television, between the first and the third stages identified above. The expansion of these secondary and tertiary markets will possibly bring in additional profits. While these businesses range widely, they typically fit into three patterns:

- Sale of programs and programming formats in domestic and foreign markets
- Film production
- Online businesses.

The sale of programs and programming formats can be broken down into two categories: domestic sales and foreign sales. Regarding domestic sales, a certain amount of demand remains today; this persists based on the history of selling programs created by non-network affiliated stations during the cross-net era. Regarding foreign sales, on the other hand, Japan is behind in terms of expanding the distribution of legitimate copies of programming. In foreign markets, since a substantial number of illegal copies are distributed, no sufficient market for licensed programs exists. To compensate for the potential loss, Japan has obtained a certain amount of profits in programming format sales. However, it has not established the sales of programs in foreign markets, where illegal distribution has been prevailing, due to the complex copyright handling and unclear licensing system for the sales of programs.

In regard to the film production, for the last 10 years, a certain system has been established in which a film production committee is launched centering on a key terrestrial station with joint investments from film companies and advertising agencies; profits will be allocated among the participants. This system is used to produce animation films for terrestrial broadcast and film adaptations of TV dramas. Additionally, terrestrial broadcasters sometimes invest in producing a film that has no connection to its broadcast offerings. In doing so, the broadcaster could obtain an opportunity for broadcasting income by securing broadcasting license after the theater screening of such a film and airing it on their station.

Various business models operate in the realm of online business. Online business is expected to bring in income outside of broadcasting or to arrest the decline in broadcasting income. A typical example of obtaining income outside broadcasting is to sell broadcasting programs on websites owned by the broadcaster for a fee. Another example is the aforementioned multiscreen model, which means transmitting programs to smartphones and tablet PCs, so that viewers are not confined to sitting in front of their TVs at home and could watch the programs while they are outside. Additional income can also be brought in through the second-screen model.

It is worth pointing out, however, that these examples only apply to the five key stations in the Kanto region or the four quasi-key stations in the Kansai region, all of which air a high percentage of self-produced programming; prefectural stations that broadcast a low ratio of self-produced programs cannot adopt these models.

Another development requires attention with regard to understanding emerging alternatives for distribution and revenue generation: a new second-screen platform created by the Multiscreen Association, not led by the public broadcaster NHK nor a key station—as a collaborative service for smart TVs and smartphones. Any station could join this platform, regardless of their affiliation with the key station networks. As of January 2015, more than 50 broadcasters (with TBS being the sole key station to join) have participated in the association.

Such a development to create a platform for a new service as the Multiscreen Association, without relying on a key station, had not been observed during the broadcasting industry's formative process. Other broadcasters than the key stations face difficulties in deploying a strategy of acquiring income outside broadcasting by selling their programs since their ratio of producing their own programs is low. Moreover, asides from key stations with the financial ability to invest in the film production committee, only the quasi-key stations in the Kansai region could invest; the prefectural broadcasters do not have the financial power to so.

4 Conclusion

Terrestrial broadcasting is the central figure in the Japanese broadcasting industry. In this chapter, the formation process of the broadcasting industry was categorized into five stages, and each stage was clarified. The main characteristic found in the formative process is the formation process of the five media enterprises centering on broadcasters and newspapers. It can be said that this type of industry formation is unique to Japan, not seen in other countries. For instance, in the USA, media conglomerates exist that include film producers, broadcasters, and internet companies; and yet, newspapers are not key players in the conglomerates.

The Japanese broadcasting industry is faced with a situation where collaboration with online businesses cannot be avoided to stabilize and enlarge the business in the fifth stage of development. This chapter considers the year 2013 to be the beginning of the fifth stage. In this period, new evolvements that cannot be explained by the previous developmental process are observed, including the telecommunication companies' entry into the broadcasting business and the development of online business by the quasi-key stations, for instance. It is crucial to pay attention to the direction of the Japanese broadcasting industry to see whether the current direction would expand to the extent that it would shatter the path dependency of the Japanese broadcasting industry or it would keep the path dependency.

References

Owen B (1975) Economics and freedom of expression. Ballinger Publishing Company, Cambridge

Sugaya M (2015) The formation of the Japanese-style terrestrial television broadcasting industry—the direction of path dependency (in Japanese). Hakuoh Bus Rev 24(2):21–34

Policy on Satellite Broadcasting

Yuichiro Ogawa

1 Introduction

Since satellite broadcasting began in Japan in 1989 with analog transmission, the transmission has been fully digitized, multichannel services with various contents have been provided, and the number of viewers and market size have expanded. In addition, satellite broadcasting has developed into a different medium from terrestrial broadcasting in that, besides free general broadcasting, various specialized channels such as movies, sports, and on-TV shopping channels are provided with high picture quality.

On the other hand, competition has been intensified between satellite broadcasting and internet video distribution services called OTT (Over The Top), and the growth in the number of viewers as well as the market size of satellite broadcasting has been slowing down. Also, as for 4K/8K satellite broadcasting that is scheduled to start in December 2018, there are issues of the dissemination of compatible receiving equipment and the increase of broadcast content. To achieve its steady dissemination, it is required to improve awareness of Japanese people on 4K/8K.

This chapter describes the history of satellite broadcasting in Japan and explains its legal system and associated issues. In addition, the new 4K/8K satellite broadcasting is discussed as an important factor for the future development of satellite broadcasting.

Y. Ogawa (✉)
Ministry of Internal Affairs and Communications, Tokyo, Japan
e-mail: y9.ogawa@soumu.go.jp

M. Sugaya (ed.), *Perspectives on the Japanese Media and Content Policies*, Advances in Information and Communication Research 2,
https://doi.org/10.1007/978-981-15-4704-1_4

2 Characteristics and History of Satellite Broadcasting in Japan

2.1 Characteristics of Satellite Broadcasting in Japan

Unlike terrestrial broadcasting, satellite broadcasting does not require the installation of relay stations in precise locations; it is a medium that can cover all over Japan with just one wave. Therefore, it is an efficient medium economically. Also, as the hardware for operating satellites and the software for broadcasting content are separate businesses, it is possible to a start satellite broadcasting business without infrastructure development. This section discusses the history of satellite broadcasting in Japan, the outline of its legal system, and the issues to be addressed.

2.2 History of Satellite Broadcasting in Japan

The history of satellite broadcasting in Japan began with the launch of an experimental broadcasting satellite in 1978. After various experiments were conducted related to satellite broadcasting technologies, Japan Broadcasting Corporation (hereinafter referred to as NHK) started test broadcasting in 1986 and shifted to practical broadcasting in 1989. In addition, the first private satellite broadcaster, Japan Satellite Broadcasting Corporation (current WOWOW Inc.), was established in 1984 and started broadcasting in 1991. NHK originally assumed satellite broadcasting as a countermeasure for viewing difficulties on terrestrial broadcasting, and therefore, they planned simultaneous broadcasting and time difference broadcasting of terrestrial broadcast content. Later, the number of channels expanded dramatically and a variety of new programs started as 124/128° east longitude CS (Communication Satellite) broadcasting started in 1996, digital BS (Broadcast Satellite) broadcasting started in 2000, and digital 110° east longitude CS broadcasting started in 2002. Details of history are described below.

2.3 Efforts Toward the Start of Satellite Broadcasting (1978–1989)

The history of satellite broadcasting in Japan began when the experimental broadcasting satellite (BS "Yuri") was launched in 1978 as a facility for educational broadcasts and broadcasts against viewing difficulties. According to the *Telecommunications White Paper 1981*, the necessary technologies had been developed through this project of the experimental broadcasting satellite for the sake of the implementation of a practical broadcasting satellite system to broadcast educational programs and to respond to broadcasting demands such as measures against viewing difficulties that could not be covered with terrestrial or wired broadcasting, and this development contributed to the establishment of technical standards for satellite broadcasting (Ministry of Posts and Telecommunications, hereinafter referred to as MPT 1981). The experimental broadcasting satellite had been used for approximately 2.5 years. Meanwhile, many experiments were conducted including the one on the operation control technology of the satellite broadcasting system, and the researchers gained positive prospects for practical use of satellite broadcasting.

After the experimental broadcasting satellite, a new broadcasting satellite (BS-2a) was launched in 1984, and NHK started test broadcasting in May of the same year. It was found that satellite broadcasting improved viewing difficulties effectively in remote island areas and mountainous areas.

While acquiring technical knowledge for practical satellite broadcasting through the test broadcasting, the MPT considered, based on the discussions at the related meetings, the following items as important points for the policies toward the start of satellite broadcasting.

Consider making full use of each medium's characteristics for improvement and diversification of broadcasting services;

To achieve fair and efficient use of radio waves and information plurality, open the opportunities for broadcasting to each layer of Japanese people and try to acquire new broadcasters in addition to the existing ones:

Secure the mutual consistency with existing broadcasters and make efforts to meet the demands of Japanese people as a whole;

Since it is assumed that competition or mutual complementary relationship between new broadcast media and existing broadcast-related media arises, it is necessary to promote policies from the comprehensive perspective of achieving mutual harmonious development (MPT 1982, pp. 65–66).

Also, according to the *Telecommunications White Paper 1982*, the MPT at that time assumed that the satellite broadcasting was used to solve viewing difficulties; provide specialized and teletext broadcasting with characteristics such as education, movies, sports, and music; and broadcast higher definition television images than the current ones (MPT 1982). On the other hand, they placed importance on securing programs with specialized characteristics, the public nature of broadcasting, diversity, and necessary financial resources based on the long-term business outlook as requirements for a business entity of satellite broadcasting. Therefore, socially trusted organizations and companies were considered as the promising entities, and it was assumed that the financial resources, in addition to advertisement revenue, would be paid by the viewers to receive specific programming.

Also, based on the suggestions by the study group, the MPT revised the related laws including the Broadcasting Act in June 1989. For smooth realization of broadcasting services utilizing communication satellites, in accordance with the actual usage condition of communication satellites, a new system was introduced that entities that intended to use satellites to provide broadcasting services should entrust its broadcast programming to the management operators of the satellites and the programs were broadcasted as they were. By preparing an environment in which willing broadcasters could enter the broadcasting market without assuming responsibility for the management and operation of the broadcasting facilities, various entities can easily start broadcasting business. Also, since the number of channels available for communications, satellite was relatively large due to its frequency, it could serve as a specialized medium to meet the various needs of Japanese people adequately, which lead to the revision of the law. This revised law resulted in the entry of various entities in the satellite broadcast market by utilizing communication satellites, and it was expected that the market would be activated by acquiring many viewers.

Looking back at these efforts, we can see that, even before practical satellite broadcasting started, specific discussions were held and plans were made on the future business type of satellite broadcasting, considering the trend in business types of other broadcast media and the viewers' needs. The efforts made at that time are reflected in today's satellite broadcasting business, and they still provide a significant perspective for discussing the development of satellite broadcasting in the future.

Also, regarding the trend in broadcasters during that period, the Japan Satellite Broadcasting Corporation was established in 1984 as a private television broadcaster with investments from about 200 private companies. Thus, the environment for satellite broadcasting was prepared not only by NHK, a public broadcasting organization, but also by private companies.

2.4 Start of Satellite Broadcasting (1989–1993)

In June 1989, NHK started to use the BS-2b broadcasting satellite and its test broadcasting was converted to practical broadcasting. This was the beginning of satellite broadcasting in Japan.[1] According to MPT (1990), by the end of March 1990, the number of NHK satellite broadcasting viewers was approximately 2.36 million households (an increase in approximately 1.7 times compared with the previous year). It is clear that public interest in satellite broadcasting gradually increased with the start of broadcasting. In November 1990, using the newly launched BS-3a broadcasting satellite, Japan Satellite Broadcasting Corp. and Satellite Digital Music Broadcasting Corp. started broadcasting, and they were the first BS private broadcaster in Japan. Japan Satellite Broadcasting Corp. started paid broadcasting services and 24-h broadcasting in April 1991 and Satellite Digital Music Broadcasting Corp. in September 1991. When paid broadcasting first started, Japan's economy was not in good shape, and private broadcasters were forced to operate with an excess of debt. It is assumed that many business efforts were made until private broadcasters could conduct solid business operations. In fact, it was not until 2007 that private broadcasters as a whole could make a profit on satellite broadcasting business.

[1] According to the NHK (n.d.), NHK broadcasts the Summit and the Calgary Winter Olympics with testing broadcast phase on its own initiative.

It was April 1992 that television broadcasting with CS started in Japan. This resulted from the revision of laws such as the Broadcasting Act in June 1989 that created an environment in which various business companies could participate in broadcasting market utilizing the communication satellite. Such new companies received approval based on the Broadcasting Act in 1991. From the following year, six channels such as news programs, sports programs, and movies, plus 18 audio programs were started sequentially utilizing the communication satellite. Also, along with the start of CS broadcasting, the MPT held many study groups with related parties and examined the policies for promoting satellite broadcasting using communication satellites. As an example of these study groups, the CS broadcast study group presented a report in September 1993 proposing a discount of the viewing fee for viewers receiving multiple satellite broadcasting services and the actualization of broadcasting services with multiple channels. Such examination results influenced the form of satellite broadcasting utilizing the communication satellite and contributed greatly to the popularization and development of satellite broadcasting.

2.5 *Digitization of Broadcasting and the Start of 110° East Longitude CS Broadcasting*

While broadcasting services advanced and viewers' needs diversified, the digitization of broadcasting began to draw attention in the 1990s. Digitization of broadcasting was expected to enhance the competitiveness of broadcasting media and result in richer lives for Japanese people. Also, the movement for standardization of digital broadcasting became active in various foreign countries and the International Telecommunication Union (herein after referred to as ITU). Under these circumstances, the MPT held many meetings including the Research group related to the digitization of broadcasting that started in May 1993 and conducted a comprehensive examination on the digitation of broadcasting including its technological conditions. Although details of the digitization technology are not mentioned here, BS broadcasting that started in 1989 and CS broadcasting that started in 1992 were both analog broadcasting. Therefore, in the abovementioned meetings, promoting policies on the digitization of satellite broadcasting were mainly discussed.

In addition to these examinations, as the digital technology advanced and the effective usage of frequencies became possible from the successful launch of the highly functional communication satellite (JCSAT-3) in August 1995, multichannel digital broadcasting started in CS broadcasting, which was for the first time in Japan. Here we should focus on the cost required for digital broadcasting: the annual usage fee of one relay device was reduced to approximately 1/5 at most compared with conventional analog broadcasting. This reduced cost required for broadcasting enabled various entities to start the broadcasting business. Highly specialized programs also started such as on-TV shopping channels that narrowed down the range of viewers.

Regarding CS digital broadcasting, the regulations were relaxed for the purpose of promoting its popularization. Specifically, in March 1997, the ownership portion that was regulated to prevent a specific entity from governing multiple broadcasting stations was reduced from less than 1/10 voting rights to less than 1/3. Also, the number of programs that could be broadcast by one broadcaster, which was restricted to 12 programs, was set unlimited within four repeaters. Also, for the change in the paid broadcasting fee, approval from the MPT used to be normally required; however, the regulation was relaxed to omit this procedure to promote competition among companies.

On the other hand, unlike CS broadcasting, digitization was not considered for BS broadcasting at first. But due to the development of digital technologies, multi-channel digital broadcasting started in CS broadcasting, and high-definition imaging became realistic through digitization. For these backgrounds, the MPT held discussions on the usage of the BS-4 broadcasting satellite to be newly launched, including on the availability of digital broadcasting. As a result, in 1997, it was determined that digital BS broadcasting was to start in 2000 using the newly launched broadcasting satellite. In addition, from the perspective of securing competition among broadcasters providing broadcast programs and entry opportunities for new broadcasters, the implementation of a system was determined to separate the company that produced and broadcast the programs and the company that operated the satellites and provided the facilities of broadcast stations. Later, seven companies that transmitted BS digital broadcasting were approved based on the Broadcasting Act in 1998, and BS digital broadcasting started in December 2000. To smooth transition from BS analog broadcasting to digital broadcasting, it is required to confirm the termination period of analog broadcasting and notify the Japanese people about the transition in advance, and therefore it was decided to end all analog broadcasting by 2011.

Furthermore, after international adjustments related to satellite radio in ITU, the operation of communication satellites in the new orbit was certified for Japan. In October 2000, a new communication satellite (N-SAT-110) was launched on the geostationary orbit at 110° east longitude, the same orbit as the BS-4 broadcasting satellite used for BS digital broadcasting. By utilizing this communication satellite, viewers could receive both BS digital broadcasting and CS digital broadcasting with the same antenna and receiver. Responding to the request from the broadcast industry, the MPT decided to utilize the new communication satellite not only for communication but also for broadcasting. This enabled the start of 110° east longitude CS digital broadcasting in March 2002 in addition to the conventional CS digital broadcasting.[2] As for 110° east longitude CS broadcasting, just like other satellite broadcasting, the system was adopted to separate the companies that created and provided broadcast programs and the companies that managed the satellites and broadcast stations, and 18 companies were approved in December 2000 as companies producing and providing broadcast programs. Initially, 110° east longitude CS

[2]The conventional CS broadcasting was using four types of communication satellites based on their position in the geostationary orbit: 124, 128, 144, and 154° east longitude.

broadcasting was expected to spread and develop as broadcast media that followed the basic broadcasting with intermediate characteristics between BS digital broadcasting that provided a variety of broadcasting by utilizing digital technology and CS digital broadcasting that provided multichannel, specialized broadcasting.

2.6 Legal System Revision Toward Development of Satellite Broadcasting (Since 2000)

As the broadcasting digitized and various services became available that did not exist in analog broadcasting, the Ministry of Internal Affairs and Communications (hereinafter referred to as MIC) revised the legal system several times to meet the changing needs of the society. This section introduces the main revisions related to satellite broadcasting.

First, based on the changes in the environment surrounding broadcasting such as the progress of digitization and advancement of the internet, a study group was held from May 2000 to May 2003 with the purpose of reviewing broadcast policies of Japan. Regarding governing through the possession of voting rights by terrestrial broadcasters over BS digital broadcasters, the study group declared a policy to relax the restriction. It was determined for the enhancement of the business foundation of BS digital broadcasters to relax the investment restriction on terrestrial broadcasters who had a more solid business foundation, considering the increasing investment burden required to start BS digital broadcasting. As a result, attractive broadcasting services could be provided. Based on the policies of this study group, the MIC revised the legal system in June 2003, and the restriction on investment from terrestrial broadcasters to BS digital broadcasters was relaxed from possession of 1/3 or more voting rights to possession of voting rights exceeding 1/2.

Next, a study group was held from July 2004 to October 2006 to discuss the smooth transition to digital broadcasting and policies for meeting the diverse needs of viewers. The study group discussed the implementation of a system for holding broadcasters as subsidiaries, and for systematizing the work of paid broadcasting contracts and customer management, and it was reported that the necessary legal systems should be arranged. This report is based on the view that the business choices for broadcasters should be expanded considering the changes in the environment surrounding broadcasting, while securing consistency with the current system. In addition, based on the increasing influence of paid broadcasting management work in satellite broadcasting, it was considered that a clear system was necessary that those who intended to conduct paid broadcasting management work needed to submit notification of such intent before starting the business in order to protect the viewers. Based on this report, the legal system was revised in 2008 for the establishment of a holding company and paid broadcasting management work, which matched the actual conditions of the broadcaster.

Furthermore, in February 2008, the legal system was revised so that BS broadcasting and 110° east longitude CS broadcasting were defined as special satellite broadcasting as both could be received with the same antenna and receiver, and the other satellite broadcasting was defined as general satellite broadcasting. In June 2011, the legal system was revised from the perspective of arrangement and rationalization in the broadcast field. BS broadcasting and 110° east longitude CS broadcasting were defined as basic satellite broadcasting and the other CS broadcasting became general satellite broadcasting. This legal system of basic satellite broadcasting and general satellite broadcasting established at that time and still remains today.

Also, the system revision in 2008 was required to review considering the social conditions 5 years later and another revision was expected if necessary, and a study group was held again from November 2012 to February 2014 to discuss and examine the system. At that time, private companies were facing financial difficulties. It was necessary to enhance the management foundation through such efforts as management rationalization since the increase in benefits from broadcasting business was hard to predict. Based on the report from the study group, the MIC relaxed the regulation so that broadcasters were enabled flexible management to enhance the business foundation such as by relaxing the restriction on concurrent appointment of executives with other companies if they prepared a plan that included early and active efforts and the plan was approved by the Minister of Internal Affairs and Communications (hereinafter referred to as MIC).

Finally, in 2016, based on the fact that 4K/8K broadcasting started on satellite broadcasting as described later, the upper limit of repeaters was determined so that an entity conducting basic satellite broadcasting could have repeaters in a separate frame from the ones already held for 4K/8K programs.

3 Legal System and Market Trend of Satellite Broadcasting in Japan

3.1 Outline of Satellite Broadcasting Legal System

As mentioned above, satellite broadcasting in Japan consists of two types, BS (broadcasting satellite) broadcasting and CS (communication satellite) broadcasting. Moreover, CS broadcasting is further categorized into 110° east longitude and 124/128° east longitude, depending on the satellite orbit. In the current Broadcasting Act, BS broadcasting and 110° east longitude CS broadcasting are defined as "Basic satellite broadcasting," which use satellites positioned on the same orbit and share the same reception antenna and tuner. 124/128° east longitude CS broadcasting is defined as "general satellite broadcasting" requiring a dedicated reception antenna and tuner, and a different discipline is applied to it. This is due to the difference in the reception environment. Specifically, as shown in Fig. 1, while approval by the MIC is required

Source: Ministry of Internal Affairs and Communications

Major disciplines \ Broadcasting division			Basic satellite broadcasting	General satellite broadcasting
Frequency assignment plan (Securing the frequencies assignable to basic broadcasting)			○	×
Plans to disseminate basic broadcasting			○	×
Plan for the usage of frequencies allocated to basic broadcasting			○	×
Entry to broadcast business	Entry procedure		Approval	Registration
Entry to broadcast business	Possibility to select HS match/separation		○	○
Entry to broadcast business	Entry requirements	Financial Base	○	×
Entry to broadcast business	Entry requirements	Technical Capability	○	○
Entry to broadcast business	Entry requirements	Technical Standards (Safety reliability/Standardized method)	○	○
Entry to broadcast business	Entry requirements	Freedom of expression possession standard	○	×
Entry to broadcast business	Entry requirements	Foreign capital restriction	○	×
Entry to broadcast business	Entry requirements	Comparative examination	○	×
Program discipline	Editorial Freedom of Broadcast Programs(§ 3) Program rules (§ 4 I) Obligation to make efforts in caption broadcasting (§ 4 II) Obligation to implement correction of broadcasts (§ 9) Agreement on re-transmission (§ 11) Obligation to provide candidate broadcasts (§ 13) Obligation to make efforts to take into consideration the natural, economic, and cultural affairs of the foreign countries and regions upon in editing broadcast programs domestic and international broadcasting (§ 14)		○	○
Program discipline	Obligation to decide program standards(§ 5) Installation deliberative bodes for broadcast programs(§ 6)		○ (Except broadcasts for extraordinary and temporary purposes)	○ (Except broadcasts for extraordinary and temporary purposes)
Program discipline	Application of the principle of mutual consistency between the broadcast programs(§ 106 I) Obligation to publicize educational program plans and contents (§ 106 II) Obligation to publicize types of broadcast programs (§ 6 and § 107) Obligation to provide broadcasting in case of disasters(§ 108) Restrictions on advertisements in broadcasting aimed at schools(§ 109) Restrictions on agreements relating to the supply of broadcast programs (§ 110)		○ (The principle of mutual consistency between the broadcast programs and publicization of broadcast program type are applied only to television broadcasting of general programs)	×
Obligation to conform to technical standards(§ 111, § 121 and § 136) Obligation to report ~~serious~~ major accidents (§ 112, § 122 and § 137)			○	○
Obligation to notify and publicly announce agreement clauses for paid broadcasts(§ 147)			○	×
Obligation to explain provision conditions of paid broadcasts (§ 148 – § 151)			○	○

Fig. 1 Application relationship of major disciplines in new broadcast legislation

to enter the market for basic satellite broadcasting, registration by the Minister is required for general satellite broadcasting. For the former, the freedom of expression possession standard, so-called the principle of preventing mass media concentration, and foreign investment restrictions are applied, but such discipline is not imposed on the latter. Also, when paid broadcasting is provided, notification of contracts is required for basic satellite broadcasting, and such obligation does not exist for general satellite broadcasting. As of September 2018, 29 television programs are being broadcast on BS broadcasting.

As of September 2018, as for basic satellite broadcasting, 29 programs are being broadcast by 21 broadcasters on BS broadcasting, and 54 programs are being broadcast by 19 broadcasters on 110° east longitude CS broadcasting. On the other hand, as for general satellite broadcasting, 4 broadcasters are broadcasting on 124/128° east longitude CS broadcasting (MIC 2019a, p. 27).

Besides the above, there is a system for paid broadcast administrators that provide platform services on customer management such as subscriptions and cancellations, billing, and so on, and requirements such as the formulation and publication of business implementation policies are imposed on these companies. Currently, the only paid broadcast administrator in satellite broadcasting is Sky Perfect JSAT Corporation.

Source: Ministry of Internal Affairs and Communications

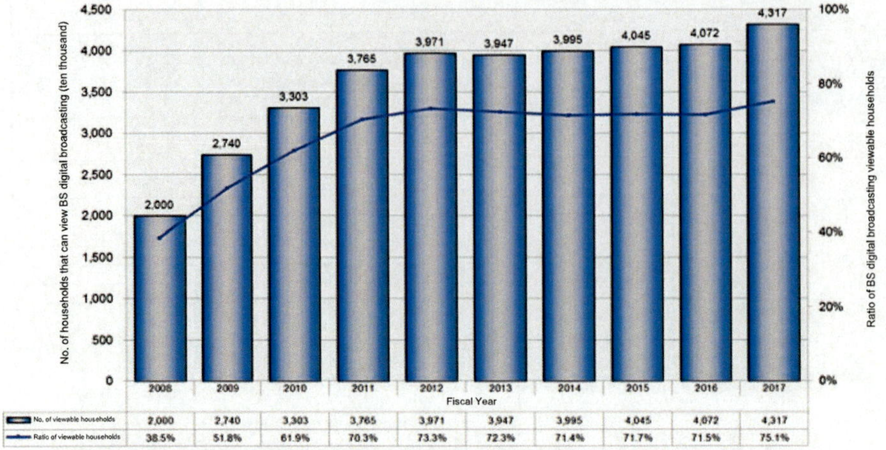

Reported by BS Nippon, BS Asahi, BS-TBS, BS Japan, BS Fuji, Nippon BS broadcasting, "Dissemination rate survey of BS viewable households"
Survey method: Phone survey through RDD (Random digit dialing)
Survey duration: Average of surveys conducted in June and August of 2008, in December and February between 2009 and 2011, December and March between 2012 and 2015, and June and December of 2016 and 2017
Subjects: General households nationwide with TV (excluding households with mass communication related jobs), 3000 households each year(allocated per prefecture)
Survey body: BS Nippon, BS Asahi, BS-TBS, BS Japan, BS Fuji, Japan BS broadcasting
Survey conducted by: Video Research Ltd. (Consigned by the survey body. Survey results belong to the survey body.)

Fig. 2 Changes in the number of households able to receive BS digital broadcasting

3.2 Market Trend

After the start of BS digital broadcasting in 2000 and 110° east longitude CS broadcasting in 2002, the dissemination of three-wave shared receivers including terrestrial digital broadcasting resulted in a rapid increase in the number of households able to watch satellite broadcasting. By 2017, it had already reached approximately 75%, as shown in Fig. 2.

Regarding the actual subscription status, the number of NHK satellite contracts was appropriately 21.66 million, about 50% of all NHK contracts, at the end of May 2018. The number of WOWOW Broadcasting Company and that of Sky Perfect JSAT Corp. contracts[3] were approximately 2.88 million and 3.19 million, respectively, as shown in Fig. 3.

Regarding the market size, the sales of private satellite broadcasters except NHK were 369.7 billion yen in fiscal year 2017, which accounted for 9.4% of the overall broadcasting market (MIC 2019b).

On the other hand, with the recent spread of internet video distribution services that compete with the satellite broadcasters over content, both the number of viewers and the market size of satellite broadcasting are beginning to level off or decrease. As for content procurement, as represented by some popular sports, there are situations in

[3]As for Sky Perfect JSAT Corp., this is the total contract number of 110° and 124/128° east longitude CS broadcasting.

Source: Ministry of Internal Affairs and Communications

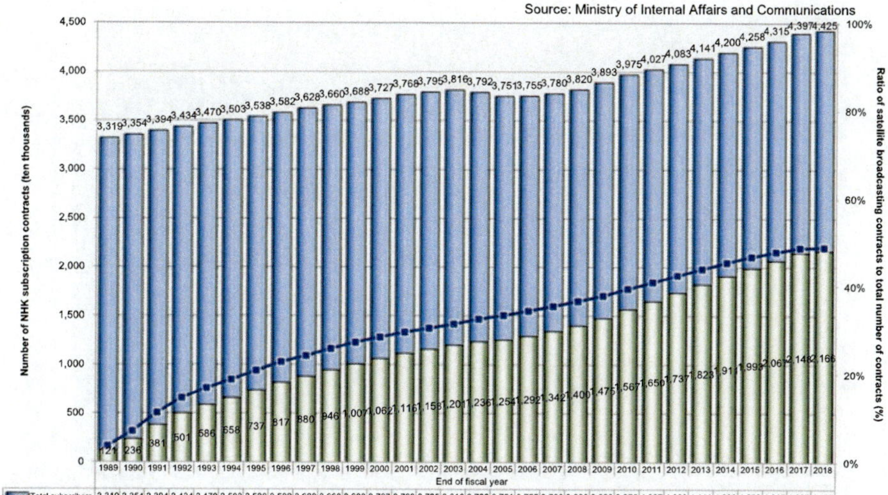

	1989	1990	1991	1992	1993	1994	1995	1996	1997	1998	1999	2000	2001	2002	2003
Total subscribers	3,319	3,354	3,394	3,434	3,470	3,503	3,538	3,582	3,628	3,660	3,688	3,727	3,768	3,795	3,816
No. of satellite subscribers	121	236	381	501	586	658	737	817	880	946	1,007	1,062	1,116	1,158	1,201
Ratio of satellite subscribers	3.6%	7.0%	11.2%	14.6%	16.9%	18.8%	20.8%	22.8%	24.2%	25.9%	27.3%	28.5%	29.6%	30.5%	31.5%

	2004	2005	2006	2007	2008	2009	2010	2011	2012	2013	2014	2015	2016	2017	2018
Total subscribers	3,792	3,751	3,755	3,780	3,820	3,893	3,975	4,027	4,083	4,141	4,200	4,258	4,315	4,397	4,425
No. of satellite subscribers	1,236	1,254	1,292	1,342	1,400	1,475	1,567	1,650	1,737	1,823	1,911	1,993	2,067	2,148	2,166
Ratio of satellite subscribers	32.6%	33.4%	34.4%	35.5%	36.6%	37.9%	39.4%	41.0%	42.6%	44.0%	45.5%	46.8%	47.9%	48.8%	48.9%

*As of the end of May in 2018

Source: Ministry of Internal Affairs and Communications

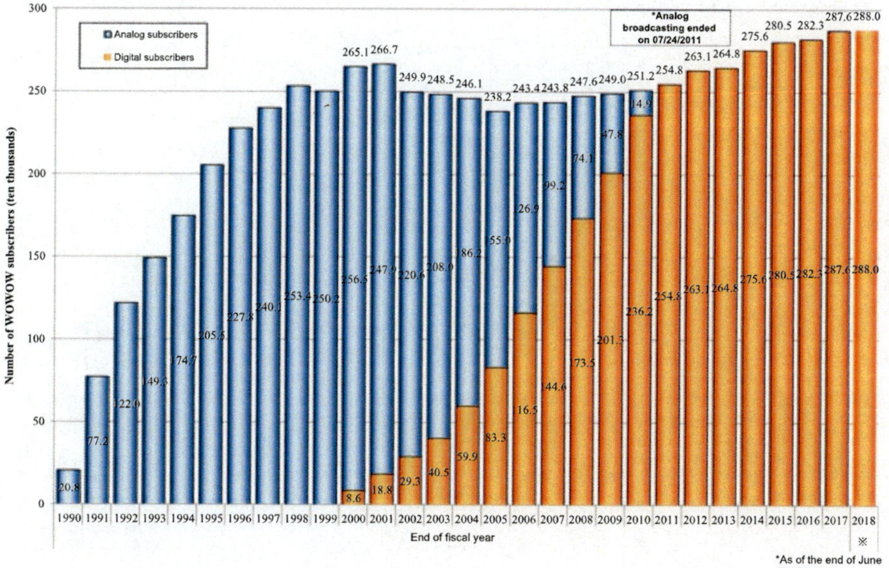

Fig. 3 Changes in the number of NHK subscription contracts, changes in the number of WOWOW subscribers, changes in the number of Sky Perfect! (110° east longitude CS broadcasting) subscribers, and changes in the number of Sky Perfect! Premium services (124/128° east longitude CS broadcasting) subscribers

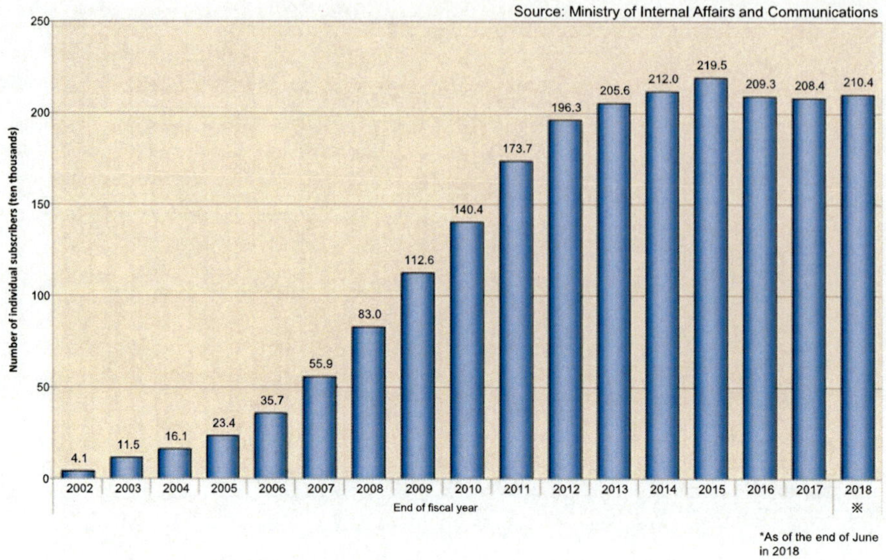

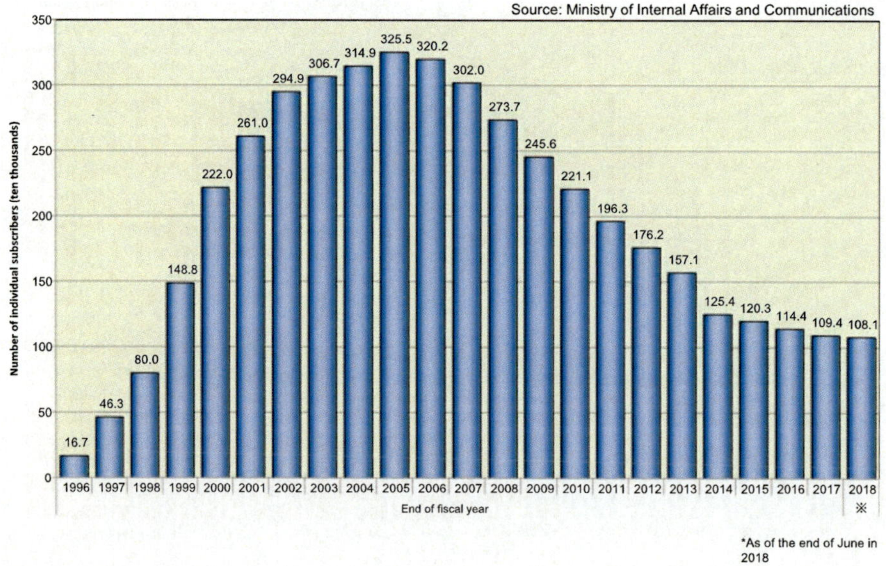

Fig. 3 (continued)

which the rights to broadcast previously held by the satellite broadcasting companies have been taken away by overseas OTT services with overwhelming capital strength. It became an issue for satellite broadcasting media how to respond to this situation.

4 Issues on Satellite Broadcasting

4.1 Effective Use of Frequency

Since July 2017, the effective use of broadcasting frequencies had been discussed in the Council for Regulatory Reform of the government. *The Second Report by the Council for Regulatory Reform* issued in November 2017 stated:

> Further effective use of bands for broadcasting should be examined amid the advanced introduction of 4K and 8K and further convergence of communication and broadcasting. With respect to frequency bands assigned in terrestrial digital broadcasting, it is pointed out that further effective use of bands is possible by utilizing new technology to dramatically assign free frequency result depending on temporal and spatial conditions. Therefore, the MIC will examine the effective use of frequency of bands assigned for broadcasting, including calling for proposals from several viewpoint such as create culture of innovation, with the vision of the future of broadcasting business, and the Council will continuously carry out examination.

In response, the MIC established the Working group on the future image of satellite broadcasting under the Study Group on Various Issues over Broadcasting, and discussions were held on the effective use of frequency for satellite broadcasting.

As for satellite broadcasting in Japan, there had been a relatively large margin in usable bandwidth. Therefore, the effective use of frequency was not examined even for approval of entry and renewal of approval every 5 years. Especially regarding renewal of approval, considering the continuity of broadcasting, the only thing to examine is the conformity with the principle of preventing mass media concentration.

In the report of the Working group on the future image of satellite broadcasting, considering the situation that the frequency of satellite broadcasting is being tightened and the fact that there are potential new entry requests, it is suggested that the system to examine the effective use of frequency should be introduced for approval of new entry and renewal of approval every 5 years. Also, in the Regulatory Reform Implementation Plan decided by the Cabinet in June 2018,

> As for the soft business of satellite broadcasting, in order to promote the diversity and competitiveness of broadcasting content by new entries, necessary system arrangement shall be conducted within fiscal year 2019[4] such as to implement a mechanism to examine the effective use of frequencies at the time of approval of basic satellite broadcasting and renewal of approval every five years.

Therefore, the MIC will take measures toward legal system development. The usable band generated through effective use of frequency will be allocated to new entries, which is expected to lead to the activation of the satellite broadcasting market.

[4]Same definition as April 2019 to March 2020.

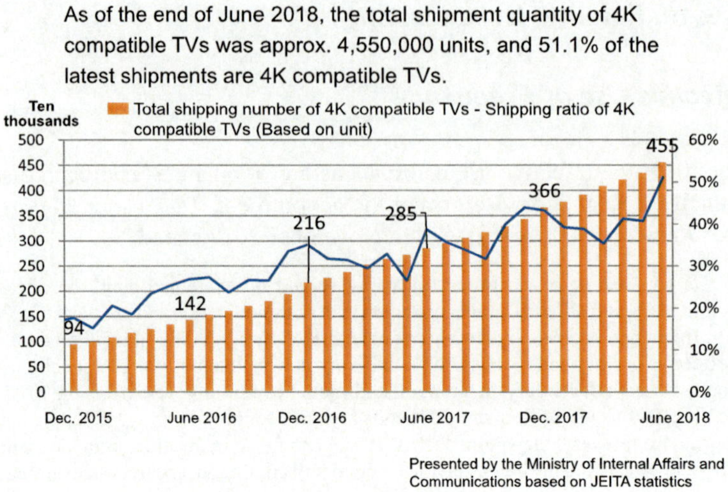

Fig. 4 Dissemination status of 4K compatible TVs

4.2 New 4K/8K Satellite Broadcasting

Satellite broadcasting in Japan has developed as medium providing high-resolution video services through digitization and high definition. Taking this background into account, the world's first full-scale 4K/8K broadcasting is scheduled to start on satellite broadcasting in December 2018. 11 broadcasters with 19 programs in total will participate in this new 4K/8K broadcasting. On the other hand, as video compression technologies for 4K/8K broadcasting are different from conventional 2K broadcasting, a new receiver is required to watch this broadcasting. Vigorous efforts had been undertaken to start this broadcasting along with content production and procurement unique to 4K/8K broadcasting. In recent years, as shown in Fig. 4, the ratio of 4K compatible televisions in the total number of TV shipments has increased gradually. The 4K/8K technologies are considered to be applicable in various fields such as medicine and crime prevention, and a large economic effect is expected. It is considered that 4K compatible TVs will be more disseminated by presenting the convenience of 4K/8K technologies to Japanese people through familiar broadcasting services.

5 Conclusion

Satellite broadcasting in Japan attained complete digitization within 30 years after its start, and it has made great progress as a medium to provide high-resolution and various contents through both BS and CS. Also, the system has been reviewed in response to changes in the society, and the separation of the hardware business that operates satellites and the software business that broadcasts content-enabled broadcasters to participate in the market without their own infrastructure development. In addition, the satellite broadcasters were divided into two types, basic satellite broadcasting and general satellite broadcasting to which different rules are, respectively, applied. In 2017, along with technology development, the percentage of households able to receive satellite broadcasting rose to approximately 75%, and satellite broadcasting has become a very familiar medium for many Japanese people.

On the other hand, due to the spread of internet video distribution services that are huge competitors for satellite broadcasting in both fees and content procurement capability, satellite broadcasting is at a major crossroads in its development. New entries by effective frequency use and new 4K/8K satellite broadcasting will enhance the existing strength, and the satellite broadcasting market in Japan is expected to grow further with these efforts.

References

Japan Broadcasting Corporation (n.d.) 60 years of television broadcasting (in Japanese). https://www.nhk.or.jp/archives/search/special/detail/?d=history008. Accessed 27 Sept 2018

Ministry of Internal Affairs and Communications (2018) Current condition of satellite broadcasting [2018 fiscal year, Second quarter version] (in Japanese). https://www.soumu.go.jp/main_sosiki/joho_tsusin/eisei/eisei.pdf

Ministry of Internal Affairs and Communications (2019a) Current condition of satellite broadcasting [2019 fiscal year, Second quarter version] (in Japanese). https://www.soumu.go.jp/main_sosiki/joho_tsusin/eisei/eisei.pdf

Ministry of Internal Affairs and Communications (2019b) Information communications white paper (in Japanese)

Ministry of Posts and Telecommunications (1978–2001a) Telecommunications white paper (in Japanese)

Regional Media Policies

Cable Television

Nami Yonetani

1 Introduction

The year 2020 marks the 65th anniversary of cable television service in Japan. The purpose of the very first cable service, which was launched at a hot spring district in Gunma Prefecture (120 km from Tokyo), was to retransmit terrestrial television signals from Tokyo to the hot spring inns. This was in 1955, just 2 years after the introduction of terrestrial television broadcasting. More recently, cable operators in Japan are providing a variety of services, including multi-channel broadcasting, internet access, fixed and mobile telephony, and home security. What is notable is that these cable services are often local oriented, which is rare worldwide as locally oriented cable service is considered to be unprofitable and tends to be avoided in many countries. Japan's locally oriented cable business model is made possible through a set of unique cable policies. In this chapter, we will examine the transition and characteristics of cable policy to provide insight into the mechanism of Japan's unique cable business model.

2 Overview of the Cable Industry

2.1 Types of Cable Operators

As of the end of the FY (fiscal year) 2017, there were 504 cable operators that broadcast both terrestrial television programs and their self-produced programs; of

N. Yonetani (✉)
Foundation for MultiMedia Communications, Tokyo, Japan
e-mail: yonetani@fmmc.or.jp

M. Sugaya (ed.), *Perspectives on the Japanese Media and Content Policies*, Advances in Information and Communication Research 2,
https://doi.org/10.1007/978-981-15-4704-1_5

these, 219 were run by public–private organizations, 183 by local governments, 76 by private corporations, 3 by public interest corporations, and 23 by other organizations (Ministry of Internal Affairs and Communications 2018). It is noteworthy that only about 20% of the cable operators are run by private corporations.

The high presence of independent cable operators also reflects the uniqueness of Japan's cable industry. While cable operators in most countries are actively engaged to join multiple-system operators (MSOs), about half of the cable operators in Japan are independent. Most of them are public–private operators or are operators who have public utility companies as their parent company. The other half of the cable operators are made up of four MSOs; these are Jupiter Telecommunications (J:COM), Community Network Center (CNCi), TOKAI Communications, and Community Cable Japan (CCJ).

2.2 *Cable Services and Market Situation*

Starting up as a rebroadcaster of terrestrial television programs in 1955, cable operators have continuously variegated their functions (see Fig. 1). They began providing self-produced broadcasting service in 1963, multi-channel broadcasting service in 1989, internet access service in 1996, fixed telephony service in 1997, mobile telephony service in 2006, and local broadband wireless access (BWA) service in 2008. Although the services vary from operator to operator, as of March 2018, 411 operators were providing multi-channel broadcasting service, 334 were offering fixed broadband service, and 242 marketing fixed telephony service. In recent years, some operators have shown a willingness to enter into the mobile telecommunications market. Here, 134 operators are engaged in mobile virtual network operator (MVNO) service, and 41 operators are involved in local BWA service.

As of March 2018, some 30,225,000 households, i.e., 51.0% of all Japanese households, were cable service subscribers, and the subscription rate has remained flat in recent years. While 97.9% of subscribing households enjoy broadcasting service, the number of households capitalizing on telecommunication service is relatively small: fixed broadband service 29.3%, fixed telephony service 24.2%, MVNO service 4.3%, and local BWA service 0.04% (Ministry of Internal Affairs and Communications 2018). On the revenue front, however, telecommunication service is expanding its presence. According to the Japan Cable and Telecommunications Association (2017), the breakdown of the cable industry's sales for the FY 2016 was telecommunications service 568.9 billion JPY (49.0%), broadcasting service 493 billion JPY (42.5%), and others 98.9 billion JPY (8.5%).

Compared with others in the media-related industry, the sales of the cable industry are considerably smaller than the terrestrial television industry and the newspaper industry but are coming close to matching sales of the publishing industry (see Fig. 2). On the pay-TV market front, cable operators enjoy a majority market share of 54.5%. IPTV operators are the runner-up with 38.7% followed by satellite broadcasting operators with 6.7% (Nomura Research Institute 2017). While IPTV operators are

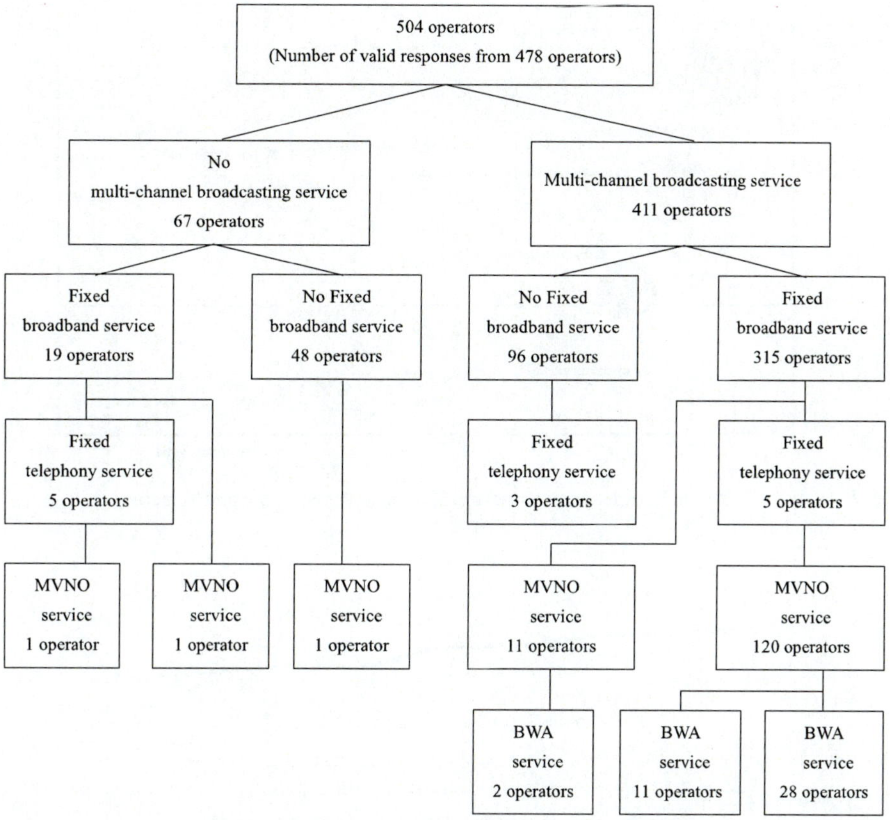

Fig. 1 Service landscape of cable operators (March 2018). *Source* Ministry of Internal Affairs and Communications (2018)

expanding their market presence as an overall trend, cable operators continue to dominate the pay-TV market (see Fig. 3). In the 2010s, over-the-top video (OTT-V) operators emerged as a new competitor for cable operators. The year 2015, when Netflix and Amazon.com launched their online streaming services in Japan, is said to be the first year of OTT-V in Japan. Although it seems that no severe cord-cutting has occurred yet, it is true that some of the consumers have started to make a decision to dump traditional television and join the growing group of people who rely on OTT-V.

2.3 *The Direction of Business Strategy*

Regardless of whether broadcasting service or telecommunications service, the local orientation of the services has been the primary focus of Japanese cable operators. According to Japan Cable and Telecommunications Association (2005), it was in

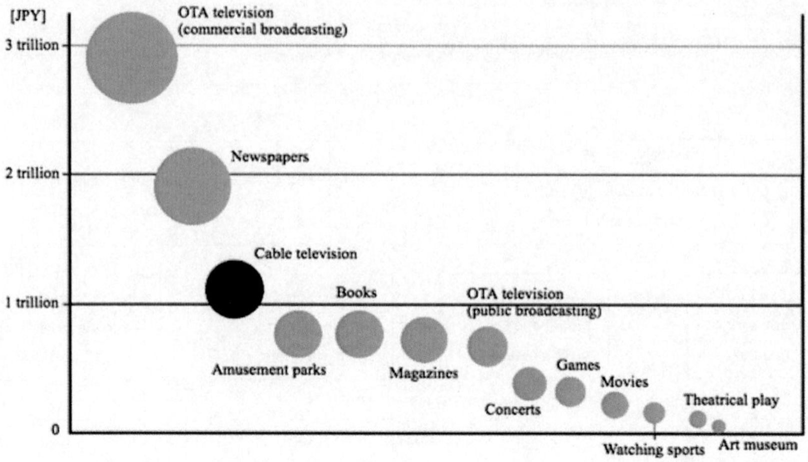

Fig. 2 Market size of media-related industry (2016). *Source* Japan Cable and Telecommunications Association (2017)

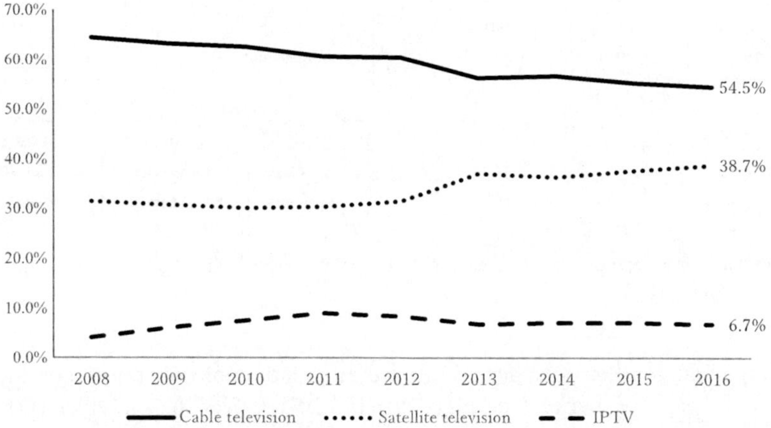

Fig. 3 Pay-TV market share by technology. *Source* Nomura Research Institute (2010-2017)

the 1970s that operators first expressed their intention to emphasize local-oriented service. Cable operators at that time, who were forefeeling the arrival of the multichannel broadcasting age, reached a common conclusion that enhancing their so-called "community channel" would become a key factor for the survival of cable television in the broadcasting market. Community channel is a channel specialized in self-produced local programs and public access programs. Fortunately, many community channels achieved a decent viewership, and cable operators gradually positioned cable television as a local-oriented media to differentiate themselves from competitors.

A valuable questionnaire study (Otani 2012) that surveyed 135 cable operators across the country to investigate their social role and prospects shows that the local-oriented attitude of cable operators still has not changed. According to the survey results, the majority of the operators answered that their purpose of operating cable business is to provide local information and their future business task is to enrich self-produced local programs and community channels. Otani (2012) concludes that cable operators in Japan "place great importance on providing local information and contributing to the local community rather than expanding and developing non-broadcasting services via cable networks."

We also cannot ignore Information Communication for the 2020s, a report published by the Japan Cable and Telecommunications Association in 2014. The association made it clear in the report that cable operators, known as "local specialists," will serve as a bridge between local governments and residents, solving local issues using a wide range of technologies including broadcasting and telecommunications (see Figs. 4 and 5). Moreover, in 2017, the chair of the association declared in the association's annual report that "cable operators are local-oriented, comprehensive service providers and shall play an essential role in the local community." (Japan Cable and Telecommunications Association 2017).

Interestingly, not only independent operators but also MSOs value their locality, for example, J:COM (established in 2005), the largest MSO, has adopted Do Local (hyperlocal) Strategy to position local-oriented services at the core of its differentiation strategy. In particular, this company set up a new department specializing in liaison between the company and local governments and local residents with the aim to build a production base for community channels and launched a smartphone application named Do Local as a new platform providing local information (J:COM

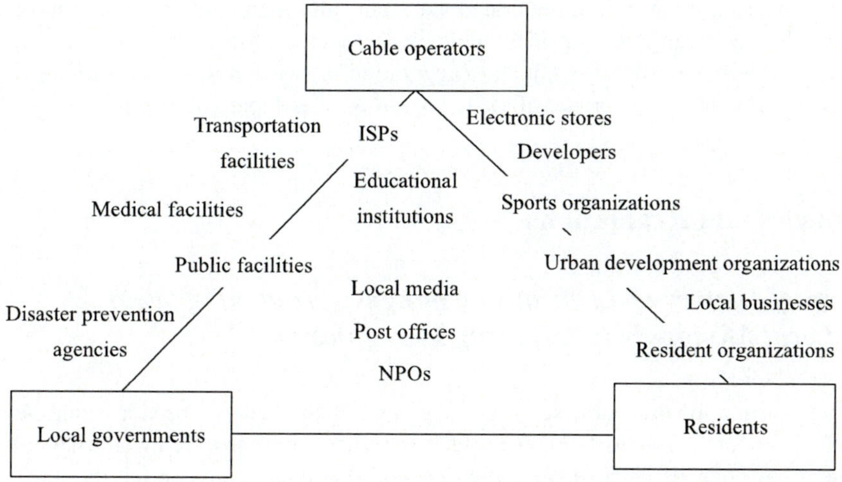

Fig. 4 Three pillars in the local community. *Source* Japan Cable and Telecommunications Association (2014)

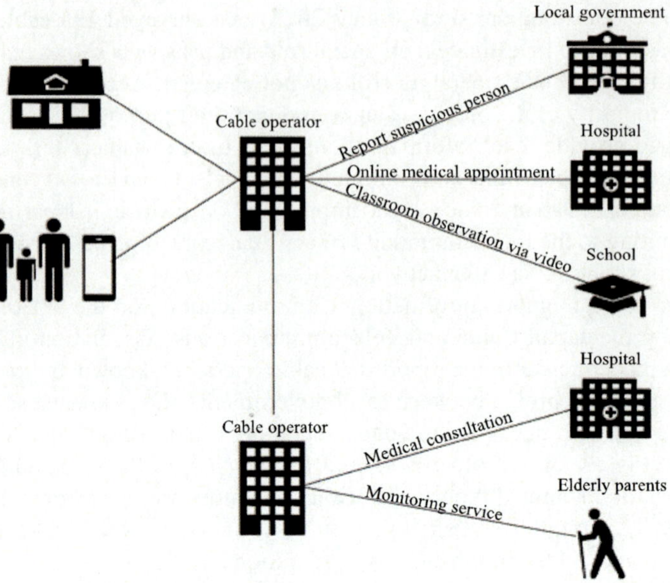

Fig. 5 Example of future local-oriented service by cable operators. *Source* Japan Cable and Telecommunications Association (2014)

2015, 2017). This smartphone application, which was developed to deliver local information to areas without broadcasting service in times of disaster, is free and open to the public. The company also launched a user-posted online video service in April 2018.

As can be seen by the aforementioned activities, although cable operators have been broadening a range of services, their local-oriented attitude has not made a difference since the 1970s. It is not an exaggeration to say that this very attitude is the most significant characteristic of the cable industry of Japan.

3 Policies and Regulations

3.1 Brief History of Legislative Changes: From a De Facto Local Monopoly to Sweeping Deregulation

As I noted earlier, the first cable service in Japan was launched to rebroadcast terrestrial television programs to Gunma Prefecture, where terrestrial television signal reception was poor, in 1955. It can safely be said that cable television at that time was nothing neither more nor less than a local common reception system. As there was no legal system designed exclusively for cable television service at that time, the Act on Regulation on Cable Radio Broadcasting Service of 1951 regulated cable television service and the Wire Telecommunications Act of 1953 set provisions for cable system facilities.

The Act on Regulation on Cable Radio Broadcasting Service required cable operators to give notification to the minister of Posts and Telecommunications (the current Ministry of Internal Affairs and Communications) when launching cable television service. The Wire Telecommunications Act, which saw cable system facility as a form of a wire telecommunications system, required cable operators to notify the minister on matters pertaining to the installation of cable system facilities.

In the 1960s, however, starting with Gujo Hachiman TV in Gifu Prefecture, cable operators had started to produce and broadcast their own local programs that were designed to meet the needs and interests of their individual communities. As the Act on Regulation of Cable Radio Broadcasting Services and the Wire Telecommunications Act assumed cable operators would only provide retransmission service of terrestrial television broadcasting, the legal system gradually became incapable of handling the changes in the cable industry.

As a remedy, the Ministry of Posts and Telecommunications presented the Cable Television Broadcasting Bill in March 1971. The bill instituted a permit system for the installation of cable system facilities and required to input the viewpoints of local governments during the screening process of permit applications. The bill also stipulated that the rules and standards of self-produced programs apply mutatis mutandis to the Broadcasting Act of 1950 and prohibited foreign ownership and management of cable operations. The bill became enforced in January 1973 as the Cable Television Broadcasting Act.

As the industry entered the 1980s, some cable operators started to broadcast programs produced by program suppliers in addition to terrestrial television programs and self-produced programs. These new-generation cable operators who engaged in multi-channel broadcasting service were called urban-type cable television operators, and they were providing more than 20 channels on average by the late 1980s (Uehara 2014). Furthermore, the door to the telecommunications market opened for cable operators when the telecommunications sector was liberalized in April 1985. This development made it possible for cable operators to provide telecommunications services based on the Telecommunications Business Act of 1984.

But despite the advancements and diversifications of cable services, the Ministry of Posts and Telecommunications adopted a package of measures to strengthen the linkage between cable operators and local communities in the 1980s. Under new rules, only one cable operator per municipal area was able to install a cable system facility. Furthermore, operators had to place the managerial arm of their organizations in the municipal area where they had set up a facility. Although there was no direct stipulation prohibiting the installation of more than one cable system facilities in one municipality in the Cable Television Broadcasting Act, the rules above turned the cable industry into a de facto locally monopolistic industry.

Perhaps the most significant change in the legal system happened in the 1990s. Along with a series of deregulation measures by the Hosokawa Cabinet, inaugurated in June 1993, the Ministry of Posts and Telecommunications announced a deregulation measure entitled Measures for Cable TV Development. The ministry first abolished the regulation requiring cable operators to place their management arms in the municipal area of their cable system facilities in December 1993 and approved more than one cable operators to run a business in the same municipal area in September 1994. As a result, cable operators became able to run business in multiple locations or to come together to form MSOs, and the scale of cable business expanded exponentially. Moreover, restrictions on foreign ownership and management had been sequentially eased since 1994 and completely abolished in 1999. With this, the legal system preserving the locally monopolistic structure of the cable industry was removed.

As information and communication technology has evolved, so too has the legal system. The Broadcast on Telecommunications Service Act came into effect in January 2002, enabling cable operators to provide telecommunications service using telecommunications carrier lines. Moreover, in line with the progress of convergence of telecommunications and broadcasting due to the digitization of broadcasting media and widespread adoption of broadband, the Cable Television Broadcasting Act, the Cable Radio Broadcasting Act, and the Broadcast on Telecommunications Service Act has integrated into the Broadcasting Act in December 2010. As of October 2018, cable operators offer broadcasting services under the Broadcasting Act and telecommunications services under the Telecommunications Business Act.

3.2 Revision of the Broadcasting Act

The Broadcasting Act, which aims to regulate broadcasting to conform to standards for the public's welfare and to facilitate sound development of broadcasting, was enforced in 1950 and revised in 1968, 2007, 2010, and 2014.

The Broadcasting Act divides broadcasters into the categories of basic broadcaster and general broadcaster, and disciplines broadcasters in each category separately. The basic broadcaster is a broadcasting operator using radiofrequency allocated either exclusively or preferentially, and the remaining broadcasters, including cable operators, fall into general broadcasters.

Compared with what applies to basic broadcasters, regulations for general broadcasters are relatively relaxed (see Table 1). While basic broadcasters must receive official accreditation by the government to launch broadcasting service, general broadcasters are only required to register or give notification. Also, general broadcasters are excused from the principle of maintaining harmony among broadcast programs so they do not have to establish cultural programs, educational programs, news programs, and entertainment programs in a balanced manner.

It is also worthy of special mention that the Broadcasting Act does not require cable operators to run a public access channel or local community channel. Public access channels and local community channels often become a mere facade in many countries where such legal obligations exist. In Japan, however, cable operators voluntarily produce local programs and broadcast them on community channels.

Table 1 Brief comparison of broadcasting regulations

			Basic broadcaster		General broadcaster		
			Terrestrial broadcaster	Satellite broadcaster (A)	Satellite broadcaster (B) Cable operator (A)	Cable operator (B)	Cable operator (C)
Entry regulation	Formalities		Licensing system	Recognition system	Registration system	Notification system	Notification system
	Requirements	No violations of laws and ordinances in the past	✓		✓	N/A	N/A
		Sufficient technical capability	✓		✓	N/A	N/A
		Compliance with the technical standards	✓		✓	N/A	N/A
		Sufficient financial base	✓		N/A	N/A	N/A
		Compliance with the standards for freedom of expression	✓		N/A	N/A	N/A
		Restriction on foreign investments	✓		N/A	N/A	N/A
Programming rules	Rules on editing programs, closed caption, and correction of broadcasts		✓		✓	✓	N/A
	Rules on rebroadcasting programs		✓		✓	✓	✓
	Rules on program standards, deliberative bodies for broadcast programs, and retention of broadcast programs		✓		✓	N/A	N/A

(continued)

Table 1 (continued)

		Basic broadcaster		General broadcaster		
		Terrestrial broadcaster	Satellite broadcaster (A)	Satellite broadcaster (B) Cable operator (A)	Cable operator (B)	Cable operator (C)
	Principle of maintaining harmony among the programs and rules on disaster broadcasting and educational programs	✓		N/A	N/A	N/A

Satellite broadcaster (A): A broadcaster who uses a satellite broadcasting station for basic broadcasting
Satellite broadcaster (B): A satellite broadcaster other than satellite broadcaster (A)
Cable operator (A): A cable operator with more than 501 drop terminals which engages in self-originated broadcasting
Cable operator (B): A cable operator other than cable operator [A] and [B]
Cable operator (C): A cable operator with more than 51 and less than 500 drop terminals which only engages in terrestrial rebroadcasting
*A cable operator with less than 50 drop terminals is exempt from the Broadcasting Act unless they do not engage in self-originated broadcasting

Meanwhile, a "must-carry" regulation that states locally licensed terrestrial television stations must be carried on a cable system, does exist in Japan as in many other countries. If there is an area with poor terrestrial television reception within cable service areas, cable operators designated by the Minister of Internal Affairs and Communications must retransmit local terrestrial television signals. When a cable operator is willing to retransmit terrestrial television signals from other local communities, the operator must acquire the approval of the terrestrial television station concerned.

4 Ties Between Cable Operators and Government

4.1 Emergence of a Close Enterprise–Government Interaction

As mentioned in Sect. 3, the current cable industry is no longer a locally monopolistic industry. Even so, as presented in Sect. 2, Japanese cable operators continue to provide local-oriented services that are considered to be unprofitable. Such a business model is possible because of governmental financial support and public–private initiative projects. Regardless of deregulation, the Japanese government and cable operators have deepened their relationships for more than 45 years, and their close ties support the role of cable television as a local media.

Almost coinciding with the time of enforcement of the Cable Television Broadcasting Act, the Ministry of Posts and Telecommunications launched the Tama CCIS Experiment, the first full-scale testing of two-way community information systems integrating computers and up-to-date communications technology in 1973. CCIS is an information system with a tree-like structured coaxial cable distribution network having the technical features of large capacity, interactivity, and geographical limitations (Kaiser et al. 1977). The system was used principally in ordinary households, not only to retransmit terrestrial television signals but also to broadcast self-produced programs and provide non-broadcasting services. The Tama CCIS experiment aimed to explore the future possibilities of cable service by experimentally providing new services based on CCIS to the residents of Tama New Town in Tokyo.

According to the White Paper: Information and Communications in Japan published in 1978, the majority of residents in Tama New Town found the service useful for their daily life and rated the experiment either "very meaningful" or "somehow meaningful." In 1978, the Experiment Evaluation Review Committee announced the Tama CCIS Experiment Report and proclaimed that CCIS is a local-oriented communication information system (Ministry of Posts and Telecommunications 1978). What is more, the committee proposed that cable operators develop their services working in tandem with local governments.

After the proposal by the Experiment Evaluation Review Committee, a significant number of financial support projects for the cable industry were launched. Most of these projects were carried out in the context of local informatization policy, ongoing across Japan since the early 1980s.

4.2 Governmental Financial Support and Public–Private Initiatives

As there was no national consensus on local informatization efforts in the early 1980s, local informatization policies were devised independently by the government agencies such as the Ministry of Posts and Telecommunications, the Ministry of International Trade and Industry (the current Ministry of Economy, Trade and Industry), the Ministry of Home Affairs (the present Ministry of Internal Affairs and Communications), the Ministry of Agriculture, Forestry and Fisheries, and the National Land Agency (the present Ministry of Land, Infrastructure, Transport and Tourism) (see Table 2). Among these policies, cable service attracted the attention of the government agencies as an effective way to realize local informatization and local revitalization, and for the local communities to receive deep-seated public financial support.

One of the well-known public support policies in Japan is the Teletopia Project that aimed at solving a variety of problems in local communities and reinvigorating their societies by introducing cable television, the internet, and community broadcasting (Ministry of Internal Affairs and Communications 2002). The project provided interest-free loans to public–private cable operators in designated areas and became an excellent incentive for launching public–private cable operator services.

Table 2 Local informatization policies in the 1980s

Name	Presiding ministry	Inaugural year	Major support measures
Teletopia Project	Ministry of Posts and Telecommunication	1983	• Interest-free loan • Low-interest loan
New Media Community Project	Ministry of International Trade and Industry	1983	• Interest-free loan • Low-interest loan
Intelligent City Project	Ministry of Construction	1985	• Interest-free loan • Low-interest loan
Greentopia Project	Ministry of Agriculture, Forestry and Fisheries	1986	• Interest-free loan • Low-interest loan
Informatization Future City Project	Ministry of International Trade and Industry	1986	• Financial support
High Vision City Project	Ministry of Posts and Telecommunication	1988	• Interest-free loan • Low-interest loan
High Vision Community Project	Ministry of International Trade and Industry	1989	• Interest-free loan • Low-interest loan

Source Fujimoto (2009)

Table 3 Public support measures for cable operators since the 1990s

Financial supports
• Subsidy program for the local governments in the urban areas with poor terrestrial reception (1993) • Subsidy program for local governments and public-private cable operators who invest in cable system facilities to advance cable services (1994) • Subsidy program for local governments and public-private cable operators who upgrade cable system facilities to secure the means of conveying information in a time of disaster (2013) • Subsidy program for local governments and public-private cable operators who lay optical cable network to support 4K and 8K broadcasting (2017)
Monetary supports
• Interest-free loans, low-interest loans, or special financing program for cable operators who are sophisticating and expanding cable system facilities (1993) • Fund loan program for cable operators who are willing to merge to support the digitization of broadcasting (2001) • Loan program for small and medium-sized cable operators who invests in 4K facilities (2015) • Low-interest financing program for small and medium-sized cable operators who are aiming to improve their managerial ability by capital investments and human resource developments (2016)

Although the government eased regulations in the 1990s, the government always had local-oriented cable business plans in mind. The Ministry of Posts and Telecommunications and the Ministry of Internal Affairs and Communications have continuously radiating policies that protect and nurture the local orientation of cable operators. The ministries have published a number of policy reports, such as the Report of the Study Group on Future Image of CATV in 1992, Report on Cable TV in the 2010s in 2007, and Cable Vision 2020+ in 2017, and represented the position that they expect cable operators to cooperate with local governments to swiftly and flexibly meet the diversified needs of each local community. In more concrete terms, they would provide continuing financial support to cable operators as part of the local informatization policy (see Table 3).

Unlike the local informatization policy of the 1980s, the local informatization policy of the 1990s aimed to bridge the digital geographic divide (Fujimoto 2009, 2010). Therefore, local governments acquired broad discretion and started to seek advances through public–private initiative projects with cable operators. Typical examples of public–private initiative projects that have been carried out include cable service via transmission lines laid by local governments and cable operators supporting local government's public relation activities.

4.3 Cable Policy Toward the 2020s

In October 2015, the Ministry of Internal Affairs and Communications launched the Study Committee on Various Broadcasting Issues to consider various concerns within the industry, such as the development of broadcasting and telecommunications convergence services, lack of local information, and evolution of the public broadcasting system. The study committee then established a Cable TV Working Group to examine the role of cable operators in the distribution of information in the local community in November 2016. The working group held a total of six meetings with stakeholders and announced its final report Cable Vision 2020+ in May 2017. As of October 2018, this report is the most up-to-date comprehensive policy report on cable businesses in Japan.

Cable Vision 2020+ is based on the following three problem areas: What kind of measures should be taken to provide stable and continuous services while responding to natural disasters and information security risk? What kind of actions should be taken to maintain and strengthen local orientations, which are the strengths of cable operators, and what is needed to enhance local information distribution? What direction should cable operators pursue to secure a stable business foundation and continuously play a public role in the local community?

In reviews, the working group pointed out the necessity for cable operators to develop not only broadcasting service and telecommunications service but also new services utilizing new technologies to survive in the market. But the group also stressed that the goal of providing new services is to meet the special needs of the local communities and that the ultimate goal is to develop the local society. Thus, as previously touched on, the government is firm in the belief that cable operators should contribute to local communities.

Recommendations presented by the working group:

- In broadcasting service, cable operators should sophisticate the cable network and set-top-boxes (STBs) and work on producing and distributing 4K content. As young audiences exhibit a trend of cord-cutting, cable operators should also cope with the demand for time-shift, place-shift, device-shift, and personalized content.
- Cable operators should develop their fixed broadband network, aggressively provide mobile broadband service, and develop a comprehensive strategy for telecommunications service.
- Cable operators should set up the third pillar of revenue in addition to broadcasting service and telecommunications service. Smart home service and smart city service, both of which utilize the Internet of Things (IoT) and individual ID numbers, are considered a possible pillar.
- Future paths of progress will open up for cable operators providing various services that meet the needs of the local community. Further development of local communities and local revitalization will realize through such efforts by cable operators (see Fig. 6).

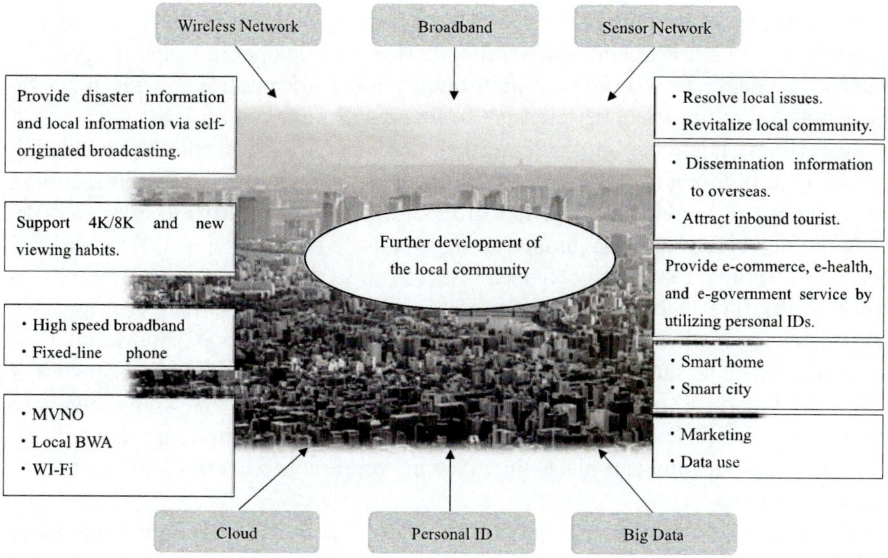

Fig. 6 Future image of Cable service. *Source* Cable TV Working Group (2017)

5 Conclusion

The characteristic of the cable business in Japan could be described as follows: Many independent cable operators are surviving in the market, private operators are small in number, and cable operators place importance on providing services that are locally oriented. This unique cable business model is achieved through a set of cable policies as typified by governmental financial support and public–private initiative projects. These cable policies, which were intended to maintain and strengthen the local orientation of cable operators, have been ongoing from the 1970s to the present.

There is no doubt that Japan's cable operators have significantly contributed to the development of local communities. Not a few operators provide local information on heavy rainfalls and high river levels using IP live camera broadcasting at times of natural disasters, and some conclude cooperation agreements for disaster management with local governments and community radio stations that disseminate emergency evacuation information. There are operators who manage local cultural facilities and operators who live-stream local festival events and local council meetings, as well. In these ways, cable operators and their services are deeply rooted in local communities as a source of local information.

However, uncertainty surrounds whether this close relationship between the government and cable operators will continue to be maintained in the future because Japan's outstanding national debt continues to increase both at the national and local levels (Ministry of Finance 2017, 2018). Given deteriorating fiscal conditions, a declining birthrate, and an aging population, local governments are expected to face a more serious financial crisis. The business model of Japan's cable operators, which provides local-oriented services by relying on government financial support, is coming to an end. While the cooperation between cable operators and the government is still necessary to produce high-quality local information, on the financial side, cable operators are under pressure to find new sources of income.

Cord-cutting is another big challenge that cable operators must address. According to a national poll conducted by the NHK Broadcasting Culture Research Institute, the frequency of television usage has dropped from 92% in 2010 to 89% in 2015 while online video usage has jumped from 34 to 50% (Kimura et al. 2015). Besides this survey, another released by Nielsen in 2015 shows that devices used for watching online videos are changing. In Japan, the number of online video viewings via smartphones exceeded the number of online video viewings via PCs in March 2014 (Nielsen 2015). The sharp rise in online video viewings via smartphones suggests that not only demand for time-shift viewing but also that place-shift viewing is likely to undergo a full-scale level of growth. Providing content for smartphones that support both time-shift viewing and place-shift viewing represents a central issue that cable operators must face.

Of course, cable operators to one degree or another are addressing the foregoing challenges. They are having a stab at creating new sustainable business models by building cooperative systems among cable operators. For example, the Japan Cable and Telecommunications Association developed an IP distribution system for self-produced local programs called AJC-CMS. This system, which started up in October 2012, can be regarded as a cable platform that enables efficient distribution of local programs produced by cable operators nationwide. Cable operators are not only able to present self-produced programs nationally but are also able to purchase unique programs produced by cable operators in other regions. Although it is difficult to quantitatively measure the contribution of AJC-CMS to the development of the cable industry, there is no doubt that it opened up a new avenue to monetizing self-produced local programs while keeping distribution costs low. Furthermore, the Japan Cable and Telecommunications Association also launched an online video distribution website based on AJC-CMS in July 2014. This site, known as Japan Interesting Motion Picture Organizer (JIMO-Tele), supports PCs, tablets, and smartphones, and more than 2,000 local programs produced by cable operators around Japan are free and open to the public (Japan Cable and Telecommunications Association 2016).

In recent years, cable operators in neighboring South Korea have been attempting to differentiate themselves from competitors by providing local-oriented broadcasting programs and online videos (Business Korea 2013). South Korean cable operators, dominated mainly by MSOs, formerly concentrated on developing telecommunications service and price cutting. However, as the content and price of telecommunications service of cable operators and competitors gradually became much the same, cable operators finally decided to try content differentiation in the broadcasting market. The Cable Vision 4.0 announced by the Korean Cable Television Association (KCTA) in 2018 described cable television as "a symbol of local communities and local cultures," and declared that cable operators would make an utmost effort to reestablish the role of cable television by strengthening its inherently outstanding characteristic of regional qualities. Specifically, cable operators will contribute to the development of local communities by expanding their function such as "local community care" (Korean Cable Television Association 2018).

Only time will tell whether the local-oriented business model developed by Japan's cable operators will be viable in the 2020s and whether it will become the savior of global cable operators aiming to combat cord-cutting.

References

Business Korea (2013) Competition for attracting mobile viewers getting fiercer among cable, telecom, terrestrial network. https://www.businesskorea.co.kr/news/articleView.html?idxno=940. Accessed 30 Sept 2018

Cable TV Working Group (2017) Cable vision 2020+ (in Japanese). https://www.soumu.go.jp/main_content/000486718.pdf. Accessed 30 Sept 2018

Fujimoto M (2009) A study of the history of Japanese regional informatization policy (part 1) (in Japanese). Stud Reg Policy 12(3):61–80

Fujimoto M (2010) A study of the history of Japanese regional informatization policy (part 1) (in Japanese). Stud Reg Policy 12(4):137–156

Japan Cable and Telecommunications Association (2005) Development history of cable TV (in Japanese). https://www.catv-jcta.jp/jcta/files/pdf/history_en4.pdf. Accessed 30 Sept 2018

Japan Cable and Telecommunications Association (2014) Information communication for the 2020s (in Japanese). https://www.soumu.go.jp/main_content/000286434.pdf. Accessed 30 Sept 2018

Japan Cable and Telecommunications Association (2016) About "JIMO-Tele", a online video distribution website of Cable TV industry (in Japanese). https://www.soumu.go.jp/main_content/000445699.pdf. Accessed 30 Sept 2018

Japan Cable and Telecommunications Association (2017) Cable TV industry report 2017 (in Japanese). https://www.catv-jcta.jp/jcta/files/pdf/catv_report2017.pdf. Accessed 30 Sept 2018

J:COM (2015) Notice of organizational and personnel change (in Japanese). https://newsreleases.jcom.co.jp/news/80050.html. Accessed 30 Sept 2018

J:COM (2017) J: COM launches local information application "Do Local" (in Japanese). https://newsreleases.jcom.co.jp/news/80611.html. Accessed 30 Sept 2018

Kaiser W, Marko H, Witte E (1977) Two-way cable television: experiences with pilot projects in North America, Japan, and Europe. In: Proceedings of a symposium held in Munich, April 27–29, 1977. Springer, Berlin; New York

Kimura Y, Sekine T, Namiki M (2015) The present state of TV viewing and media use from the 2015 public opinion survey (in Japanese). NHK Mon Rep Broadcast Res 65(8):18–47

Korean Cable Television Association (2018) Cable Vision 4.0. https://www.kcta.or.kr/kcta_new/comm/htmlPage.do?SEQ=35#page04. Accessed 30 Sept 2018

Ministry of Finance (2017) National and local accumulative long-term debt (in Japanese). https://www.mof.go.jp/budget/fiscal_condition/basic_data/201704/sy2904g.pdf. Accessed 30 Sept 2018

Ministry of Finance (2018) International comparison of outstanding obligation (in Japanese). https://www.zaisei.mof.go.jp/pdf/04-k02.pdf. Accessed 30 Sept 2018

Ministry of Internal Affairs and Communications (2002) Information and communications policy in Japan 2002 annual report (in Japanese). https://www.soumu.go.jp/main_sosiki/joho_tsusin/eng/Resources/AR2002/ar2002.pdf. Accessed 30 Sept 2018

Ministry of Internal Affairs and Communications (2018) Current state of cable TV (in Japanese). https://www.soumu.go.jp/main_content/000504511.pdf. Accessed 30 Sept 2018

Ministry of Posts and Telecommunications (1978) White paper: information and communications in Japan (in Japanese). https://www.soumu.go.jp/johotsusintokei/whitepaper/ja/s53/pdf/index.html. Accessed 30 Sept 2018

Nielsen (2015) YouTube viewers via smartphones reached more than 30 million (in Japanese). https://www.netratings.co.jp/news_release/2015/02/Newsrelease20150224.html. Accessed 30 Sept 2018
Nomura Research Institute (2010–2017) IT navigator (in Japanese). Toyokeizai-sha, Tokyo
Otani N (2012) Cable TV in the digital age (in Japanese). Bull Fac Sociol Toyo Univ 50(1):37–50
Uehara N (2014) Cable TV market and dominant independent operators in Japan (in Japanese). In: Sugaya M (ed) Local media power: digital-network formation in Japan and Asia. Chuokeizai-Sha, Tokyo, pp 6–29

Community Radio Broadcasting

Tomoko Kanayama

1 Introduction

Community radio broadcasting in Japan uses the frequency of ultrashort wave broadcasting. So, it is also called community FM because of FM broadcasting. Since the community radio broadcasting regulations were set in the broadcasting law in 1992, the number of community radio stations has reached 320 nationwide as of July 2018, and the number will continue to increase in the future. For 26 years, community radio broadcasting regulations have continuously changed, and such changes have greatly and directly influenced the operation of community radio broadcasting. Since the study of community radio broadcasting has not focused on the side of the policy and policy-making, this section, first of all, tries to take a general overview of the related communication policy-making trends in Japan.

After Japan had a period of deregulatory movement influenced by the USA and the UK, particularly in the 1980s, the Ministry of Posts and Telecommunication (hereinafter referred to as MPT) started realizing the next stage of advanced broadcasting systems, such as Direct Broadcast Satellite. During this period, Japan's government and business partnerships were highly respected around the world and Japan's broadcast policy and policy-making were applied in other countries (Gershon and Kanayama 1995). Okimoto (1989) used the term "Japan, Incorporated" to draw the images of a big and ubiquitous state, not trusting laissez-fair capitalism and relying on centralized planning and administrative guidance.

T. Kanayama (✉)
Institute of Advanced Media Arts and Sciences, Ogaki, Japan
e-mail: kanatomo@iamas.ac.jp

M. Sugaya (ed.), *Perspectives on the Japanese Media and Content Policies*, Advances in Information and Communication Research 2,
https://doi.org/10.1007/978-981-15-4704-1_6

On the other hand, when looking back from the late 1960s to the 1970s, Japan was supposedly placed in a political arena influenced by the society-centric policy-making approach. During that time after Japan's realizing aggressive industrial policies and their executions between 1950 and 1960s, they caused serious pollution-related diseases. The general public started wondering whether they could find the public interest in state-centered public policy-making. Obviously, the trend of public policy and policy-making in Japan shifted from a state-centric to a society-centric approach and the government was forced to comply as well.

They say that before the deregulatory movement happened during the 1980s, the US and the UK influenced Japan being pulled back from the society-centric policy and policy-making approaches due to the fact that deregulatory policy-making needed critical authoritative leadership, which refers to the state-centric policy-making approach. The Liberal Democratic Party, then-leading political party of Japan was revived from the struggled situation under the strong leadership by Kakuei Tanaka (1972–1974) administration by adopting the pork-barrel politics to win over voters. This led Japan's deregulatory policy and its policy-making to realize the era of Japan's deregulatory movement in the 1980s.

Being synchronized with the society-centric policy-making atmosphere in the early 1990s, establishing the community radio station was allowed under the new political rules and orders by MPT of Japan. In other words, it might say that the society-centered movement affected Japan's broadcasting policy-making in regulation.

At that time, the political actors involved were comprised of business, politics, local governments and authorities, academics, and mass media. They orchestrated their voices that Tokyo-centered in all aspects of centrally controlled phenomena should be adjusted and the Japanese government should allocate the centralized power to more diverse local authorities across Japan. This meant that Japan should realize more pluralistic society-centered policy and policy-making. This type of policy and policy-making was put into effect to open another new broadcasting area for the community-based media.

During the 1990s, all political actors except elite bureaucrats emphasized the importance of "decentralization of power" and eventually came to the idea that many voices through the establishing community radio stations in each community of Japan could be explicated people's thoughts and sometimes beliefs towards what happened in their communities. In 1992, the government information policy enacted the community broadcasting rules and orders under the revised broadcasting law.

Thus, community radio broadcasting was initiated by the government and the business sector in order to close the information gap between rural and urban areas. However, changes in society and the environment in Japan strongly influenced the policy of the government. Particularly, the risk in a Japanese society increased due to frequent catastrophes after the 2011 Great East Japan Earthquake. The government has since strengthened policies that utilize information media and technology, which has resulted in the Broadcasting Network Resilience. Community radio broadcasting inevitably is involved in this. In this regard, the policy related to community radio broadcasting has gradually changed again from society-centric approach to state-centric.

As mentioned above, when the community radio station was allowed to be established in each community throughout Japan, to a greater or lesser extent general public policy and its policy-making trends in Japan impacted community radio broadcasting. Therefore, this chapter looks at the changes in community radio broadcasting policy and how they have affected community radio broadcasting over the past 26 years.

2 Community Radio Broadcasting Under Broadcasting Act

2.1 Purpose

In the beginning of the 1980s, community information policy was promoted to bridge the economic gap between urban and rural areas. In 1983, the Teletopia plan was proposed by MPT for the development of regional information and telecommunications infrastructure across the country using CATV and telecommunication media (Ministry of Internal Affairs and Communication (hereinafter referred to as MIC: former MPT) 1987). Many local FM stations were newly established under the trends of deregulation in the 1980s, and social demand for the institutionalization of smaller scale FM broadcasting was fostered with the diversification of radio (Japan Community Broadcasting Association (hereinafter referred to as JCBA) 2004).

In May of 1985, "a Round-table conference on a broadcast in the new medium era" (Broadcast policy discussion meeting) was installed as an advisory body to MPT. It consisted of 15 experts including the president of DENTSU INC., the chairman of Sony Corporation, and the chairman of the Japan Commercial Broadcasters Association. The result of deliberations by various aspects was reported to the Minister of Posts and Telecommunications. It included the analyses of the current broadcasting legislation and the current situation of broadcasting, the prospect of changes in the social environment in the future, and the expected role of broadcasting in such circumstances. Based on that, the report proposed widely about issues and direction of the broadcast policy in the future with regard to organization, business entity, licensing system, public broadcasting, broadcasting program, etc. (VR Digest 2017). In this proposal, it was described that it should be considered with the possibility of the introduction of FM, etc., which would be smaller than the prefecture area (local FM), for example, a municipality unit including a village, town, or city as a broadcast target area. This was the beginning of the community radio broadcasting in Japan.

Since the 1980's catchphrases such as "age of local autonomy" began to get popular, and radio has appeared as part of the movement. In addition, with the extension of radio handicraft, Mini FM, which is nonlicensed micropower broadcasting, boomed, and Mini FM broadcasting was conducted at stores and event venues. In 1988, "temporary purpose broadcasting stations" (often called event broadcasting) targeting small output and limited areas for a limited time were legislated under the Broadcasting Act.

In 1988, "survey workshop on the public interest of broadcasting" began to be discussed for more than 2 years with a result proposed as follows.

> In order to flexibly respond to the diverse needs of the region, it is necessary to consider introducing something like community broadcasting with a smaller area as broadcasting target area, in addition to broadcasting for current prefecture unit (JCBA 2004).

In 1991, the special administrative reform promotion council requested to introduce community radio broadcasting to promote multilateralization of broadcasting in rural areas and to remedy the regional disparity in information communication infrastructure development. In order to respond to these requests, MPT has institutionalized community radio broadcasting, which is ultrashort wave broadcasting aimed at providing information closely related to the area, for a part of the municipalities.

The basic way of thinking in community broadcasting is as follows (Tanaka 1992).

1. To allocate one frequency to one municipal town village and to implement this in all countries
2. To alleviate daily broadcasting obligations due to the fact that it is a small broadcasting station
3. To make it possible for the same business operator to open multiple community broadcasters in the same municipality in order to be able to provide common information such as administrative information etc.

MPT articulated the purpose of the community radio broadcasting that is to provide local information including community information, local government information, community welfare information, local economy information, and tourism information to local people, contributing to the local development and revitalization as well as to improve the social welfare. It should be noted that information of disaster prevention was not mentioned in the purpose of the statement when the government enacted it.

2.2 *License*

In order to open a community broadcasting station, procedures as specified in the relevant laws such as the Broadcast Law and the Radio Law are required. MIC requires license applicants for opening the community radio station to take the cooperation of local residents, local governments, the business community in accordance with the purpose of the system and to proceed as a whole regional initiative. The most concerned by MIC is the scale of funds and how to procure them for smooth business operations without any difficulty (MIC 2015). An applicant has to make a financial plan and 5-year income and expenditure estimate in the business plan when applying for opening the station. The applicant has to follow the process as shown in Fig. 1.

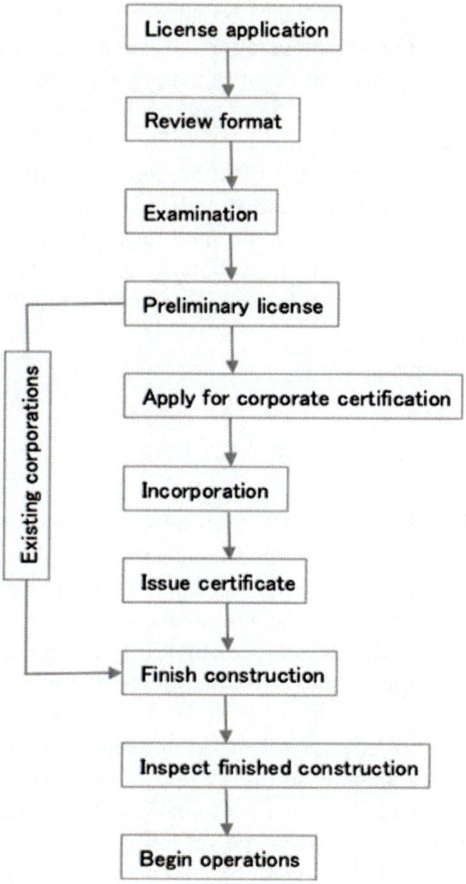

Fig. 1 Process by which community radio stations are opened (*Source* MIC 2015)

An applicant has to take such complicated steps when making preparations that it takes more than a year to apply. In addition, community radio broadcasters have to conform to the broadcast's community basis (MIC 2015). Some of them are shown as follows.

- Broadcasts responding to the needs of the local population, e.g., programs containing information directly related to the region (regional politics, city information, traffic information, sightseeing information) shall occupy 50% or more of weekly broadcast time (limited from 8 am to 8 pm each day) as far as possible.
- Founders and officials (included those scheduled to be appointed) shall, as far as possible, reside in the region where the broadcast takes place. Principal investors shall, as far as possible, reside in the region (or, have a base of business activity, e.g., a branch office or store, where the broadcast takes place).
- Members of the deliberative committee shall, as far as possible, reside in the area where the broadcast takes place.

Community radio broadcasting is based upon the existing radio broadcasting model in which operation fees are earned through advertising revenues. MIC always emphasizes that because radio waves are a public limited resource, the community radio broadcaster has a responsibility to use it for its own broadcasting. This means that once the community radio station begins to broadcast, they cannot easily stop broadcasting. This is the reason why MIC severely checks the scale of funds and how to procure them as well as the preparation of broadcasting equipment.

The license shall be valid for no more than 5 years after its issuance. It has been determined that the validity period for broadcast stations to conduct community broadcasting shall expire on October 31, 2015, as well as October 31 every 5 years thereafter.

2.3 JCBA and Lobbying

Technically, ultrashort wave for the use of broadcasting was assigned by community broadcasting and the frequency allocations were determined by MIC. The scale of output power for transmitting signals is extremely important for community radio broadcasters to reach residents in the community. In other words, the scale of output power influences the reason for the existence of community radio broadcasters. This section describes how the community radio broadcasters have endeavored to increase the scale of output power for their existence.

Currently, the rule sets, "antenna power shall be no more than 20 w; and, furthermore, shall be no higher than is minimally required to reach the broadcast area." However, when the community broadcasting rule was enacted, only 1 W or below transmitting electric power range, which could reach a radius of only 2–3 km, was permitted. This was essential for the scale of output power for the community radio operations in order for all communities in Japan to have their own stations. However, the electric transmission power of community radio was so small that local residents could not fully enjoy community radio programs as listeners. In fact, FM Iruka, which began broadcasting as the first community radio station, was assigned only the power of 0.1 W. In addition to the cost to open a community radio station was so expensive that government financing was needed. However, such very small-scale output power could not attract local governments.

In 1994, JCBA was established by nine community broadcasters in order to promote community broadcasting and to solve common issues among broadcasters. JCBA held a summit the same year, which had 400 participants. In the summit, two important and urgent issues were clarified: (1) upgrading the scale of output power and (2) mitigation of investment from local government and freedom of speech. JCBA has begun to play a central role in lobbying for deregulation with the government (JCBA 2004).

By that time, government and community broadcasters were no longer focused on the role of disaster prevention; however, this changed when the Great Hanshin-Awaji Earthquake occurred in 1995. Community radio received attention from society in providing disaster information in responding to natural disasters since then. News and information by mass media are typically unbalanced, so that disaster victims often become frustrated due to the lack of information that they need for their lives in the local communities in the disaster-stricken areas.

For that particular purpose, local governments have financially engaged in community radio broadcasting operations of their local areas, by utilizing community radio broadcasting as a means of information communication to execute their policies for disaster prevention. Right after the earthquake, the government allowed the increase in the range of output power for the disaster-stricken area's community radio station from 1 to 10 W. By doing so, a radio station in a disaster-stricken community could reach a radius of 5–10 km, which eventually led to a boom in launching community radio stations in those days. In 1998, 116 broadcasters opened community radio stations nationwide.

As a member of the government advisory committee, JCBA endeavored to improve the technical conditions of radio broadcasting, including a replacement of transmitters and receivers. As a result, an improvement of radio standards for community broadcasting was submitted to the government, and it led to increase the scale of output power from 10 to 20 W in 1999. The number of community broadcasters at that time reached 124 stations and more than a half of which was jointly financed by local government bodies and private local enterprises.

With the increase of the station numbers and necessity of improving their organizational footing in operation, JCBA had started to prepare for incorporation. In 2002, JCBA was incorporated as an industry group, which was nonprofit and nonpublic. New JCBA set the object to visualize "raison d'être (reason for existence)" of community broadcasting especially with convergence of the telecommunication in the era of digitalization as well as the change of the community itself. In the JCBA pamphlet for PR, it emphasized that community radio broadcasting was for on-air topics of your community at your community (JCBA 2004).

In 2004, the Niigata Chuetsu Earthquake struck, the large disaster once again was an alarm call to local communities and governments to consider the effectiveness of community radio for preventing and responding to disasters. Although many of the newly opened community broadcasters aimed to contribute disaster prevention in their local area and local government financed them for that purpose, MIC still had not changed its position that community broadcasting was not mainly for disaster prevention, but for providing community information to the community.

In 2009, MIC accepted the need to exceed 20 W in exceptional cases. Regarding such exception, it clearly states the criterion that there is no interference to other radio stations, there is no technical method for improving household coverage rate besides an increase in antenna power, and there is no influence on the relay station of the community broadcasting or general broadcasting company in the prefecture area (commercial FM) when a new launch is scheduled. In 2012, MIC was allowed to output from 50 to 80 W for the mute station in Hokkaido where there are no other broadcasting stations in the vicinity (i.e., FM Wappi) as well as the islands of Okinawa Prefecture (i.e., FM Kumejima) in exceptional cases.

The conditions for content have also been improved gradually. Particularly, copyright fees for music so seriously influenced on the small scale of the business that JCBA had to severely negotiate with the Japanese Society for the Rights of Authors, Composers, and Publishers (JASRAC) for years. Such negotiations finally brought about an agreement with their favorable conditions. Thus, the emergency situation empowered the community radio to inevitably become an important communicator for local government.

The environment surrounding community radio broadcasters has been improved by JCBA through negotiations since 1992. In other words, MIC had listened to the voices of community radio broadcasters.

3 Current Community Radio Broadcasting

Since community radio broadcasting regulations were set in the broadcasting law in 1992, the number of community radio broadcasters has reached 320 nationwide as of July 2018. A recent study showed that this number tended to increase after a natural disaster in which the community radio plays an important role in disseminating information related to disaster recovery as well as support victims emotionally in the stricken area (Miyata 2017). Figure 2 also shows this tendency. As such, the enhancement of the scale of output power directly has affected the increase of this.

As already explained, MIC has prioritized securing business continuity of the community radio station when approving the opening of radio station. In general, a

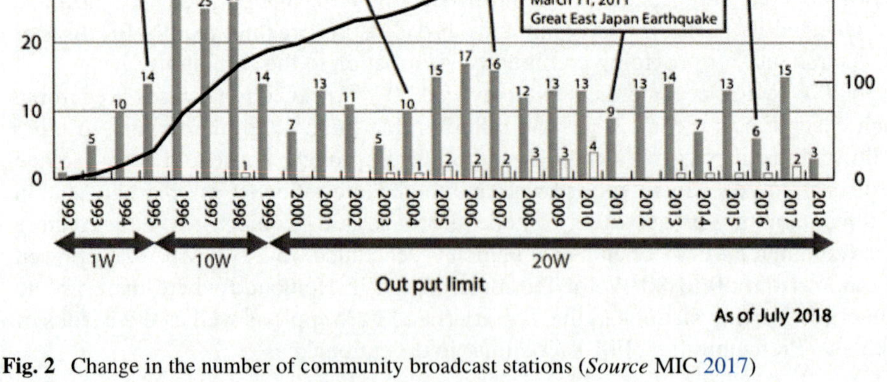

Fig. 2 Change in the number of community broadcast stations (*Source* MIC 2017)

community radio station broadcasts in a relatively small-sized local area, so that they are unable to raise revenues for operation. It should note that there is no subsidy for opening and operating community radio stations. It is not easy for a community radio station to operate on its own. At the beginning of the enforcement of the regulations, community radio stations tend to be the joint public–private sector, which includes investments from local government.

In December 1998, the Act on the Promotion of Specified Non-profit Activities was enacted, and the number of nonprofit organizations has gradually increased in society. When the first nonprofit community radio station (Kyoto community radio broadcasting) applied to open a radio station, MIC was confused on how to deal with a nonprofit broadcaster that did not exist other than Japan Broadcasting Corporation (NHK) at that time. Since the first public broadcast after World War II opened for the first time, the broadcasting business has only been approved as a joint public–private sector and private enterprise (Sakata 2007). So, it is not easy for nonprofit broadcasters to provide the scale of the funds and its stability for operating a station as a nonprofit.

The growth of community radio broadcasting is divided into three periods: (1) the first period of community radio emerged (1992–2001), (2) the development period (2002–2010), and (3) the transition period (2011–present) (Miyata 2017). The first period of community radio emerged when local residents realized the importance and usefulness of community radio broadcasting as information media during disaster. In this period, half of the stations belonged to the joint public–private sector. In the development period, the improvement of broadcast ethics and mutual enlightenment was promoted by JCBA. 70% of the stations were private enterprises or corporations (Miyata 2017). In the transition period, community radio broadcasting was positioned as a major broadcaster in the Broadcasting Act. The details of this will be explained in the next section. The number of nonprofit community radio broadcasters increased in this period.

As shown in Fig. 3, there are four types of community radio broadcasters: private broadcaster (53%), joint public–private (33%), nonprofit (10%), and CATV operation (3%) as of 2017 (MIC 2017). In terms of investment, relatively small investments are dominant (see Fig. 4).

A study also showed that financial resources depend on five main sources: advertisements (46%), broadcasting business (30%), subsidies (5%), events (14%), and donation/membership (4%) (Matsuura 2017).

Typically, a small number of staff conduct daily operations for community broadcasting (Miyata 2017). 85% of the community radio broadcasters have less than 10 employees and the overall average counts 6.8 (persons for daily operations). As such, the community radio broadcasters have to face their real station in operating daily broadcasting activities with limited human and financial resources in a stringent environment.

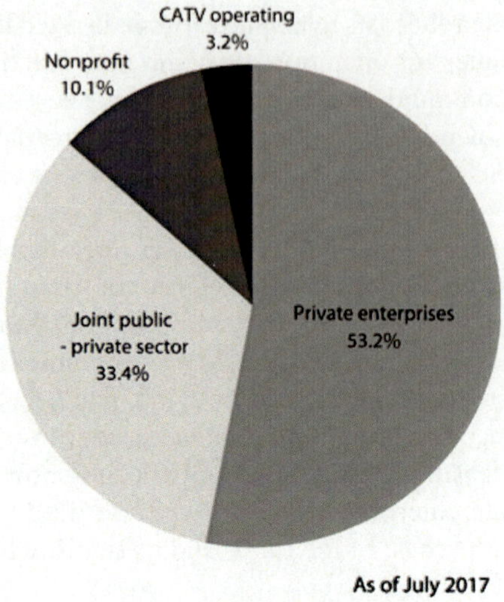

Fig. 3 The type of community radio broadcaster (*Source* MIC 2017)

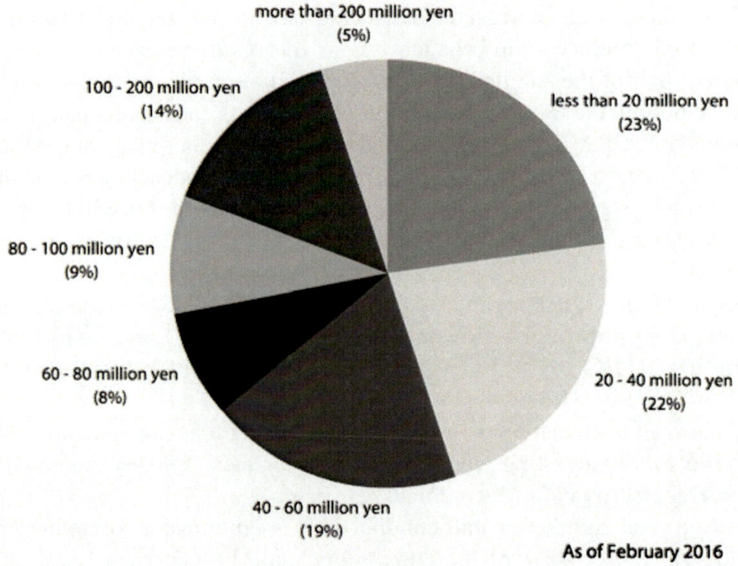

Fig. 4 The investment of community radio broadcaster (*Source* MIC 2016)

4 Disaster Broadcasting as a Main Broadcaster

MIC has revised to merge four different legal systems broadcasting law and communication—with the rapid innovation of information communication technology. This was the first time to amend the Broadcasting Act in 60 years since it was enacted. In the Act, the terrestrial main broadcaster is newly defined as one that uses electronic waves for broadcasting in national, regional, prefectural, and community areas and is prioritized in terms of frequency allocation. As such, the community broadcaster is positioned as same as mass media. There is criticism about the way in which the community broadcaster is positioned as a main broadcaster automatically and formally. Obviously, this policy change was the most influential and significant policy change for the community radio broadcasting in 26 years. With regard to the situation, JCBA took the position that this was a favorable condition for the community radio broadcasting to be guaranteed the frequency allocation even though it was not easy for them to deal with the regulatory requirement by MIC (Kanayama 2017).

Nakamura (2015) mentioned that a community broadcaster should focus on a function to convey disaster and recovery information to their local residents. As a country known as a disaster powerhouse, earthquakes can occur almost anywhere and at any time throughout Japan. Typhoons also occur almost every year from June to November and leave serious damages in certain regions after running from south to north in Japan. So, crisis communication has become considerably important for Japan to reduce damages for people's lives as well as overcoming environmental adversity from the disasters. Various community media have been utilized to send warning or evacuation advisories to certain community residents and yet the community radio broadcasting is one of those to reach residents in the stricken area as a pushed media.

Most community radio broadcasters have tried to equip hardware such as private power generators (Uninterruptible Power Systems, hereinafter referred to as UPS) and automatic starting devices from local government with a disaster agreement for emergency broadcasting purposes (Kanayama 2007). They have also formed a structure under an emergency broadcasting situation that includes training, updating manuals, maintaining networks for information gathering, multilingual broadcasting, and so on. Community radio broadcasters have maintained and improved emergency systems in preparation for urgent broadcasting operations by spending their own expenses. Thus, most community radio broadcasters had already prepared for disaster prevention and disaster broadcasting; however, the amendment of the Broadcasting Act consequently has forced community radio broadcasters to strengthen preparations for disaster broadcasting.

In 2011, the Great East Japan Earthquake struck and led to the Fukushima No.1 nuclear power plant accident following immediately after. The unprecedented disasters had an extraordinary impact on the whole nation. MIC granted permission to special emergency broadcasters to operate, when providing earthquake-related information as well as information related to recovery and reconstruction, to residents of 30 communities in the Tohoku and North Kanto regions. Ten of the community radio broadcasters have used the existing FM radio frequencies in their community for emergency broadcasting while 20 local governments set up newly established community-based radio stations by themselves. The total of 30 emergency community broadcasters was recorded in the past. Needless to say, the community radio broadcasting has received a great deal of attention from the nation since then (Kanayama 2014).

Before the 2011 Great East Japan Earthquake, MIC had not changed its nationally official position that the community radio broadcasting not only existed for disaster prevention but also for providing community-based unique and necessary information for the sake of the community. MIC changed its policy-making direction in that community broadcasting should function in the case of natural disaster situations at any moment. This was the reverse course by the MIC-led public policy that more loosely controlled whether any more community broadcaster's operations would be allowed. Therefore, community broadcasters were suddenly restricted in their daily operation with decent broadcasting operation equipment and transmission systems.

All community broadcasters have to inspect this hardware and systems with the inspection items made by MIC and submit the annual results to a regional office. The inspection has become more severe with an increasing number of the items that need to be inspected, for instance, dual equipment, monitoring systems for the equipment, UPS, and seismic proofing, fireproofing, waterproofing, and studios and stations using fireproof materials, all of which are for the purposes of disaster preparation.

It is easy to imagine that such an inspection would become a considerable burden on all community radio broadcasters. Even though MIC has subsidized community radio broadcasters and local governments in response to fill in the desired budgets to maintain and prepare for the regulatory requirement, such an overburden has not been eased on the community radio broadcasters with the small and limited number of staffs that they manage. The survey on the community radio broadcasters showed that while 41% of respondents answered that the responsibility as a terrestrial main broadcaster was to convey useful information at the time of disaster, some respondents answered that the technical requirements proved to be too heavy a burden for most small-scaled community broadcasters to operate with few financial supports in their local community (Kanayama 2017). Many of the community radio broadcasters regularly test the feasibility and function of interrupt emergency community radio broadcasting.

Regardless of the limited number of staff, all of the stations are required to form and maintain their own operation systems that can react to any emergent situation as much as possible. In fact, FMYY, a community radio broadcaster located in Nagata, Kobe-city, stopped its broadcasting operations as terrestrial radio broadcasting in March 2016. One of the reasons why FMYY stopped broadcasting was that it was financially and mentally burdened to reach the technical conditions required by the government regulation since FMYY started broadcasting to promote multicultural and coexisting town development from the grassroots level (Hibino 2017).

In addition to the equipment and systems, community broadcasters have entered into a cooperation agreement on disaster management (or disaster prevention agreement) with the local governments where the broadcaster is located, and with neighboring villages/towns/cities. In the agreement, local government is able to conduct interrupt broadcasting in the case of an emergency. Since the 2011 Great East Japan Earthquake struck, this agreement has been promoted by MIC in regulations. The community radio broadcasters that have received financial compensation from their local government(s) already have the agreement, and the community radio broadcasters with no investment from any local government(s) have also proceeded to

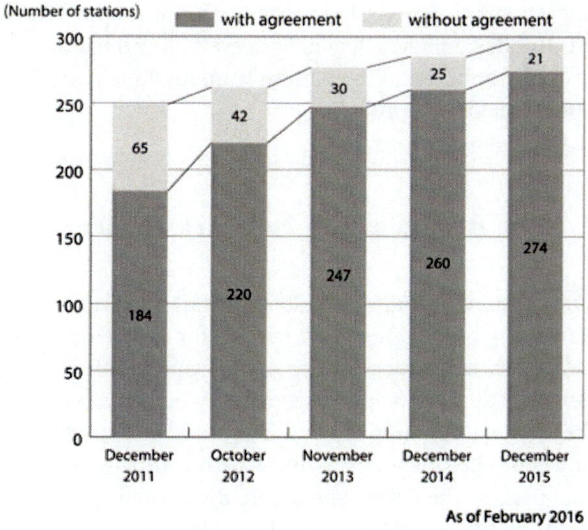

Fig. 5 The disaster agreement with local governments (*Source* MIC 2016)

conclude agreements with their local government. As shown in Fig. 5, 92.9% of 295 community broadcasters had the agreement and 65.4% of those have interrupt broadcast equipment as of 2015 (MIC 2016).

In general, the broadcaster and the local government(s) negotiate the timing of interruptions with consideration to sponsors of their program and the media editorial rights during an interrupt broadcast conducted by the local government. As a result, they set a rule between two for conducting an interrupt broadcast about the who, when, how it would be do that. In other words, how the community broadcasters should maintain their role as community media to communicate with the community they serve.

The policy change also has promoted the broadening of broadcasting. In general, the regulation permits the only one community radio broadcaster to sign off the air only in one local area (either village, town, or city). However, since a huge disaster would damage a potentially wide area and involve multiple local governments, community radio broadcasters come to need to cover a wider area beyond the regulatory defined conventional listening area. They often set up agreements with multiple municipalities in case a serious disaster happens. Some of the community radio broadcasters make a disaster agreement with seven municipalities. In such a case, the community radio broadcasting may convey information related to seven local areas during and after disaster. Since community radio broadcasters are needed in municipalities facing decreasing population and municipalities with weak economic activity municipalities for disaster broadcasting, this tendency is predicted to increase. This could obviously be an excessive burden for community radio broadcasters.

Disaster prevention has already become institutional pressure in Japan, so that community radio broadcasters and local governments, regardless of their purpose and operational situations, have to take actions for that (Kanayama 2017). Otherwise, they are afraid of being criticized by society. As seen, this whole situation has caused a shift in public policy-making pattern from the society-centric approach to the state-centric policy-making approach.

5 The Broadcasting Network Resilience

The community radio broadcasting has been required to strengthen the operation in terms of the equipment and system for disaster prevention as aforementioned. MIC in 2013 received recommendations from the advisory body, "the Study Group for the Broadcasting Network Resilience," which is a part of the decision-making body for the National Resilience Plan. The study group defined a significant role for community radio broadcasters as the first informants for realizing disaster mitigation and also pointed the issues and future discussions to overcome and realize the resilience situation in community radio broadcasting under the emergent situation.

MIC has executed the policy implementation since 2013 as a government-led development project. Based on the policy implementation by MIC, all community-based broadcasting networks would be supported or subsidized to realize well-equipped and well-organized information networks fulfilled by the decent broadcast equipment and systems.

Among those systems, MIC nationally proposed to launch the National Early Warning System, commonly known as J-ALERT, which was developed as a satellite-based system allowing national authorities to quickly broadcast and disseminate alerts through local- and community-based media to local and community citizens via direct loudspeaker communication systems set up in the localized cell community. According to Japanese government officials, it takes about 1 s to inform local officials, and between 4r and 20 s to relay the message to all citizens living in Japan. Although the warnings were broadcast via J-ALERT when the 2011 Great East Japan Earthquake happened, less than a half of the local governments in the stricken area had adopted the J-ALERT system at that time.

J-ALERT was to be developed and utilized to cover ballistic missile launches and guerrilla/special forces attacks when the Civil Protection Law was established in 2004 assuming similar circumstances as the September 11 attacks in the USA and North Korean unidentified ship missile launches at any time. The law stipulated the responsibilities of the national and local governments and MIC has expanded the function of J-ALERT to various telecommunication systems including community radio broadcasting to send the national warning to all community people (see Fig. 6).

In 2016, all local governments introduced J-ALERT. MIC has included J-ALERT in the inspection items that community radio broadcasters comply with every year. Even though J-ALERT is an inspection item, rather than legally enforced, the community radio broadcasters might consider broadcasting nationally alerted messages through the urgent notice radio system that activates a receiver in a standby state and conveys emergency information through the community radio broadcast channel.

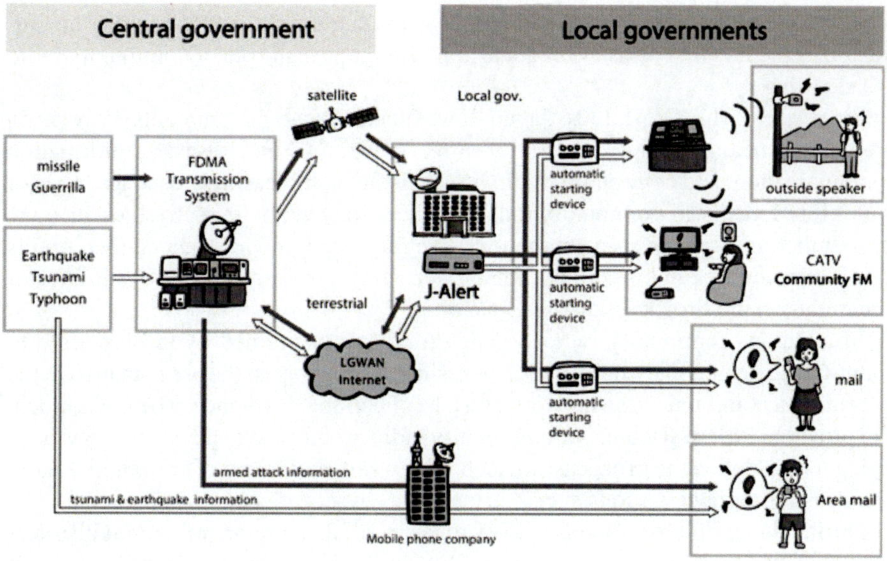

Fig. 6 J-ALERT system (*Source* MIC 2014)

Because of the low diffusion rate of the urgent notice radio system, MIC has subsidized the cost in developing and/or adopting the urgent notice radio system of utilization for local governments.

MIC's intervention and attitudes connotatively and/or denotatively toward the community radio broadcasting operation have motivated community radio broadcasters to adopt an urgent notice radio system and distribute urgent messages to local residents at low prices. In this sense, the community radio broadcasters did not see the government intervention negatively due to the fact that all community radio broadcasters believe they can contribute to the public service by committing nationally secured broadcasting operations. Rather, it seemed that this would be a chance for them to make their broadcasting environment and operation better.

6 Conclusion

Since community radio broadcasting was institutionalized for the purpose of rectifying regional information disparity in 1992, its role has expanded dramatically. In addition to the role of communicating detailed information to the local community, revitalizing the community, and communicating local culture, social expectations that such broadcasting will serve a role in promoting safety and security through disaster prevention and disaster broadcasting have been growing year by year. In such a context, the revision of the Broadcast Act in 2010 to position the community radio broadcaster as one of the main broadcasters using radio waves actually institutionalizes the fact that disaster broadcasting is an important role of community radio broadcasting.

Since the 2011 Great East Japan Earthquake, local governments have been promoting media multiplexing for disaster prevention and disaster information communication, and community radio broadcasting is increasingly used as a type of multiplexed media. If community radio broadcasting cannot be realized on its own, the number of local governments that realize this through wide-area cooperation is also increasing. It can be said that the broadcasting services and responsibilities of community radio broadcasting are expanding.

In addition, community radio broadcasting was positioned as the last mile to communicate emergency information to residents, not only in the area but also in the information communication network as a part of national resilience. The government had provided little assistance for community radio broadcasters; however, it has been trying to strengthen the broadcasting technology and equipment of community radio broadcasting through various subsidiary policies in recent years.

During the period from January to October in 2018, a number of natural disasters have occurred including heavy snow, multiple volcanic eruptions, four major earthquakes, five typhoons, heavy rain, and landslides, which caused a number of casualties and damage to houses and facilities (Fire and Disaster Management Agency 2018). In the affected areas, MIC has taken the initiative to launch temporary disaster broadcasting stations in order to prompt disaster broadcasting. Community radio broadcasters in these areas have conveyed information about disaster and recovery to victims and supported them emotionally. However, more than 30 community radio broadcasters in the affected areas had to stop their broadcasting because of long-term power outages or equipment damage and malfunctions caused by the disaster. MIC has to consider how to strengthen the technological environment for community radio broadcasting with no more burdens.

Thus, in a risk society whose scale has expanded and in which the number of natural disasters has increased, policies that utilize small community radio broadcasting will be promoted in the future.

References

Fire and Disaster Management Agency (2018) Disaster information list (in Japanese). https://www.fdma.go.jp/bn/2018/. Accessed 5 Oct 2018

Gershon R, Kanayama T (1995) Direct broadcast satellites in Japan: A Case Study In Government-Business Partnerships (in Japanese). Telecommun Policy 19(3):225–226

Hibino J (2017) FMYY changed to an online broadcaster by overcoming the perseveration of transmission line (in Japanese). In: Matsuura S (ed) Community broadcasting in Japan: between ideal and reality. Koyo Shobo, Kyoto, pp 196–211

Japan Community Broadcasting Association (2004) 10 years history of Japan Community Broadcasting Association (in Japanese). Japan Community Broadcasting Association, Tokyo

Kanayama T (2007) Community media: community FM makes connections in local area (in Japanese). Keio University Press, Tokyo

Kanayama T (2014) What required in case of unexpected disaster—the role of community radio (in Japanese). In: Research Group of Disaster and Community Radio (ed) Regeneration of a small radio broadcaster and its local community. Ohsumi Shoten, Shiga, pp 9–19

Kanayama T (2017) The role of disaster prevention from the viewpoint under institutional pressure (in Japanese). In: Matsuura S (ed) Community broadcasting in Japan: between ideal and reality. Koyo Shobo, Kyoto, pp 2–17

Matsuura S (2017) New resource procuring (in Japanese). In: Matsuura S (ed) Community broadcasting in Japan: between ideal and reality. Koyo Shobo, Kyoto, pp 52–63

Ministry of Internal Affairs and Communication (1987) 1987 white paper information and communications in Japan (in Japanese). https://www.soumu.go.jp/johotsusintokei/whitepaper/ja/s62/html/s62a03020100.html. Accessed 15 Sept 2018

Ministry of Internal Affairs and Communication (2014) 2014 white paper information and communications in Japan (in Japanese). https://www.soumu.go.jp/johotsusintokei/whitepaper/ja/h26/html/nc263230.html. Accessed 15 Sept 2018

Ministry of Internal Affairs and Communication (2015) Guide for opening a community broadcast station (in Japanese). https://www.tele.soumu.go.jp/resource/j/system/bc/commu/tebiki.pdf

Ministry of Internal Affairs and Communication (2016) Current situation of community broadcasting (in Japanese). http://www.soumu.go.jp/main_content000401159.pdf. Accessed 15 Sept 2018

Ministry of Internal Affairs and Communication (2017) Local community examples of automatic start radio by using community broadcasting (in Japanese). https://www.soumu.go.jp/main_content/000495078.pdf. Accessed 15 Sept 2018

Miyata N (2017) From the result of nationwide survey (in Japanese). In: Matsuura S (ed) Community broadcasting in Japan: between ideal and reality. Koyo Shobo, Kyoto, pp 18–31

Nakamura H (2015) Publicness of community broadcasting as a main broadcasting (in Japanese). J Law Polit Sci Univ Kitakyusyu 42:2–4

Okimoto D (1989) Between MITI and the market: Japanese industrial policy for high technology (in Japanese). Stanford University Press, Redwood City

Sakata K (2007) A readjustment of perspective concerning the study of community radio. Ritsumeikan Rev Ind Soc (in Japanese) 42(4):155–163

Tanaka H (1992) Policy of broadcasting and telecommunication (in Japanese). Telev Acad J 46(7):799–802

VR Digest (2017) Report of the round table conference for broadcasting in new media era (Broadcasting policy conference) (in Japanese). https://www.videor.co.jp/digestplus/tv/2017/04/1822.html. Accessed 15 Sept 2018

Content Policies

Film and the Other Video Contents (TV program and Internet Video)

Takashi Uchiyama

1 Introduction

Generally speaking, the policy on film, television program, and internet video by the Japanese government can be summarized as below.

in twentieth century	just Laissez-Faire!
in 2000s	turning point to positive commitment
in 2010s	considerable political investment by the government

Compared with European policies that have involved a heavy commitment by government and with American policy that was affected by strong lobbying activities by Hollywood majors, the long history of Laissez-Faire or sparse relationship between industry and government and sparse relationship between film and television industries have formed quite free audience markets in film and in television and Japan's domestic market is quite a free one in institutional terms even now, both in terms of domestic productions and imports (of course the natural barrier of the Japanese language cannot be ignored). I believe the eyes of this trained audience can appeal internationally.

T. Uchiyama (✉)
Department of Cultural and Creative Studies, School of Cultural and Creative Studies, Aoyama Gakuin University, Tokyo, Japan
e-mail: T2uchiya@sccs.aoyama.ac.jp

M. Sugaya (ed.), *Perspectives on the Japanese Media and Content Policies*, Advances in Information and Communication Research 2,
https://doi.org/10.1007/978-981-15-4704-1_7

2 Background and History

2.1 The History and Relationship between Film and TV

The case of Japan is unique and the relationship between film and television industries was inactive at first. It is a voluntary and pure commercial relationship and does not involve governmental regulative relations like European states nor hostile ones like Hollywood major film studios and major TV networks in 1950–80s.

Japanese TV broadcasting was started in February 1953 by Japan Broadcasting Corporation (hereinafter referred to as NHK). It was a time when the number of admissions to the cinema was still increasing and continued to increase until 1958 (Fig. 1).

As in other countries, the film industry neglected the television industry in the beginning. The characteristic of Japan is that it has long been neglected, and no one has arbitrated, allowing it to be just Laissez-Faire! Because of the admission increasing during that time, it is thought that the attitude of it being disrespected by the film sector has become stronger.

In the early stages of the beginning of television, some film companies supplied their theater films to television. But Japanese film industry started to refuse to supply their theater films and actors and actresses to television industries despite the demand

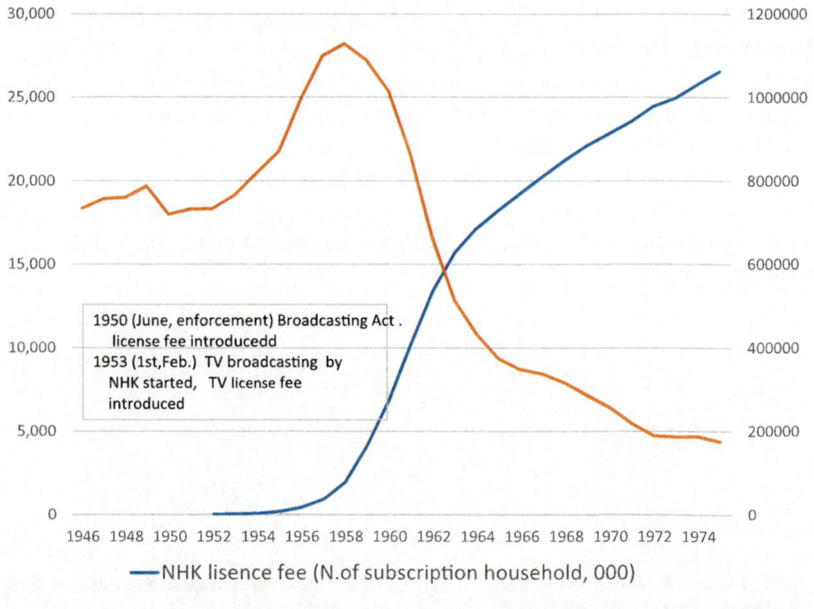

Fig. 1 Diffusion of TV and decline of cinema. (*Data Source*) NHK lisence fee from *MIC* Long-term time series data. Theatre admission from *Motion Picture Producers Association of Japan, Inc.* (Graphic) by author

of the television industry as observed in other countries. Particularly in the 6 years from September 1958 to September 1964, The six major film company members of Motion Picture Producers Association of Japan, Inc., signed an agreement concerning the above. The direct trigger was an ending of disagreements over broadcasting royalties. Royalties had risen dramatically till 1958 and this was unacceptable for television. More essentially as was the case in foreign countries, it is fully conceivable that this was due to film industry's neglect of early television, low qualities, low budgets, etc.

Film companies made television movies for television with very low budgets as in other countries. This was not so attractive for film companies due to low profitability, and it was a low-priority activity among film companies.

After September 1964, film companies started to supply theater films to TV networks again. At that time, the following agreement was decided.

= Films 7 years after theater exhibition were permitted to be broadcast.
= Up to 100 films per year per film company.

That is to say, it would be a first formal window control strategy in Japan. Moreover, the royalties of broadcasting rights began to increase again. The gap in quality, budget, and extensive production period between film and TV program was still large and the ratings broadcasted on TV were good.

There were corporative aspects too. New TV networks Fuji Television and Nippon Educational Television Co., Ltd. (hereinafter referred to as NET) started to broadcast in February 1959 and Mar. 1959 each. These are invested by Japanese film majors.

1960s–70s were two decades in which the independent movement relative to majors was active in the world, like Nouvelle Vague in France, American New Wave in USA, and Punk subculture in UK compared with these, the movements in the Japanese film scene were mild and more commercial.

Of course, there were similar phenomena in the Japanese film industry to those in western nations. The market share of major's dropped and, instead, independents and imports rose. One of the majors Shin-TOHO became bankrupt in 1961 and DAIEI led by Masaichi NAGATA in 1971. Vertical integrated organizations could not be kept and divisions production, actors/actresses were separated (collapse of studio system).

Some directors became independent. For example, the famous Japanese director Akira KUROSAWA first signed an exclusive contract with TOHO but eventually became independent in 1965.

Another example of independents involved the activities of Haruki KADOKAWA, the president of KADOKAWA a large publishing company. He made their own novels into films (the first one being the *Inugami Family* (1976) and the second ranking in box-office revenue of Japanese film in 1976) through the second half of 1970s and much of the advertising costs were placed on TV spot CMs. This was called a "media-mix strategy" at that time. His strategy stood out because the other film companies were not active on TV. In 1980s, he added the so-called star-system to their filmmaking. Three teen-age actresses were found under his film productions, played the leading role in the films, and were promoted as multitalents (photo-visual, music activities, etc.). These films were also ranked within the top five box office hits each year.

Animation films also became popular in the 1970s. From the view of box office rankings (in Japanese films), the animation films below were listed.

10th 1975 *Hans Christian Andersen's The Little Mermaid*
2nd 1978 *Farewell to Space Battleship Yamato*
1st 1979 *Galaxy Express 999*
8th 1979 *Lupin the Third.*

Needless to say, the target audience of *the Little Mermaid* was kids, *Yamato, 999 and Lupin* were popular among not only kids but also teenagers, including university students.

2.2 The 1980s—The Beginning of Investment by TV Stations

The attractiveness of high-quality films and their commercial success and avoidance of the high costs of broadcasting right of film and high risk whether the rights could be obtained or not, caused TV stations to voluntary begin investing in films. An example is *Antarctica* (1983) invested in by FUJI television. Of course, there were some films invested in by TV stations 1960s and 70s, but this could be said to be the first full-fledged work. Theoretically, the effectiveness of the participation on film productions by TV stations induces large number of advertisements and promotions by media-mix strategy. *Antarctica* (1983) produced by FUJI television was the first successful one. The box-office ranking of it in 1983 was 2nd only to *E.T. The Extra-Terrestrial* and superior to *Star Wars: Episode VI Return of the Jedi.* Many films by FUJI Television were produced and became popular after this and other TV stations followed suit.

2.3 The 1990s—The Recovery Season of Japanese Film Industry

The 1990s was an era in which cinema complexes were popularized in Japan. First, one of the American style multiplexes was introduced in EBINA, a suburb of Tokyo, on 24th April 1993 by Warner Mycal Cinemas, one of the major theater chains, which is Aeon Cinema now. After a long absence of investment in the exhibition sector, the clean image and environment of the new cinema complex had become a chance to regain the audience. And the drastic increase in exhibition supply against distribution flow and audience demand was also an opportunity to change old business customs. Ministry of International Trade and Industry (hereinafter referred to as MITI) was

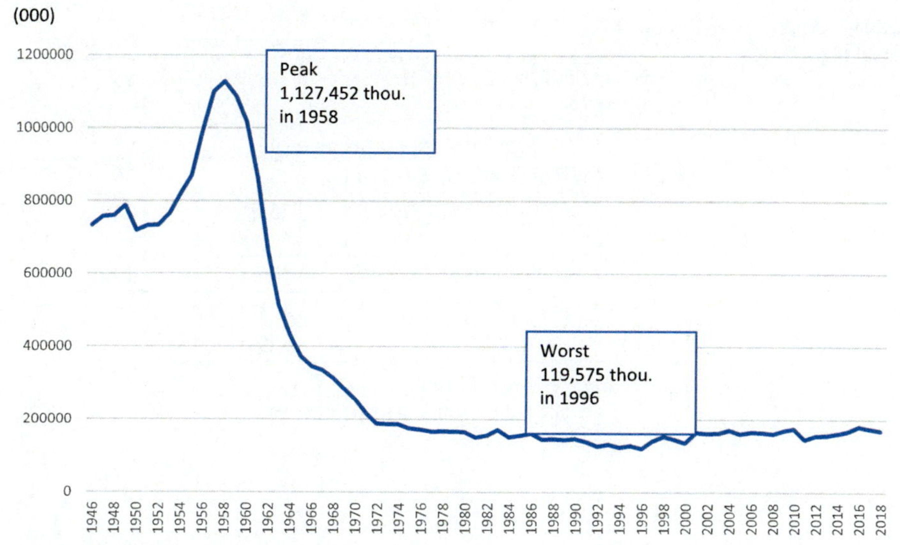

Fig. 2 Admissions film theatre in Japan. (*Data source*) *KINEJYUN and Motion Picture Producers Association of Japan, Inc.* (Graphic) by author

concerned about such old customs like fixed admission fee, inflexible time tables, and block-booking by distribution companies (Fig. 2).

3 The Relationship Between Government and Media Industries in the Second Half of the Twentieth Century

In Japan after the Second World War, democratization became a central social issue for Japan as a whole, and the policy was intended to make the government independent and independent of the methods of the media. This was in contrast to the situation in European countries. In the interwar period and in European countries, and in the trade war of motion pictures with Hollywood, various protection and promotion policies were struck, and even after WW2, they were passed. However, in Japan, the relationship between the government and the cinema and the broadcasting industry is also strongly linked to the Laissez-Faire relationship.

So, policies like the Paramount Decree in 1948 in the USA have not been implemented. The Paramount decree aimed to achieve fair trade through the vertical separation of distribution and exhibition functions of major studios. The same scheme was never considered as a problem by either the government or industry sides of the public discussion and even now there is no rule to separate them. So Japanese film majors, each has their own theater chains even now (Table 1).

Rather, the business of custom block-booking was regarded as a problem. The block-booking business custom itself is also observed in western countries as a

Table 1 Multiplex chains in Japan (Dec. 2016)

	No. of screens	No. of sites
AEON ENTERTAINMENT CO. LTD	718	85
TOHO Cinemas[a]	588	67
UNITED CINEMAS CO., LTD	333	36
Shochiku Multiplex Theatres, Ltd.[a]	253	25
Tokyu Recreation Co., Ltd.	175	19
T-Joy Co., Ltd.[a]	131	14
Corona World	129	13

Source Kinema Junpo
[a]are subsidiaries or a division of majors

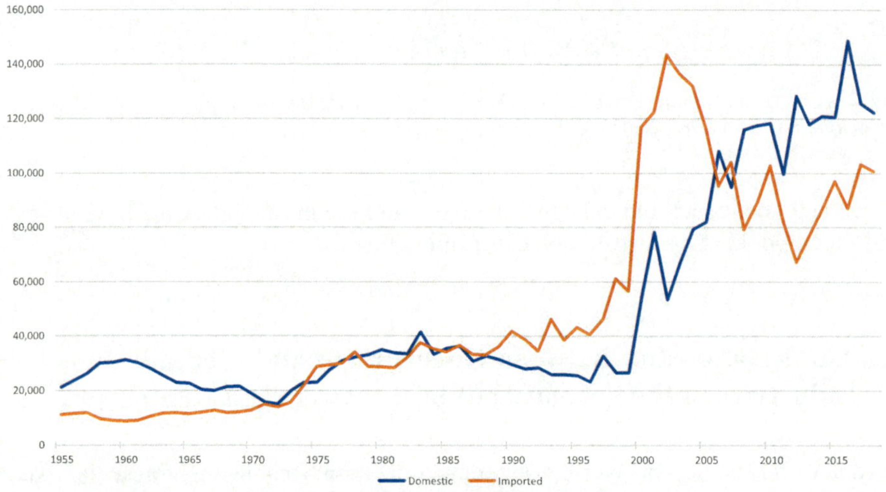

Fig. 3 The maket share of domestic and inported films (on distribution rev. up to 1999 and on box office rev. since 2000). (*Data source*) *Motion Picture Producers Association of Japan, Inc.* (Graphic) by author

means of a full-time theater programming system to cover all screenings with films of the same company. In addition, a characteristic that long-term (generally said to be one year ahead) contracts cause loss of theater programming flexibility has been added. Theaters have to break off films with a good reputation and must continue to show films of a poor quality based on the contracts. Although MITI came to see it as an obstacle to fair trade later, the exclusivity of it has been lost practically in environmental changes such as the expansion of the cinema complex and/or some of the majors themselves voluntary abolishing the custom.

As shown below (Fig. 3), the market share of imported films had been superior to domestic for around 30 years from 1975 to 2005 when Hollywood high concept and block buster films were popular around the world. Although European countries have considered reversal of market share domestically as a cultural problem, there were no governmental actions taken in Japan. The Japanese government was occasionally interested in exports but was completely indifferent to imports. Because of the nonseparation of distribution and exhibition, whether domestic or imported, profitable films in both distribution and exhibition sectors are important for Japanese film companies. This may help form their free market status.

In one of the reports shown here, the UK's past regulator Independent Television Commission (hereinafter referred to as ITC) published a report "Comparative Review of Content Regulation," (1st May 2002) that analyzed the policy stance of some countries (ITC 2002). Among them, the position of Japan is the opposite of that in France. If France has a content-intensive policy, Japan's broadcasting policy is analyzed as a transmission-intensive policy (Fig. 4).

As an example, there was a discussion about the introduction of screen quota rules when Japan was about to join Organisation for Economic Co-operation and Development (hereinafter referred to as OECD) in 1964 and this finally resulted in self-regulation, rather than governmental regulation in 1965. Because of the discussions accompanying OECD affiliation, MITI committed this issue on the table of the industrial structure council and discussed the matter of screen quotas in the phase of the decline of the film industry. The OECD allowed screen quota rules at that time. After discussion, the industry refused governmental hard regulation because of Japanese complex distribution business customs and this resulted in an agreement Japanese movie special screening system in 1965 that had very loose provisions and lost its meaning within a few years under the environmental change of the film market. The stances of industry and government were so different from those of

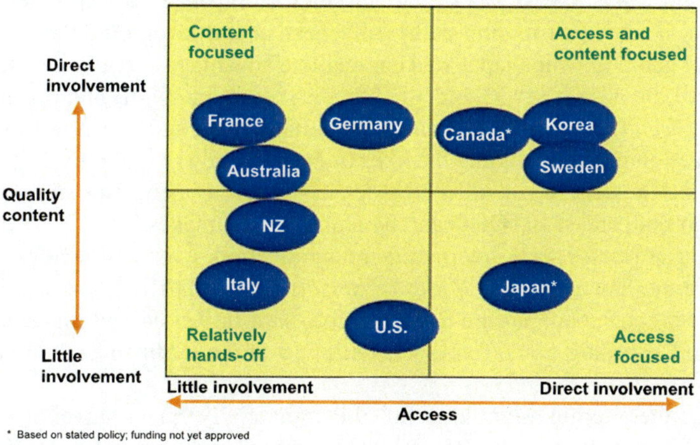

Fig. 4 Country classification: approaches for regulating quality and access. *Source* ITC (2002), p. 12

continental European countries where screen quotas were available. On the discussion among industry and between industry and government, the protection of industry rather than Japanese cultural promotion was emphasized. This is also the difference between Japan and Europe and a reason for the difference.

One exception to this is the case of Japan Film Export Promotion Association (in the form of an incorporated association, April 1966–March 1972). According to Tanigawa (2016), the government (responsible: MITI too) responded to requests for financing loans from the film industry that was in a recession and setup "export film promotion financial measures." The organization became a fund trustee. The scheme was such that the organization reviewed members' films that had qualified as exports and passed financially. There were 61 films in 5 years (and 60 films produced), 7,333 million JPY was provided in finance. The evaluation of the organization was negative. As they were unable to achieve the target export amount at all, suspicion was raised as to whether it was simply for the relief of poor management companies.

Under the qualifying procedures, the estimation of the distribution and sales abroad was an important attribute. So, the genres Japanese film had a competitive advantage in, like SFX (special effect films) or monster (Kaijyu), films tend to be pass the qualifying procedure. Before the introduction of this policy, typically *Godzilla, king of monsters!* (1954) and a series of 12 films by TOHO were already successful films for export. What is more, coproduction films between Hollywood producer, Henry G. Saperstein and TOHO in 1960s were also good examples of international expansion. Companies other than TOHO followed the trend and made monster films. *DAIEI's GAMERA* series, *NIKKATSU's Gappa: The Triphibian Monster* (1967) *and SHOCHIKU's The X from Outer Space* (1967) were typical examples and, as such, became the candidate films of the loan. Six monster films were financed by the association.

If you find a positive aspect to the activities of Japan Film Export Promotion Association, it would be finding competitiveness in and leveraging the SFX genre and monster genre in which japan had competitive advantage according to Tanigawa (2016). Until the advent of CG and VFX that is required to withstand practical use, Japanese SFX had actual internationally competitive genre, and even now in 2018, the superhero action genre, including the likes of *Power Rangers*, and movies conscious of monsters (Kaijyu) are sometimes made and *Godzilla* itself also continues to be produced on both sides, at TOHO and by Hollywood remakes.

The other attributes were international coproduction, overseas locations, and/or foreign casting. For example, *Malenky Beglets* (1966, DAIEI) was a coproduction film between Japan and the Soviet Union, shot in Russia and financed by the association. Regarding casts, foreigners act in 16 of the 60 financed and produced films.

Although the attempt might have failed commercially, quantitative international exports (rather international friendship) had continued in the private sector. In particular, there were the animation programs and films in 1980s during the season of privatization of the European broadcasting market. Famously, such concentrated exports alongside Hollywood soap operas caused the introduction of the *Television without frontier directive* in 1989 (89/552/EEC) on EU states, which have the nationality programming quota among stations in EU. Under the regulatory Reform Dialogue between Japan and EU, Japan is formally in a position to request deregulation from the view of "cultural exchanges" between Japan and EU ((see Ministry of Foreign Affairs, hereinafter referred to as MoFA (2007) pp. 53–54).

There are two cases for overseas development to be introduced. The Japan Foundation and Japan Media Communication Center (hereinafter referred to as JAMCO). Both were not primarily for commercial promotion, but for international exchange and friendship.

3.1 Japan Foundation

According to the statement of the Japan Foundation itself, "To cultivate friendship and ties between Japan and the world, the Japan Foundation creates global opportunities to foster friendship, trust, and mutual understanding through culture, language, and dialogue. The Japan Foundation was established in October 1972 as a special legal entity supervised by the MoFA. In October 2003, it was reorganized as an independent administrative institution. Based on a government endowment of 78 billion JPY, the activities of the Japan Foundation are financed by annual government subsidies, investment revenue, and donations from the private sector.

There is a category "film and broadcast" in their business domain "art and cultural exchange." The Japan Foundation supports overseas TV stations in the broadcast of Japanese TV programs. They also hold Japanese film festivals in collaboration with local institutions and encourage the screening of Japanese films at international film festivals.

Regarding film, the Japan Foundation provides and distributes Japanese feature films (foreign-language versions) and cultural films (dubbed into foreign languages) in order to provide assistance to the cultural activities of its overseas offices and Japanese embassies. Under the title of "Overseas Screenings of Japanese Feature Films", the Japan Foundation cooperates in the submission of films and participation at overseas international film festivals and organizes screenings of Japanese film retrospectives under joint sponsorship with film specialist organizations in various countries. Depending on the project, lectures by film directors or film critics may also be held. The first one was started by the director feature series "*Ozu Yasujiro*" in 1980.

3.2 JAMCO (Japan Media Communication Center)

JAMCO was established as an incorporated foundation with funds from NHK and 123 private broadcasting stations, members of the Japan Commercial Broadcasters Association (hereinafter referred to as JBA), in April 1991. The organizational status was changed to general incorporated foundation on 29th, March, 2013.

As a part of international exchange, JAMCO is seeking programs and works to be expanded overseas from domestic broadcasting companies, etc. and then bear the costs of subtitling and dubbing for localization. On the other hand, JAMCO negotiates with broadcasting stations, countries economically disparate with Japan and are offering these Japanese programs. Their financial resources are profits from fund investments.

3.3 The 2000s—The Beginning of Positive Commitment by Japanese Government

The 2000s was a turning point for positive commitment. See the details in Uchiyama et al. (2009).

3.4 The Policy by Ministry of Economy, Trade and Industry (Hereinafter Referred to as METI), the Successor of Ministry of International Trade and Industry (Hereinafter Referred to as MITI)

At the end of the 90s, a study group "A study for revitalizing the film industry" was held in MITI concerning the promotion of the Japanese film industry, which discussed the financing, export, and audience service of the film industry and so on (see Murakami and Ogawa (1999)). Before and after this, new divisions for the cultural industry were established in MITI by article 98.3 "regarding film industry" in revision of the *Order for Organization of the* MITI in 1997. MITI became METI by 2001 central government reform in 6th January 2001. The policies were inherited and the division was renamed the "Media and content industry division."

3.5 The Policy by Agency for Cultural Affairs (Hereinafter Referred to as ACA)

The ACA, Agency for Cultural Affairs of the twentieth century and the ACA of the twenty-first century differ greatly in their domains of activity. Whereas the former focused exclusively on the preservation of ruins and heritage etc., the latter would start to take charge of the modern media arts domain. The symbol of this is the establishment of the Basic Act for the Promotion of Culture and the Arts (Act No. 148 of 2001), amended to the Basic Act of Culture, and the Arts in 2017. In an article about the promotion of media art in this law (Article 9), it is clearly stipulated that measures necessary for production support and screening support of media art including film will be taken, and in conjunction with this, backups by local governments were stipulated in Article 35.

3.6 *The Policy by the Cabinet Office, IP Strategy Headquarters*

The Cabinet Office also began a commitment under Prime Minister Junichiro KOIZUMI with the establishment of the IP (Intellectual Property) strategy headquarters based on the Intellectual Property Basic Act (Act No. 122 of December 4, 2002).

(https://www.kantei.go.jp/jp/singi/titeki2/) (in Japanese).

Cabinet Office Intellectual property strategy headquarters.

2002. 2.25 Decision of conference of Intellectual property strategy.
2002. 7. 3 Decision of outline of Intellectual property strategy.
2002.12. 4 Promulgation of Intellectual Property Basic Act.
2003. 3. 1 Enforcement of Intellectual Property Basic Act.
2003. 3. 1 Establishment of Intellectual property strategy headquarters.

Since 2003, the office has published the Intellectual Property Strategic Program 20XX every year. As the office itself has not had a sufficient political budget, the actual policies are enforced by the ministries in charge. So, the role of the office is to coordinate among ministries.

3.7 *The Policy of Ministry of Internal Affairs and Communications (Hereinafter Referred to as MIC)*

The e-Japan strategy has been discussed by the Strategic Headquarters for the Promotion of an Advanced Information and Telecommunications Network Society (IT Strategic Headquarters) in the cabinet office from 2000 till now (https://japan.kantei.go.jp/policy/it/index_e.html in English) and MIC, taking charge of telecommunications and broadcasting, has committed to this. At that time, Japan had a top-class high-speed internet infrastructure based on the high diffusion rate of ADSL and optical fiber networks, and rather than content transmitted in narrowband, the focus was on the broadband network.

In parallel with this, the activities of content development office in the MIC have been observed since 2002. From the view of production, preservation (archive), and distribution of intellectual property or content, the division has attempted to provide menus in the three fields. For example, for production, there have been some experiments involving copyright clearance of television programs in digital networks.

The office was promoted to a division (Promotion for Content Distribution Division) in 2007.

3.8 Industrial Promotion by the Private Sector

The Tokyo International Film Festival (hereinafter referred to as TIFF), the most historical and largest film festival in Asia since 1985, which is operated by Public Interest Incorporated Foundation (hereinafter referred to as UNIJAPAN) now, was reformed under general producer and chairman Tsuguhiko KADOKAWA who was CEO of the KADOKAWA group, one of the Japanese film majors, in the mid 2000s.

One of the features of the 17th TIFF in 2004 was the introduction of the B2B film and TV program market. The first Tokyo International Film and Contents Market (hereinafter referred to as TIFCOM) 2004 and Tokyo Entertainment Market 2004 (ENTAMA 2004, deal with comic, anime and game content) were held and have become the Japan Content Showcase now. It is a multicontent market featuring music, TV, film, and animation, combining the three markets of TIFFCOM (rename of TIFCOM, film, and TV program market), Tokyo International Anime Festival (TIAF) Autumn, and Tokyo International Music Market (TIMM).

METI has subsidized this market for the promotion of the export of Japanese content and intellectual property, since then. Although around 20 thousand people (sellers, buyers, and visitors) visit this market every year, thanks to the subsidy of METI and efforts of UNIJAPAN who operates this market, there are fiscal difficulties. TIFF is held in the second half of October every year. It is just before the AFM (American Film Market), the largest film market in the world, in Santa Monica in early November. So many sellers and buyers would tend to choose AFM due to limited budget and time when circling the film markets. Indeed, TIFF has many sellers and buyers from Asia, but relatively few from western countries. Of course, the global film market and festival schedule are tight and are also difficult for TIFF to move to another season. As a result, it is also very close in terms of season to the festival and market of Busan, S.Korea (festival since 1996, market since 2006) in the first half of October.

As mentioned above, neither government nor industry has had concerns about heavy governmental promotion policies like European states in twentieth century, and this has changed gradually. Another feature of the 17th TIFF was the review of international governmental film promotion policies. A symposium regarding this was held. The panelists—the Chairman of the U.K. Film Council, Assistant Representative of CNC, Chairman of Huaxia Film Distribution Co., Ltd, Director of China Film Museum, and Secretary-general of Korean Film Council (hereinafter referred to as KOFIC)—were invited and their policies were announced there. Although the policies shown by these institutes have not been achieved yet in Japan, these have provided hints for the activities of Visual Industry promotion Organization (hereinafter referred to as VIPO) afterward. VIPO was established in December 2004 just after this.

As an association from that name, UNIJAPAN is an organization like Uni-France. It was established in 1957 as the Japan Film Promotion Association (Uni Japan Film) and integrated with Tokyo International Video Culture Promotion Association in 2005. Its organizational status was changed from incorporated foundation to Public interest incorporated foundation in 2010. As the former name indicated, the mission of the organization is the promotion of Japanese film in foreign countries. So, the operation of TIFF is one of their major businesses. And support for exhibition or application of filmmakers for film festivals and markets in foreign countries is also an important one with the cooperation of JETRO.

As mentioned below, in addition, in recent years, UNIJAPAN also supports international coproduction and disseminates Japanese movie information for overseas-, survey-, and research-related fields. It is a comprehensive organization aiming for the development of the film industry.

Such positive movements in the government sector stimulated the private sector and JapanBusiness Federation (hereinafter referred to as KEIDANREN, the largest business association in Japan) have also considered the promotion of the entertainment industry since August 2003 under the chairman of the entertainment & Content division Tatsumi YODA. As a result of this discussion, they decided on the establishment of a new organization VIPO.

VIPO started their activities in June 2005. It is nonprofit private organization and receives policy money from government in biddings for public offerings and member fees from the private sector. At the point of this beginning, they had four main business domains, human resource development, market development domestically and overseas, support for production, and support for entrepreneurs, and now two, Human resource development (hereinafter referred to as HRD) and market development. There is no systematic money or ecosystems to support the production and support of entrepreneurs, like the French system (special tax and automatic support, for example).

In the second half of 2000s, the policies of S.Korea (KOFIC; Korean Film Council, KOCCA; Korea Creative Content Agency) became a benchmark, because of the Korean Wave in many Asian countries including in Japan that stood out at that time and some of their numbers regarding content exports were superior to Japan.

3.9 The 2010s—The Beginning of Positive Investment by Japanese Government

After the Great East Japan Earthquake in March/2011, the cabinet of Democratic Party of Japan was replaced by the Liberal Democratic Party of Japan and Shinzo ABE became Prime Minister. One of the policies adopted by the new Cabinet was the Cool Japan policy, a term inspired by Cool Britannia, which Tony Blair used in the election campaign in late 1990s.

3.10 Export, Cool-Japan

Content export is an important policy for Japan in our history. Regarding the international trade of film and media content, major disputes have continued from the interwar period between USA and other countries (France, Canada, South Americas, and so on) on GATT, WTO/GATS, UNESCO, FTA negotiations, and so on.

It would not be going too far to say that Japan has stayed out of the abovementioned international disputes and that the Japanese government and Japanese industry have remained uninvolved.

As an outsider, until at least the end of the Democratic Party of Japan era (till 2012),

- there were no restrictions or special taxes relating to film and television imports and exports (these have not been introduced yet as of 2018)
- there were no domestic systems favoring domestically produced content such as screen and broadcasting quotas (these have not been introduced yet as of 2018).
- The government budget for promotion of domestically produced content was around 4 billion JPY/year in the 2000s, on a par with midsize countries in Europe.
- Via the Structural Impediments Initiative (SII) talks, the US-Japan Framework Talks, the US-Japan Regulatory Reform and Competition Policy Initiative, and the US-Japan Economic Harmonization Initiative, domestic laws, such as copyright law, had come relatively close to US systems, and
- the policy focus with regard to media tended strongly toward distribution & transmission channels rather than content production.

Because of the above, Japan did not become embroiled in the dispute between the USA versus Europe and others. In other words, just as there were no WTO/FTA-type tariffs or non-tariff barriers in film and television that were obstacles to free trade, Japan's domestic film and television market was based strongly on free competition, including domestic productions and imports. However, as aggressive protection and support policies of the type discussed in the UNESCO Universal Declaration on Cultural Diversity (Convention on the Protection and Promotion of the Diversity of Cultural Expressions) have been modest in relation to the size of the country, in Japan, this issue did not become an international problem. International coproduction agreements between countries were also rare, and a sense of exclusivity in relation to other countries was not created.

However, to avoid any misunderstanding (rather than my unclear views outlined above), Japan's legal stance in relation to WTO/GATS is that it is, "opposed to the argument that measures for protecting the "cultural value" of audio-visual services should be allowed as GATS exceptions, because audio-visual services represent a major area of trade in services and excluding them from the scope of GATS based on the ambiguous concept of "cultural value" would be inappropriate." (METI 2013):439. On the other hand, it has failed to ratify the UNESCO declaration. In other words, superficially Japan has adopted a stance similar to that of the USA, with its measures vis-a-vis content being more industrial than cultural.

In all this, I think I should note that Japan's domestic market is quite a free one in institutional terms, both for domestic productions and imports (of course the natural barrier of the Japanese language cannot be ignored). I believe the eyes of this trained audience can appeal internationally.

See more details in Uchiyama (2012) and Uchiyama (2017).

4 Policies in the Present (2012–)

4.1 Organization

Unfortunately, the Japanese political structure (organization) is neither simple nor centralized. Basic players are MIC, METI, ACA, and Cabinet office IP headquarter (Fig. 5).

4.2 Acts and Regulations Policy Menu

The Japanese TV, film, and video content market are very open and are almost completely regulation-free and market-driven, with a low entry barrier. Perhaps the

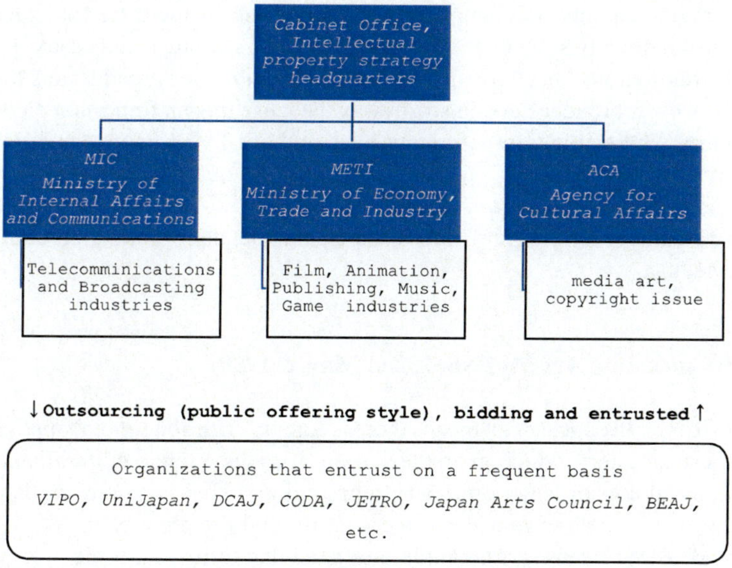

Fig. 5 Political organizations related to media content

Japanese language and its location in the far east can be considered its greatest entry barriers.

There are acts regarding the broadcasting system. Particularly in terms of the Broadcasting act, some content regulations do exist, but there are no direct acts for the film industry. From the view of media content in a broad sense, there are basically three other acts.

4.2.1 Censorship

There is no government censorship where broadcasters are concerned, only self-regulation by broadcasters and the Broadcasting Ethics & Program Improvement Organization (hereinafter referred to as BPO). Guidelines and broadcasting codes are published by NHK (Japan Broadcasting Corporation 1998) and by the Japan Commercial Broadcasting Association (see JBA (n.d.)). Where necessary, rulings can be given by a private organization the BPO.

4.2.2 Quotas

Regarding film, there are no actual screen quota rules in Japan as mentioned above, and many are surprised to learn that there are no broadcasting quotas between domestic programs and foreign programs—unlike in EU states, for example. Therefore, there is no need for a cultural test system in Japan.

There are no content-windowing control regulations, as there are for example in France. The windowing strategy is governed by business strategy and customs, rather than public regulation. There are also no legal obligations for broadcasters to invest in films. However, broadcasters do so anyway, because it is an important element of their business. There are no import quota rules on both TV programs and films.

Additionally, regarding TV programs, there are no quota rules for independent productions in Japan as there are, for example, in the UK, where broadcasters must include a percentage of programs produced by independent production companies in their schedules.

4.2.3 Broadcasting Act (Act No. 132 of May 2, 1950)

Article 106 of the Broadcast Act means there is a genre criterion (quota) applicable to generalist broadcasters, which guarantees room for educational, cultural, and news programming alongside entertainment programming. This is to ensure that basic broadcasters are operating in accordance with official directive of the *MIC*, which issues broadcasting licenses. The guidelines state that terrestrial basic broadcasters must dedicate 10% of broadcast hours to educational programming and 20% to cultural programming.

4.3 Act and Promotion Policy Menu

Basic policies of the three ministries regarding film and broadcasting (Table 2).

The basic acts regarding content-promotion established in twenty-first century are as below.

Intellectual Property Basic Act (Act No. 122 of December 4, 2002).

It is a law that aims to promote measures concerning the creation, protection, and utilization of intellectual property and determines the measures to be taken for that purpose. It was promulgated on December 4, 2002 and this came into effect on March 1, 2003.

"Intellectual Property" and "Intellectual Property Rights" (Article 2)
Clarify the responsibilities of the national government, local governments, universities, etc. and the business entities concerning the handling of intellectual property (Articles 5–8)
Basic policy

Promotion of R & D (Article 12)
Promotion of the transfer of research results (Article 13)
Accelerated granting of rights (Article 14)
Enhancement and acceleration of court proceedings etc. (Article 15)
Strengthening measures against infringement of rights (Article 16)
Construction of international institutions (Article 17)
Protection of intellectual property in new fields (Article 18)
Improvement of the environment for utilizing intellectual property (Article 19)
Provision of information (Article 20)
Promotion of education (Article 21)
Securing personnel (Article 22)
Preparation of a "Promotion plan concerning creation, protection and utilization of intellectual property" (intellectual property promotion plan) (Article 23).
Establishment of Intellectual Property Strategy Headquarters (Article 24).

Act on Promotion of Creation, Protection and Exploitation of Contents (Act No. 81 of 2004)

It defines the responsibilities of the national and local governments and the general public to contribute to the revitalization of the content industry. Content is defined as "films, music, theater, literary arts, photographs, cartoons, animations, computer games and other characters, figures, colors, sounds, motions or videos, or combinations thereof. Or a program for providing information related to these via a computer, which is produced by human creative activities."

- The development of human resources
- Promotion of R&D on advanced technologies
- Proper protection of intellectual property rights related to contents

Table 2 Representative and long-term policies of each ministry

	Production Support	Export	Festival	Human Resource Development	Piracy problem	Bargaining among nations	Technology	Budget
Cabinet office, IP headquarter	Review of Japanese film industry (Export, finance, film commission, etc.)				Site blocking problem			
METI		*JLop* & new scheme Intl. Co-production support	*CoFesta* (Collaboration of multiple festivals)		Support for the activities of *CODA*	Dialogue among Japan–China-S.Korea	CG, VR/AR development Business matching Standardization of animation production	
ACA	Subsidy for film production Support for location database	Intl. Co-production support Support for entry on festivals	*Japan Media Arts Festival* Subsidy for festivals	Animators Directors live action	Problem of reaching sites			
MIC	Subsidy for export of TV programs						ICT general 4K8K promotion	

(summarized by author)

- Promotion of smooth distribution of contents
- Promotion of proper preservation
- Correct the disparity of utilization opportunities etc.
- Establishment of a system to raise funds
- Measures against infringement of rights
- Promotion of overseas business development

etc.

Basic Act for the Promotion of Culture and the Arts (Act No. 148 of 2001, renamed Basic Act of Culture and the Arts since 2017)

What became a major point for the cultural promotion policy of the ACA was the Basic Act for the Promotion of Culture and the Arts established and enforced in 2001. The law sets out the basic philosophy concerning the promotion of cultural arts including media art (which states media art as being "art using cinema, cartoons, animation and computers and other electronic devices"). Furthermore, it clarifies the responsibilities of the national government and local governments and sets out the basic matters of measures for cultural art promotion. It is intended to promote the voluntary activities of persons engaged in cultural and artistic activities and to promote comprehensive promotion of measures concerning the promotion of cultural arts.

4.4 METI

METI takes charge of cinema, game, music, publishing, ad-agency, and information processing industries according to Article 90 in revision of the Order for Organization of the METI in 2017. In particular,

(1) Content overseas expansion
(2) International Content Trade Fair Project
(3) Cool Japan Fund
(4) Intergovernmental dialogue
(5) Measures against intellectual property right infringement (pirated contents)
(6) Content technology promotion

(according to "about content industry policy" by media and content industry division, 2018 edition.)

specifically comprise their policy menu now. To summarize, oversea export is a central issue for METI. As mentioned above, fair trade issues have been traditionally one of the agendas in MITI and METI, and overseas exports have become more critical. Human resource development, particularly that of producer function (artist and creator are the domain of ACA), was another important issue in METI in past.

The core policy menu for oversea expansion by METI was Japan Contents Localize & Promotion support subsidy (hereinafter referred to as J-LOP) programs from 2013 to 2017. Around 6 billion JPY/per year had been spent on promotion activities overseas and for subtitling and/or dubbing. After the Abe administration took office in December 2012, a major subsidy scheme called J-LOP, which was based on the FY2012 supplementary budget, was announced (Table 3). The budget was of the order of several billion JPY per year. This was of course far larger than any previous budget in the history of Japan's measures related to film and television content. Initially, METI and MIC jointly managed the scheme at first. Today, however, it is a fund and subsidy scheme run by METI's Media and Content Industry Division (subcontracted out to the VIPO. The budget is not only limited to film and broadcasting but also used to subsidize localization (subtitling, dubbing, including music and games) and promotion (exhibition in international trade fairs) (subsidy ratio: 1/2, later 2/3 in some cases).

J-Lop was renewed to a new scheme "Creation of global content ecosystem focusing on creators" in 2018. The budget scale is half that of J-Lop (around 3 billion JPY/per year) (Fig. 6).

From the view of industrial organization, there are the other aspects to METI taking charge. First, there are institutions regarding fund raising for film production.

Table 3 4 years J-LOP subsidy programme

Abbreviation	Period in effect	Official name	Budget
J-LOP	2013.3 –15.3	FY2012 supplementary budget, METI, MIC fund for "Promoting Content Worldwide"	12.33bn JPY (METI), ¥3.20bn JPY(MIC)
J-LOP+	2015.3 –16.3	FY2014 supplementary budget METI "Fund for promoting content produced by Japanese broadcasters worldwide that contributes to regional revitalization"	5,997.44 M JPY
JLOP	2016.2 –16.11	FY2015 supplementary budget, METI "Subsidy for expenses arising from establishment of foundation for distribution of locally produced content overseas"	6,694.00 M JPY
J-LOP4	2016.12 –17.11	FY2016 supplementary budget, METI "Subsidy for expenses arising from establishment of foundation for creating global demand for content"	5,999.00 MJPY

(summarized by author)

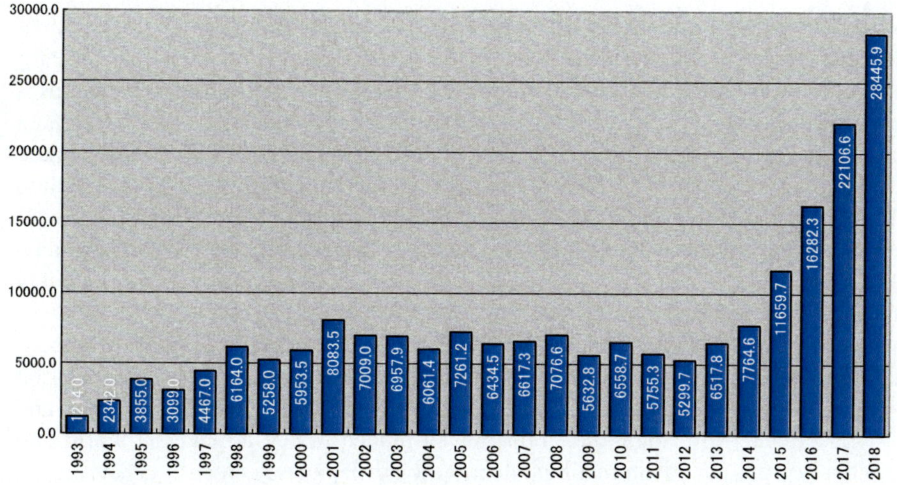

Fig. 6 Film Export by Japanese Film Majors (10 thousand USD). *(Data source) Motion Picture Producers Association of Japan, Inc.* (Graphic) by author

Japanese unique production alliance "film partnership" widely used for the production of Japanese films and animations (TV, movie). Film partnership has the function of fund raising. In general, as one of the means of raising funds for films in the world, it emphasizes a method of producing a film by organizing investment funds. This is achieved due to the creation of movie investment opportunities by ordinary people and foreign investors, securing fairness and fairness of returns commensurate with investment, and inducing and expanding funds for cinemas through tax incentive systems for investors.With respect to the fund composition of films, the METI has took a strong interest from around 2002 to 2005, and through the subcontract payment law, the amendment of the trust business law, the creation of a limited liability partnership (LLP) system, etc., a set of policies was launched that aimed to simplify organization. However, the film partnership is still the mainstream way for Japanese films and Limited Liability Company (hereinafter referred to as LLC)/LLP are rarely used. According to METI (2016), "The Production Partnership is a consortium formed and financially contributed to by various companies including a television broadcaster, a film distributor, a film production company, a publisher, an advertising agency and a video production company with a shared aim of jointly operating and producing and exporting a film. In most cases, it is in the form of a partnership under the Civil Code (voluntary partnership); although the members are usually not individual persons, the legal structure is considered to be a partnership, not a joint venture, unless otherwise agreed between the partners. Partners decide matters pertaining to the Production Partnership by counseling each other and reaching an agreement. Partners are coowners of any right relating to the Production Partnership including copyright: each partner owns undivided interest with no right to assign or sever one's interest unless otherwise agreed between the partners." So, it is different from LLP and LLC under the LLC act and companies act which are ways for film production in western countries. Film production partnership is suitable for usual member companies under the Japanese media ecosystem, but is less open system than LLC/LLP for new entrants to Japanese film production. The operational cost of film partnerships is less than that for LLC/LLP. Although exports have been promoted on the government side, the money invested in the project has been recouped in the domestic market. Considering the Japanese domestic market size, the budget of around 0.1–1 billion JPY is reasonable and film partnerships can collect enough money. Finally, there is no tax incentive, and it is not necessary to be a tax vehicle and to open financial statements widely. These are the reasons why the film partnership is more widely used than LLC/LLP.

Piracy problem is one of their domains. Regarding this matter, *CODA* is subcontracting organization for *METI*. The Content Overseas Distribution Association (CODA) was founded as an organization through which content holders and copyright-related organizations cooperate to reduce piracy around the world and to actively promote the international distribution of Japanese content, such as music, films, animation, TV programs, and video games. While *CODA* was formed to counter content piracy, the organization is now expanding its enterprise in cooperation with domestic and international government agencies, industry organizations, and content holders. On December 2, 2013, CODA merged our secretariat office with that of the Anti-Counterfeiting Association (ACA) in order to strengthen our capability to protect copyright and offer comprehensive measures against copyright infringement in Japan as well as overseas.

Fair Trade issue is another domain. Particularly, there is a subcontracting problem involving animation production companies, animators and film & TV companies (platformers). Because of Japanese business customs, a type of labor union or guild by company is mainstream and unions by business function are relatively weak, so independent or personal creators are in a weak position for negotiations. In addition to this, with the separation of content production and platform function in the age of convergence of telecom and broadcasting, the relationship between production and platform should be considered. METI and MIC (regarding broadcasting programs) have been instructed by the Cabinet office to consider what this should be and create guidelines for contracts. METI is aiming to achieve fair trade through the method of formulating model contracts and publications.

Intergovernmental dialog is also an area in which METI has had a strong interest. Recently METI and MoFA succeeded in signing an agreement about coproduction with China (May 2018). Even before that, negotiations have taken place with East Asia (China and S.Korea) and ASEAN nations. Regarding the former, content industry forums involving Japan, China and S.Korea have been held since 2002 and the 10th was held in Japan in June 2017. The latter, Asia Content Business Summit (ACBS) has been held since 2008 and the 5th was in Malaysia in September 2016.

HRD was the one of the main issues. HRD at the METI was characterized by being interested in the (business) producer function as a ministry of commerce. The position or power of the producer in Japanese film production is not as strong as in the Hollywood system and it was considered that the enhancement of the producer function would contribute to the expansion of market and/or export of Japanese films.

Many research projects and studies were done and the awareness of the importance of the producer function has increased during this decade. However, METI has lost interest in recent years as it does not appear as a clear policy outcome.

There is a rule for the central bureaucracy system to produce policy evaluations and results within 3 years. It is because the METI seems to be particularly conscious of this rule. In reality, however, there are many time-consuming policy issues such as improvement of international competitiveness, human resource development, countermeasures against piracy, and so there seems to be a situation where there are dilemmas within the METI's own organization culture.

4.5 ACA

The ACA (Agency for Cultural Affairs) is an external agency of the Ministry of Education, Culture, Sports, Science and Technology, and it is the agency that promotes and diffuses culture, conservation and utilization of cultural properties, copyright, administration relating to religious corporations, etc. Film and video policy at the ACA is conducted as part of "Promotion of Arts and Culture." The total budget amount of the ACA has steadily been around 100 billion JPY. The budget composition can be divided into "enhancement of cultural property protection" and "promotion of arts culture," but in the twenty-first century, the proportion of "promotion of arts and culture" is increasing.

As mentioned above, the Basic Act for the Promotion of Culture and the Arts changes the character and the business domain of ACA. The political menu recently includes.

1. Human Resource Development

Development projects for young film directors and animators. NDJC for live action film shoot by 35 mm films (subcontracted by VIPO) and Animemirai or Anime Egg for animation (See Chapter "Anime Policy: Various Aspects and the Importance of Industry" for details)

2. Subsidies through the Japan Art Council (for cinema production and cinema festival)

This is not so large as the European system and typical selective support system, no automatic systems

3. Subsidy for coproduction (with UNIJAPAN)

4. Support for entry on foreign film festival

5. Organizing Japan Media Arts Festival (https://j-mediaarts.jp/).

Regarding the promotion of cinema policies, following the enforcement of the act, the "Roundtable on Cinema Promotion" was held in 2002. Discussions were held on the main conference, "Human Resources Development," "Production," "Distribution & Exhibition," "Preservation/Dissemination" four subcommittee compositions. When considering the promotion of the cinema at this roundtable discussion, the meaning of film today is defined as "cinema as total art," "cinema in national life," "cinema as a leading visual work of the IT era" "cinema as a mean" for disseminating Japanese culture abroad. After this discussion, the final report "*For the promotion of future Japanese cinemas ~ For the revival of Japanese cinemas ~*" was released in April 2004. In the report, as a basic policy of national film promotion, 4 policies were outlined,

"Preservation of movie films as a cultural heritage"
"Establishment of an Autonomous Creative Cycle of Film Industry"
"Construction of a system based on the importance of human resources training"
"Valuable evaluation of the arts field of a movie"

and 12 actual tasks were proposed as a cinema promotion measure that the government should promote in order to realize the above.

1. Establishment of a system to preserve Japanese cinema film
2. Introduction of a new production support forum
3. Cooperation with location attraction in the region
4. Expansion of screening opportunities utilizing noncinema facilities
5. Formation of a place for encounters of screeners with diverse cinema work information
6. Improvement of domestic film festival spreading function
7. Support for overseas deployment
8. Reconstruction of personnel training measures closely tied to the site
9. Opening of the cinema plaza
10. Appropriate evaluation of cinemas in the field of art
11. Promotion of the spread of children's cinema appreciation
12. Independence of Film Centre

In response to the report, the Japan Cinema & Video Promotion Plan started in FY 2004 in order to concretely implement the 12 actual tasks. The budget amount of the plan was 2,510 million JPY in FY 2004, 2,452 million JPY in FY 2005, 2,286 million JPY in FY 2006, 2,222 million JPY in FY 2007, and 2,050 million JPY in FY 2008. These were very large political budgets in Japanese film promotion policy history, but very small compared with those of European states.

Regarding subsidy menus, those of ACA are small in scale but have meaning in terms of its continuity. Specifically, there are subsidies for film production and film festival that are performed through the Japan Art Council, subsidies for international coproduction that is carried out with the METI and UNIJAPAN.

The financial source of subsidies for film production and for film festivals are from the Japan Arts Fund composed of ACA investment and private donations to the Japan Art Council and ACA's "Cultural and arts promotion expenses subsidy." The Japan Arts Fund has 68.1 billion JPY in basic funds and is run in every year using the profit on investment and money from government every year for various cultural activities. Regarding films, around 500 million JPY has been subsidized for two categories from two money resources. These are typical selective subsidies (selection committee held) and an amount from 2 million JPY up to a max of 20 million JPY is subsidized per film.

Subsidies for international coproduction also use a typical selective subsidy. Policy budget is around 200 million JPY by ACA. UNIJAPAN holds the selection committee and qualifies eligibility.

The New Emerging Artist Overseas Study Abroad Program is aimed at providing young artists and others in various fields with the opportunity to engage in practical training overseas to nurture personnel who are responsible for promoting future cultural arts in our country. It is a system that supports travel expenses and stay expenses when field training is conducted at overseas universities and arts organizations. Along with fields such as art, music, performing arts, the film field has been established to support several people every year.

4.6 MIC

(See Chapter "Assistance for International Coproductions and Overseas Broadcasts of Japanese Broadcast Content" and others for details.)

4.7 Cabinet Office, IP Headquarters

The domain of IP headquarters is broad, ranging from industrial patent matters to old and new media content matters, and there has been a strong interest in cinema recently.

Review meetings on overseas development of the cinema industry (2016–2018)
Japan–China Film Co-Production Agreement (2018)
Review Conference on Promotion Measures of Cinemas (2016)
Government Liaison Meeting on Environmental Improvement of Location Shooting (2017).

The establishment of the agreement on coproduction with China in 2018 is a big result. In the report on the "The report of review meeting on movie promotion measures (Cabinet office 2017)," three issues were pointed out.

1. Current status and issues surrounding film production support and financing
2. Current situation and issues surrounding overseas deployment support
3. Current situation and issues surrounding location supporting.

4.8 Budget

Generally speaking, the scale of budgets of ministries is not so large compared with European states, France, Germany, U.K. Italy, Spain, etc. But it became bigger than the past budget until 2000s. This is the result of the policy of Prime Minister Abe. Under the Abe administration since 2012, approximately 8 billion JPY/year has been invested by three ministries through general and supplementary budgets. There is no special tax for media content and no special accounts for film and media in Japan.

5 No Systems/Weak Systems in Japan

Compared to European system where the political promotion menu is substantial, there are many policies Japan has not introduced and/or has not been active.

Tax Incentives for film and TV program productions are not found in Japan. This is one of the core and central promotion political methods among EU states, British Commonwealth countries, and states in the U.S. and Canada invite rich shooting crews and generate ripple effects through the film exhibition and broadcasting as in so-called film-tourism and investment promotion for investors. The invitation competition among governments has heated up around the world and it is easy to imagine that the political cost will increase and efficiency will drop. So, USC researcher Thom and An (2017) and Thom (2018) criticize such excess competition. Needless to say, MPAA refuses it (MPAA 2016). As the Thom and An (2017) indicate that "the more money that a state has invested in a program, the more entrenched the program becomes, even when the returns are small," competitive government had invested a significant degree of political resources and had a long history, Japan seems to have lost the chance to enter this competition. Technically it will be necessary to keep the tax incentive system for a long time to generate the effects, and Japan could not find stable financial resources for this policy.

Automatic subsidies have never been introduced throughout history. As mentioned above, the subsidies by ACA/Japan Art council are in the selective subsidy style. Because public subsidies must be fair and just, tax incentives and/or automatic subsidy systems are superior to selective subsidies. As in the social discussion about automatic support and selective support in France in 1959–1960, a balance should be considered.

Thus, the Cultural Test system is not necessary because the incentive systems are not so substantial as Europe. Additionally, the nationality of Japanese works has been very clear compared with continent European works. The cast and staffs are almost all Japanese and the money also comes from Japanese sources. The location and language are also Japanese. Due to the unique position of Japan (island nation, economic status, cultural uniqueness), the degree of cultural sharing with surrounding countries is low. Moreover, the domestic market size for Japanese film majors is sufficient to produce works for domestic market without foreign sales. This is another reason why international coproduction is sluggish.

There is similar rule in coproduction subsides by ACA/UNIJAPAN. There is a point rule when measuring the nationality of the film.

Co-Production agreements are not as prevalent in Japan as they are in many other countries, particularly in continent Europe, with similarly active audiovisual sectors. Japan has only three coproduction agreements—for example, with Canada, established in 1994, and with Singapore, an agreement active since 2002. These agreements are signed by the MoFA and are for both TV programs and for films. A reason why coproduction is not so prominent in Japan is that tax incentives and subsidies here are scarce and there is no reciprocity with other countries and producers where such incentive systems are in place.

However, since the Liberal Democratic Party returned to cabinet in December 2012, the policy slogans COOL JAPAN and VISIT JAPAN have been strengthened and the government is investing more in cultural activities. For example, the MIC introduced coproduction subsidies for TV programs genre since 2013, with a view to increasing the export of Japanese content. Coproduction is one way to develop programming exports and south-east Asian countries are a particular target where this strategy is concerned.

As mentioned above, the third agreement was signed with China, in 2018. Famously, the Chinese film market has numerical restrictions and censorship for foreign films, Japan hopes that coproduction films can be treated as domestic Chinese films in China under this agreement. As the scheme of coproduction subsidy by ACA/UNIJAPAN, UNIJAPAN will perform certification work in the Japan–China Film Co-Production Agreement.

There are no obligations for TV stations to invest in and broadcast films on TV programming including the public broadcaster NHK. This is one of the common rules in the EU state. At this moment, films are not such strong programs in terms of TV ratings compared with in the past, and TV stations have decreased motivation to invest in films now, which will make it difficult to introduce such a rule in Japan now.

The norm for internet video distribution like the discussion in European commission since 2009 or revision of AVMSD in EU has not been discussed adequately. Compared with western countries, the diffusion of internet video distribution has been delayed. For example, the launch of Amazon prime and Netflix in Japan was later than in the USA (about 5 years) and the European Union (about 1–2 years), and the reversal in the TV advertising market scale and internet advertising market has not occurred yet although it has already occurred in the USA and many European states (Fig. 7 and Table 4).

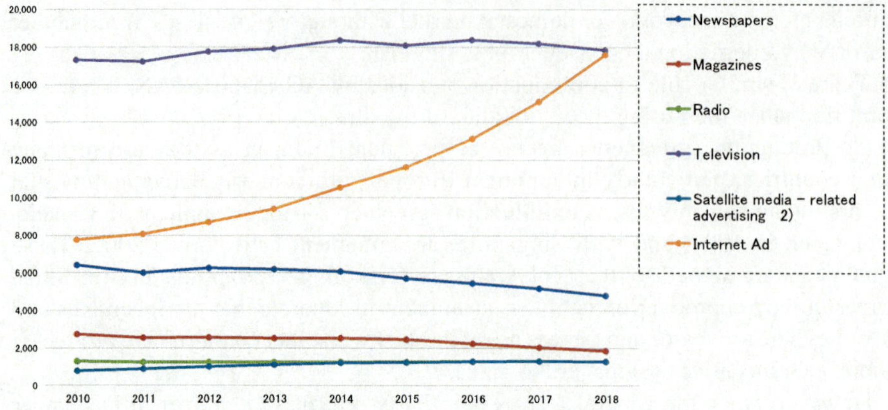

Fig. 7 Japanese Advertising market. (*Data source*) *MIC* Long-term time series data (Graphic) by author(Data Source) MIC Long-term time series data (Graphic) by author

Table 4 Global players entering the multi-screen business from each country (year of entry)

	Countries, states (North America, Europe)	Japan
Netflix	U.S. (2007), Canada (2010) U.K., Ireland, Sweden, Denmark, Finland, Norway (2012) Netherlands (2013) France, Germany (2014) Spain, Portugal, Italy (2015)	2015
Amazon Prime	U.S. (2011) U.K., Germany, Ireland (2014)	2015
sky	U.K., Germany, Italy (2014)	n.a.
WUAKI TV	Spain(2010), U.K. (2013) France, Germany (2014) Italy, Austria, Ireland (2015)	n.a.

(summarized by author)

References

Agency for Cultural Affairs (2003) For the promotion of future Japanese cinemas ~ For the revival of Japanese cinemas ~. https://www.bunka.go.jp/seisaku/bunkashingikai/kondankaito/eiga/eigashinko/pdf/korekara_nihoneiga_shinkou.pdf. Accessed 11 Dec 2019

Cabinet Office (2017) The report of review meeting on movie promotion measures (in Japanese). Task force on promotion measures of films in IP strategy headquarters of Cabinet office

Independent Television Commission (2002) Comparative review of content regulation. A McKinsey Report for the Independent Television Commission UK

Japan Broadcasting Corporation (1998) NHK broadcasting ethics, amended in 1998 (in Japanese). https://www.nhk.or.jp/pr/keiei/kijun/index.htm. Accessed 11 Dec 2019

Ministry of Economy, Trade and Industry (2009) A report of study group for business models in Film industry (in Japanese)

Ministry of Economy, Trade and Industry (2016) Survey on overseas development of video content and procurement of funds—Issues and countermeasures plan in our content industry (in Japanese)
Ministry of Economy, Trade and Industry (2013) "Service trade," 2012 unfair trade report, Chap. 11, (22 April 2013):439 (in Japanese)
Ministry of Foreign Affairs (2007) Japan's proposal for regulatory reform dialogue (between Japan and EU). https://www.mofa.go.jp/region/europe/eu/overview/dereg0712.pdf. Accessed 11 Dec 2019
Motion Picture Association Inc. (2016) When analyzing data on film incentives, you have to start with the right data. https://www.mpaa.org/press/when-analyzing-data-on-film-incentives-you-have-to-start-with-the-right-data/. Accessed 11 Dec 2019
Murakami Y, Ogawa N (1999) The forefront of the Japanese film industry (in Japanese). Kadokawa, Tokyo
The Japan Commercial Broadcasters Association (n.d.) Broadcasting ETHICS, amended 1996, 1999, 2014. https://www.j-ba.or.jp/category/english/jba101019. Accessed 11 Dec 2019
Tanigawa K (2016) Japan Film Export Promotion Association and contents for export. Monster film production by using government funds and its story. In: Tanigawa K (ed) Industrial space of postwar films. Capital, entertainment, exhibition (in Japanese), Chap. 2. Shinwasha, Tokyo
Thom M (2018) Lights, camera, but no action? Tax and economic development lessons from state motion picture incentive programs. Am Rev Public Adm 48(1):33–51
Thom M, An B (2017) Fade to black? Exploring policy enactment and termination through the rise and fall of state tax incentives for the motion picture industry. Am Polit Res 45(1):85–108
Uchiyama T, Ishikawa T, Shirayone E (2009) Japanese film & video content policy. In: Sugaya M, Nakamura K, Uchiyama T (eds) Video content industry and film policy, Chap. 14 (in Japanese). Maruzen, Tokyo
Uchiyama T (2012) Oversea expansion of Japanese content industry. In: Regeneration of Japan through technology and culture (in Japanese). Research and Legislative Reference Bureau of National Diet Library. https://dl.ndl.go.jp/view/download/digidepo_3533035_po_20120110.pdf?contentNo=1. Accessed 11 Dec 2019
Uchiyama T (2017) Global film and TV distribution policy disputes and overseas development of Japanese TV programs. In: The current state and challenges of international broadcasting in key countries. 25th JAMCO online international symposium. https://www.jamco.or.jp/en/symposium/25/7/. Accessed 11 Dec 2019

Film Works

Honda I dir. Godzilla, king of monsters! 1954, TOHO produced and distributed
Ichikawa K dir. The Inugami Family. 1976, Office of Haruki KADOKAWA produced, TOHO distributed
Katsumata M dir. Hans Christian Andersen's The Little Mermaid. 1975, TOEI Animation produced, TOEI distributed
Kinugasa T, Bocharov E dir. Malenky Beglets. 1966, DAIEI & GORKY FILM produced
Kurehara K dir. Antarctica. 1983, Antarctica Film Partnership produced, Nippon Herald Films distributed
Marquand R dir. Star Wars: Episode VI Return of the Jedi. Lucasfilm Ltd. Produced
Masuda T, Matsumoto R, Katsumata M dir. Farewell to Space Battleship Yamato. 1978, Yoshinobu NISHIZAKI produced TOEI distributed
Nihonmatsu K dir. The X from Outer Space. 1967, SHOCHIKU produced and distributed
Noguchi Y dir. Gappa: The Triphibian Monster. 1967, Nikkatsu produced and distributed
Rin T dir. Galaxy Express 999. 1979, TOEI Animation produced, TOEI distributed
Spielberg S dir. E.T. The Extra-Terrestrial. Universal Studios & Amblin Entertainment produced

Yoshikawa S dir. Lupin the Third. 1979, Tokyo Movie produced, TOHO distributed

Acts Related to Content

Act on Promotion of Creation, Protection and Exploitation of Contents. Act No. 81 of 2004. https://www.japaneselawtranslation.go.jp/law/detail/?vm=04&re=01&id=1581. Accessed 11 Dec 2019
Basic Act for the Promotion of Culture and the Arts. Act No. 148 of 2001, amended to Basic Act of Culture and the Arts in 2017. https://www.japaneselawtranslation.go.jp/law/detail/?vm=04&id=1494&re=02. Accessed 11 Dec 2019
Broadcasting Act. Act No. 132 of May 2, 1950. https://www.japaneselawtranslation.go.jp/law/detail/?id=2954&vm=04&re=01. Accessed 11 Dec 2019
Intellectual Property Basic Act. Act No. 122 of December 4, 2002. https://www.japaneselawtranslation.go.jp/law/detail_main?vm=&id=129. Accessed 11 Dec 2019

Anime's Economic Value: the Government's Response to a Changing Environment

Mariko Koizumi

Abstract This chapter aims to provide the overview of Japan's anime policy. Japanese animation, popularly known as "anime," is distributed not only in Japan but throughout the world. The industry has drastically expanded over the last half century. What role has public policy played in this development? The government had started to implement industrial promotion initiatives since only around the year 2000 in response to a Japanese economic recession, the advancement and spread of IT, and the increase in anime's global popularity. Since then, the government has been primarily focusing on the economic value of anime rather than its cultural value. The initiatives intended to eliminate the inherent problems of the industry which had consisted of the weak financial base of production companies, the lack of animators, and more. Despite these, the policy's achievements have been limited and also Japanese policy has been needing a clear vision. A significant improvement in social recognition of anime may be the most profound effect of the policy so far. This chapter consists of information on the current state and characteristics of the industry, the difficulties the industry faces, anime's history, and specific initiatives which the government implemented.

1 Introduction

Japanese animation, popularly known as "anime," is distributed not only in Japan but also throughout the world. Figure 1[1] shows the proportion of viewers who cited anime as their favorite genre of TV programs in Japan, suggesting that anime is popular among men and women of all ages. Also, the anime industry in Japan has been continually growing. Figure 2 exhibits the transition of the scale of the Japanese

[1] All figures presented in this chapter are for Japan unless otherwise noted in the title of the figure.

M. Koizumi (✉)
Faculty of Manga, Kyoto Seika University, Kyoto, Japan
e-mail: mariko123@ark.ocn.ne.jp

M. Sugaya (ed.), *Perspectives on the Japanese Media and Content Policies*, Advances in Information and Communication Research 2,
https://doi.org/10.1007/978-981-15-4704-1_8

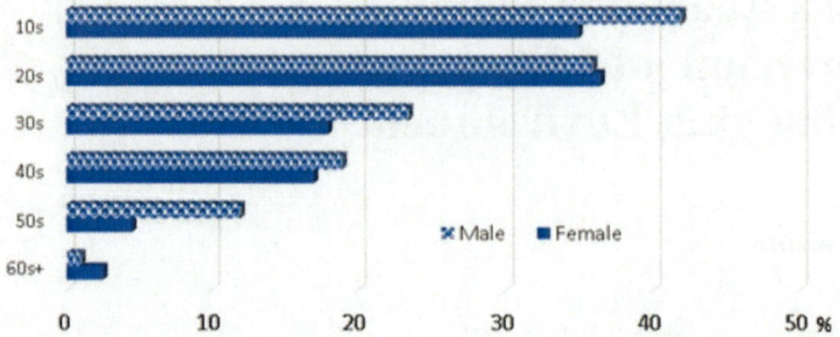

Fig. 1 Proportion of viewers who cited anime as their favorite TV program genre (2016). *Source* Based on JDS Co., Ltd. (2016); The Association of Japanese Animations (2017), p. 52

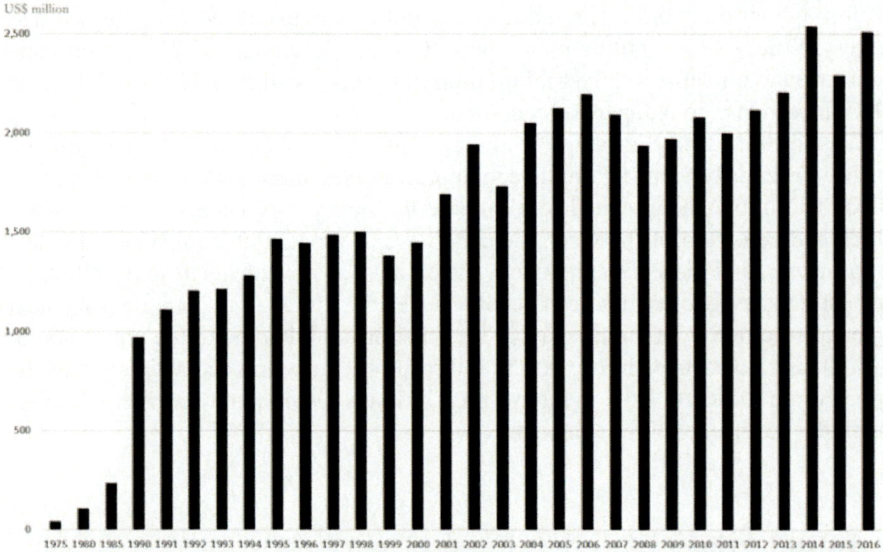

Fig. 2 Transition of scale of the Japanese anime industry (Total of films, TV, videograms, and Internet). *Source* Dentsu Communication Institute Inc. (2001), p. 64; Id. (2014), p. 110; Dentsu Media Innovation Lab (2018), p. 102

anime industry from 1975 to 2016.[2] These numbers indicate the total size of the film, TV broadcast, videogram, and Internet distribution industries, since anime is viewed in various ways. The scale of the anime industry, which was only 42 million USD in 1975, started growing rapidly in the late 1980s. It reached 2.5 billion USD in 2016 and it is still growing. Figure 3 demonstrates that anime is an important part of the entire Japanese film industry including the live-action film industry, accounting for

[2] 1USD was converted to 110 JPY in this chapter.

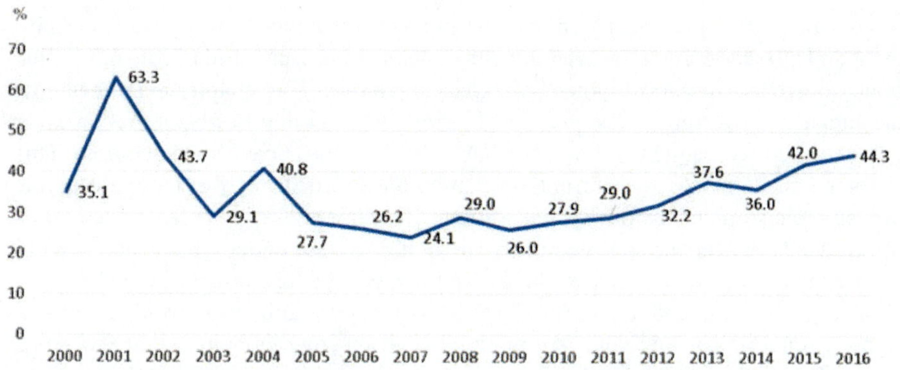

Fig. 3 Proportion of anime in box-office revenue. *Source* The Association of Japanese Animations (2017), p. 9

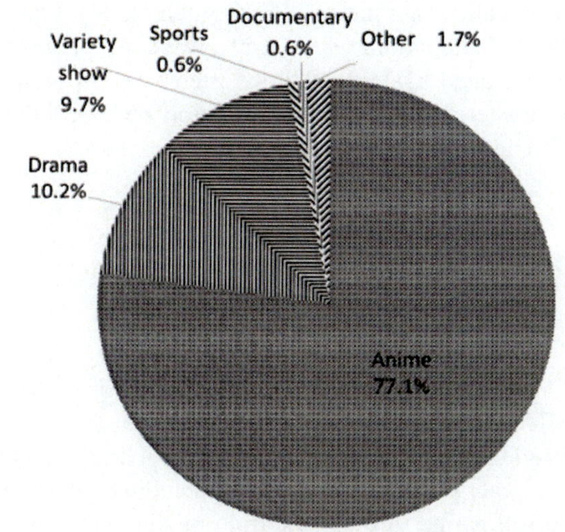

Fig. 4 Breakdown of broadcast content export by genre (FY2016). *Source* Ministry of Internal Affairs and Communications (2018), p. 2

around 25–40% of the total box-office revenue every year.[3] The amount for 2001 was notably high as a result of the hit film *Spirited Away* produced by Studio Ghibli Inc., winner of the Oscar for Best Animated Feature Film and all-time box office winner in Japan. In addition, as shown in Fig. 4, anime represents as much as 77.1% of exported Japanese broadcast content, suggesting that anime is essential for the TV industry as well.

[3]The data in the anime industry report provided by the Association of Japanese Animations are the aggregated numbers for production companies that belong to the association. The association was founded in May 2002 with the aims of protecting and developing animation culture, in which Japan takes pride, and assisting its spread around the world as an industry. It is the largest industrial body of the Japanese anime industry with 36 regular members and 42 associate members (as of 2018) and it conducts activities in cooperation with the government as well.

As can be seen previously, anime is significant for Japan culturally as entertainment and also economically as an industry. Meanwhile, what kind of role has public policy played in the development of Japanese anime? This chapter examines how the Japanese government has perceived anime, what policy has been the basis for specific initiatives, and how the policy has influenced the current state of anime. This chapter first describes the current state and characteristics of the Japanese anime industry and some of the difficulties it faces. Based on these, it explains what kinds of initiatives the Japanese government has implemented, under what policy, and to what extent. Finally, it discusses the future prospects of Japanese anime policy.

Note that in this chapter "anime" refers to Japanese animation to distinguish it from "animation" as a whole. "Animation" is an imaging technique that projects a series of still images to create the illusion of movement. "Animation" is the noun form of "animate" and is derived from the Latin word "anima," which means "vitalize." Films made up of pictures drawn frame by frame to express movement came to be called "animated cartoons" to distinguish them from live-action movies and then later were called "animation" (Yamaguchi 2004). Japanese animation is characterized by limited animation, which uses only eight pictures per second, while full animation represented by Disney films often uses 24 pictures per second. Because of these characteristics, Japanese animation became known as "anime" within Japan and abroad.

2 Current State and Characteristics of the Japanese Anime Industry

One distinct aspect of the anime industry is that it has a huge economic spillover effect since a variety of businesses can be deployed based on anime. Anime was originally produced for a single purpose such as films or TV broadcasts; however, the emergence of new media including DVDs and the Internet made it possible to sell anime through multiple media, expanding the scale of the anime industry. Moreover, the first Japanese TV anime series, *Astro Boy*, generated income by selling character merchandise to make up for the insufficient production budget. This practice spread within the industry and numerous kinds of character merchandise have been produced. Anime is utilized in various forms of content such as game software and manga. Therefore, the anime industry consists of the primary market, which sells anime, and the secondary market, which sells anime-related goods and services. According to Fig. 5, the sales breakdown for anime production companies in 2016 indicates that anime brings about a wide variety of income sources. The total anime sales amount is 2.1 billion USD, with the largest part coming from TV broadcasts and other parts from moving images for films, videograms, and Internet distribution as well as character merchandise, music, entertainment, and live performances. Income from overseas is also a significant part, representing 19.9% of the total sales.

Fig. 5 Breakdown of sales of anime production companies (2016). *Source* Based on the Association of Japanese Animations (2017), p. 12; Dentsu Media Innovation Lab (2018), p. 102

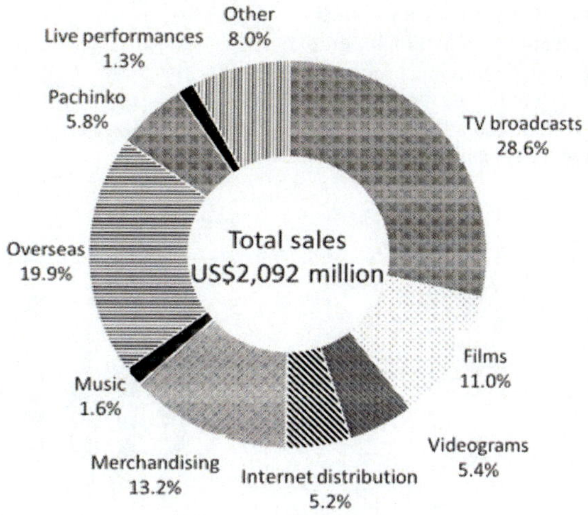

When looking at the state and characteristics of anime by distribution format, the core of the anime industry is moving images, as generally expected. Figure 6 indicates the size of Japanese markets by distribution format. Although the TV and videogram markets are large, the differences among these four markets have shrunk in recent years. Figure 7 shows the box-office revenue of animated films (including overseas animation) in Japan, and Fig. 8 indicates the changes in the number of anime films released. Both the revenue and number have grown in the long term, although the figures vary with the year. Since a single successful movie can generate huge

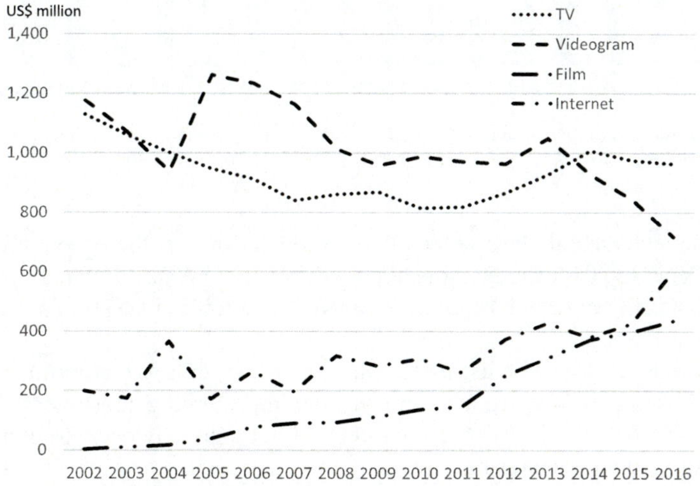

Fig. 6 Transition of size of anime market by distribution format. *Source* The Association of Japanese Animations (2017), p. 28

Fig. 7 Estimated box-office revenue of animation. *Source* Dentsu Communication Institute Inc. (2014), p. 111; Dentsu Media Innovation Lab (2018), p. 103

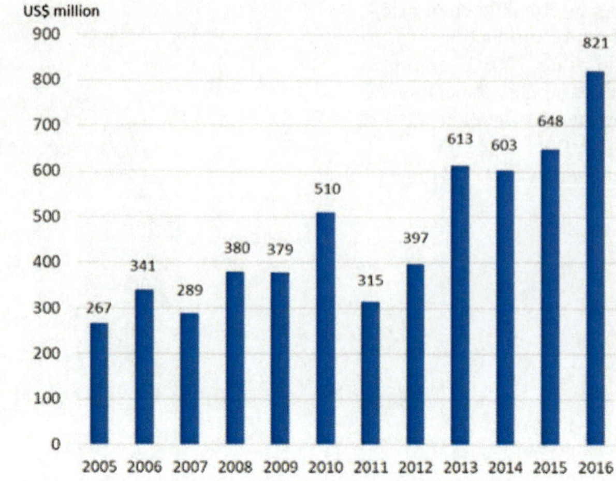

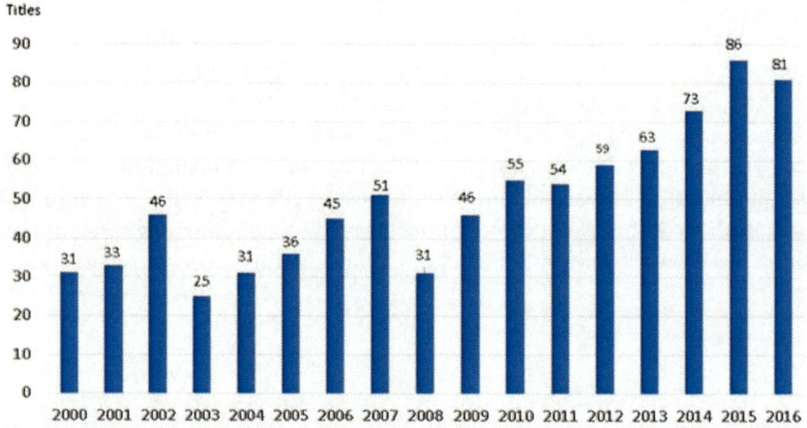

Fig. 8 Transition of number of anime film titles. *Source* The Association of Japanese Animations (2017), p. 36

revenue, the total annual revenue largely depends on whether there were hit movies during the year. In 2016, for example, the success of *Your Name* directed by Makoto Shinkai (finalized box-office revenue in Japan: 227.5 million USD) raised the total sales.

TV broadcasts, which also use moving images, often serve as the starting point for secondary businesses, playing a significant role in promoting consumer awareness of anime titles. As seen in Fig. 6, its market size has gradually decreased in the last 15 years. TV audience shares have recently been decreasing year by year. Although they slightly increased in 2014 and 2015, they fell again in 2016. The number and running time of broadcast titles have also decreased every year, from 3,045 titles and 89,196 min in total in 2012 to 2,473 titles and 73,264 min in 2016. One suggested

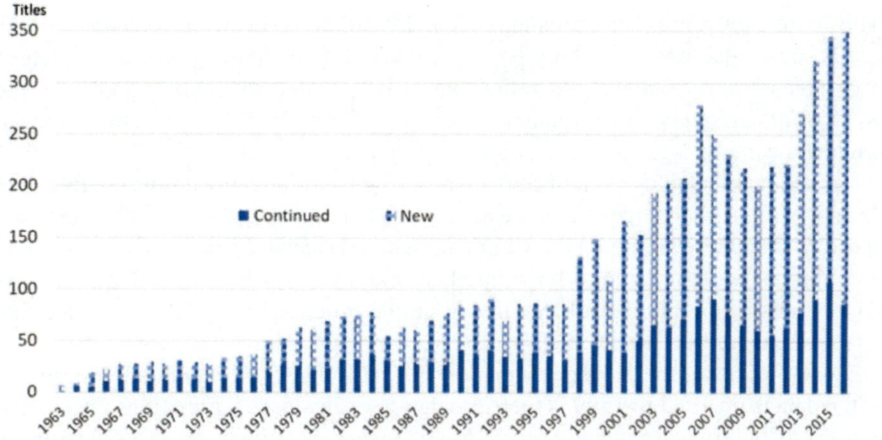

Fig. 9 Transition of number of TV anime titles. *Source* The Association of Japanese Animations (2017), p. 29

cause for this decline is the lower quality of anime due to a shortage of production workers (Dentsu Media Innovation Lab 2018). Looking back now on the history of Japanese anime using Fig. 9, the number of titles broadcast since 1963 with *Astro Boy*, Japan's first TV anime series, reveals that more than 300 titles have been broadcast per year for the last few years and the proportion of new titles has been rising. New titles are increasing more rapidly than the growth speed of the market, because more and more titles have become short lived.

The history of world animation started after 1900. In Japan, the first short animated film was locally produced in 1917 (Yamaguchi 2004). The predecessor of today's Toei Animation Co., Ltd. was established in 1956 with the vision of becoming an oriental Disney and released the first Japanese color animated feature, *Hakujaden*, in 1958. After TV broadcasting started in Japan in 1953, animation started being used in commercials. The same year, the previously mentioned *Astro Boy*, which formed the foundation of the Japanese anime industry, started being broadcast on TV and was also exported to the USA. Osamu Tezuka, who had succeeded as a cartoonist, established Mushi Production Co., Ltd. for anime production. Since TV programs at that time were made on low budgets, he kept the production cost low by reducing the number of pictures used and developed the bank system which was a production technique that used the same pictures repeatedly. These techniques led to Japanese anime having a distinct style of expression. He also established a scheme for generating royalty income from character merchandise to obtain additional funds for production.

Astro Boy triggered the anime boom. While the running length of TV anime was 2,625 min in 1963, it reached 8,865 min in 1964. Following a record-high audience share of 40.3% for the 30-min *Astro Boy* program, the running length rapidly grew to 14,640 min in 1965 and 21,985 min in 1967. *Little Ghost Q-Taro* gained an audience share of 36.7% in 1966 and *Perman*, 35.6% in 1967 (Masuda 2016). As with *Astro Boy*, a number of manga-origin TV anime series were produced. In the 1970s, anime that became highly popular included *Space Battleship Yamato*, which was targeted at a younger generation but also appealed to a wider audience and *Mobile Suit Gundam*, which focused on not only anime itself but also anime-related products, namely, figures of the robots that appear in the story. The foundation of the mixed-media deployment business was formed and Japanese anime continued to develop with a broad target audience not limited to children, which is a characteristic of today's Japanese anime. In the world, animation is usually perceived as something for children, while in Japan, a large number of anime titles are targeted at adults. As Fig. 10 shows, the number of minutes of anime produced for adults exceeded that for children and families in 2015.

Next, the size of the videogram market shown in Fig. 11 is examined. The source of the data from 1983 to 1999 is the Association of Japanese Animations (2011) and that from 2000 onward is the Association of Japanese Animations (2017), between which the data calculation methods slightly differ. The market size peaked at around 2005–2006 and exhibited a declining trend thereafter. In 2016, it was 716 million USD, which is almost the same level as 15 years ago. This downward trend can be observed in not only anime but also the entire videogram market. Anime accounts for approximately 30% of the videogram market and is an important genre within videograms as a whole, although it is not as important as movies.

While the sales of videograms declined, Internet distribution grew, as Fig. 12 indicates, reaching 645 million USD in 2016, up 20.1% year on year and comparable to videogram sales of 716 million USD. Numerous businesses became involved in Internet video distribution and competed for anime to differentiate their services. In particular, Netflix, Inc. and Amazon.com, Inc., global distribution platforms, are expanding their investment in anime to actively produce their own anime or obtain the rights for exclusive distribution. According to the Digital Content Association

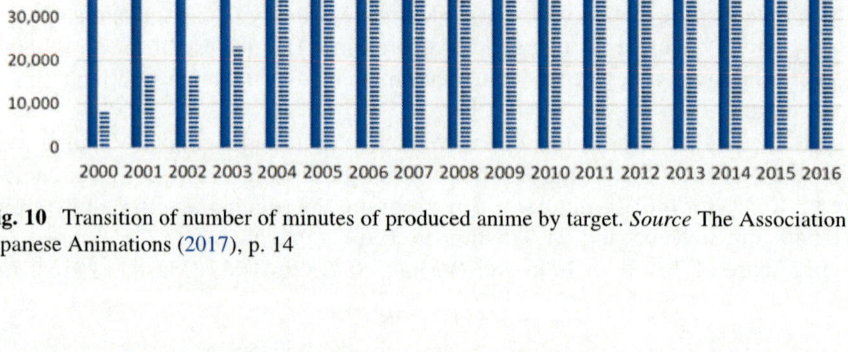

Fig. 10 Transition of number of minutes of produced anime by target. *Source* The Association of Japanese Animations (2017), p. 14

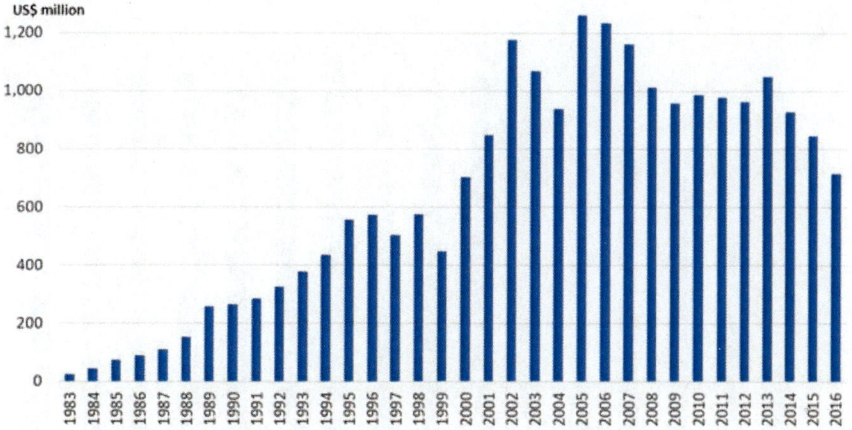

Fig. 11 Transition of sales of anime videograms. *Source* The Association of Japanese Animations (2017), p. 40; Id. (2011), p. 28

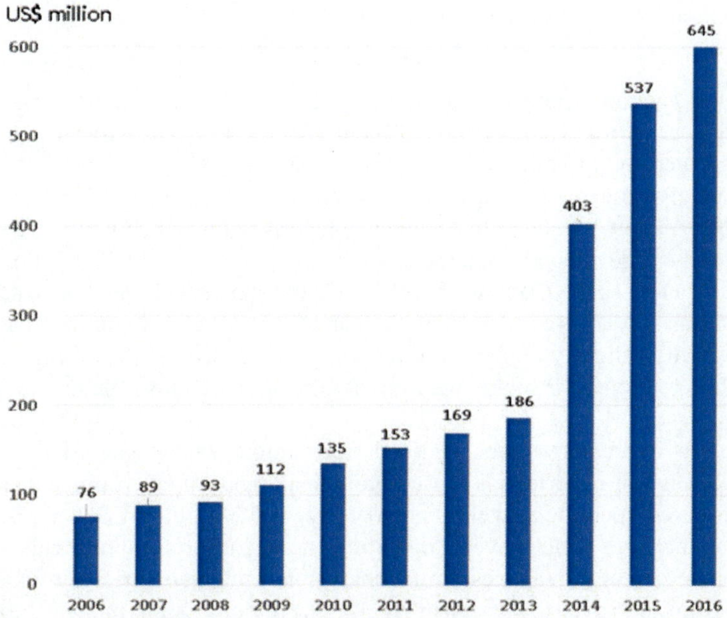

Fig. 12 Transition of market size of Internet anime distribution. *Source* Dentsu Communication Institute Inc. (2015), p. 112; Dentsu Media Innovation Lab (2018), p. 106.
Note the counting method changed from 2014

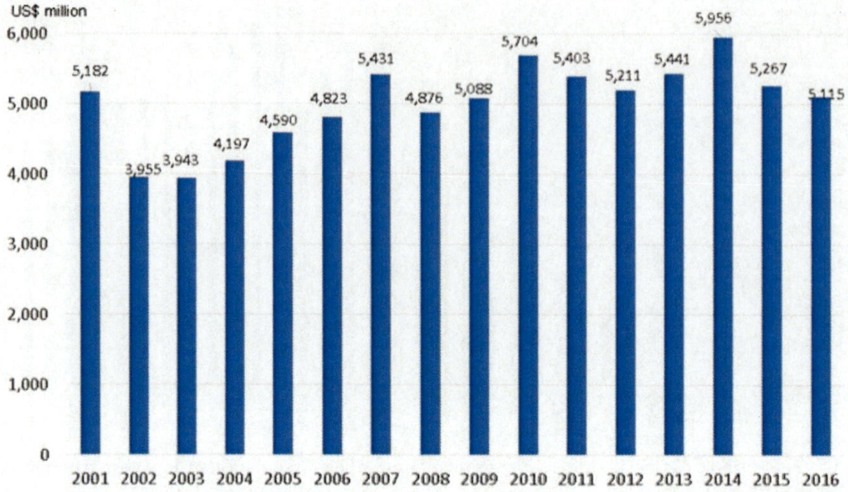

Fig. 13 Transition of market size of anime character-based goods. *Source* The Association of Japanese Animations (2011), p. 36; Id. (2017), p. 49

of Japan (2017), a different source from that of Fig. 12, the Japanese Internet video distribution market was 1,482 million USD in 2016 (+16% year on year), of which anime accounted for 435 million USD (+9.4% year on year).

Consider also the markets that do not create moving images. The character merchandise market remains almost unchanged, as shown in Fig. 13. The most common products developed as character merchandise are toys (37.7%), followed by household articles (12.9%), accessories (12.4%), and apparel (11.6%) (Dentsu Media Innovation Lab 2018). Around 60% of all character merchandises are purchased by females, which is slightly higher than the proportion of males. Regarding age, the younger the age group, the higher the ratio of purchasers (Dentsu Media Innovation Lab 2018).

Looking at live entertainment derived from anime, recent years have seen a growing demand for experiential consumption in all kinds of entertainment and this trend is observed in anime as well. Its market size is 559 million USD, as shown in Fig. 14, and there are various events including anime concerts and musicals.

Finally, the size of the Japanese anime market in foreign countries shrunk during the period from 2006 to 2012, as seen in Fig. 15. The reasons for this include the appreciation of yen and the fact that a decrease in videograms could not be compensated by the growth of Internet distribution, for which the unit price is low. The market started expanding again and grew rapidly in 2016, reaching approximately 7 billion USD, up 31.6% compared to the previous year. The proportion of sales in overseas markets increased to 20% of the total sales of production companies. This growth has been supported by distribution license fees from Netflix, Amazon, and other Internet distribution networks as well as strong sales in Asian nations, mainly China. When looking at the number of overseas contracts closed by production companies in Fig. 16, the top

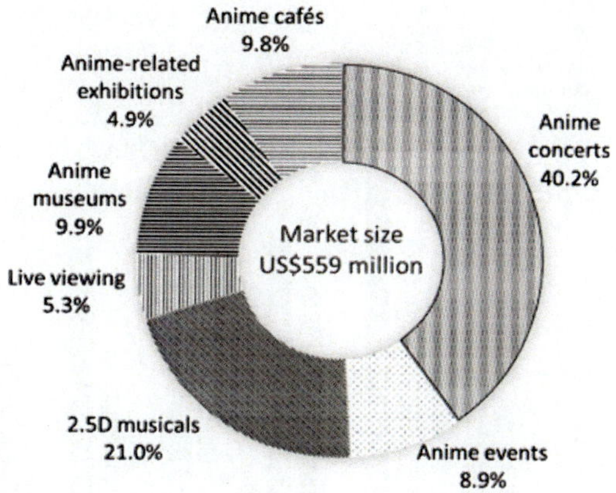

Fig. 14 Anime live entertainment market (2016). *Source* The Association of Japanese Animations (2017), p. 62

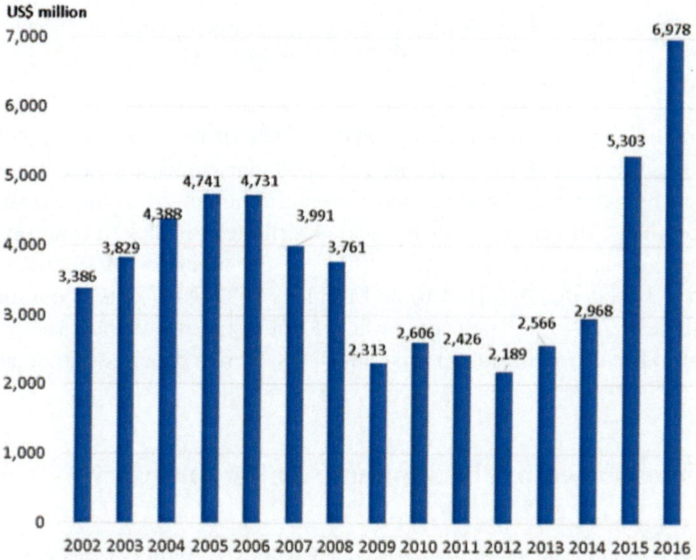

Fig. 15 Transition of overseas market size of Japanese anime. *Source* The Association of Japanese Animations (2017), p. 77

three countries in the total number of contracts in 2016 were China, South Korea, and Taiwan. The USA, which had often ranked first, fell to fourth. As for export destinations by region, Asia (38.4%) was the largest, followed by Europe (25.4%), Oceania (11.7%), Latin America (7.2%), and North America (6.8%) (The Association of Japanese Animations 2017). The most common contracted distribution format is Internet distribution, followed by TV, merchandising, and then videograms (The Association of Japanese Animations 2017). In some Asian nations including South Korea, Taiwan, Hong Kong, and Thailand, Japanese anime titles are released soon after their release in Japan, heightening their popularity.

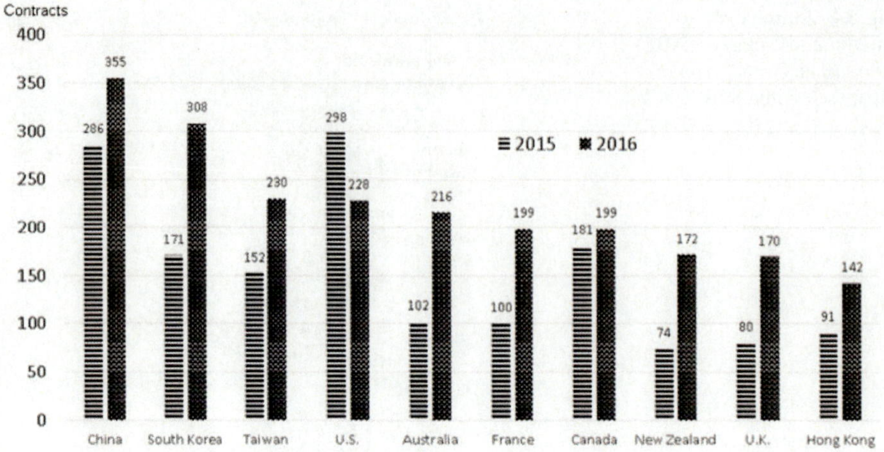

Fig. 16 Y/Y comparison of number of contracts for Japanese anime by country. *Source* The Association of Japanese Animations (2016), p. 65; Id. (2017), p. 71

As discussed earlier, the anime industry consists of the primary market, where animated images themselves are sold, and the secondary market, where related products such as character merchandise and live entertainment are sold. Unlike general industrial products, the anime industry also contributes to sales in other industries. According to the Economic Analysis Office, of the Ministry of Economy, Trade and Industry (hereinafter referred to as METI) (METI 2017), its economic effect is approximately 7.5-fold. Such a significant effect is one of the reasons for the government to focus on promoting this industry, which is described in detail later.

3 Problems Faced by the Japanese Anime Industry

The animation industry is labor-intensive, since a huge amount of in-between animation and key animation must be created frame by frame in the production process. Therefore, reduction of the labor cost is an important management issue for production companies. In the 1960s, the pictures were drawn in-house, but by the 1970s, the production process was being divided and outsourced to cut costs due to increased competition. As a result, there emerged small production companies specialized in specific production processes such as illustration and background layout as well as a large number of freelance animators. This led to the multilayered subcontracting structure of today's Japanese anime industry, shown in Fig. 17. A large production company as a principal contractor subcontracts production to medium-sized companies, and medium-sized companies subcontract to smaller production companies or individuals. The majority of production companies are medium, small, or very small companies with annual sales of less than 9 million USD (Mizuho Bank 2014) and

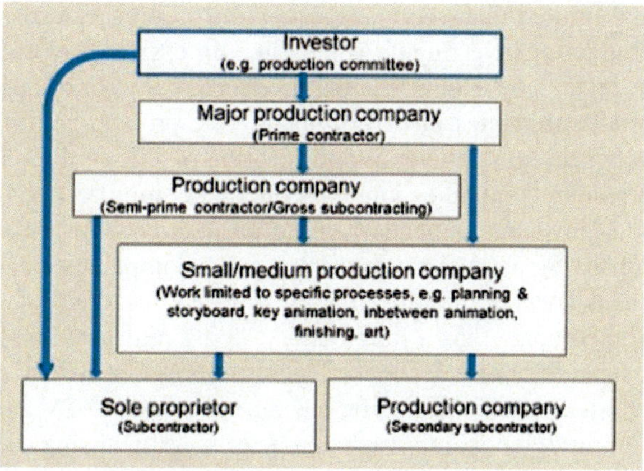

Fig. 17 Multilayered subcontracting structure of anime industry. *Source* Ministry of Economy, Trade and Industry (2017), p. 4, Modified by author

their financial standing is fragile. This multilayered structure makes it difficult for subcontractors to secure a profit, inevitably resulting in difficult working conditions for animators. The creation of in-between animation and key animation is typically paid as piecework at a rate of 1.6–1.8 USD per piece on average as a whole (Mizuho Bank 2014). In fiscal 2009, the average annual income for all animators was 23,200 USD. Although compensation for high-skilled positions such as director (45,000 USD) and storyboard creator (41,300 USD) is higher than that for general workers (national average: 39,700 USD), compensation for less-skilled positions is extremely low. For example, compensation for key animation artists is 21,100 USD and in-between animation artists, 9,540 USD (Japanese Animation Creators Association 2009). Due to production companies now subcontracting the downstream processes of production to South Korea, China, Vietnam, and other overseas countries to seek cheaper labor, it is difficult to cultivate high-skilled animators in Japan.

The Anime business is high-risk high-return. Since additional production does not cost much, successful anime generates huge profits. On the other hand, since production costs are high and the possibility of success is low, unpopular anime causes a sizable loss. Small- and medium-sized production companies with a weak financial base cannot afford to take investment risks and have no choice but to rely on funds from companies that are able to take risks. This means that small- and medium-sized production companies are unable to obtain sufficient profit or the copyrights even when the titles they make are successful, making it hard to establish a firm foundation of their business.

Figure 17 illustrates a "production committee," which places orders with a major production company. A production committee is an organization formed for the purpose of funding production and is a main financing means for today's anime. Businesses related to anime titles, e.g., TV stations, major production companies, video sales companies, advertising agencies, and toy manufacturers, get together to form a production committee for joint funding. The purpose of such investment is to participate in anime-related businesses or obtain the copyrights of anime titles. In the anime business, which is high-risk high-return due to the high production costs and limited chance of success, joint funding can distribute the risks and ease the production investment. At the same time, since the production committee as a whole owns the copyrights, the deployment of copyright business requires the agreement of all companies involved, making the process complicated. In addition, there is a drawback in that overall optimization of a committee is difficult to achieve because investing companies join a production committee for their own interest.

Many large Japanese anime production companies are a group of companies consisting of major filmmakers, game companies, or broadcast stations. The largest one is Toei Animation Co., Ltd., whose sales totaled 418 million USD in fiscal 2017. The company has a long history, being registered in 1948 and founded in 1956 as a subsidiary of a Japanese leading filmmaker, Toei Co., Ltd. (Toei Animation Co., Ltd. n.d.). Toei Animation has the advantage in TV anime and generates significant copyright income through character merchandising. It grew steadily from 2004 and its growth rate especially expanded from 2011, with its current profits also having increased. Its business comprises video production and sales 35%, copyright income 52%, merchandise sales 10%, and overseas sales 42%, and it has 695 employees on a consolidated basis (as of March 2018) (Toyo Keizai Inc. 2018). Its representative works include *Sailor Moon*, *Precure*, *Dragon Ball*, and *One Piece*. In recent years, it has focused on production investment in its original films and overseas business. In fiscal 2017, it achieved strong results in video distribution in China and the adaptation of *Dragon Ball*, one of the main works of the company, to application games (Toyo Keizai Inc. 2018).

IG Port, Inc., an independently listed company and the parent company of Production I.G, Inc., is engaged in production and sales of anime for films, TV, and DVD, and planning and production of comics. IG Port's sales is 69 million USD in fiscal 2017. Its predecessor, I.G Tatsunoko Ltd., was founded in 1987 and established a US affiliate, Production I.G., LLC, in 1997 (IG Port, Inc. n.d.). Its sales comprise video business 59%, publication 21%, and copyright 15% (Toyo Keizai Inc. 2018). IG Port has 295 employees (consolidated, as of February 2018) and its representative works include the universally popular *Ghost in the Shell* series directed by Mamoru Oshii, *The Basketball which Kuroko Plays* and *Haikyu!!* (Production I.G, Inc. n.d.). For the last few years, it has enhanced its anime distribution business in partnership with NTT Plala Inc. as well as forming a multiyear business alliance with Netflix (Toyo Keizai Inc. 2018).

While labor and outsourcing costs of TV anime production are high because its production is time-consuming, the sales price is low; therefore, it is hard to earn a profit. As a result, neither Toei Animation nor IG Port is able to generate revenue from TV anime alone and they rely on copyright income to keep their business running.

Another company is the world-famous Studio Ghibli Inc. It started operations in June 1985 as a subsidiary of Tokuma Shoten Publishing Co., Ltd. for the purpose of animated film production by two directors, Isao Takahata and Hayao Miyazaki. It became independent from Tokuma Shoten Publishing in 2005. The company name "Ghibli" comes from a word that means "hot wind blowing through the Sahara Desert." Many of their representative anime titles are globally popular, including *Nausicaä of the Valley of the Wind* (1984), *My Neighbor Totoro* (1988), *Prince*

Mononoke (1997), and *The Tale of the Princess Kaguya* (2013) (Studio Ghibli Inc. n.d.). *Spirited Away* (2001) won the Golden Bear award in 2002 and the Academy Award for Best Animated Feature in 2003. The film was ranked fourth in the 21st Century's 100 Greatest Films, which was organized by the BBC in 2016 and voted on by 177 film critics from all over the world.

One company that has notably grown in recent years is Aniplex Inc., which was established in 1995 as a 100% subsidiary of Sony Music Entertainment (Japan) Inc. The company founded Aniplex of America Inc. in the USA in 2005. Aniplex is engaged in planning, production, and sales of video titles centered on anime, distribution of films, and in recent years, planning and production of games for smartphones. It employs 150 workers (as of 2018) and its sales and operating profits for fiscal 2017 were 1,826 USD and 465 million USD, respectively (Aniplex Inc. n.d.).

According to the Economic Analysis Office of the METI (2017), anime production companies capitalized at 270,000 USD or more had sales of about 33 million USD, produced 20 titles, and employed slightly less than 100 workers, on average in fiscal 2015. Approximately 90% of those firms outsource production and regular employees account for around 60% of the total, and the rest, approximately 40%, are contracted employees including freelancers.

As described previously, the anime business has characteristics such as labor-intensiveness, high-risk, and high-return, and there are industry practices arising from historical backgrounds such as that TV anime is sold at low prices. As a result, there is now the problem that the Japanese anime industry is underpinned by numerous financially fragile small and medium production companies.

4 Policy for Promoting the Anime Industry

4.1 Policy on Economic Aspects Which Started After 2000

Stemming from the aforementioned situation of the Japanese anime industry, the Japanese government has taken steps to improve its policies. To put it succinctly, the government focused mainly on the economic value of anime rather than its cultural value and has actively implemented industrial promotion initiatives since 2000 (Uchida 2006). Various ministries and agencies were involved, mainly including the Cabinet Office, the METI, the Ministry of Internal Affairs and Communications (hereinafter referred to as MIC), the Agency for Cultural Affairs (hereinafter referred to as ACA), and the Ministry of Foreign Affairs. The Cabinet Office plays a role in defining and supervising the overall policy. Policy implementation was prompted by the establishment of the Intellectual Property Strategy Headquarters in the Cabinet Office in March 2003 as an organization related to anime policy. The headquarters aimed to promote initiatives regarding the creation, protection, and exploitation of intellectual property intensively and according to plan, in light of the increased need for boosting the industries' international competitiveness. To accomplish its purpose, the Intellectual Property Strategy Headquarters of the Cabinet Office releases a yearly Intellectual Property Promotion Program, which is a policy for the entire nation.

Policies for anime are often implemented as part of the policies for "content" and "Cool Japan" rather than through a framework for anime alone. The word "content" here refers to the content of information distributed through media such as publications, TV programs, films, games, and also anime. "Coolness" of Japanese cultural power was noticed by "Japan's Gross National Cool," a paper by US journalist Douglas McGray published in a US foreign affairs journal in 2002 (McGray 2002). By modifying the term GNP (Gross National Product), McGray proposed "Gross National Cool (Gross National Cultural Power)" as a new index of a nation's ability, and the paper mentions that Japan has a strong cultural superpower as demonstrated by its globally popular anime, music, fashion, and the like. The global popularity of Japanese pop culture represented by anime, manga, and video games was often mentioned in global media at that time. Until then, many Japanese people perceived anime and manga as children's entertainment and a variety of media did not really recognize them as culture. However, because their cultural value was recognized abroad through the word "Cool," anime's cultural value was acknowledged within Japan as well and anime started being incorporated in policies. The Japanese government has actively promoted anime within the frameworks of the "content industry" and "Cool Japan Strategy" since 2000.

The most significant background that activated the promotion of anime from around 2000 was the economic recession in Japan. The manufacturing industry, which drove the Japanese economy after World War II, became sluggish and the bubble economy collapsed around 1990. In addition to the decrease in export competitiveness of Japanese industrial products, there were problems of low domestic demand and shrinking workforce due to the dwindling birthrate and aging population. However, the anime industry continued to grow amid the stagnation of the Japanese economy. This is clearly shown in Fig. 18, which indexes the transition of the Nikkei Stock Average from 1990 to 2010 and the scale of the anime industry. Furthermore, what accelerated the promotion of content creation was the advancement of information technology from the 2000s. Information technology drastically changed the forms of production and the distribution of content and at the same time expanded their size.

Additionally, the government started considering not only anime's economic value but also its cultural value. From around 2000, in response to changes in the international environment, the new importance of international cultural exchange was recognized and ways to implement it diversified. Factors including the progress of globalization and democratization and the advancement of digital technology made the government realize, in the context of foreign diplomacy, the importance of shifting from the traditional diplomatic approach of state-to-state negotiation to the concept of public diplomacy, which directly targets the citizens of the other country and the "soft power" derived from culture. This public diplomacy is "diplomatic activities to reach out directly to citizens of the other country rather than its government as in the traditional approach, for the purpose of heightening the presence of the home country in international society, driving its positive image, and deepening foreigners'

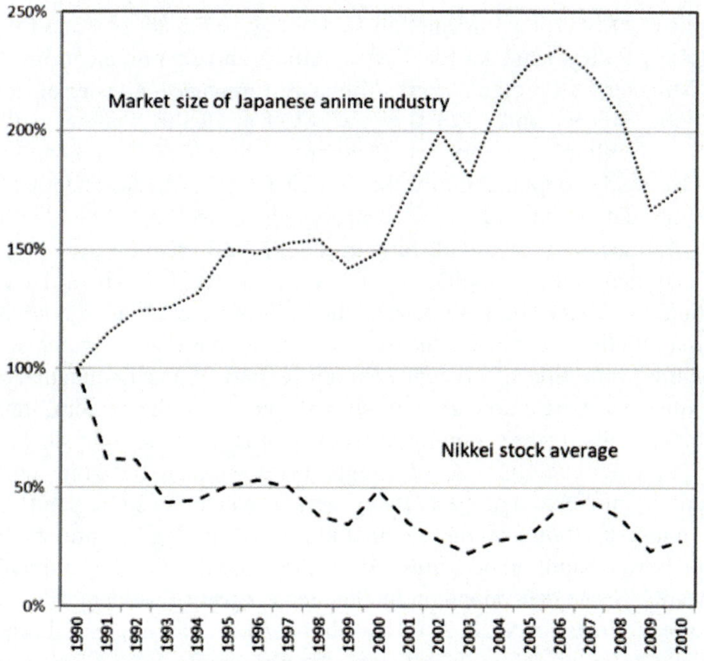

Fig. 18 Growth of anime industry in the sluggish Japanese economy. *Source* Digital Content Association of Japan (2011), p. 212. etc. Modified by author

understanding of the country" (Hoshiyama 2008). Also, soft power was coined by Professor Joseph S. Nye Jr. at Harvard University in the USA as "the ability to get what you want through attraction rather than through coercion or payments." Nye explained that soft power arises from the attractiveness of a country's culture, political ideals, and politics, and that soft power had become important in international relations as opposed to hard power such as military force and economic power (Nye 2004). Expectations were heightened for building international relations through culture and the Japanese government took notice of anime, which was already popular worldwide, as one of the measures to improve the image of Japan.

With these social changes as a backdrop, how exactly were policies implemented from 2000 and how have they been implemented recently? In February 2002, the then Prime Minister Koizumi declared a "nation built on intellectual property," stating in his policy speech, "Japan already holds world-leading intellectual property such as patents. I will make it a national goal to strategically protect and utilize the outcomes of research and creative activities as intellectual property and enhance the international competitiveness of our industries. For this purpose, the Strategic Council on Intellectual Property will be formed to powerfully drive the necessary policies." It was the first time that intellectual property was a topic of discussion in the Diet. A month later, the Strategic Council on Intellectual Property kicked off with the Prime Minister, Chief Cabinet Secretary, Minister of State for Economic and Fiscal

Policy, Minister of State for Information Technology, Minister of State for Science and Technology Policy, Minister for Internal Affairs and Communications, Minister of Justice, Minister for Foreign Affairs, Minister of Finance, Minister of Education, Culture, Sports, Science and Technology, Minister of Health, Labour and Welfare, Minister of Agriculture, Forestry and Fisheries, Minister of Economy, Trade and Industry as well as 11 scholars. In July, the council published the Intellectual Property Policy Outline that aimed to address "concerns about declining industrial competitiveness," "the necessity of establishing an intellectual creation cycle," and other issues by becoming a "nation built on intellectual property." With regard to concerns about declining industry competitiveness, the outline states, "Japan is highly evaluated internationally in content industries such as animation and game software." It calls for the promotion of content creation as part of the intellectual property strategy while perceiving anime as an important element of the content, stating, "As a strategy for revitalizing the economy and society of Japan, where physical resources are limited and labor and other costs are high, it is essential to have the viewpoint of a nation built on intellectual property that generates wealth by strategically creating, protecting, and exploiting content, etc. including outstanding inventions, manufacturing know-how, design, brands, music, films, broadcast programs, animation, and game software" (Strategic Council on Intellectual Property, Cabinet Office 2002). In his policy speech in January 2003, Prime Minister Koizumi expressed high regard for the artistic value of anime, mentioning that the movie *Spirited Away* won the prize for best film at the Berlin International Film Festival and the award for best animation from the New York Film Critics Circle. In March of the same year, the Intellectual Property Strategy Headquarters headed by Mr. Koizumi was established. Policy development started with the aim of making intellectual property the industrial foundation, which used to be formed mainly by the manufacturing industry. This was a significant turning point for Japanese industry policy. The Task Force on Content, which was formed within the Intellectual Property Strategy Headquarters in July of the same year, defined the dramatic expansion of content business as the pillar of policy. Although the initial objectives of the Intellectual Property Strategy Headquarters were centered on the protection of patents for inventions and copyrights, it was soon recognized that the content industry was the base of the copyright business and had profound spillover effects on other industries. As a result, promotion of the content industry became the headquarters' main objective. In the following year, it formulated the "Policy for Promotion of Content Business," which served as a pillar of promotion afterward. Although it mainly covers the promotion of industries, it also indicated its aim to promote international understanding of Japan through the dissemination of Japanese culture, as expressed in its subtitle, "National Strategy in the Age of Soft Power" (Task Force on Contents, Intellectual Property Strategy Headquarters, Cabinet Office 2004).

This way, Mr. Koizumi led the promotion of the content industry within the framework of the intellectual property strategy against the background of the transformation of industrial structure and worldwide recognition of pop culture. In 2004, the Act on Promotion of Creation, Protection and Exploitation of Content was enacted. To take an example, this act allows a production company to hold the copyright when a state orders content production from the company, whereas the ordering party held it previously. There are also mentions for fair business in Article 20 "Building fair trade relations" and Article 21 "Consideration for small- and medium-sized companies." (e-Gov n.d.). Many of the initiatives at that time were implemented by the METI since they were centered on industrial promotion. Initiatives for technological development and intellectual property protection, which underpinned industries, were under the control of the Ministry of Education, Culture, Sports, Science and Technology and the ACA, and those for communications infrastructure were under the control of the MIC. Specifically, those initiatives included tightening the Antimonopoly Law in order to promote fair trade and revising the Act against Delay in Payment of Subcontract Proceeds, etc. to Subcontractors, because existing content sales channels tended to be monopolized by TV stations, film distribution companies, etc., and content producers often relied on them for funding, marketing, etc., resulting in unfair contract relations (the revised Act against Delay in Payment of Subcontract Proceeds, etc. to Subcontractors was enforced in April 2004). With regard to this point, the initiatives particularly focus on the anime industry among all content industries. And, to fund modernization and new business development in the content industry consisting of mainly medium, small, and very small companies, financing means were further diversified. The METI promoted, for example, securitization through the Development Bank of Japan's special purpose company scheme, facilitation of procedures required by the Commodity Fund Act, and the copyright trust system through a revision of the Trust Business Act. As an incentive for content production, preferential taxation was considered. Other efforts included protection of intellectual property, creation of curriculum for fostering producers as a human resource development measure, and changes to the university system conducted by the Ministry of Education, Culture, Sports, Science and Technology.

As described earlier, in response to social changes that occurred around 2000, the then Prime Minister Koizumi started and actively drove the promotion of anime in the context of intellectual property and content. Especially, such initiatives focused on the aspect of industrial promotion and, as for anime, aimed to solve the problems with the industrial structure. Meanwhile, in terms of cultural aspects, anime was recognized as leading to a better image of Japan. Since then, the perception of anime and the purposes of promotion have almost been maintained; however, more and more initiatives have been implemented within the "Cool Japan" framework.

The second Abe administration (2012–) considered it important how to take in the growth of the ever-growing overseas markets within the trend of the shrinking domestic market and set the goal of linking Japanese characteristics such as Japanese culture, cuisine, and services with the revenue of Japanese firms, clearly presenting the "Cool Japan Strategy," another framework of the current activities of anime promotion. In 2011, the Cool Japan Promotion Office was created in the METI, which was reorganized and expanded as the Creative Industries Division in July of the following year. After the second Abe administration commenced, the Minister of the Cool Japan Strategy was assigned and the Cool Japan Fund was established in 2013. In 2015, the Cool Japan Strategy Public–Private Collaboration Initiative was also founded. As a result, the strategy was promptly and actively implemented.

According to the METI (2013), the aim of the Cool Japan policy is "Under the severe economic environment such as decreasing domestic demand, changing the appeal of Japanese culture and lifestyle, clothing, food and housing, and content (anime, drama and music) into additional value (commercialization of the Japanese appeal) in addition to the traditional industry such as cars, home electronics and devices in order to achieve Japanese economic growth (job creation and community vitalization) by capturing vibrant overseas demand including that from emerging nations." As for the promotion structure of the Cool Japan Strategy (as of 2018), the Cabinet Office serves as its secretariat, the Minister of the Cool Japan Strategy leads the strategy, and public and private sectors jointly conduct initiatives. Offices and ministries involved are the MIC, the Ministry of Foregin Affairs, the Ministry of Finance (National Tax Agency), the Ministry of Education, Culture, Sports, Science and Technology (ACA), the Ministry of Agriculture, Foresty and Fisheries, the METI and the Ministry of Land, Infrastructure, Transport and Tourism (Japan Tourism Agency).

The private entities involved 46 bodies and 43 enterprises, etc. The objectives include supporting the Japanese content industry, promoting overseas deployment, introducing Japanese food culture, and promoting tourism. The government perceives Cool Japan as "Japanese unique appeal that foreigners think is cool (content such as anime, manga, and video games, fashion, cuisine, traditional culture, design, robots, environmental technology, etc.)" (Office of Strategy for Intellectual Property, Cabinet Office 2018).

The Office of Strategy for Intellectual Property, Cabinet Office presented five principles for the Cool Japan Strategy in April 2018.

1. Enhancement of design: Enhance the ability to design and edit things to add sensitivity value such as design or texture in addition to functional value such as quality and performance of products and services
2. Business Partnership between governmental policy and private businesses
3. Building of talent hubs: Attract human resources in Cool Japan-related fields from all over the world and accumulate and sophisticate creativity, thereby building a hub to disseminate information
4. Incorporation of foreigners' viewpoints: With regard to overseas dissemination and deployment of Cool Japan, increase foreigners' acceptance of Japanese appeal by re-editing it from the viewpoint of foreigners in collaboration with foreign Japan fans and influencers
5. Production of regional appeal: Discover regional Cool Japan resources and produce them as products for overseas by accumulating and editing them in a way that appeals to overseas as the appeal of all of Japan

The objective of these principles is to comprehensively disseminate the characteristics of Japanese culture to overseas, capture overseas demand, and achieve Japan's economic growth such as by job creation and community revitalization. Five focus areas are listed: the content industry, fashion industry, clothing, food and housing industry (e.g., daily goods, cuisine, beauty), service industry (e.g., tourism, education, welfare), and regional products.

Here, some concrete anime-related initiatives are examined. As mentioned earlier, anime accounts for approximately 80% of the total exported broadcast content. For the purpose of supporting its export, the J-LOP (Japan Localization and Promotion) project was implemented from fiscal 2013 to 2017 to assist with localization for adapting the content to foreign cultures and customs and the promotion of content. A total of 6,591 projects were adopted during those five years and 543 businesses newly entered the overseas markets. The project's budget for fiscal 2017 was 54.5 million USD (Visual Industry Promotion Organization n.d.). Additionally, the Japan Content Showcase, a comprehensive international trade show for content, is organized every October. For stronger collaboration among state governments in promoting the content industry, the Japan-China-Korea Cultural Content Industry Forum was held ten times from 2002. Other activities include taking countermeasures against infringement of intellectual property rights and awarding prizes for advanced technologies that contribute to the content industry's development. The most focused initiative is the Cool Japan Fund formed in November 2013. The fund supplies risk money for building sites and distribution networks as a base for capturing overseas demand, which could not previously be achieved by the private sector. As of April 2018, it was operating with a total investment of 630 million USD, consisting of 533 million USD from the government and 97 million USD from banks, broadcasters, printing companies, department stores, and other leading enterprises. The fund is formed as a stock corporation. As of May 2018, the total investment amount of the fund was 488 million USD for 28 projects, of which 216 million USD (44.3%) for nine projects was content related. Three major anime-related investments are listed below (Commerce and Service Industry Policy Group, METI 2018).

1. Japan content-related online sales to overseas: 13.6 million USD (the fund subsidy amount)
   Media and EC business that distribute popular culture such as anime and manga to foreign nations. This investment has doubled the number of registrations with the EC site and products dealt with, making progress in its operation in China. It was an investment in TOM (Tokyo Otaku Mode), a venture company that delivers content to 18 million overseas users on Facebook in four different languages: English, Chinese, Spanish, and Indonesian. The government expects that this business will become a platform for selling Cool Japan works abroad. Additionally, the business also aims to eliminate pirated products and copycats by selling genuine content.
2. Genuine anime-related online sales: 9.1 million USD (the fund subsidy amount) (total project cost: 45.5 million USD)
   The fund invested in entities including Bandai Namco Holdings Inc. for a multilingual, simultaneous distribution business for genuine Japanese anime, which ended in March 2017.
3. Creator development abroad: 4.1 million USD (the fund subsidy amount) (total project cost: 9.1 million USD)
   The fund invested in KADOKAWA Contents Academy Co., Ltd., a school business that develops creators of Japanese content in Asia and other areas. The first

schools were established in Taiwan and Thailand with plans to open in an additional 12 countries and regions. Courses are provided to develop the necessary skills because, although there are a large number of fans overseas, there is a lack of human resources who are knowledgeable about overseas markets and local creators who understand Japanese content and can work based on their local culture or needs. Graduates of the academy are expected to enter Japanese firms or become talented artists who work with Japan to create content at local companies.

The third reshuffled Abe administration, which commenced in 2017, established the Headquarters for Japan's Economic Revitalization in the Cabinet Office in order to enable the whole government to work as one to implement economic measures for revitalizing the Japanese economy and realize its growth strategy. It also developed the "Future Investment Strategy 2017" and "Future Investment Strategy 2018." While both strategies mention "content" and "Cool Japan" only in some parts, these topics touched on anime in the context of the expansion of broadcast content export and the enhancement of the cultural industry centering on content (Headquarters for Japan's Economic Revitalization, Cabinet Office 2018).

4.2 Policy Regarding Anime's Cultural Aspects

The anime promotion policy has two objectives. As described earlier, one is industrial promotion to develop the content industry including the anime industry as a single industry sector comparable to the manufacturing or distribution industries. The main organizations in charge of this objective are the METI and the MIC. The other objective is cultural promotion, for which the ACA[4] is primarily responsible. The ACA treats anime as part of the framework of media arts. Media arts refer to art, entertainment, animation, and manga by the ACA. According to the ACA, media arts are widely loved by the public and stimulate the creation of new art and the revitalization of the country's art as a whole as well as being highly regarded internationally, which in turn serves to deepen interest and understanding with respect to Japan. Not only do the media arts promote culture, but they also contribute to the promotion of the content industry, tourism, and international cultural exchange. Anime-related initiatives fully started shortly before 2000. The ACA budget for media art promotion was 10 million USD for fiscal 2018. The amount has remained almost the same in recent years and is significantly lower than that for industry promotion. There are

[4]An official in charge of anime policy from the ACA was interviewed for this research. Details of the interview are as follows: Date: Tuesday, November 6th, 2018. Place: ACA (Tokyo). Interviewee: Mr. Tetsuya Ino, Deputy Director to the Counselor, Arts and Culture Division, ACA. Most of this section is based on six materials provided in the interview ("Media arts global deployment project," "Promotion of media arts," "Nurturing young animators, etc.," "Anime Tamago 2018," "Project to support development of media arts creators in fiscal 2017," and "Japan Media Arts Festival at Annecy 2018").

two pillars of initiatives: "support for creation and dissemination" and "support for human resource development."

First, as for the former, "support for creation and dissemination," the total budget for this initiative is 7.8 million USD (fiscal 2018) and there is a project for global deployment of media arts through organizing comprehensive festivals, a project to facilitate interaction on media arts, and support for production of animated films. The core of the project for global deployment of media arts is the Japan Media Arts Festival, which has been held every year since 1997. The festival publicly seeks works in four categories: art, entertainment, animation, and manga and awards prizes to outstanding works as well as providing the public with opportunities to appreciate prize-winning works. The 21st festival (2018) received 4,192 applications (including 2,262 from overseas) from 98 countries and regions all over the world and 41,295 visitors to the exhibition of prize-winning works. In recent years, special exhibitions related to the festival have been held in not only Tokyo but also other areas. Such exhibitions were held in Ishigaki Island, Kyoto, and Aichi in fiscal 2017 and were attended by 45,009, 157,733, and 15,863 visitors, respectively. The Japan Media Arts Festival has continued to evolve into an international festival focused on diversified modern expression and is strengthening cooperation with overseas entities by holding exhibitions and screening events related to overseas media festivals such as the Festival international du film d'animation d'Annecy in France.

In addition to "support for creation and dissemination," there is also the pillar "support for human resource development," which consists of a project to support the nurturing of media arts creators and a project to nurture young animators and other talent. The total budget for this initiative was 2.2 million USD (as of fiscal 2018). As for support for creation by domestic young creators, the project invites creators who have won awards or were highly recognized at media arts festivals to submit a plan for a new work, subsidizes the production costs, and provides opportunities for obtaining expert advice and presenting their works. The project invites young creators from overseas to Japan where they engage in production activities while experiencing Japanese creative culture and also interacting with domestic creators. In fiscal 2017, 169 people from 51 countries and regions applied for only three places, making the screening process very competitive. It was mentioned earlier that the anime industry is labor-intensive and that talent is the key. Also, as for the animators' working environment, there is a fixed negative image of low wages and long working hours, which makes it hard for capable young people to dream about working as an animator. Furthermore, due to the increasing number of works produced, experienced animators cannot afford to guide young workers. Therefore, more and more simple production processes such as in-between animation are being subcontracted to low-wage Asian nations. As a result, a worker's subsequent career path, that is, the path to key animator, illustration director, and then director, is difficult to form, creating a structure where few animators can gain experience or knowledge. To improve the situation, the ACA implemented a scheme to subsidize production costs in 2010 for the purpose of developing young animators and commend outstanding works created under the subsidy. The subsidy for production costs allows creators leeway in their time and budget, enabling them to nurture young animators on the job at their production sites. The creators are also provided with opportunities including screenings of their works. The ACA commissioned the implementation of this scheme to the Japanese Animation Creators Association (JAniCA) from fiscal 2010 to fiscal 2013 and the Association of Japanese Animations from fiscal 2014. Every year, the scheme selects four companies from among all the applicants and nurtures about two dozen young animators who belong to the selected companies. Their finished works are broadcast on TV, distributed via the internet, or screened in theaters. Its budget for fiscal 2018 was 1.9 million USD.

As explained previously, initiatives such as the Japan Media Arts Festival have been steadily executed since shortly before 2000 although the budget for cultural promotion is smaller than that for industrial promotion. Such initiatives are characterized by an emphasis on talent development.

5 Conclusion

As described earlier, the Japanese anime industry has dramatically expanded over the last half century. Distribution channels of videos have been broadened utilizing technological innovations from films to TV, DVD, the Internet, etc. Besides video, multifaceted businesses including character merchandise and live entertainment have been deployed. There are also a growing number of types of relevant businesses beyond anime. Additionally, the social position of anime has rapidly improved in recent years. Until around 2000, anime was perceived as "merely anime" created for children and its value was recognized only in terms of popular culture. Its social position was not very high and its artistic or economic value was not appreciated. For instance, it was hard to imagine learning anime in university. However, society's evaluation has notably improved. How did anime develop like this?

The first reason is that the original form of expression, namely, anime with high-quality content, was established. The content of anime is characterized by, for example, unique characters, complicated stories, rich expression, artistic depiction of emotions, and themes based on everyday life to which viewers can easily relate. Another advantage of Japanese anime is that it can serve a broad audience range since there are various anime genres including not only those for children but also for young adults and adults. Behind this is the diversity of manga, as demonstrated by the fact that the first Japanese TV anime series, *Astro Boy*, was based on manga. The Japanese anime industry has developed despite its huge structural and financial problems, because of its high-quality content and originality. Works with excellent content are enjoyed by people and compensate for the business disadvantages. These outcomes have been achieved by private business activities.

What has Japanese governmental policy done for this anime's growth? The government's promotional measures taken in response to the development of anime started around 2000. Amid the Japanese economic recession and against the background of advancement and spread of IT, anime as a form of "content" attracted attention in the context of policy as well. The basic idea was to develop a new industry that would replace the manufacturing industry as a driving economic force. The initiatives intended to eliminate inherent problems of the anime industry. Specifically, they steadily addressed issues including the weak financial base of small- and medium-sized production companies, lack of animators, and poor working environment. However, their achievements are presently limited to a narrow range and have not fundamentally resolved those problems. In recent years, with declining domestic demand as a backdrop, the focus has shifted to promoting exports as part of the Cool Japan Strategy. Although this also generated some pinpoint effects, it may be too early to evaluate the overall policy results.

Japanese policy needs a vision for the future state of Japanese anime. Previous initiatives promptly responded to social changes and steadily addressed problems faced by the anime industry. From a different perspective, however, they were passive. Those initiatives were designed to solve problems that spanned across the anime industry's inherent aspects of human resources, funds, culture, and the like and appropriately, they were implemented through an interministerial support structure. Anime has developed largely because of the content of anime titles. It is hoped that the government will discuss which direction to lead anime and how to elevate the value of anime as works. Animation film director Gisaburo Sugii[5] states, "In anime production, we should not forget the cultural aspect of what to deliver to people's hearts while it needs to make good business sense." Although anime cannot reach people unless it is commercially viable, the influence of its content on the public should be taken into account along a defined principle.

In addition, significant improvement in social recognition of anime may be the most profound effect of the policy, albeit indirect. Until around 2000, anime was not recognized as either an industry or a culture; however, society as a whole began noticing its economic value after the government seriously implemented its policy and also its cultural value as its popularity increased abroad. Anime has now become widely recognized as an integral part of Japanese society.

The following is a summary of changes in the environment surrounding anime to which the anime industry itself as well as policy must respond in the future. The first one is the response to overseas markets and cooperation with overseas entities. Looking at the numbers alone, the export of Japanese anime has steadily grown. However, many anime titles were planned and produced on the assumption that they would be sold in the Japanese market. As previously mentioned based on Fig. 10, in Japan, the number of minutes of anime produced for adults exceeded that for children. However, overseas markets have different conditions and cultures such as that anime for children is still in high demand, and Japan has not yet responded to such differences.

Also, the spread of digital technology continues to have an impact. The target audience has expanded as a result of the construction of worldwide distribution networks associated with the penetration of the Internet. Global platform operators now not

[5]An animation film director was interviewed to research the anime industry. Details of the interview are as follows: Date: Thursday, October 11th, 2018. Method of interview: phone. Interviewee: Animation film director Gisaburo Sugii.

only buy anime works targeted at the Japanese market but also are producing their original works and have started investing in production to obtain the distribution rights in the global market. Some have established a collaboration structure where Japanese productions are allowed to retain the rights. A US-based distributor specializing in anime began investing in Japanese production committees to more actively engage in anime planning and production. These moves will become a huge force for the transformation of the anime industry that has so far operated within Japan only. The industry is expected to produce works that can be adapted to overseas markets. Also, production companies with outstanding production ability may be able to obtain the rights without relying on TV stations or others that have traditionally held the power. Since global distributors invest in anime as a strategy of differentiation from competitors, the importance of maintaining the quality of anime content should not be forgotten.

Furthermore, entrants in the existing anime industry are not limited to overseas companies. In recent years, an increasing number of video games derived from anime have been developed for smartphones and game companies are starting to enter anime production. Digitalization has resulted in changes to the form of distribution as well as that of production. Relocation of production companies to nonurban areas is now easier. Nearly 90% of production companies are currently based in Tokyo because the problem of transporting a large amount of drawings made production in nonurban areas difficult. Today, however, deliverables can promptly be transferred and work can be performed anywhere thanks to digitalization. Unlike areas around big cities, the cost of living in nonurban areas is low and therefore labor costs are also lower, which broadens the range of opportunities for obtaining skilled employees.

It is hoped that those parties involved will continue with proper support and efforts in order for anime to strengthen its status, continue to provide pleasure for the public, and contribute to the economy, while adapting to diverse changes in environment.

References

Aniplex Inc. About us (in Japanese). https://www.aniplex.co.jp/company/index.html. Accessed 1 Sept 2018

Commerce and Service Industry Policy Group, Ministry of Economy, Trade and Industry (2018) About the cool Japan policy (in Japanese). https://www.meti.go.jp/policy/mono_info_service/mono/creative/file/180509CooljapanseisakuMay.pdf. Accessed 1 Sept 2018

Dentsu Communication Institute Inc. (ed) (2001) Research for information and media society 2001 (in Japanese). DENTSU INC., Tokyo

Dentsu Communication Institute Inc. (ed) (2014) Research for information and media society 2014 (in Japanese). Diamond Inc., Tokyo

Dentsu Communication Institute Inc. (ed) (2015) Research for information and media society 2015 (in Japanese). Diamond Inc., Tokyo

Dentsu Media Innovation Lab (ed) (2018) Research for information and media society 2018 (in Japanese). Diamond Inc., Tokyo

Digital Content Association of Japan (ed) (2011) Digital content 2011 (in Japanese). Author, Tokyo

Digital Content Association of Japan (2017) Video distribution (VOD) market research report 2017 (in Japanese). Author, Tokyo
Economic Analysis Office of the Ministry of Economy, Trade and Industry (2017) Comparing the actual state of production companies producing two major Japanese contents, games and anime (in Japanese). https://www.meti.go.jp/statistics/toppage/report/minikeizai/pdf/h2amini083j.pdf. Accessed 1 Sept 2018
e-Gov (n.d.) Act on promotion of creation, protection and exploitation of contents (in Japanese). https://law.e-gov.go.jp/cgi-bin/idxsearch.cgi. Accessed 1 Sept 2005
Headquarters for Japan's Economic Revitalization, Cabinet Office (2018) Future investment strategy 2018—transformation toward "Society 5.0" and "Data-driven society" (in Japanese). https://www.kantei.go.jp/jp/singi/keizaisaisei/pdf/miraitousi2018_zentai.pdf. Accessed 1 Sept 2018
Hoshiyama T (2008) Japanese diplomacy and public diplomacy (in Japanese). Institute for International Policy Studies, Tokyo. http://www.iips.org/research/data/bp334j.pdf. Accessed 1 Sept 2018
IG Port, Inc. (n.d.) https://www.igport.co.jp/. Accessed 1 Sept 2018
Japanese Animation Creators Association (2009) White paper on labor (animators) 2009 (in Japanese). Author, Tokyo
JDS Co., Ltd. (2016) Comprehensive preference survey—comprehensive version (in Japanese). Author, Tokyo
Masuda H (2016) Anime business that digitalization changes (in Japanese). NTT Publishing Co., Ltd., Tokyo
McGray D (2002) Japan's gross national cool. Foreign Policy May/June:44–54
Ministry of Economy, Trade and Industry (2013) About cool Japan fund (tentative name) (in Japanese). https://www.cas.go.jp/jp/seisaku/fund/dai2/siryou3.pdf. Accessed 1 Sept 2018
Ministry of Economy, Trade and Industry (2017) Guidelines for promoting fair subcontracting, etc. in the animation production industry (in Japanese). https://www.chusho.meti.go.jp/keiei/torihiki/2014/140313shitaukeGL9.pdf. Accessed 1 Sept 2018
Ministry of Internal Affairs and Communications (2018) Analysis on the current situations of overseas deployment of broadcast contents (fiscal 2016) (in Japanese). https://www.soumu.go.jp/main_content/000554642.pdf. Accessed 1 Oct 2018
Mizuho Bank (2014) Mizuho industry research 48, Prospects of the content industry – for further development of the content industry (in Japanese). Author, Tokyo
Nye JS Jr. (2004) Soft power. PublicAffairs, New York
Office of Strategy for Intellectual Property, Cabinet Office (2018) About the cool Japan strategy (in Japanese). https://www.cao.go.jp/cool_japan/about/pdf/cj_initiative. Accessed 1 Sept 2018
Production I.G, Inc. (n.d.) About us (in Japanese). https://www.production-ig.co.jp/company/index.html. Accessed 1 Sept 2018
Strategic Council on Intellectual Property, Cabinet Office (2002) Intellectual property policy outline (in Japanese). https://www.kantei.go.jp/jp/singi/titeki/kettei/020703taikou.html. Accessed 1 Sept 2018
Studio Ghibli Inc. (n.d.) https://www.ghibli.jp/. Accessed 1 Sept 2018
Task Force on Contents, Intellectual Property Strategy Headquarters, Cabinet Office (2004) Content business promotion policy (draft)—National strategy in the age of soft power (in Japanese). https://www.kantei.go.jp/jp/singi/titeki2/tyousakai/contents/dai5/5siryou5-1.pdf. Accessed 1 Sept 2018
The Association of Japanese Animations (2011) Anime industry report 2011 (in Japanese). Author, Tokyo
The Association of Japanese Animations (2016) Anime industry report 2016 (in Japanese). Author, Tokyo. https://aja.gr.jp/english/japan-anime-data (Summary, in English). Accessed 13 Feb 2020
The Association of Japanese Animations (2017) Anime industry report 2017 (in Japanese). Author, Tokyo. https://aja.gr.jp/english/japan-anime-data (Summary, in English). Accessed 13 Feb 2020
Toei Animation Co., Ltd. (n.d.) Corporate information (in Japanese). https://corp.toei-anim.co.jp/company/. Accessed 1 Sept 2018
Toyo Keizai Inc. (2018) Quarterly corporate report 2018, summer issue (in Japanese). Author, Tokyo

Uchida M (2006) Content policy in Japan: various aspects and the importance of industry (in Japanese). J Cult Econ 5(1):39–47
Visual Industry Promotion Organization (n.d.) Japan localization and promotion project (J-LOP) (in Japanese). https://www.vipo.or.jp/project/j-lop/. Accessed 1 Sept 2018
Yamaguchi Y (2004) Whole history of Japanese anime (in Japanese). Ten-Books Co., Ltd., Tokyo

Video Games: the Once Sustainable Industry is in Need of Policy

Mariko Koizumi

Abstract This chapter aims to provide an overview of Japan's video game policy. The Japanese video game industry has expanded greatly and has gained popularity around the world in the last 40 years. However, it had been unclear what role the government had played to support this industry. This chapter concludes that there have been no radical policy measures that drive the industry, even though the government has recognized the magnitude of the industry's economic ripple effects, video game's importance as an export industry, and its cultural value. In fact, the industry had traditionally been centered on home video games and Nintendo and Sony, the market leaders, had continued to grow on their own, so there was little need for any policy aid. However, due to the recent emergence of online games, government policy is now needed. This chapter consists of information on the explanation of history, the characteristics, and the current situation of the industry; on how video games are treated within the policy framework; and on specific video game measures.

1 Introduction

This chapter provides an account of Japan's policy on video games, with references to Japan's policy on anime described in the Chapter "Anime's Economic Value: the Govenment's Response to a Changing Environment". There are two commonalities between anime discussed in the previous chapter and video games dealt with in this chapter: both are forms of content and segments of the Cool Japan wave which are currently enjoying popularity overseas. As explained in the previous chapter, when the economic value of anime started getting noticed, Japan's anime policy came together quickly. This happened after the year 2000 and was led primarily by the Ministry of Economy, Trade and Industry (hereinafter referred to as METI). Nowadays, anime policy has been pursued aggressively within the frameworks of content

M. Koizumi (✉)
Faculty of Manga, Kyoto Seika University, Kyoto, Japan
e-mail: mariko123@ark.ocn.ne.jp

M. Sugaya (ed.), *Perspectives on the Japanese Media and Content Policies*, Advances in Information and Communication Research 2,
https://doi.org/10.1007/978-981-15-4704-1_9

and Cool Japan. The Agency for Cultural Affairs (hereinafter referred to as ACA) has led anime policy on the cultural side, around the beginning of 2000, within the framework of media arts. Video games and anime share a similar background to their respective policy implementations—their value as industries, the impact of IT progress and proliferation, and their popularity outside of Japan. It is interesting to examine here whether Japan has actually implemented video game policy measures within the same frameworks as anime: namely, content, Cool Japan, and media arts, and other distinctive policy measures for video games.

This chapter starts by explaining the history, characteristics, and current situation of Japan's video game industry, which are closely related to the implementation of video game policy. It then describes specifically how video games are treated within the policy frameworks of anime—content, Cool Japan, and media arts. Finally, some specific video game measures taken in Japan as well as the future outlook for video game policy in Japan are presented.

2 Scope of Video Games Considered in This Chapter and the History of Video Games in Japan

Video games can be categorized by their platform configuration, as shown in Fig. 1. This chapter considers all types of video games other than arcade games, i.e., games where the player owns or possesses the platform. Arcade games that were located in amusement arcades, cafes and other locations gave birth to home video games. In Japan, companies dealing in jukeboxes began developing mechanical game machines in the mid-1960s (Fujita 1999), with two of the most well-known arcade games being *Space Invaders* (released by Taito Corporation in 1978) and *Pac-Man* (released by NAMCO Ltd. in 1980). Gaming technology grew more sophisticated through the 1980s, with home video games attempting to emulate arcade games. In the 1990s,

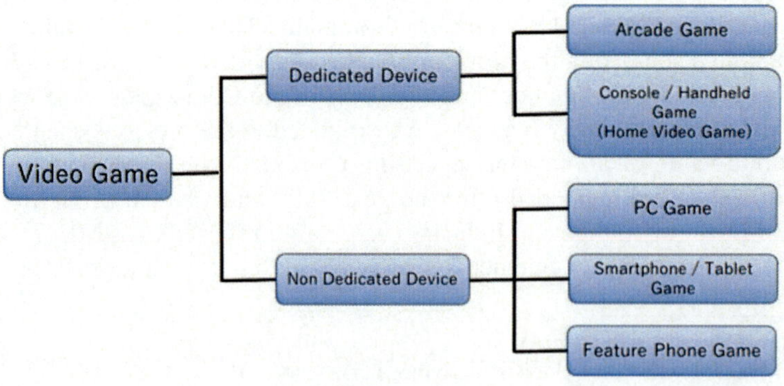

Fig. 1 Video game types. *Source* Koizumi (2016), p. 18.
Note: "Console" refers to floor standing game machine in this chapter

however, in terms of image quality and the processing speed, the technological gap between the two types narrowed considerably, due to the progress in semiconductors and display technologies as well as greater data storage capacities, leading to the rapid development of home video game consoles (Koizumi 2016).

The release of the Nintendo Entertainment System home video game console (NES, colloquially called the Famicom) by Nintendo Co., Ltd. in 1983 initiated and drove the expansion of the Japanese home video game market. The first home video game consoles were tethered devices such as the NES and the PlayStation (PSX), released by Sony Computer Entertainment Inc. (SCE, currently Sony Interactive Entertainment Inc. (SIE)) in 1994. The consoles had to be connected to a television or other types of monitors to be used, but with the subsequent progress of compact, high-performance electronic components, handheld game devices with a built-in screen sold rapidly. The Game Boy (GB), released in 1989 by Nintendo, was the first handheld game device to find major success; this was followed by the release and immediate popularity of the Nintendo DS (DS) and the PlayStation Portable (PSP) in 2004. In 2016 SIE held 57.8% of Japan's home video game console market by units sold, followed by Nintendo at 42.1% and Microsoft at 0.1%. Nintendo, backed by the success of the Nintendo Switch, dramatically increased its market share in 2017 to 70.7%, followed by SIE at 29.2% and Microsoft at 0.1%; Microsoft's Xbox has made little headway in the Japanese market. The handheld game devices are distinctively popular in the Japanese market. Regarding home video game devices by type from 2015 to 2017 on the basis of units sold, tethered consoles accounted for 57.3% of the market versus 42.7% for handheld devices in Japan, compared with 83.2% and 16.8%, respectively, overseas (CESA 2018).

A huge number of software titles have been developed for home video game devices, with many categories of games including role-playing games (RPGs), action games, massively multiplayer online role-playing games (MMORPG), shooting games, real-time strategy games, business and educational simulation games, adventure games, sports games, puzzles and quizzes, racing games, and romance-simulation games. Video games that are particularly popular in Japan are RPGs with strong stories and characterization and action games. Japanese users tend to favor 2D computer graphics over 3D and do not necessarily seek high-resolution games: the titles selling more than five million units in 2013 were all 2D computer graphic games.

Video games have continually evolved to meet the demands of more people, driven by advances in semiconductors and image technology that gave video games a richer range of expressions. The Internet, however, has further disrupted the video game industry in recent years. Online games, a new game type, started to spread globally around 2000. Online games are usually played on smartphones or other general-purpose devices and differ greatly from dedicated game devices not only in the nature of the games themselves but also in their business structures and market players. This chapter generally follows the definition of online games from the Japan Online Game Association (established in 2004): "Games in which the same title is played by multiple players via the Internet." Social games, namely games that are played on social media platforms, are grouped with online games (Digital Content Association of Japan 2014).

The first games with communication functions were often battle games, where a cable connected two video game devices to exchange game data. The first games that could be played by connecting to the internet were *Diablo*, released in the USA in 1996 by Blizzard Entertainment Inc., and *Ultima Online*, released in the USA in 1997 by Electronic Arts Inc. These titles were imported to Japan, but aside from a core of passionate fans, they never gained widespread acceptance. This was because, in addition to buying the package at a physical store, players had to pay a monthly fee to play the video games. Another reason was the underdeveloped communication infrastructure at the time; only about 30% of Japanese households had Internet access around 2000. Starting around 2001, however, a succession of online computer games with large fanbases in South Korea made thier way to Japan, including such titles as *Lineage*, *Ragnarok Online*, and *MapleStory*. These titles were structured differently in order to appeal to new users. The software could be downloaded for free and required a monthly fee to play. In 2003, services offering item purchases, which is the primary billing method for most games today, started in South Korea and were soon adopted in Japan. Item purchases enable the title developer to bill users: the games are provided for free and are free to play, but certain desirable tools or skills that help the player in the game can be bought. Thus, the Japan online game market was formed mainly through the import of South Korean computer games. Until this time, home video game consoles were the choice for gaming in Japan, rather than computers. In 2002, online games for home video game consoles started to be sold, such as Square's development of *Final Fantasy XI* for PlayStation 2. Online games, however, took off in Japan beginning around 2005 (Koizumi 2016).

Social games started to become popular around 2007 in Japan. Approximately 70% of game software downloads have been dominated by free titles based on an item-purchase business model in 2012 (Koizumi 2016). Players who pay to play games spend an average of approximately 50 USD a month on game items. Players between 20 and 49 are most likely to pay to play, with between 20 and 30% of players in this age bracket paying to play games (Digital Content Association of Japan 2014). In addition to social games, native gaming apps, another form of online games, began to appear in significant numbers in 2012. With native gaming apps, which are ordinarily called smartphone games, the game processing is done directly on the device. Unlike social games, these apps do not rely on social media platforms and are sold on the iTunes Store, Google Play, and other online stores.

Online games, as interactive entertainment, let large numbers of players play the same game over the Internet. As the players form deeper connections through the video game, it becomes even more interactive, and the Internet's growth has produced a number of general-purpose communication devices that can be used as gaming platforms. Such developments have fundamentally transformed the video game industry. The next section describes the recent state of Japan's home video game market and online game market, which have been affected by these disruptions.

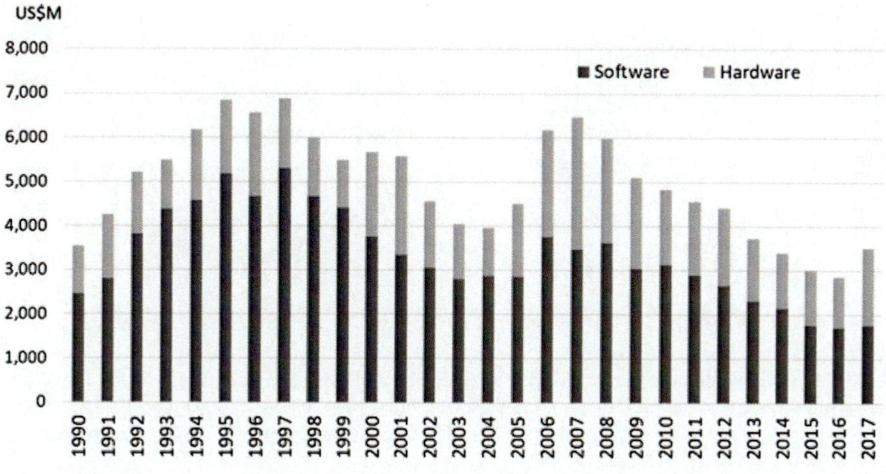

Fig. 2 Market scale of console/handheld games in Japan, 1990–2017. *Source* Data from Dentsu Institute for Human Studies (2001), p. 69, Digital Content Association of Japan (2014), p. 103, Computer Entertainment Supplier's Association (CESA) (2015), pp. 58–59 and CESA (2018), pp. 54–55

3 Current State of Japan's Video Game Industry

Regarding the home video game market in Japan, Fig. 2 illustrates the changing size of the market from 1990 to 2017,[1] with market size being defined as the total value of consumer purchase prices. The market grew steadily from 1990, reaching a peak of 6,893 million USD in 1997. After a period of decline, the market grew again around 2006, but has never recovered to its 1997 levels. The industry had a series of hits, with the NES, Super Nintendo Entertainment System (SNES), and PSX, leading up to 1997, but this momentum was lost due to growing disinterest in gaming. Nintendo responded by developing the Nintendo DS series and the Wii. These devices could be easily used and enjoyed by anyone and aimed to expand the gaming segment to middle-aged and older people and to women, and their popularity led to a comeback that peaked around 2006. The market has waned since 2007, apart from 2017, when the hit Nintendo Switch drove up the market's value to 3,515 million USD. The home video game market is thus susceptible to large swings, depending on whether there is hit hardware product in any given year, making the video game industry cyclical and unstable in comparison with other leading industries.

Figure 3 plots the shipping value of Japanese home video game exports over time, defined as the total based on the manufacturers' selling prices. Although exports have fluctuated greatly, they have grown substantially over 21 years, unlike the domestic market. Over the period 2004–2007, hardware exports surged by 5.4 times and software exports by 2.4 times. This was followed by a steep drop that lasted until 2012.

[1] 1 USD was converted to 110 JPY in this chapter.

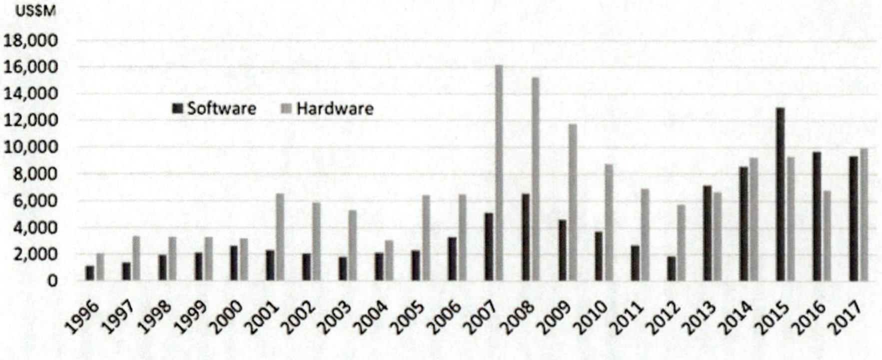

Fig. 3 Console/handheld revenue shipped overseas by Japanese companies, 1996–2017. *Source* Data from CESA (1998), pp. 30–31, CESA (2001), pp. 45–46, CESA (2004), pp. 77–79, CESA (2007), pp. 107–109, CESA (2009), pp. 143–145, CESA (2012), pp. 123–125, CESA (2015), pp. 78–80, and CESA (2018), pp. 74–76

Japan's video game industry is known as having developed into a sizeable export industry, but at the same time, it is unstable, as the tremendous variations in shipping value highlight. The total export value of hardware and software combined in 2017 was 25,346 million USD, accounting for 3.6% of Japan's total exports of 712 billion USD and making it a significant export industry (Yano Tsuneta Kinenkai 2018).

Figure 4 shows the export ratios of the home video game industry over the same time period, revealing that the industry is heavily dependent on exports, especially hardware. Figure 5 ranks the 2017 home video game (hardware and software) market

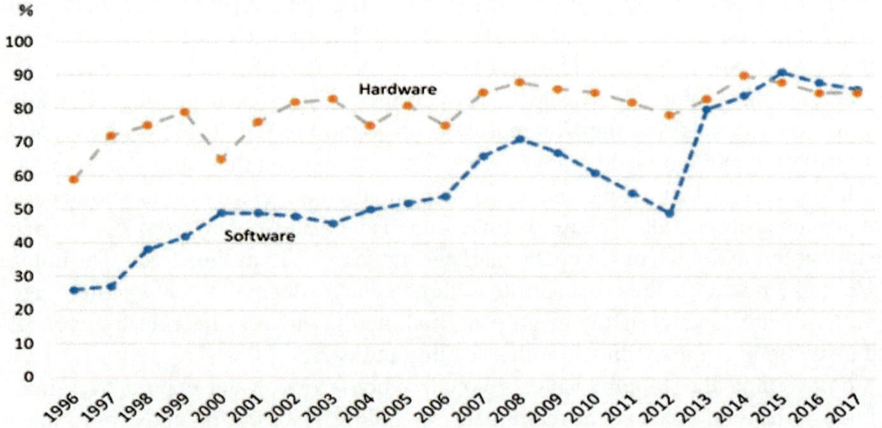

Fig. 4 Export ratio of console/handheld software and hardware from Japan, 1996–2017. *Source* Data from CESA (1998), pp. 27–31, CESA (2001), pp. 38–39, 45–46, CESA (2004), pp. 73, 75, 77, 79, CESA (2007), pp. 103, 105, 107, 109, CESA (2009), pp. 139, 141, 143, 145, CESA (2012), pp. 119, 121, 123, 125, CESA (2015), pp. 73, 75, 78, 80, and CESA (2018), pp. 69, 71, 74, 76. Note: Software data in 2011 and 2012 excludes overseas revenue shipped by overseas offices

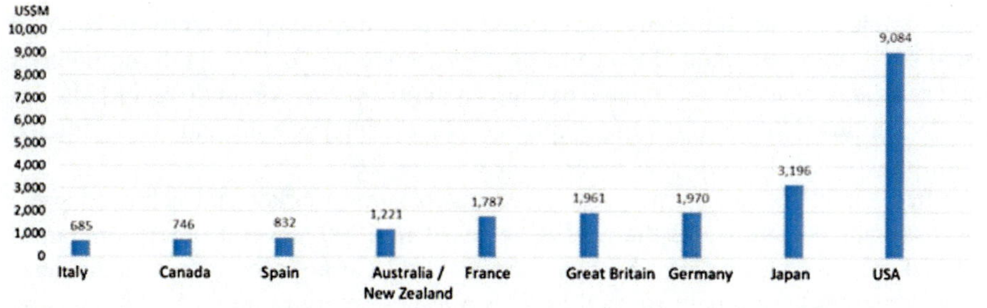

Fig. 5 Market scale of console/handheld game software and hardware by country, 2017. *Source* Data from CESA (2018), pp. 147–148

sizes in several countries, placing Japan second after the USA. The figures previously mentioned illustrate that the home video game industry is a large industry sector for Japan and that it is heavily dependent on exports. The industry has cycled through boom years and lean years because hardware companies develop new video game devices every few years, incorporating advances in technology, which are followed by popular software titles that run on the devices. A handful of hardware companies drive the video game industry, and numerous software companies have grown by supporting the lead taken by the hardware companies.

Japan has essentially two hardware companies: Nintendo and SIE. Nintendo was founded in 1889 in Kyoto as a manufacturer of *hanafuda* playing cards; Ninten means "to leave luck to the heavens." Nintendo later moved into the toy business to remain relevant in the changing times and started manufacturing toys using electronic technology, such as the *Laser Clay Shooting System*, a commercial entertainment system, in 1973. The company created an arcade game machine in 1978 and gradually entered businesses related to home game devices. In 1980, Nintendo released GAME&WATCH, its first handheld video game device. GAME&WATCH was an enormous success, selling over 40 million units worldwide. The palm-sized video game device with a liquid crystal display screen had its video game software embedded in ROM which could not be interchanged. The then-president Hiroshi Yamauchi was determined to create a company policy where Nintendo completely devotes itself to entertainment (Hatakeyama and Kubo 2000). Under this consistent policy, Yamauchi guided the company to constantly adapt to the times, irrespective of the form product development took. These moves enabled Yamauchi to turn Nintendo into a global company. The great-grandson of Nintendo's founder, he joined the company in 1949 at the age of 22 and stayed with the company as president for over 50 years, before stepping down in 2002.

Nintendo's sales reached a record high of 16,714 million USD in the fiscal year ending in March 2009. After a period without a hit product however, sales fell to 4,446 million USD in the fiscal year ending in March 2017. The company then made a remarkable recovery with the Nintendo Switch, reaching 9,597 million USD in the fiscal year ending in March 2018, and has maintained this momentum. In 2015, Nintendo partnered with DeNA Co., Ltd. (DeNA), a leading Japanese online game software company and entered the smartphone game sector in 2016. In fiscal 2017, with dedicated video game devices accounting for 96% of the company's total sales and smart-device-related business making up 4%, Nintendo recorded sales of 9,597 million USD on operating profit of 1,614 million USD and had a consolidated workforce of 5,501 employees (Toyo Keizai Inc. 2018).

After Nintendo had created the home video game market and achieved great success with the NES and the SNES, released in 1990, several other companies entered the market, one of which was SCE. Sony Corporation and its subsidiary Sony Music Entertainment formed SCE as a joint venture to enter the video game device business. In December 1994, SCE released the 32-bit PlayStation. Sony had apparently had some previous experience in the video game industry, developing the sound-generation system for Nintendo's SNES (Yanagawa and Kuwayama 1999). To counter the market-dominating Nintendo, Sony decided to make high-performance image processing its strength on the product side and to take a different software strategy from Nintendo on the sales side (Shintaku, Tanaka and Yanagawa 2003). PlayStation 2 (PS2), released in 2000, sold a total of 155 million units globally; PlayStation 4 (PS4) was released in 2013. In 2016, SCE consolidated all its planning, development, and sales operations for PlayStation-related hardware, software, content, and network services and renamed the organization SIE. Software sales totaled 4,180 million USD in fiscal 2014, but the figures since then have not been apparent. On the hardware side, the combined sales of all PlayStation models reached 525 million units as of July 2018 (SIE 2018).

Today, Nintendo and SIE are the only Japanese hardware companies in the home video game industry, although there are many software companies. Leading software companies, as listed in Table 1, include Koei Tecmo Holdings Co., Ltd., Capcom Co., Ltd., Square Enix Holdings Co., Ltd., Konami Holdings Corporation, Sega Sammy Holdings Inc., and Bandai Namco Holdings Inc. Many of these major video game software companies started out developing and selling arcade game machines in the 1960s and 1970s and applied this knowledge to enter the home video game software market in the 1980s. Since 2000 there has been a succession of restructurings among software companies, due to skyrocketing development costs as video game devices have increased in performance, and due to the stagnant domestic market (Koizumi 2016). Video game development is sophisticated and uses state-of-the-art technology, and so companies are making enormous R&D investments to strengthen their technological capabilities (Mizuho Bank 2014). Notable smaller and mid-sized Japanese video game software companies include Nippon Ichi Software, Inc., Marvelous Inc., Nihon Falcom Corporation, Broccoli Co., Ltd., Level 5 Inc., Spike Chunsoft, Co., Ltd., MAGES. Inc., and FromSoftware, Inc.

Japan's online social game market, in which games are normally played on general-purpose devices, has become an important industry sector in recent years on par with the home game market. Figure 6 shows the market's development, including its surging growth since 2010. In contrast to Fig. 2, this market was only 15% the size of the home video game software market in 2006, but it had expanded to 384% by 2016.

Table 1 Large software companies in Japan

Company name	Established	Sales (US$M, fiscal 2017)	Operating Profit (US$M, fiscal 2017)	Features	Major software
KOEI TECMO	2010 with acquisition by KOEI (established 1978) of TECMO (established 1967)	353	106	Its main business is game software production; puts significant resources into smartphone games; known for its historical simulation games	Nobunaga's Ambition
CAPCOM	1979	859	146	Sales of game software accounting for 78% of total sales (fiscal 2018); known for combat sports game software	Street Fighter; Resident Evil; Rockman; Monster Hunter

(continued)

Table 1 (continued)

Company name	Established	Sales (US$M, fiscal 2017)	Operating Profit (US$M, fiscal 2017)	Features	Major software
SQUARE ENIX	2003 with the merger of ENIX Co., Ltd. (established 1975) and SQUARE Co., Ltd. (established 1986)	2,276	347	Successful management of online game website. Digital entertainment business, 76%; Amusement business, 17%; Publishing, 4% (fiscal 2018)	Dragon Quest; Final Fantasy
KONAMI	1973	2,177	411	Wide business range (sports gyms, arcade game facilities, arcade game machines and home video game software), Digital entertainment business, 50%; Amusement, 11%; Health services, 27% (fiscal 2018)	Metal Gear; Winning Eleven

(continued)

Table 1 (continued)

Company name	Established	Sales (US$M, fiscal 2017)	Operating Profit (US$M, fiscal 2017)	Features	Major software
SEGA SAMMY	2004 with aquisiton by SAMMY (established 1975) of SEGA, (established 1951)2004 with aquisiton by SAMMY (established 1975) of SEGA, (established 1951)	2,942	161	Former development of home video game consoles (SEGA); pachinko business	Sonic; Puyo Puyo
BANDAI NAMCO	2005 with the merger of BANDAI CO., Ltd. (established 1950) and NAMCO LIMITED, (established 1955)	6,166	682	Manufacturing and sales of toys and operation of amusement facilities; copyright holder of prominent content such as GUNDAM	Tekken; Tales series

Source Adapted based on Koizumi (2016) p. 42, Toyo Keizai Inc. (2018) pp. 520, 1120, 1457, 1834, 1838, and 1858 and each company's official website

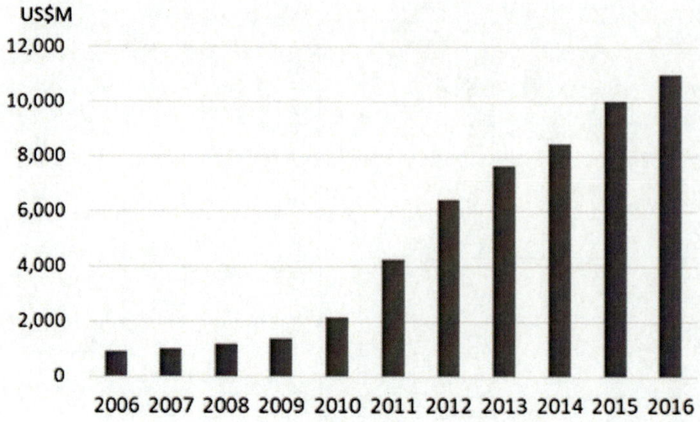

Fig. 6 Transitions in sales of online/social games in Japan. *Source* Dentsu Media Innovation Lab. (2018), p.112

Figure 7 shows the transitions in sales over the past 18 years at leading Japanese online game software companies. Three of these companies—DeNA, mixi, Inc., and GREE, Inc.—are social game companies. None of these companies are home video game software companies; they are companies operating online sales and social media sites. As startups, they have grown briskly since 2009. Item purchases are streamlined in Japan because of a system in which mobile carriers collect payments for item purchases on behalf of online game software companies. Consequently, online game software companies earn revenue from item purchases, instead of relying solely on advertising revenue.

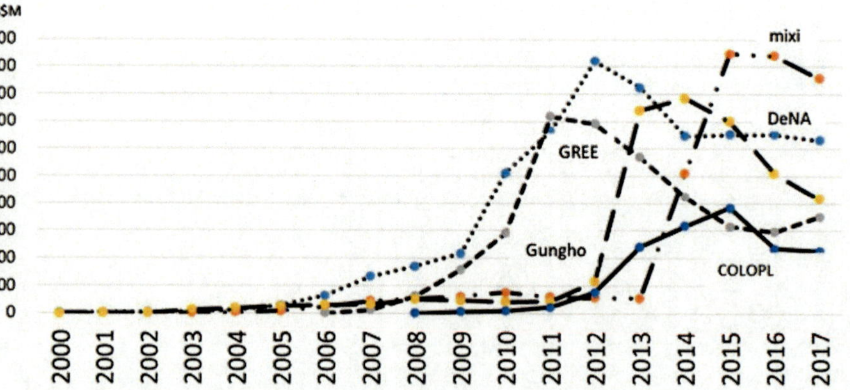

Fig. 7 Sales transition of Japanese major online game enterprises. *Source* Data from Nikkei Inc. (2005), pp. 252, 457, Nikkei Inc. (2009), 171, 263, 519, 541, Nikkei Inc. (2012), pp. 161, 243, 485, 515, Nikkei Inc. (2015), pp. 165, 244, 498, 513, 541, and Toyo Keizai Inc. (2018), pp. 175, 250, 518, 533, 560

Table 2 Top 10 companies by game revenues, 2017, worldwide

Rank	Company name	Annual revenues (US$B)
1	Tencent	18.1
2	Sony	10.5
3	Apple	8.0
4	Microsoft	7.1
5	Activison Blizzard	6.5
6	NetEase	5.6
7	Google	5.3
8	Electronic Arts	5.1
9	Nintendo	3.6
10	Bandai Namco	2.4

Data from Wijman (2018)

Japanese companies driving the market with native gaming apps include GungHo Online Entertainment, Inc., publisher of *Puzzle & Dragons*, and COLOPL, Inc. as well as large companies also involved in home video game software such as Konami Digital Entertainment Co., Ltd., Bandai Namco Entertainment Inc., Sega, and Square Enix. GungHo started out as an online auction company in 1998, but withdrew from the business in 2002 and shifted to the online game business, where it has enjoyed a string of hit products. COLOPL was founded in 2008 and, starting from a mobile-phone location data service, it successfully branched out into online games in 2011 and now online games are the main source of revenue (Koizumi 2016).

Table 2 lists the world's top companies in 2017 by revenue from video games, which includes both home video games and online games. Three Japanese companies made the list—Sony in second, Nintendo in ninth, and Bandai Namco in the tenth spot. The list indicates that Japan has a leading presence in the global video game industry, alongside Tencent Holdings Ltd., China in first place followed by major US companies.

4 Japan's Video Game Policy

4.1 Video Game Policy in the Frameworks of Content, Cool Japan, and Media Arts

Around 2000, Japan quickly rolled out stimulus measures for the content industry and Cool Japan-related industries. Details on the background of this policy development are given in the Chapter "Anime's Economic Value: the Government's Response to a Changing Environment". Video games, like anime, are a leading content industry. The popularity of Japanese video games outside of Japan has been outlined in the previous section and in the previous chapter which describes Cool Japan. Japanese video games held 20.0% of the global market in 2016 (Media and Content Industry Division, Commerce and Information Policy Bureau, METI 2017). Nye (2004) described the relevance of video games to Japan's soft power and that cultural soft power increases a country's economic growth. According to Nye, Japan's revenue from sales and royalties of cultural products, such as TV games, anime, movies, and fashion, reached 12.5 billion USD in 2002 which was an increase of 300% for 10 years. It was further mentioned that Pokémon conveys a soft, friendly image of Japan to children around the world.

Pokémon was originally developed as a video game software title, and it has inevitably received mention for its enormous economic ripple effects in materials on measures to stimulate the content industry published since 2000 by METI (e.g. METI 2006). *Pokémon* was the brainchild of a single creator who had been a fan of video games in his youth. Game-device-maker Nintendo supported the *Pokémon* idea, which took six years to develop. *Pokémon* was eventually released as a video game title in 1996 (Hatakeyama and Kubo 2002). To let fans have multiple ways of enjoying *Pokémon* and to boost sales, the owners paired the video game software with manga magazines aimed at children and teens and sold them together, which proved to be highly successful. Manga magazines are a magazine format unique to Japan, publishing ten or more serial stories per issue on either a weekly or monthly schedule. Following this success, the *Pokémon* franchise expanded into TV anime series, card games, character goods, movies, and books on game tactics. The franchise was launched in the USA and other overseas markets and today is loved by children around the world. The cumulative market sales for *Pokémon* as of March 31, 2017 totaled over six billion USD, 35% of which has come from sales in Japan and 65% from sales abroad.

As the *Pokémon* example illustrates, the video game business is closely linked to the anime business. Video game sales alone contribute a significant portion to the whole, although not to the same extent as that of anime. Extending a title across multiple media platforms greatly magnifies the scale of the business, and the Japanese government closely monitors the size of these ripple effects. The Pokémon franchise has expanded in many directions. The foundation of all Pokémon expansions however, regardless of size or characteristics, is the role-playing game, in which players catch and raise Pokémon and trade and battle with their friends. The total number of Pokémon-related software units shipped exceeds 300 million units worldwide (as of March 31, 2018). Pokémon anime, first broadcasted on Japanese TV in April 1997, are now broadcasted in 124 countries and regions. The first Pokémon movie was released in July 1998, and the total audience in Japan for the first movie through the 20th movie (released in 2017) was approximately 77.36 million, with box-office earnings of about 748 million USD. The Pokémon card game pioneered card games in Japan in October 1996 by recreating the video game's gameplay with cards. Over 25.7 billion cards have been shipped worldwide, and they have been translated into eleven languages and sold in 74 countries and regions (as of March 31, 2018). There are now 550 companies licensed to sell Pokémon character goods, including candy, stationery, and apparel (The Pokémon Company 2018).

The METI (2009) formulated a basic policy on revitalizing the video game software industry in 2007 with the understanding that:

> Video games are one of Japan's leading content formats and a type of world-class entertainment. The current state of Japan's video game software industry is, unfortunately, not encouraging. In global markets, international competition has increased in recent years, with US companies rapidly entering home video games and South Korean and Chinese companies entering online games. In Japan, the home video game market is seen as sluggish.

The METI organized the issues confronting Japan's video game market from three perspectives.

- Changes in the domestic market: shrinking gamer population due to a declining birth rate; proliferation of online games
- Changes in overseas markets: Japan's video game exports are flat, even though overseas video game markets are witnessing booming growth
- Increasing competition with overseas companies: the presence of Japanese video games has dwindled: seven of the top ten best-selling video game titles in the USA in 1998 were Japanese, compared to only two in 2005.

The METI also indicated that it believed aggressive policy formulations were necessary for the video game industry, given that video games are the largest export sector in the content industry, that global video game markets have high growth potential, and that the video game segment drives the content industry from the technological side.

These examples show that the METI recognizes the importance of the video game industry for the Japanese economy, as well as its issues and promise. Nevertheless, examining the actual measures taken since 2000 confirms that video games have received less attention than anime. For instance, the Cool Japan Fund—the prime investment vehicle within the Cool Japan Strategy discussed in the previous chapter—has not invested in a single project directly related to video games. Only two of the Fund's projects are even marginally associated with video games: *Japan content-related online sales to overseas* (the fund subsidy amount: 13.6 million USD), and *Creator development abroad* (the fund subsidy amount: 4.1 million USD (total project cost: 9.1 million USD)) (Commerce and Service Industry Policy Group, METI 2018). Other assistance to the video game industry includes the J-LOP (Japan Localization and Promotion) project described in the previous chapter. The J-LOP project, which ran from fiscal 2013 to fiscal 2017, aided the export of Japan content by subsidizing the localization and promotion of content to match the culture and customs of overseas markets, and helped video game companies cover the costs of localizing video games and exhibiting at international exhibitions. In addition, the METI is a sponsor of the Tokyo Game Show, an international video game exhibition held every September that drew 300,000 visitors in 2018. Therefore, it is possible to identify some finely focused policy measures like these that have benefited the video game industry. However, no radical policy measures exist that explicitly address the industry, despite the METI extolling its importance.

Aside from economic aid to the industry, regarding cultural aid, the ACA[2] has treated video games as part of the media arts framework in the same way as anime. The ACA divides the media arts into four categories: art, entertainment, animation, and manga, with video games placed under the entertainment category. Since video games are not named as a category however, it is apparent that video games do not have the same central presence as anime and manga in the ACA's media arts framework. An examination of the cultural stimulus measures directed at video games reveals the Media Art Database, a project that has a category for video games along with animation and manga. The Media Art Database is the result of five years of work by the ACA's Media Art Digital Archive Initiative launched in 2010. The database collects information on past works of Japanese manga, animation, and video games, as well as past media art events, and makes this information available online. In the video game category, the database has information on video game titles compatible with home video game consoles sold as recently as December 2016, arcade games released from 1972 through 2016, and video game software compatible with the PC-8801 series of home computers. After the completion of the database, the ACA initiated the Media Art Archive Promotion Support Project. Three of the 19 accepted projects are related to video games: The Game Preservation Society's *Entry of information into a database of Japanese retro computer games* (10.2 thousand USD); the Komaki Highway Kikaku's *Project to restore, preserve, and archive arcade games* (59.1 thousand USD); and the Ritsumeikan Trust's *Survey project toward the creation and application of video game bibliographic records* (63.6 thousand USD) (as of fiscal 2017). The Media Art Cooperation Promotion Program initiates research studies and the creation of new domains through the cooperation and collaboration of industry, academia, and government crossing fields and domains in the media arts. The program's aim is to consistently apply and develop cultural assets in the media arts. Two of the eight projects accepted by the program in fiscal 2017 were related to video games: Hitotsubashi University's *Cross-discipline oral history project on innovation generated by the video game industry* (approximately 49.5 thousand USD), and the Ritsumeikan Center for Game Studies' *fiscal 2017 survey project on coordination among collections of video game archives* (approximately 165 thousand USD) (ACA n.d.). These programs show that the ACA provides assistance for several archive projects involving video games as a category of the media arts. However, the ACA has policy measures tailored for developing anime creators but no similar measures for video games, and any budgets are very small.

Why are fewer policy measures directed at video games than anime? One major reason is that the anime industry has developed primarily for a domestic audience in close alliance with the TV and film industries, whereas the video game industry has moved forward independently targeting overseas markets. The Economic Analysis Office of the METI (2017) performed a comparative study of video game software

[2]An official in charge of video game policy from the ACA was inteviewed for this research. Dates: November 6th, 2018. Place: ACA (Tokyo). Interviewee: Mr. Tetsuya Ino, Deputy Director to the Counselor, Arts and Culture Division, ACA.

production companies versus animation production companies (surveying companies with a capitalization of at least 272 thousand USD). The industries were compared on the average sales per company, the number of employees, their capitalization, the number of content titles produced, the percentage of full-time employees, the copyright retention and the orientation toward markets outside Japan. The survey found both industries had multiple layers of subcontractors, relying on very small subcontractors at the bottom. Video game software production companies, however, tended to be about twice the size of the animation production companies on a lot of comparison indices, suggesting a greater degree of autonomy among video game companies. The size of the video game's revenue shipped domestically and internationally, counting both hardware and software, was 28,861 million USD (in 2017, CESA (2018)), compared to 19,576 million USD for the anime-related market domestic and overseas (in 2017, the Association of Japanese Animations (2018)), suggesting that the diferences are not big in size. However, after subtracting multimedia development, character goods, and other related merchandise, the market for anime films alone totaled only 2,428 million USD, and thus is significantly smaller than the video game industry.

Another major difference between the two is copyright retention by production companies and their orientation toward markets outside Japan. In fiscal 2015, 90% of video game software production companies retained 100% of the primary usage rights to their software, whereas the same was true for only around 5% of anime production companies. Furthermore, about 80% of video game software production companies held 100% of the secondary usage rights of their titles, while a similarly low percentage of anime production companies retained secondary usage rights as those that had held onto primary usage rights. Thus, retention of copyrights among video game software production companies is dramatically higher than among anime production companies. In a survey of attitudes on overseas expansion, almost 80% of video game companies had plans to expand overseas and over 50% were considering outsourcing production overseas. In contrast, less than 40% of anime companies were considering selling their titles in overseas markets (The Economic Analysis office of the METI 2017).

This section has shown that video games are treated in the same frameworks as anime—content, Cool Japan, and media arts—in terms of industry stimulus measures and cultural stimulus measures. Video game production companies, however, tend to have more solid business platforms in place, which is one reason that actual policy measures for the video game industry are less prominent than those for the anime industry.

4.2 *Specific Policy Measures on Video Games*

This section examines what specific policy measures for video games have been developed outside of the frameworks of content, Cool Japan, and media arts. One area of the video game industry that has drawn considerable attention in recent years is e-sports.[3] E-sports are organized competitions in which multiple players or teams compete on a specific video game using computers, home video game consoles, or mobile devices. The term e-sports arose due to the sports-like nature of the competitions, where players battle using their keyboard, video game controller, and tapping skills. E-sports have become a worldwide phenomenon, and even the International Olympic Committee (IOC) announced at the October 2017 Olympic Summit that it would study the inclusion of e-sports as an Olympic event. The global e-sports market was estimated to be worth 493 million USD in 2016 and 906 million USD in 2018, and is expected to expand rapidly to 1.65 billion USD by 2021 (Kaneda 2018). E-sports, however, have been slow to take off in Japan, which the Japan video game industry and the government see as a problem. This is evidenced by e-sports' low public awareness, just 14.4% as of August 2017, and its near invisibility, apart from news reporting, on leading broadcasting media platforms (Ministry of Internal Affairs and Communications 2018). Competitive e-sports events in Japan have gradually increased in number since 2015, delayed in part by the slow establishment of the online game market itself. Structures to promote e-sports have been put in place, first with a succession of new e-sports organizations, such as the Japan eSports Association (JeSPA) in April 2015, the e-sports Promotion Organization in October 2015, and the Japan eSports Federation (JeSF) in March 2016. In 2017, these three organizations collaborated with the Computer Entertainment Supplier's Association (CESA) and the Japan Online Game Association (JOGA) to launch a new organization to tackle the development of e-sports together. In February 2018, the three e-sports organizations were dissolved and the Japan esports Union (JeSU) was formed. JeSU has since been involved in aiding the Japanese e-sports industry and sending professional gamers from Japan to international competitions (Digital Content Association of Japan 2018), and a number of TV broadcasters and newspapers have announced they will enter e-sports following JeSU's founding. Furthermore, more competitions are being held and are beginning to show signs of success. In February 2018, tournaments were held in Tokyo for such video game titles as *Winning Eleven 2018* (Konami Digital Entertainment), *Street Fighter V Arcade Edition* (Capcom), *Puzzle & Dragons* (GungHo), and *Monster Strike* (mixi) (Digital Content Association of Japan 2018). In 2019, an e-sports competition was held at the 2019 National Sports Festival in Ibaraki Prefecture as a cultural program. E-sports are finally gaining traction in Japan, but the gap with other countries remains large, both in terms of popularity and the scale of competitions. Nobuyuki Umezaki—president of SunGence Inc, a company that manages pro e-sports teams in Japan—described the state of e-sports in Japan: "Japan has few competitions, the prize money is small, and the gap is huge in terms of social recognition of pro gamers with that of the USA and other countries" (Watanabe 2018).

[3]The following two people were interviewed to study the video game industry for this research.

Dates: December 2018 and January 2019. Method: Social media. Interviewees: Reo Yonaga, Special Projects Officer attached to the President's Office of GMO Internet, Inc., and Itaru Kaneko, Visiting Associate Professor at Nagoya City University.

The spread of e-sports is also hampered by several legal issues. The Ministry of Internal Affairs and Communications (2018) pointed out that, unlike soccer matches or shogi tournaments, hosting a video game competition is complicated by the need to obtain consent from the rights holder to the video game title used in the competition. Japan also has a number of laws that limit the activities of businesses in the interest of consumer protection, most of which were enacted prior to the existence of online games, so it is not clear how to interpret and apply these laws to e-sports and whether legal amendments are necessary. The three laws problematic for e-sports competitions in Japan are the Penal Code, the Act against Unjustifiable Premiums and Misleading Representations, and the Act on Control and Improvement of Amusement and Entertainment Business (Ministry of Internal Affairs and Communications 2018).

- Penal Code (administered by the Ministry of Justice)
  The Penal Code restricts gambling, and under Article 185, it may be illegal for players who pay an entry fee to then collect prize money if this act is characterized as gambling. It is legal, however, for a player to collect prize money when entry is free.
- Act against Unjustifiable Premiums and Misleading Representations (administered by the Consumer Affairs Agency)
  This law restricts the provision of excess giveaways with products and services to allow for the fair choice of products by consumers. It may be illegal for video game publishers or developers to provide prize money at e-sports competitions if the provision of prize money is interpreted as a means to entice customers and as ancillary to their product or service transactions. It is legal, however, for a business other than companies benefiting from the competition to provide prize money. If the value of the transaction is less than 46 USD, the prize value is limited to 20 times the transaction value, and if the transaction value is 46 USD or more, the prize value is capped at 909 USD. Under the current law, it is impossible to host competitions that offer prize money exceeding one million dollars like those outside of Japan.
- Act on Control and Improvement of Amusement Business, etc. (administered by the National Police Agency).
  This law regulates the running of amusement centers, darts bars, and similar establishments. Article 23–4 of the Act states: "A person operating a mahjong parlor as provided for in Article 2–1(IV) or a business as provided for in Article 2–1(V) shall neither offer nor provide, in relation to said business, prizes accompanying the results of games under the provisions in the previous Article" (e-gov 2019). When a promoter holds a competition in a non-permanent venue, the venue may be viewed as a permanent establishment if the competition lasts two days or longer. As most e-sports offline championship competitions last two days or longer, they will likely be subject to the Act on Control and Improvement of Amusement Business, etc.

It is illegal in Japan to hold competitions offering the large prizes widely found overseas. The total prize money at some overseas e-sports competitions can be enormous. For example, in August 2017, *The International 2017* offered 24.78 million USD, the *2017 League of Legends World Championship* offered 2.25 million USD, and the *2017 Call of Duty World League Championship* had a total of 1.52 million USD. In contrast, September 2017′s *RAGE Vol. 5* offered 91 thousand USD and the *All Campus Series* offered 182 thousand USD in prizes, not cash (Hamamura 2018). Since it is nearly impossible to hold large e-sports competitions in Japan with significant prize money, it is difficult both to develop gamers and to build a following among ordinary viewers.

Considering how the Japanese government is addressing e-sports, the government has regarded e-sports as an important growth segment of the nation's video game industry and recognizes that the laws discussed earlier are an issue for e-sports, but actual concrete policy measures have not yet been developed. As described in the previous chapter, the Intellectual Property Strategy Headquarters, which resides within the Cabinet Office, has released an Intellectual Property Strategic Program paper each year since 2004. The Intellectual Property Strategy Headquarters (2018) was the first to consider the topic of e-sports:

> E-sports is gaining attention as a new growth domain in the content field and is a business development born out of digital communications, which is today the prime form of communications. The government quickly recognized this new trend and will seek to address, as necessary, the arrangement of proper conditions to ensure the sound development of e-sports.

There are other elements connected with video games in which policy moves are hoped to be achieved. These include adjustments to the copyright system to meet the changing times, prevention of the adverse effects of gaming on youths, and assistance for technology development. First, there are two means of accomplishing copyright protection for video game software: technical means and legal means. The course of legal protection is summarized with reference to the Association of Copyright for Computer Software (2015). Legal protection was first applied to computer programs, including video game software, in 1985 when copyrighted works gained protection under the Copyright Act. This was a major step forward, since prior to the Copyright Act, owners of computer programs could only retain protective rights by filing for a patent. In 1997, public transmission rights were first instituted. Public transmission rights are a part of copyrights and allow copyrighted works to be transmitted for the purpose of direct reception of the works by the public. These rights govern acts of public transmissions by entities other than the copyright holders.

In 2002, the Provider Liability Limitation Act was established. This legal system permits providers to take down or delete information in cases where information distributed over the Internet violates the rights of other people, while carefully balancing relief for victims versus the freedom of expression for information posters. Under the law, a victim can demand that the provider, which is a third party to the distribution of information, disclose to the victim information on the poster of the information that was purported to violate the victim's rights. Such disclosures enable the victim to identify the perpetrator and file a claim for damages as a means of recouping losses or damages caused by the distribution of rights-violating information. Information on posters must ordinarily be protected to maintain the privacy of posters, the freedom of anonymous expression, and the secrecy of communications, and so providers and other businesses are not permitted to disclose such information without a lawful reason. The Provider Liability Limitation Act, however, makes it possible for providers or other businesses to disclose information on posters legally, provided that certain strict conditions are met, and also defines the conditions under which providers and other business are exempt from legal liability.

The government set up the Intellectual Property High Court in 2005 specifically to hear patent cases and intellectual property cases, which has supported the handling of legal cases related to intellectual property. Later, the Copyright Act was amended in 2012 to impose criminal penalties on illegal downloads. Through these moves, the government has addressed the changing times by enacting and revising legislation that aims to protect video game software.

In regard to the adverse effects of gaming on society and youths, a rating system, which indicates the appropriate age range for individual home video game titles, was instituted, since such a broad range of people play home video games. To avoid direct involvement of the government in rating video games, the Computer Entertainment Rating Organization (CERO), a neutral, voluntary organization launched in 2002, rates video games sold on the Japanese market. The ratings consist of five age classifications: A (all ages), B (aged 12 and older), C (aged 15 and older), D (aged 17 and older), and Z (aged 18 and older). The Z classification was added in 2006, and video games with a Z rating are prohibited from being sold or distributed to people under the age of 18 (Watanabe 2010). CERO had rated 8,200 titles by April 2010, covering nearly 100% of the video games on the market—an astonishingly high percentage. CERO, since its inception, has worked to improve its rating methodology in keeping with the times, but the video game industry has undergone immense changes and new challenges have emerged, particularly with the sharp rise of online games. Online games are played on smartphones and other devices that differ substantially from home video game consoles, making it much harder to manage online games, as multiple businesses are involved. Other key issues that have emerged are the nature of managing games and the way services are provided, such as charging high prices for adding features to games or tactics that entice players to gamble (Fujiwara 2017).

5 Conclusion

This chapter has analyzed the last 35 years of Japan's video game industry, during which it has grown enormously, from a scale so small it could not be called an industry to today, when it contributes 3.6% of Japan's total exports by value. Nintendo and SIE, along with Microsoft, have constructed a triumvirate that dominates the global market for home video game consoles. An examination of the current state of affairs, however, reveals many salient problems. The biggest is the emergence of online games. Numerous new firms with no connection to the companies that pioneered home video games have entered the video game industry, increasing international competition. Since home video games and online games differ in content, playing methods, and player demographics, they do not occupy the same territory. Nevertheless, since the rapid ascent of China, South Korea, and other countries in online games, the strong position that Japan had built up is on the decline across the entire video game industry. Government policy is needed urgently to halt this decline and revitalize the video game industry.

In the days when the video game industry was centered on home video games, there was little need for policy aid because Nintendo and SIE continued to grow under their own power due to their scale advantages, financial strength, and technical capacity. Even though many video game software companies had weak financial footings, hardware companies backed their development. Today the video game industry is in an increasingly tough environment. Despite this, many new business opportunities have opened up due to the continued move to online platforms and quickly advancing technological innovations in VR and AR, for example. The video game business of the future will require more than just sales of video game devices and video game software; companies will need integrated competitiveness across different industries, such as communication equipment, communication devices, VR and other imaging devices, and electronic components. Fostering such competitiveness will benefit not only just the video game industry but also the advancement of many other related industries. Individual industries acting alone, however, are unlikely to enable these related industries to develop through mutual synergy. Instead, integrated support on the policy side is likely to be effective.

This chapter has looked at the video game policy measures implemented by the Japanese government to date. Although the government partly recognizes the magnitude of the video game industry's economic ripple effects, its importance as an export industry, and its cultural value, there have been no radical policy measures that aim strongly to drive the video game industry. This chapter outlined Japan's video game industry and considered what can be accomplished and what needs to be done in terms of government policy to further advance video games as an industry and as a culture. To play video games, platforms that pool technological knowledge will be necessary. The current rapid pace of technological innovation is expected to increase and the conditions surrounding the video game industry will evolve even faster. In this so-called fourth industrial revolution, in which science and technology progress at an accelerated rate and the economic landscape undergoes tremendous disruptions, the video game industry requires prompt and strategic assistance.

References

Agency for Cultural Affairs (n.d.) Promotion for media arts (in Japanese). https://www.bunka.go.jp/seisaku/geijutsubunka/media_art/. Accessed 1 Dec 2018

Bandai Namco Holdings Inc. (2018) https://www.bandainamco.co.jp/about/index.html. Accessed 1 Dec 2018

Capcom Co., Ltd. (2018) https://www.capcom.co.jp/ir/company/. Accessed 1 Dec 2018

Commerce and Service Industry Policy Group, Ministry of Economy, Trade and Industry (2018) Cool Japan fund (in Japanese). https://www.meti.go.jp/policy/mono_info_service/mono/creative/file/180402CooljapanfundApr.pdf. Accessed 10 Dec 2018

Computer Entertainment Supplier's Association (ed) (1998) 1998 CESA game white paper (in Japanese). Author, Tokyo

Computer Entertainment Supplier's Association (ed) (2001) 2001 CESA game white paper (in Japanese). Author, Tokyo

Computer Entertainment Supplier's Association (ed) (2004) 2004 CESA game white paper (in Japanese). Author, Tokyo

Computer Entertainment Supplier's Association (ed) (2007) 2007 CESA game white paper (in Japanese). Author, Tokyo

Computer Entertainment Supplier's Association (ed) (2009) 2009 CESA game white paper (in Japanese). Author, Tokyo

Computer Entertainment Supplier's Association (ed) (2012) 2012 CESA game white paper (in Japanese). Author, Tokyo

Computer Entertainment Supplier's Association (ed) (2015) 2015 CESA game white paper (in Japanese). Author, Tokyo

Computer Entertainment Supplier's Association (ed) (2018) 2018 CESA game white paper (in Japanese). Author, Tokyo

Dentsu Institute for Human Studies (2001) Information media trends in Japan 2001 (in Japanese) Dentsu, Inc., Tokyo

Dentsu Media Innovation Lab (ed) (2018) Research for information and media society 2018 (in Japanese). Diamond Inc., Tokyo

Digital Content Association of Japan (ed) (2014) Digital content 2014 (in Japanese). Author, Tokyo

Digital Content Association of Japan (ed) (2018) Digital content 2018 (in Japanese). Author, Tokyo

e-Gov (2019) Act on Control and Improvement of Amusement Business, etc. (in Japanese). https://elaws.e-gov.go.jp/search/elawsSearch/elaws_search/lsg0500/detail?lawId=323AC0000000122. Accessed 1 Sept 2020

Economic Analysis Office of the Ministry of Economy, Trade and Industry (2017) Comparing the actual state of production companies producing two major Japanese contents, video games and anime (in Japanese). https://www.meti.go.jp/statistics/toppage/report/minikeizai/pdf/h2amini083j.pdf. Accessed 1 Sept 2018

Fujita N (1999) The Japanese video game industry prior to the release of Famicom - the formation process of the present-day video game industry (2) (in Japanese) Kyoto University Economic Society, Kyoto. The Economic Review 163(3):59–76

Fujiwara M (2017) Issues and transitions in digital game rating systems:-comparing CERO, PEGI, and IARC- (in Japanese). J Digit Games Res 9(2):1–13

Hamamura K (2018) The expanding global e-sports market and market prospects in Japan (in Japanese). Japan e-sports Union. https://www.kantei.go.jp/jp/singi/titeki2/tyousakai/kensho_hyoka_kikaku/2018/contents/dai4/siryou1.pdf. Accessed 11 Dec 2018

Hatakeyama K, M Kubo (2002) Pokémon story (in Japanese). Nikkei Business Publications, Tokyo

Kaneda A (2018) Outside view of e-sports entertainment and issues with market entry (in Japanese). Deloitte Tohmatsu Financial Advisory LLC, Tokyo. https://www2.deloitte.com/jp/ja/pages/consumer-and-industrial-products/articles/sb/esports.html. Accessed 11 Dec 2018

Koei Tecmo Holdings Co., ltd. (2018) https://www.koeitecmo.co.jp/company/history/. Accessed 1 Dec 2018

Koizumi M (2016) Japanese video game industry: history of its growth and current state. In: Lee SA, Pulos A (eds) Transnational contexts of development history, sociality, and society of play video games in East Asia. Palgrave Mcmillan, Cham, pp 13–64

Konami Holdings Corporation (2018) https://www.konami.com/corporate/ja/. Accessed 1 Dec 2018

Media and Content Industry Division, Commerce and Information Policy Bureau, Ministry of Economy, Trade and Industry (2017) Content industry policy measures (in Japanese). https://www.soumu.go.jp/main_content/000534166.pdf. Accessed 1 Sept 2018
Ministry of Economy, Trade and Industry (2006) International expansion of Japanese content (in Japanese). https://www.kantei.go.jp/jp/singi/bunka/dai3/3siryou7.pdf. Accessed 11 Dec 2018
Ministry of Economy, Trade and Industry (ed) (2009) Basic policy on revitalizing the video game software industry (in Japanese). Author, Tokyo
Ministry of Internal Affairs and Communications (2018) Research study on the e-sports industry (in Japanese). https://www.soumu.go.jp/main_content/000551535.pdf. Accessed 10 Dec 2018
Mizuho Bank (2014) Mizuho industry research 48, Prospects of the content industry—for further development of the content industry (in Japanese). Author, Tokyo
Nikkei Inc. (2005) Nikkei company information spring (in Japanese). Nikkei Publishing Inc, Tokyo
Nikkei Inc. (2009) Nikkei company information summer (in Japanese). Nikkei Publishing Inc, Tokyo
Nikkei Inc. (2012) Nikkei company information winter (in Japanese). Nikkei Publishing Inc, Tokyo
Nikkei Inc. (2015) Nikkei company information summer (in Japanese). Nikkei Publishing Inc, Tokyo
Nye JS (2004) Japan's soft power: its limits and potential (in Japanese). Gaiko Forum June: 12–15
Sega Sammy Holdings Inc. (2018) https://www.segasammy.co.jp/japanese/pr/corp/data/. Accessed 1 Dec 2018
Shintaku J, Tanaka T, N Yanagawa (2003) An economic analysis of the video game industry (in Japanese). Toyo Keizai Inc., Tokyo
Sony Interactive Entertainment Inc. (2018) https://www.sie.com/corporate.html. Accessed 1 Dec 2018
Square Enix Co., Ltd. (2018) https://www.jp.square-enix.com/company/ja/. Accessed 1 Dec 2018
The Association of Copyright for Computer Software (ed) (2015) Current state of copyright violations through circumvention of technical protective means on home video game software (in Japanese). Author, Tokyo
The Association of Japanese Animation (2018) Anime industry report 2018 (in Japanese). Author, Tokyo. https://aja.gr.jp/english/japan-anime-data (Summary in English). Accessed 1 Sept 2020
The Intellectual Property Strategy Headquarters (2018) Intellectual property strategic program (in Japanese). https://www.kantei.go.jp/jp/singi/titeki2/kettei/chizaikeikaku2018.pdf. Accessed 1 Dec 2018
The Pokémon Company (2018) https://www.pokemon.co.jp/corporate/about/. Accessed 1 Dec 2018
Toyo Keizai Inc. (2018) Quarterly corporate report 2018. Summer issue (in Japanese). Author, Tokyo
Watanabe K (2010) Age rating system for home video game software: for the selection of video game software matching the mental development of children (in Japanese). Commun Oper Res Soc Jpn 55(8):479–483
Watanabe T (2018) Booming e-sports industry prints money from video game competitions (in Japanese). Weekly Toyo Keizai 6779: 66–69
Wijman T (2018) Top 25 Public Game Companies Earn $94.1 Billion in 2017. Newzoo. https://newzoo.com/insights/articles/top-25-public-game-companies-earn-94-1-billion-in-2017/. Accessed 1 Dec 2018
Yano Tsuneta Kinenkai (2018) Nihon Kokusei Zue 2018/2019 (in Japanese). Kokuseisha, Tokyo
Yanagawa N and J Kuwayama (1999) An economic analysis of the home video game industry (in Japanese).The Research Institute of Economy Trade and Industry, Tokyo. http://wwww.rieti.go.jp/jp/publications/act_dp.html#jp. Accessed 1 April 2015

Music

Stevie Yoshida

1 Introduction

This chapter will provide insight into Japanese public policies surrounding music content and will provide the background to the policies being implemented and its effects. Section 2 will detail the competition law in the record market and will look into how retail price maintenance (hereinafter referred to as RPM) was established and its current state. The chapter will also outline the clashes between the Fair Trade Commission (hereinafter referred to as FTC), which is against RPM, and the record industry, which wishes to maintain RPM. Section 3 will address educational policies, looking at the changing demands for music education in compulsory education, and assess the establishment and impact of the Committee for Music Education Promotion Act. Section 4 will also make observations and comments on the successes and limits of lobbying for the music industry. Section 5 will focus on the policy discussions regarding the artist management industry and use the agreement adopted by the film industry in 1953 to explain the business structure of the artist management industry. This chapter will also analyze the practice of artist management companies registering stage names as trademarks and compare it to the report presented by the FTC in 2018. In Sect. 6, we will look into policy amendments made in regard to the music copyright collecting agencies and explain why music copyright collecting was changed based on the competition in the domestic market. Section 7 will summarize and reflect on the entire article and discuss future pathways for Japanese policymaking in regard to audio content.

S. Yoshida (✉)
The Glendon Partners LLC, New York, USA
e-mail: syoshida@alum.mit.edu

M. Sugaya (ed.), *Perspectives on the Japanese Media and Content Policies*,
Advances in Information and Communication Research 2,
https://doi.org/10.1007/978-981-15-4704-1_10

2 RPM

2.1 The Birth of RPM for Records

In 1953, 8 years after the end of World War II, Japan implemented the Antimonopoly Act. While the Act considered RPM to be illegal, "daily necessities for consumers" and "copyrighted work" were exempt from the rule. According to academic Kinoshita (2003), the cosmetics industry lobbied strongly to have cosmetics included in the definition of daily necessities and eventually succeeded in having them exempted from the rule. Fearing that the masses will accuse them of playing favorites to the cosmetics industry, lawmakers copied West Germany's stance on copyrighted work, by similarly classifying copyrighted work as exemptions to the Antimonopoly Act. Initially, the goods defined as copyrighted work were books, magazines, newspapers, and records. CDs and music cassettes eventually joined the list to make six goods exempt from the Act. By following the example of the cosmetics industry, the Japanese record industry enjoyed a market environment without price competition, for many years after 1953.

2.2 The First Review of the RPM

In 1963, an industry organization for retail record stores, the National Record and Commerce Federation, was accused by the FTC of violating Antimonopoly Act, a violation to which the Federation later admitted. According to Wada (1994), the Federation requested record companies to not sell their records to retail record stores outside of the Federation. While the RPM itself was not the issue here, the very nature of the request by the Federation inhibited competition of the retailers and FTC's accusation brought the spotlight on the record industry and how records were distributed.

Since 1966, the FTC had been calling for a review of the RPM, and in 1978, the chairman of the FTC even quoted "We will be looking into the situation regarding the distribution of books and records with the objective of eliminating RPM and revising the Antimonopoly Act" (Kinoshita 2003). The FTC went on to comment that the Japanese retail price for records was too expensive compared with those in foreign countries.

However, the elimination of the RPM that the FTC wished for did not happen, and policymakers opted instead to put a time limit on products eligible to be sold with an RPM.

From 1977, a parliamentary group of policymakers supporting the arts was formed Parliamentary Association for Music to support laws promoting culture and the arts. The continuation of the RPM was the result of the influence of the Parliamentary Association exercising their political clout.

2.3 The Second Review of the RPM

In 1991, a government inquiry consisting of academic experts recommended the revision of the RPM for records, cassettes, and CDs. In the following year, the FTC commented on the need of the government to narrow the definition of what classified as copyrighted works, and promised to investigate the actual state of the distribution of books, magazines, newspapers, and CDs.

Fearing this action would be taken by the FTC, the music industry offered to limit the RPM of records to 2 years after release, starting from 1992. However, in 1995, the government voted to clearly define the scope and limits of the definitions of copyrighted works by the end of 1997 as part of its "Socio-Economic Plan for Restructuring" (Cabinet Office 1995). The FTC, following the government's plan, also pledged to make clear definitions of content classified as copyrighted work in the Antitrust law by the end of March 1998. The likelihood that the RPM for CDs would be eliminated was higher than ever.

Once again, the music industry responded with more lobbying to maintain the RPM for CDs. Numerous organizations within the music industry including the Recording Industry Association of Japan (RIAJ), Japanese Society for Rights of Authors, Composers and Publishers (hereinafter referred to as JASRAC), and Japan Council of Performers Rights & Performing Arts Organizations (Geidankyo), hosted a Music and Arts Gathering and the attendants all signed a petition requesting the government to maintain the current law regarding the RPM. In the same year, the Parliamentary Association for Music signed a resolution to maintain RPM in the case of records.

In response to those actions from the music industry, the FTC established a research group to investigate the resale issues in February 1997. The research group concluded its findings by stating that "there are few reasons to support maintaining RPM for copyrighted works, and the objective should be to eliminate it in the long run. However, considering the parties involved, an immediate elimination would cause problems" (Kinoshita 2003).

The FTC's recommendation was for the elimination of CD resales in the long run. To fight back against this recommendation, the music industry ramped up their lobbying and tried to win the favor of the public. In June 1997, the Parliamentary Conference for Music and Arts was created by lawmakers. They acted as representatives of the music industry in the political world. The industry also reached out to other similar industries such as book and newspaper publishers that were also facing the threat of having the resale clause eliminated, to form the Conference for RPM. In 1997, the Conference for RPM hold multiple events with both members from the industry and of the public, to garner support for the continuation of the resale law. The Parliamentary Conference for Music and Arts organized an emergency resolution in regard to continuing RPM for music copyrighted works in March 1998.

Due to the lobbying by the music industry, in March 1998, the FTC released a statement, stating that "while eliminating RPM would be favorable when considering the effects on competition, we must also consider the effects doing so will have on promoting culture and the spreading of said culture" and the FTC decided to "give more time to examine the issue." (Kinoshita 2003).

Further later, in 2001, when the FTC conducted a public survey regarding RPM on copyrighted works, an astounding 94.6% of respondents supported the continuation of RPM and this was the same for RPM for books, magazines, and newspapers. And to no surprise, when the FTC conducted an industry hearing on the matter, industry insiders expressed their support to the continuation of the RPM. Therefore, even with 64 consumer groups opposing RPM in March 2001, the government decided to continue RPM for copyrighted works for the foreseeable future.

3 Education

3.1 Music Taught in Compulsory Education

Including music studies as part of compulsory education is one of the key pillars of promoting and expanding the music industry. By having students get accustomed to music, it is expected that they will be consumers of music in the future. Not only that, students must be exposed to music from a young age to foster musical talents and future professional musicians, so there is also an educational value to it. From both viewpoints, music studies in compulsory education play a crucial part in the long-term growth of the music industry in Japan.

The constitution of Japan stipulates children's rights to education and obligation of their parents or guardians to have their children go to school. Compulsory education is provided to children between the ages of 6 and 15. During this 9-year period, children go to elementary school for the first 6 years and then to junior high school in the last 3 years. As the competent authority, the Ministry of Education, Culture, Sports, Science and Technology (hereinafter referred to as MEXT) announces the Curriculum Guidelines and updates it from time to time. These Guidelines define what should be taught in and how many hours should be spent on music classes at elementary, junior high, and high schools in Japan.

In terms of objectives of music education in compulsory education, the Guidelines state as follows for elementary and junior high schools:

> To encourage pupils to cultivate their sentiments, fundamental abilities for musical activities, a love for music as well as a sensitivity toward it, through music-making and appraising. (elementary schools) (MEXT-a)
>
> To encourage pupils to cultivate their sentiments, a love for music as well as enrich their sensitivity to music, develop fundamental abilities for musical activities and deepen understanding of music culture, through a wide variety of music-making and appraising activities. (junior high schools) (MEXT-b)

In terms of hours spent in compulsory education in Japan, music education has been emphasized less and less over time. According to new Curriculum Guidelines to be effective in 2020 at elementary schools and 2012 at junior high schools, students will be studying for 6,876 h during the 9-year compulsory education period. 364 h, or 5.3% of total, will be allocated for music classes. When the guideline was first set by new government after World War II, 490 h of total 6,799 h, or 7.2%, was assigned for music. In the long run, the share of music education among other subjects has decreased. In the whole history of post-war Japanese education, except one revision to the Curriculum Guidelines made in 1961, both the hours and share of music classes have continually decreased. In 1961, hours spent on music increased by 4.8% from 490 to 514 h. However, in the revision made in the following year, the number of hours was cut to 514, which was lower than the previous level. Since 1962, the hours allocated for music have declined three times; to 459 h in 1980, to 430 h in 1993, and then to 364 h in 2002.

The reason behind the decline of music education is the diversification of subjects. Currently, major subjects such as mathematics, Japanese, science, social studies, and English also have fewer hours allocated to them than before. In contrast, new subjects were introduced to the compulsory education system recently and their shares as part of the total curriculum have increased over time. One example is living environment studies, which were introduced to elementary schools in 1992 with 155 h. Ten years later, the allocation for this subject was almost doubled to 287 h. Another instance is integrated studies, which were introduced to both elementary and junior high schools in 2002 with 498 h. With this interdisciplinary and experiential learning, MEXT aims to allow pupils to proactively learn international affairs, information technology, environmental issues, social welfare among other up-to-date subjects. While the allocation for integrated studies was cut by 26% to 368 h in the transition period from 2011 to 2012, 655 h have been assigned to living environment studies and integrated studies since then. This is the key reason why the time for music education is shrunk along other key subjects.

If we consider the importance and influence of music studies in compulsory education in regard to the music industry in Japan, the decrease in overall lesson times of music classes in schools is indeed a troubling sign.

3.2 Music Education Promotion Act

To combat the declining lesson times of music classes in compulsory education, the National Conference for Music Education was established in 1987. Shibi Oku, a specialist in music education at Wakayama University, spoke at a conference in 1995 to encourage fellow educators in the music education field to come together to form a committee to push a law for the Promotion of Music Culture. In 1994, 7 years after the Conference was established, the Parliamentary Association for Music responded to the requests from the Conference and established the Committee for Music Education Promotion Act, which presented "suggestions to create an environment to promote music education" which were later used as the basis for the Music Promotion Act, passed in the same year.

The law stipulated that local municipalities must host musical performances, provide classes on music to the public as part of social education, and for schools to open their facilities to the public for music education so long as it did not impede with the learning environment for students. The law was not about music education for children, but for all citizens to have music as part of life-long learning, and it did nothing to solve the problem of the declining time of music education classes in compulsory education. Even the Parliamentary Association for Music was not able to find a way to increase lesson times in the curriculum itself.

4 The Issues Surrounding the Artist Management Industry: Five-Company Agreement

The creativity of an artist is the most important resource in the music industry and thus, laws in regards to artist management companies are vital to the well-being of the entire music industry.

In February 2018, the FTC's investigative commission presented their claims that restricting the transfer of individuals and professional entertainers was in violation of the Antimonopoly Act. The findings also cite the "Five-Company Agreement" antitrust issue that occurred in the film industry back in 1963. This chapter will begin by analyzing the Five-Company Agreement as the first step before getting into the issue of artist management.

The Five-Company Agreement was an agreement between five major film studios in Japan at the time. The agreement was that any actor signed with a major studio will not have his or her movie screened in any cinema affiliated with the major studio if they were to star in a movie with a nonmajor independent film studio. This made it virtually impossible for a movie star to sign a contract with other film studios than the one he or she has already signed with. The reasoning behind this agreement was to limit the poaching of movie stars, as the stars themselves were usually the deciding factor of whether people watched a particular film or not back then, and also to limit the poaching race to secure stars, which could lead to astronomical performance fees for actors from a studio. While this meant that actors were unable to maximize their economic opportunity to the fullest extent, because the film studios had so much more bargaining power than actors when it came to production, advertisement and distribution, most actors ended up staying with their respective film studios.

In 1957, another company joined the Five-Company Agreement and all the six major film studios refused to screen or distribute films created by an independent film studio who hired an actor that was signed with one of the major studios. According to Hoshino (2016), the independent film studio claimed that the Five-Company Agreement was in violation of the Antimonopoly Act and reported it to the FTC. In 1963, the FTC did admit that the Five-Company Agreement was in breach of Antimonopoly Act, but the authority decided not to investigate further as the major studios had already removed that particular clause out of the agreement by then.

4.1 *The Business Model of Artist Management in Japan*

In the entertainment industry, businesses operate on a very skewered structure where the success of a handful of hit movies and songs generate the majority of the profit. Therefore, the success of this industry lies in product portfolio management. If a producer is lucky enough to create a hit, they must then distribute that product through as many channels as possible to maximize the profit within the limited copyright duration of the work. Then the profits from that product are then reinvested in creating the next big hit, to eventually create a type of "catalogue" of intellectual property that can sustain and finance that entertainment company for years to come.

The artist management industry operates with the same structure. Of all the artists that belong to a management company, only a few if any have their breakout moment to rake in the profits. The profits that a popular artist makes are then reinvested into that artist or spread across the management company to recuperate costs from other artists. In the case of Japan, it is the management company that pays for the training of an artist by enrolling he or she in voice training classes and may even pay a monthly salary to him or her. Therefore, Japanese management companies have to collect a significant amount on their investments from their successful artists. And thus, the Japanese business model is structured with a high breakeven point with long-term investment returns, whereas in the USA, artists themselves usually pay for their own training and living costs and management agencies simply collect a small portion of the artist's earnings. American management companies have a business model that has a low breakeven point and is based on collecting commission fees.

One of the Japanese management companies I conducted a hearing on told me that their top 13% of registered artists made 102% of their operating income and the bottom 58% lost money, with the middle 29% of artists just breaking even. In the short run, it may seem like a sound business decision to cut off the loss-making artists and only focus on the moneymakers, but artists live in a competitive world where eventually their popularity will fade with time, so it is important for managers to keep their loss-making artists who may have their breakout moment in the future. Especially in the case of Japan, where the industry actively blocks the transfers of artists between agencies, management companies must cultivate and train their own stars of the future.

4.2 *Stage Names and Trademark*

Because Japanese management companies adopt a long-term investment model, the worst-case scenario that they all want to avoid at any cost is for their artists to jump ship to another management company just after they have their big break. However, because of the constitutional right of an individual to choose their careers and the principle of freedom of contract, it is impossible to keep a person tied to their job. One method Japanese management companies adopted to counter this situation is to give all of their artists a stage name, which the company then registers as a trademark of its own. Since the company owns the trademark, even if the artist tries to leave the agency, he or she will not be able to work using the stage name that they have used up until that point, essentially losing the marketing value that he or she previously had. This ensures that most artists are grounded in the agency that they first signed with.

There are cases of an artists' old management company registering an artist's real name as a trademark, then suing the new management company for using the artist's name after he or she has transferred to a new management agency. The courts ruled that the artist is allowed to use their own name in a scope that is not covered by the trademark or if the trademark expires (Intellectual Property High Court, Judgment, July 30, 2015). But there are also cases where artists are unable to use their own given name. In 2016, when a popular actress transferred to a new management company, she stopped using her stage name, which was also her real name, and began work using a new stage name. On inquiry, a patent office stated that her real name was not registered as a trademark, but perhaps there was a clause in the contract with her old management company preventing her from using her real name. Regardless, actions like these that restrict an artist's transfer by trademarking their name are a common practice in the industry and only surfaces to the public when such news of an artist being unable to use their name occurs.

4.3 Report on Competition Policies and Workforce by the FTC

In January 2018, the Asahi Shimbun, a newspaper, posted an article titled "Restriction against Entertainers' Freedom to Change Management Company 'may be Illegal': Fair Trade Commission to Announce" (Yajima 2018). In the following month, the FTC posted their investigative report about individuals who work on their own and this included not just artists, but also athletes, system engineers, journalists, designers, consultants etc., and analyzed the legality of their situation. But the way that the article emphasizes "artists" in its header and in its writing was a way to play on public curiosity regarding the issue.

As I quoted in the beginning of this chapter, the FTC's report concluded that the "methods of restricting transferring may be illegal" and did not go any further. However, while the article simply acted as a warning to the reader, there were some points in the report that may be beneficial to artists. The FTC stated that regardless of whether an artist transfers or not, there is no guarantee to that the costs associated with the training of the artist will be recuperated anyway. Therefore, the paper concludes that the very nature of investing in the artists is a risk on its own and it should be unfair to virtually prohibit an artist from changing his or her management company.

More so, in February 2018, Kyodo News reported that after the FTC report was published, the most powerful industry body of artist management companies,

Japan Association of Music Enterprises (hereinafter referred to as JAME), revised its contract template and plans to remove the clause that grants a management company an option to extend the contract by a year (Kyodo 2018). At the same time, JAME also released a statement in March to counter some of the claims made in the FTC report. JAME argued that the relationship between an artist and the management company is different from that of a contractor and employer, and it is inappropriate to treat artists as independent contractors.

The important point to note is the debate whether the power lies with the management company or with the artist. The FTC report argues that the power lies in the management company and JAME refutes that it does not. In reality, it is a case by case situation. A new and unproven artist is more dependent on his or her management while receiving lessons and a stipend and has practically no bargaining power. But once an artist breaks and becomes popular, he or she will then gain power to negotiate better terms or even change the contract to suit his or her way. However, in general, management companies still do have ways to solidify their power and could still remain a threat with a considerable amount of influence. The FTC report admitted that it had not looked into particular companies or industries but will need more investigation before they make any decisions about the artist management industry.

5 Policy Revisions Regarding Music Copyright Collection

5.1 The Birth of the Copyright Management Service Act

In 1928, the Berne Convention was revised, and Japan followed in its wake and made revisions to reflect the changes in 1931 to protect performance rights as well. This phenomenon will eventually be known throughout Japan as "Plage Furore." According to Ohie (1992), Wilhelm Plage, a German national representing the audio copyright collecting in Japan for composers from England, France, Germany, Austria, and Italy, confronted NHK, Japan's then only broadcaster, to pay for the performance rights to the recordings they played. Plage charged a yearly fee of 7,200 JPY and NHK complied. Since NHK only paid 1,489 JPY to Japanese copyright holders, Plage's fee was an astounding figure. The following year, Plage billed NHK for 18,000 JPY for the performance rights. NHK refused the payment and it resulted in no foreign music being played in Japan for a year.

Plage also acted as an intermediary for Japanese composers by collecting royalties in Europe when Japanese music was performed. AntiPlage sentiments rose for this side of Plage's business as well, and in 1939, the Japanese government introduced laws to make the copyright intermediary services businesses based on registration with the government. As antiPlage entities, two organizations sprung up from these laws and were awarded licenses to provide copyright intermediary services as soon as within five days of their establishment following the new government policy. Meanwhile, Plage's request for a license was immediately rejected.

According to Ando (2016), the reason why the government kept rejecting Plage's application was because of their desire to create one governing body to oversee all of the copyrights. And thus, since 1939, all music copyrights have been handled by JASRAC.

However, in 1990, the monopoly that JASRAC held over the copyrights became a social issue. In March 1998, a famous musician Ryuichi Sakamoto, wrote an article in a national newspaper saying "monopolizing the market, JASRAC cannot adjust to changing styles of the business and \readjust its fees and it is unable to respond to meet the demand of users" (Sakamoto 1998). In his post, Sakamoto wrote that he participated and offered testimony to the Copyright Council at Agency for Cultural Affairs, a government arm overseeing copyright issues, in regards to the matter. The Council stated in January 2000, that the Copyright Management Service Act needed to be reviewed and recommended that the permission method should be replaced by a registration method. As a result, in 2001, the Copyright Management Service Act was revised to a registration-based system and the permission-based system was scrapped. With the birth of the revised Copyright Management Service Act, other than JASRAC, E-License, and Japan Rights Clearance (hereinafter referred to as JRC) also became new copyright collecting agencies.

5.2 The Cease and Desist Order by the FTC to JASRAC

The collection of broadcasting fees is a big moneymaker for copyright owners. Because it is a very profitable opportunity for the copyright owner, it is just as profitable for the agent that represents them. In 2009, JASRAC collected 27 billion JPY from broadcasters. This was 25% of JASRAC's 109 billion JPY operating profit and was their biggest source of revenue. It was even larger than the 17 billion JPY they made from copyrights from CDs.

In February 2009, the FTC claimed that JASRAC's contracts with broadcasters prevented other players from entering the copyright collecting business and issued a cease and desist order against JASRAC. JASRAC and broadcasters had an agreement where the broadcasters will pay 1.5% of their broadcasting earnings to JASRAC as royalties in exchange for being able to use any song of which the copyright was managed by JASRAC. JASRAC will then pay the copyright owners their share of the royalties collected based on the number of plays of the copyrighted work on the air. This structure was worked out when JASRAC was the only player in the market and represented virtually all musical works. But 2001 brought new entrants into the market, and JASRAC's business model became a problem. The problem was that JASRAC charged flat a 1.5% fee to the broadcasters regardless of the number of songs the broadcasters choose to play or the number of times they choose to play it. This means that if a broadcaster wanted to use music from another collecting agency, they will still have to pay JASRAC their 1.5% fee and pay additional fees to the other copyright collecting agencies. Therefore, JASRAC's flat fee acted as a deterrent for broadcasters to sign with other copyright collecting agencies and the

FTC cited this blanket agreement between JASRAC and broadcasters as an obstacle for new entrants entering the market.

5.3 *Agreement Between Stakeholders*

After receiving a cease and desist order from the FTC in February 2009, JASRAC appealed to the FTC. It claimed that it had not made any anticompetitive demands to broadcasters, that the FTC had not provided an alternative solution for broadcasting fees to be calculated, that it was impossible for JASRAC to arbitrarily change the contract without the cooperation of the broadcasters, and that it was only natural that broadcasters will have to pay additional fees to use songs that were not in the copyright collecting coverage of JASRAC and were managed by other companies. After a 3-year hearing process, the FTC decided to retract their cease and desist order, an outcome that shocked many people.

Claiming that FTC's retraction of their cease and desist order was unjust, a new entrant copyright collecting agency, E-License, took the FTC to court. The trial went all the way to the Supreme Court, which ruled on April 2015 that JASRAC's blanket agreement with broadcasters was anticompetitive because the agreement made it extremely difficult for new collecting agencies to enter the market. Based on that judgment, the cease and desist order was reissued, and at the same time, the copyright collecting agencies JASRAC, E-License, JRC, public broadcaster NHK, and the Japan Commercial Broadcasters Association formed an investigative commission to discuss the best method to calculate the usage ratio of music. In September 2015, the commission agreed to calculate the broadcasting fees as multiplied by the duration the song was played on a pro rata basis.

From 1939 until 2001, JASRAC held a monopoly over the music copyright collecting market. And while new entrants were theoretically able to enter the business, due to the law revisions in 2001, it was not until 2009 that they were practically able to even out the playing field in terms of broadcasting fees. The policy changes were brought about this time due to the widespread use of the Internet, the demands by artists to generate royalties on the internet, and JASRAC's inability to accommodate the artists' requests. In regard to music copyright collection, the development of technology was what led to the changes in policies.

6 Conclusion

In conclusion, what we can observe from the changes in policies regarding music content is that technological advancements have always been the catalyst for a lot of these changes. Even when technological changes may not play the melody that directly affects the policies; they play a thorough bass that defines the background of policymaking.

The Copyright Management Service Act was established to accommodate the widespread use of the internet and a decision was made that one music copyright collecting agency was not enough to handle all the requests by artists and thus, the law allowed new music copyright collecting agencies to enter the market. For other policy changes, much of it started as an antiPlage initiative when Japan was in the middle of its exclusionist policy, but even those were originally related to technological advancements. Plage was said to have set his eyes on the Japanese market because Japan was still struggling to adapt to the new technology known as radio. He took advantage of Japan's lack of knowledge regarding the radio for his business opportunities.

The reason why the music industry prefers to operate with the RPM in the same way that newspapers, magazines, and books are sold is due to the structure of its business. The marginal manufacturing costs to create audio content are incredibly low. Even with physical audio disks, the costs are not high, and when you consider digital copies, the costs become extremely low. In that situation, the natural laws of economics will bring down the retail value of the audio content unless a RPM is set. As digitization further brings down the marginal manufacturing costs of audio content, the need for the RPM to maintain a high retail value will become greater.

Furthermore, artist management companies trying to restrict the transfer of their artists are based on the core structure of their business. In the business of content creation, an individual artist's creativity is the basis for competition and the supplier of that is individual. But companies cannot own individuals like capital assets in other businesses. With this business structure, even if the distribution of content was in a state of oligopoly, the producers downstream had more bargaining power than the artists themselves. However, the split up of the most popular boy band in Japan last year from their management company and the members starting their own internet streaming activities proves that the distribution channels for artists are becoming more plentiful with the development of technology and that their bargaining power is also being influenced by the internet.

In regard to the decline in allocated class times for music classes in compulsory education, the development in technology will not apply in this case. However, if the core curriculums are going to be changed in the future to a more STEM-focused curriculum, then it is expected that curriculum like music classes will continue to decline in terms of attendance and acceptance. But in recent years, some argue that "creative" subjects like the arts are needed to foster creativity that will apply with the STEM subjects, and there are groups pushing for a STEM + Art to form a STEAM curriculum (Eger 2011). Nobel laureates Albert Einstein and Werner Karl Heisenberg both played the violin and piano, respectively. If the demand for STEAM picks up pace, then we could expect further interest and demand for music classes and there may be policy changes that will accommodate this rise in demand in the future.

References

Ando K (2016) The current situation and issues on music copyright collecting agencies: why can no one abolish the monopoly position of JASRAC? (in Japanese). Toyo Hogaku, pp 162–134

Cabinet Office (1995) Economic and social plan for structural reform (in Japanese)

Eger JM (2011) National science foundation slowly turning STEM to STEAM. https://www.huffingtonpost.com/john-m-eger/national-science-foundati_b_868449.html. Accessed 12 Oct 2018

Hoshino Y (2016) Why entertainers can get sidelined (in Japanese). Rokusaisya, Tokyo

Japanese Society for Rights of Authors, Composers and Publishers (2009) A hearing request to the Fair Trade Commission (in Japanese). https://www.jasrac.or.jp/ejhp/release/2009/0227.html. Accessed 5 October 2018

Kinoshita O (2003) The RPM for copyrighted works and the chronology of that system of Japan (in Japanese). J Law Polit Sociol 76(1):281–334

Kyodo News (2018) Restriction of entertainers' transfer to be revised: JAME to amend contract template (in Japanese)

MEXT-a. The curriculum guidelines of elementary school (in Japanese). MEXT

MEXT-b. The curriculum guidelines of lower secondary school (in Japanese). MEXT

Ohie S (1992) Plage furor (in Japanese). In A. G. Faculty of Law, Record and Laws

Sakamoto R (1998) Change monopolistic management of musical copyright (in Japanese). The Asahi Shimbun

Wada T (1994) Trade association activities and antimonopoly law (in Japanese). Econ Rev

Yajima D (2018) Restricting transfer of entertainer "may be Illegal": fair trade commission to announce (in Japanese). Asahi Shimbun

Copyright Clearance

Yu Terada

1 Introduction

Triggered by digitization and information technology, content distribution in Japan is becoming rapidly active. Even broadcast programs, which have an important market scale as video content, have seen significantly expanding opportunities for use (multiuse), as viewing them through delivery services has become common (Ministry of Internal Affairs and Communications, hereinafter referred to as MIC 2018).

Since the past, broadcast programs have been called a "bundle of rights" (National Association of Commercial Broadcasters in Japan 2018). This is because, in addition to programs themselves being copyrighted works, there are a countless number of rights included in programs, including many copyrighted works. To use a broadcast program, it is necessary to obtain permission from copyright owners. To distribute programs, transaction costs for this "copyright clearance" are essential.

Schwan Inc., founded in 1988 and celebrating its 32th anniversary this year, is a company that specializes in copyright clearance of video copyrights, such as broadcast programs. Following changes in the viewing environment, it has transformed how copyright clearance is performed.

Thus, from the perspective of actual copyright clearance, this paper investigates what hinders the smooth distribution of broadcast programs, and among them, what is unique to the digital network era.

First, in Sect. 2, as a means of sorting out the current situation, we reflect on the path of expansion and institutional improvement of opportunities to use contents, such as broadcast programs. How broadcast programs have come to be put to multiuse,

Y. Terada (✉)
Schwan Inc, Tokyo, Japan
e-mail: yu@schwan.co.jp

M. Sugaya (ed.), *Perspectives on the Japanese Media and Content Policies*,
Advances in Information and Communication Research 2,
https://doi.org/10.1007/978-981-15-4704-1_11

revision of the Copyright Act and Broadcasting Act in relation to copyright clearance, copyright management organizations, and a centralized management system are discussed.

Next, in Sect. 3, we examine the "walls" in copyright clearance when distributing broadcast programs. "Walls" that are encountered in actual work, such as when submitting applications to copyright management organizations, performing individual clearance, handling unknown copyrighted works, and those for which clearance judgment is difficult, are discussed.

Finally, in Sect. 4, we look at trends in challenges presented in actual copyright clearance work of broadcast programs as well as proposed measures in relation to the "wall" of copyright clearance and the digital network era. First, we categorize the trends in delivered contents in actual copyright clearance work and review worrisome challenges for each type of content, using model organization by Associate Professor Tatsuhiro Ueno of Waseda University's Faculty of Law as support. On top of this, we will also consider solutions that can be realized in actual work.

The abovementioned material includes many topics for discussion, such as future revision of laws. Facts have been organized, with the desire to overcome "walls," even by just a little bit, in actual work. This is because there is the fear that solutions must be drummed up somehow in the information explosion era caused by digital networking, otherwise, it will be too late.

2 Expansion of Opportunities for Using Contents and the History of System Development

For broadcasting organizations such as TV stations, one of the factors that inhibits the smooth distribution of broadcast programs is copyright clearance.

Since copyright clearance is essential to the legal use of programs, this challenge has existed since 30 years ago. As usage opportunities for programs have increased due to the development of digitization and networking, copyright clearance costs have increased more and more as well. Regardless of the fact that laws have been revised and content distribution platforms developed, and the "wall" of copyright clearance not resolved, why do costs continue to increase?

This is because conventional copyright clearance methods are overwhelmingly unsuited to explosive expansion of information volume and its distribution means.

To sort out the circumstances up until now, we will look back on (1) expansion of opportunities for use of contents, (2) broadcast programs processing and revision of laws (Copyright Act), (3) the same with Broadcasting Act, and (4) commissioning businesses and centralized management systems.

2.1 *Expansion of Opportunities for Use of Contents*

Multiuse of contents such as broadcast programs, etc. has expanded in an extended manner due to the evolution of media and changes in viewing environments. Broadcast programs require copyright clearance for each new mode of use. Over the past 30 years, how have new uses and copyright clearance of programs changed? We will take a look back on this, focusing on key topics.

- 1988: Opening of the "Kawasaki City Museum"

In 1988, the Kawasaki City Museum (Kawasaki Prefecture) (Kawasaki City Museum 2013) opened the first video library in Japan (Kawasaki City Museum 2013). This represented a collection and publishing of documentaries that won awards at the "Age of Regionalism" Video Festival (photos from 1988 are introduced on the Japan Broadcasting Corporation (hereinafter referred to as NHK) site (NHK 2018c). The first business that Schwan Inc. contracted after it was founded was copyright clearance to store and publish these programs. The programs included many delicate contents on challenges encountered by local companies, and there were programs that could be stored but for which permission to publish could not be obtained. (Even today, the "Age of Regionalism" Video Festival is ongoing albeit in a different format ("Age of Regionalism" Video Festival Executive Committee 2011), but the video library is not made public).

In the middle of the bubble economy, local public organizations established public cultural facilities in various locations through cultural administration. There were some who voiced that public video libraries are necessary, and based on a partial revision of the Broadcasting Act in 1989, the institution of Broadcast Programming Center of Japan for gathering, storing, and publishing broadcast programs was defined. In 1991, the Broadcast Library (Yokohama City, Kanagawa Prefecture) for receiving programs from NHK and commercial broadcasting stations (Broadcast Programming Center of Japan 2000) was established.

On the other hand, within TV stations, tapes were used repetitively during the period when VTRs were expensive (NHK 2018b); thus, there are no many videos of programs from the 1960s to 1980s. In the 1990s, video archives were built within commercial television stations and databases for program information, and contracts were also enriched (NHK implemented a database in 1985 (NHK 2018d)).

Schwan Inc. cooperated in various ways with advice on rights when the abovementioned Library and station archives were launched as well as with the organization of resources and information.

- 2003: Start of NHK's Program Publication Library

50 years after starting TV broadcasting, NHK established NHK Archives in Kawaguchi City, Saitama Prefecture as a base for storing, utilizing, and publishing past programs (NHK 2018c). 2,000 programs were released to the public, as part of

the Program Publication Library (jointly operated with Saitama Prefecture). Because of a new usage method, copyright clearance started off by trial and error.

Today, in 2018, there are 900,000 programs stored in the Archives, and 6,000 TV and radio programs are published, including many valuable programs that can be screened only within the Archives building, such as documentaries related to wars.

Afterward, opportunities for secondary use of programs expanded, from the development of videograms (around 2006, the core of the market changed from VHS to DVD (Japan Video Software Association 2018)), to sales of domestic programs (CS, BS) and overseas sales. In particular, for videograms, the scope of sales is large if they become a hit once, and copyright clearance fees can be recovered. Departments that carry out secondary use of programs at various broadcasting stations have expanded their business operations. With regard to license conditions and usage rates that differ for each medium used, copyright holders, performers, rights organizations, and broadcasting stations have created rules while negotiating on a case-by-case basis.

- 2008: Start of paid delivery service NHK On Demand (hereinafter referred to as NOD) for Japan (NHK 2018a)

As the multiuse of TV programs progressed, commercial television stations started video-on-demand distribution. Due to a revision of the Broadcasting Act in 2007, NHK enabled programs that had already been broadcast to be provided to the general public, based on the conditions of "non-profit management" and "separating accounting for this service from reception fees" (Tokoro 2009).

To prepare 1,200 programs at the start of NOD and to provide a varied lineup, from documentaries such as NHK specials, to morning serial TV dramas and long-running period dramas, copyright clearance was carried out. At the time, both NHK and commercial broadcasting stations moved forward with copyright clearance while developing operational rules for "distribution" that differ from "broadcasting".

Today, when combining the "Show Catch-up Service" where programs are distributed immediately after they are broadcast, and the "Choice Library" of selections from the archives, approximately 6,000 programs and new features can be viewed at any time (as of December 2017) (NHK 2018c).

Around 2013, video distribution services expanded rapidly. Billing methods also diversified, and contents started to include TV programs, movies, internet videos, etc. OTT-business operators serving the global market, such as Netflix and Amazon, also became prominent (Murakami 2017).

- 2018: Today

TVer (TVer 2015), which was launched in 2015 based on coordination among the five key commercial broadcasting stations in Tokyo, is a free catch-up service for TV programs with advertisements. In July 2018, the TVer app exceeded 13 million downloads (Fuji Television Network, Inc. 2018), establishing the roots for a custom of making distribution of TV programs available on official sites (MIC 2018).

Since before TVer was formed, each station had carried out its own unique method of providing opportunities for viewers to catch up on shows and had been accumulating know-how on how to carry out copyright clearance within an extremely short clearance time. Since there are multiple platforms today, all stations are required to carry out complicated paperwork, in terms of submitting applications to rights organizations and making complex calculations for allocating usage fees.

In addition, a variety of discussions are conducted today on simultaneous distribution. Although NHK wishes to implement simultaneous distribution at all times, this requires revising the Broadcasting Act, and NHK has been experimenting with the simultaneous distribution since FY (Fiscal Year) 2015 (Murakami 2017). On the other hand, commercial broadcasting stations have been experimenting with simultaneous distribution of some programs, but a business model for simultaneous distribution has not been built, and they have not reached judgments on how to tackle this issue. In Review Committee on Promoting the Production and Distribution of Broadcast Contents by the MIC, it has been deemed that future examinations are required by NHK and commercial broadcasting stations as to how copyright clearance of constant and simultaneous distribution should be conducted.

2.2 Clearance of Broadcast Programs and Revisions of Laws: Copyright Act

To adapt to the evolution of technology, limitation rules in the Copyright Act have been individually and repeatedly revised. Among these revisions, those in recent years that have impacted copyright clearance of broadcast programs are as follows.

2009: Measure to promote smooth use of copyright materials utilizing the internet, etc.
"Smoother use when the right holder is unknown".

2012: Revision of limitation rules on copyrights, etc. (smoother use of copyrighted works).
Development of rules related to so-called "accompanying copyrighted works".

2018: Support of development of digitization and networking.
Development of flexible rights limitation rules.

- 2009 Revision of the Copyright Act

If carrying out secondary use of past broadcast programs, etc. on the internet, the unknown whereabouts of the copyright holder or performer (actor) may inhibit the ability to gain permission. This revision aims to resolve this point (Agency for Cultural Affairs 2010).

In the ruling system in the Copyright Act before this revision (system in which rulings are made by the Commissioner for Cultural Affairs in cases where the whereabouts of the copyright holder are unknown, etc.), there were issues such as (1) performers not being addressed and (2) the lengthy time it takes until ruling results are presented.

As a result,

(1) Even in cases where the whereabouts of the performer are unknown, the ruling system can be used.
(2) Requirements (considerable effort) are clarified (*specified by Cabinet order).
(3) By depositing a deposit when submitting an application for a ruling, provisional use is recognized even before ruling results are presented (created based on data from the Agency for Cultural Affairs (2010)).

After this revision, the copyright clearance team for NOD has been able to use the ruling system for unidentified performers.

- 2012 Revision of the Copyright Act

A large impact on actual copyright clearance work for broadcast programs was the fact that a certain number of specific examples were indicated as judgment standards as to whether the so-called "accompanying copyrighted works" (use of ancillary applicable copyrighted material) is illegal (Agency for Cultural Affairs 2012a).

In this revision, with regard to development of rules related to so-called "accompanying copyrighted works," etc., restricted rights provisions that comprehensively specify the purpose of use and requirements to a certain extent, as described in (1)–(4) below, were established, to clarify that while the use of copyrighted material that does not unfairly impair the gains of the copyright holder is formally illegal, it does not infringe on copyrights, etc. (created based on data from Agency for Cultural Affairs (2012b)).

(1) Use of ancillary applicable copyrighted material
(2) Use in the process of examination
(3) Use for provision in development of technology or experiments for practical application
(4) Use for information clearance required in preparations for information provision using information and communications technology.

In particular, (1) is important in actual copyright clearance work for broadcast programs. In program production, for example, when recording a video, a copyrighted character may be reproduced in the background. Although the use of copyrighted works that appear in such a way in the background do not normally unfairly impair the gains of the copyright holder, there was a chance of this being questioned as an infringement of copyright.

In cases of secondary use of programs in which such copyrighted works appear, normally, one much choose whether to give up, obtain permission from the right holder by paying some fees or cut out the scene in which the copyrighted work appears. The fact that concrete examples are presented in this revision was a large help in that production sites are now able to have definite judgment criteria regarding infringement risks.

- 2018 Revision of the Copyright Act

Although this revision has four main points, the one that relates to copyright clearance is the point that flexible restricted rights provisions were developed for certain uses of copyrighted works, etc. that do not negatively affect the market for the copyrighted work, etc., so that flexible approaches can be made to the development, etc. of information and communication technology (Agency for Cultural Affairs 2018a). Specifically, as indicated below, flexible provisions that are appropriate for types of actions that do not normally impair the gains of right holders ((1) and (2) below), and types of actions that cause a minor disadvantage to right holders ((3) below) were developed.

(1) Use of which the purpose is not to enjoy the ideas or emotions expressed in the copyrighted work
(2) Use, etc., that is ancillary to the usage of the copyrighted work in a computer
(3) Minor use, etc., that is ancillary to information clearance by a computer and provision of results of such clearance.

The three "tiers" of classification corresponding to the extent of disadvantage to the right holder and the scope covered under "flexible restricted rights provisions" are indicated in the Agency for Cultural Affairs' materials related to the revision of the Act (Created based on data from Agency for Cultural Affairs (2018b)).

The following three themes are being reviewed as ideals for the copyright system in the future (Agency for Cultural Affairs Chief Cabinet Secretary Copyright Section 2018).

(1) Verification projects for consolidating rights information for contents
(2) Ruling system
(3) Extended collective licensing.

These themes are discussed in further detail together with their challenges in Sect. 4.

2.3 *Clearance of Broadcast Programs and Revision of Laws: Broadcasting Act*

Among the revisions to the Broadcasting Act in recent years, the following also have impacts on actual copyright clearance work.

2010: Revision to organize/rationalize systems that support the development of digitization in the communications and broadcasting field.

2014: Expansion of NHK's internet utilization services.

- 2010 Revision of the Broadcasting Act

This revision is a "revision to organize and rationalize systems that support the development of digitization in the "communications and broadcasting field," and is normally known as the "communications/broadcast convergence legislation." This is the first revision of communication and broadcasting laws in 60 years (MIC 2015). Based on this, the rights of broadcasting organizations in the Copyright Act were reexamined in the revision to the Copyright Act in 2012 (Kimizuka 2016).

- 2014 Revision of the Broadcasting Act

Due to this revision, NHK defined its own internet utilization services, and based on "implementation criteria" for which approval was obtained from the MIC, it became possible to promptly and flexibly deliver (1) broadcast programs that were "already broadcast," (2) broadcast programs "currently being broadcast," and even broadcast programs "before broadcast" (MIC 2015). Up until then, services utilizing the internet were positioned to complement the original broadcasting business of public broadcasting. However, as the development of social infrastructure for communications progressed, implementation of simultaneous delivery of programs during large-scale disasters became recognized.

Currently, at NHK, experiments on simultaneous distribution targeting limited audiences are being carried out, such as of breaking news, the World Cup and Winter Olympics, but regular simultaneous distribution is not recognized. On the other hand, there are no restrictions in the Broadcasting Act on whether private broadcasting companies can implement internet services. Thus, private broadcasting companies have already started to implement the simultaneous distribution of high school baseball and some programs on economic information, etc. (Murakami 2017).

One of the reasons that broadcasting organizations give for simultaneous broadcasting not being carried out up until now is copyright clearance. Since 2016, the MIC has established the Review Committee on Promoting the Production and Distribution of Broadcast Contents in the Information and Communications Policy sectional meeting of the Information and Communications Council and has been carrying out discussions involving broadcasting organizations, right holders, and knowledgeable persons (MIC 2016).

2.4 Copyright Management Organizations and Centralized Control Systems

Copyright management organizations (copyright management businesses, etc.) are organizations that are registered with the Agency for Cultural Affairs based on the Act on Copyright, etc. Management Service (formerly Intermediary Business Act) (as of April 2018, there are a total of 27 such businesses (Agency for Cultural Affairs 2018c)). Based on trust agreements or mandate contracts (based on intermediation or a proxy) with consignors, centralized management is carried out by having the organizations aggregate various copyrighted works, etc. as shown in Fig. 1 and serving as the contact window for relevant parties, for the convenience of right holders as well as the users of their copyrighted materials, etc.

Copyright management organizations include the following, for example (Kanai and Tatsumura 2011; Nomura Research Institute, Ltd. 2016):

Language	The Japan Writers' Association Writers Guild of Japan Japan Writers Guild
Music	Japanese Society for Rights of Authors, Composers, and Publishers (hereinafter referred to as JASRAC) NexTone
Records	The Recording Industry Association of Japan.
Performance	Center for Performers' Rights Administration (hereinafter referred to as CPRA)

As trends in recent years, the audiovisual Rights management association (hereinafter referred to as "aRma") (aRma 2018) was established, and unification and systemization of copyright clearance contact window functions for performers have been carried out. Reinforcement of centralized management has also been accelerating, such as through the joint establishment of the Copyright Data Clearinghouse by content providers' and right holders' organizations (Copyright Data Clearinghouse 2018), with the objective of creating data on the state of use of copyrighted works.

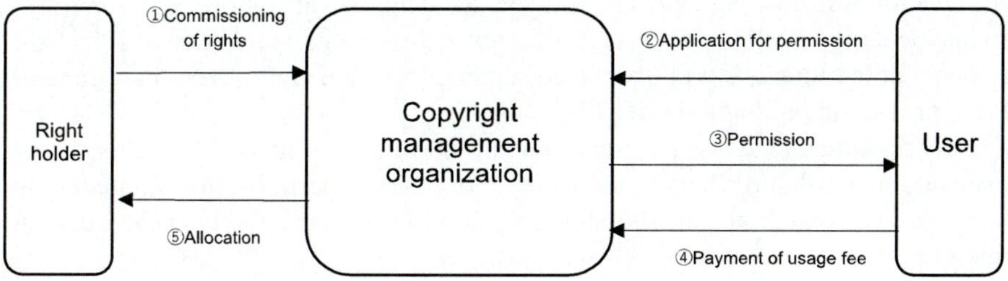

Fig. 1 Conceptual diagram of centralized management (Interim Summary of Expert Group in Subcommittee on Centralized Management of Rights of Copyright Council Created by revising July 1999 Materials by CRIC (2018))

3 What is the "wall" Known as Copyright Clearance?

In the previous two sections, we have looked at approaches toward expanding opportunities for use of contents and the development of systems. At the same time, in the multiuse of broadcast programs, copyright clearance rules differ for each form of use in the value chain. Although there may be cases where copyright clearance is carried out on a case-by-case process for each form of use, there are also others where one faces complicated copyright clearance in an attempt to cover all forms of use and obtain rights.

If the complicated copyright clearance rules and increased costs of clearance work are thought of as a "wall," what kind of wall, concretely, is it? (Fukui 2014).

As examples where the cost of copyright clearance work is extremely high, there are (1) submission of application to copyright management organizations and individual clearance; (2) approaches toward unclear copyrighted works, etc.; and (3) cases where clearance judgment is difficult. We will look at how these are implemented in terms of actual work.

3.1 Submission of Application to Copyright Management Organizations and Individual Clearance

As we discussed in the preceding section, copyright clearance has become extremely simple due to centralized management by copyright management organizations. However, individual negotiations with right holders referred to as nonmanaged (nonmembers, outsiders), who do not commit to copyright management organizations, arise. As usage opportunities have increased, the number of submission of applications to copyright management organizations has also increased, but the number of individual clearance items has also increased proportionally.

Currently, most broadcast programs are centrally managed, and for internet distribution of programs that have already been broadcast and that are currently being broadcast, operative procedures are being carried out for actual work, centering on comprehensive license agreements with broadcasting organizations and copyright management organizations. Figures 2 and 3 show the essential operation of copyright clearance in the music and performance sectors, in which centralized management has progressed in particular (MIC 2018).

If distributing broadcast programs on the internet (Archive/VOD) after being broadcast, or distributing them on the internet for a certain period of time immediately after broadcast (catch-up, missed shows), this kind of operation is carried out, in principle.

In the future, if simultaneous (and regular) broadcast and distribution are initiated, it is necessary to carry out an enormous amount of distribution clearance in a short period of time, making it unrealistic. As a result, the creation of new rules is sought after.

Right Type	Right holder	Law and actual state	Broadcast (Example of initial terrestrial broadcast)	Internet distribution (Example of non-simultaneous distribution such as VOD)
Copyright	**Composer/lyricist**	Copyright Act	Right of public transmission	Right of public transmission
	JASRAC NexTone, etc.	Actual operation	Blanket permission (Various broadcasting organizations)	Blanket permission (Various broadcasting organizations)
Neighboring right	**Record producer/ Record performer (audio)**	Copyright Act	Right to remuneration	Right to make transmittable
	Recording Industry Association of Japan CPRA, etc.	Actual operation	Blanket permission (NHK / commercial broadcasters)	Blanket permission (Various broadcasting organizations)

Fig. 2 Principle operation of copyright clearance in the music industry

Right Type	Right holder	Law and actual state	Broadcast (Example of initial terrestrial broadcast)	Internet distribution (Example of non-simultaneous distribution such as VOD)
Neighboring right	**Performer (visual)**	Copyright Act	Broadcasting right	Right to make transmittable
	aRma, etc.	Actual operation	Individual permission (Production company⇔ broadcasting organization)	Individual permission (aRma⇔broadcasting organization)

Fig. 3 Principle operation of copyright clearance in the performing industrys

- Clearance of music

– Copyright clearance of lyricists and composers

Lyricists and composers who create music (copyrighted works) possess copyright.

Broadcasting organizations obtain permission related to broadcasting by preliminarily concluding annual comprehensive license agreements with JASRAC and NexTone, which are music copyright management organizations (MIC 2018). In other words, theme songs and BGM used in programs and can be used freely if they are songs managed by JASRAC, etc. Even with regard to distribution (catch-up/VOD), licensing has been obtained since comprehensive agreements are concluded preliminarily with JASRAC for each service (consultations are underway with NexTone).

Depending on the song, however, there are many cases where subdivided rights for broadcasting are entrusted to JASRAC, but those for distribution are not. In actual work, it is necessary to confirm the state of rights for each song in the JASRAC database when distributing.

– Copyright clearance for phonogram producers and phonogram performers

Clearance of music does not only apply to lyricists and composers. Record producers who create records (master disks) onto which music is fixed and phonograph performers who perform music on such records have neighboring rights. If a record (sound source such as a CD) is used as a theme song or BGM of a program, copyright clearance of the record producer and record performer is also necessary.

As with songs, comprehensive license agreements are concluded beforehand between broadcast organizations and recording associations/CPRA) regarding broadcast and distribution (catch-up/VOD). Accordingly, broadcast can be used freely if within the scope contracted with recording associations/CPRA.

On the other hand, with regard to nonmanaged (outsider) commercial records that are not managed by recording associations or the CPRA, it is necessary for the broadcasting organization to individually obtain permission from the right holder when distribution. In terms of actual work, when distributing a BGM record for which confirmation was not necessary for broadcasting, it is necessary to investigate whether the record is outside the control of recording associations. This work is extremely complicated, due to the fact that not all song/CD information remain from the time that broadcast programs were produced. If simultaneous restreaming is to be carried out, major creation of rules must be carried out, otherwise, such works will not be cleared.

- Clearance of performers (video)

Performers appearing in program videos possess neighboring rights, requiring copyright clearance.

When broadcasting, it is common for broadcasting organizations to carry out appearance negotiations for each program with the individual productions with which performers are affiliated and obtain permission. For internet distribution (catch-up/VOD), applications are commonly submitted as an organization to aRma, which is the centralized contact window for secondary use (differs partially between NHK and private broadcasting).

However, for nonmanaged performers (outsiders) of which management is not commissioned to aRma, separate copyright clearance is required.

Currently, actual application work is extensive, such as submitting applications for multiple forms of use for the same program and submitting them to multiple platforms even for internet distribution.

At the moment, aRma does not officially carry out copyright clearance of simultaneous distribution, since the simultaneous distribution of TV programs is in the experimental stage.

- Challenge of individual clearance of outsiders

Presently, even in copyright clearance of internet distribution (catch-up/VOD) of broadcast programs, there are cases where record companies and performers must be investigated and processed separately.

In the case of video performances, payment procedures are made after individually contacting production companies and obtaining understanding. For production companies that are prudent when it comes to internet distribution, it may take a considerable amount of time up until permission is obtained. In cases such as old programs, etc., it is often found that performers have changed production companies and it is difficult to track them down.

For music clearance, it takes time to investigate whether a performer is outside the management of JASRAC, etc. and whether he/she is outside the management of record companies. It is difficult to establish contact with Indies performers, etc. who are not entrusted to record companies, and there are also cases where the clearance deadline is not met. For overseas LP records that are not released in Japan, it may also be difficult to determine the record company name.

When clearance of simultaneous (and regular) distribution using current operational rules as described above is carried out, it is inevitable that complicated work is necessary for a short period of time, both beforehand and afterward.

3.2 Approaches to Copyrighted Works, etc. With Unknown Right Holders

Copyrights for which the right holder cannot be specified are referred to as "copyrighted works with unknown right holders" and "orphan works." There are more copyrighted works with unknown right holders than one generally thinks there are, and the use of orphan works is a major issue throughout the world. Then, a system to prevent the hoarding of copyrighted works due to reasons such as right holders being unknown, etc., and to protect the gains of right holders by making users deposit compensation becomes necessary (Nakayama 2014). Even in Japan, in cases where clearance is carried out for a massive amount of simultaneous (regular) delivery of broadcast programs, how to perform copyright clearance of copyrighted works with unclear right holders is a large issue.

Complex cases that are encountered in the clearance of broadcast programs include the following examples.

Although the name of the author is known, due to his/her death, the rights successor is unknown.

- There is no song information due to the program being old, and the BGM song is used in such a way that it cannot be detected even by using fingerprinting (there is overlapping narration, etc.).

- Even though a song as part of location sound is of a level where it can be well heard, the song title, etc., cannot be determined.
- Contact information for a performer who appears in an old program is unclear, due to retirement or closure of his/her production company.
- CD information, etc. for a program is not known, and although the copyright for a famous piece of classical music is P.D. (public domain), it is impossible to pinpoint the performing orchestra (rights have not been extinguished).

- Ruling system

When copyrighted works with unknown right holders, etc. exist within a program, it is not possible to obtain individual permission, thus making distribution impossible. In such cases, there is a method of using the ruling system for when the copyright holder is unknown, etc. (MIC 2018).

According to the MIC (2018), the ruling system for when the copyright holder is unknown, etc. is a system that makes it possible to use copyright works, etc. legally, by receiving a ruling from the Commissioner for Cultural Affairs and depositing a compensation in the amount specified by the Commissioner for Cultural Affairs for the copyright holder, in cases where it is not possible to contact the right holder even through considerable efforts, due to reasons such as the copyright holder being unknown, etc.

With regard to "considerable efforts," which is a requirement for use, there did not use to be a clear stipulation in past laws, and the requirement was unclear. In FY2009, the "considerable efforts" requirement was clarified. In addition, to shorten the period of time from when an application is submitted to when it is possible to actually use the copyrighted work, etc., a system where the copyrighted work, etc. for which an application for ruling was submitted could be used even before the ruling was received by depositing collateral specified by the Commissioner for Cultural Affairs was established. In the 2016 revision, this was expanded to neighboring rights, which are the rights of record producers and performers. In the 2016 revision, the requirements for reusing copyrighted works, etc. for which a ruling had been received in the past were significantly alleviated, and on the Agency for Cultural Affairs website, a searchable database for copyrights that had received a ruling in the past was developed. Furthermore, in FY2017, a revision was made to reduce the application clearance fee for rulings.

Although the ruling system has been considerably improved, actual circumstances at the current point in time are such that clearance deadlines for secondary use of programs are still not met, and thus, a resolution is sought after (Agency for Cultural Affairs Chief Cabinet Secretary Copyright Section 2018).

- aRma's search for unknown right holders

If there are unknown performers in a program, broadcasting organizations such as NHK are commissioning searchers for unknown right holders related to video contents to the aRma to fulfill the "considerable efforts" requirement in the ruling system. According to the MIC (2018), concretely, the procedure is as follows.

First, if a broadcasting organization is carrying out secondary use of a past program, a provisional application for secondary use is submitted to the aRma. The aRma checks the list of performers sent to them and provides a response as to whether the performer is under the aRma's management. Afterward, when an actual application is submitted by the broadcasting organization, the aRma initiates a search if there is a request to search for unknown right holders regarding performers outside of aRma's management.

Search work is performed in a manner that fulfills the ruling system's requirement of "considerable efforts" and is carried out in 14 days, including listing on the aRma website.

If contact information for the right holder is found as a result of the search, solicitation for delegation of rights is carried out by aRma first. If aRma is able to obtain delegation, consent for secondary use is conducted through aRma. In this case, aRma's scope of delegation is expanded, and the effects of the promotion of centralization management arise. On the other hand, if delegation could not be obtained despite carrying out solicitation of the delegation of rights, aRma notifies the broadcasting organization to that effect, and the broadcasting organization may renegotiate with the right holder afterward.

- Trans-Pacific Partnership Agreement (hereinafter referred to as TPP)

In June 2018, a law related to the TPP was established. As such, the Copyright Act was also revised, and protection was extended from 50 years after death to 70 years (Agency for Cultural Affairs 2015). Copyrighted works with unknown right holders could be used after rights expire and extinguish, but due to a longer protection period, the period during which the right holder is unknown also becomes longer.

The "wartime extension" for copyrighted works was not dissolved even in the TPP, and a period of 10 years and some months is added to the protection period (Ootaka 2018). There remains an issue where, even if the author is the same, there is a mix of works with rights that have expired and those that have not yet expired, depending on when the work was released.

3.3 *Works for Which Clearance Judgment is Difficult*

In clearing the rights of broadcast programs, there are cases where it is difficult to judge whether rights will be infringed. When there is the possibility of rights infringement, depending on how a program is used, the program ultimately cannot be distributed.

For example, there are parodies (moral rights of authors), such as the so-called accompanying copyrighted works and works that take human rights into consideration, such as the right of publicity and privacy. In the case of accompanying copyrighted works, it is possible to move forward if there is an exception where there are no rights depending on the purpose of how a work is used. The right of publicity, privacy, and parody (moral right of the author) requires individual and concrete approaches.

In addition, even cases that are referred to as "pseudo copyrights" may be one where judgment on copyright clearance is difficult (Agency for Cultural Affairs 2015).

- Accompanying copyrighted works

As stated in the item in Sect. 2 entitled 2012 Revision of the Copyright Act, in cases where a copyrighted work is unintentionally reproduced in the background of a program video, there was the possibility of it being considered an infringement of copyright. However, the provision related to accompanying copyrighted works (use of incidental copyrighted works) was clarified (Agency for Cultural Affairs 2012a).

> When creating a copyrighted work based on a method of shooting photos, etc., other copyrighted items that are incidental subjects of the work (incidentally included works) because they are difficult to be separate from the item that is a subject of the said copyrighted work (copyrighted work of photography) may be copied or translated along the work being created, which shall not correspond to an act of infringement. (Paragraph 1)
>
> Copied or translated incidentally included works may be used along with the use of the copyrighted work of photograph, which shall not correspond to an act of infringement. (Paragraph 2)

Examples of acts of use of copyrighted works subject to this Article are as follows.

- Cases where, upon shooting a photograph, a poster or drawing is unintentionally captured in a small size in the background, in addition to the photograph's originally intended subject.
- Cases where, upon shooting, a video recording of a street scene, posters, drawings, and music that was playing in the street are also recorded, in addition to the video's originally intended subject.
- Cases where a photograph containing a small image of a drawing in the background is featured on a blog.
- Cases where a video containing posters, drawings, and music that was playing on the street is broadcast or shown on the internet.

On the other hand, the following acts of use of copyrighted acts are not subject to this Article; in principle, permission from the copyright holder is required.

- Cases where a photograph of a poster or drawing shot as the originally intended subject of the photograph is featured on a blog.

- Cases where a drawing is set up in the set of a TV drama with the intention of actively showing it to viewers in an important scene, and a video recording of this scene is broadcast or shown on the internet.
- Cases where a sticker of a photo in which a cartoon character appears incidentally to the originally intended subject of the photo is sold, under the condition of using the cartoon character to attract customers.

By having these concrete examples, which are given by the Agency for Cultural Affairs (2012b), it has become easier for persons in charge of producing programs and those in charge of secondary use to make judgments based on having grounds, and it has also become possible for work to progress more smoothly. Even so, there are many puzzling cases that do not fall under the examples described here.

- Portrait rights

Portrait rights refer to the "freedom to not have one's appearance or figure photographed or published, without consent and due cause" (Umeda and Nakagawa 2016). This is a right that has come to be recognized in court, as a type of human right that is constitutionally guaranteed to everyone.

The judgment criteria for infringement of portrait rights by the Supreme Court is "infringement of moral interests of the photographed person exceeds the allowable limit in social life," and cases where such infringement that exceeds this is considered as being "unlawful."

Cases that formally fall under infringement of portrait rights but that are "within the allowable limit" of the photographed person in terms of social acceptance are permitted as a legitimate act of expression.

Judgment as to whether an infringement is "within the scope of the allowable limit" is made by comprehensively considering the following.

① Social status of the photographed person, ② activity contents of the photographed person, ③ photography location, ④ photography purpose, ⑤ photography condition, ⑥ necessity of photograph, etc. (Judgment made by Supreme Court dated November 10, 2005) (Wakayama Curry Poisoning Incident/appeal hearing).

Occasionally, there are cases involving secondary use of old programs, where understanding regarding performance was obtained at the time of the program's broadcast, but now, the performer is embarrassed about his/her past appearance and does not want it to be shown. There are also cases where performers regret having performed, due to a change in circumstances after the program's broadcast. It is not possible to predict whether such opinions will arise unless contact is made with performers for permission for secondary use.

(Portrait rights may also be referred to as publicity rights. Publicity rights are "rights to use a portrait, etc. of a celebrity for the sole purpose of attracting customers to promote sales of a product, etc." Although publicity rights should also be processed individually, assumptions can be made beforehand to some extent in the clearance of secondary use.)

- Publicity rights

On the other hand, publicity rights are "rights or benefits to not have facts or information about one's personal life that he/she does not want others to know published" (Umeda and Nakagawa 2016). Similar to portrait rights, privacy rights are rights that have come to be recognized in court, as a type of human right that is constitutionally guaranteed to everyone.

Not all information in one's personal life is protected; rather, the four requirements below must be satisfied.

(1) There is a circumstance such that the information is perceived as a fact or can be perceived as a fact of one's personal life, (2) using the sense of a general person as a standard, the fact is one that the person does not want to be publicized, (3) the fact is not yet generally known, (4) the person will suffer mental anguish (displeasure, insecurity) based on the fact becoming publicized (Tokyo District Court Judgment dated September 28, 1964).

Additionally, in recent years, the "right to control one's personal information" has started to become recognized (MIC 2009). According to the MIC (2009), to make protection of personal information sufficient in a society where informatization has been progressing, privacy rights, which had been understood in the past as a passive right, should be understood more actively and aggressively, but there are also various views regarding this.

There are cases where a cooperator from whom understanding had been obtained at the time of a program broadcast does not permit secondary use since there is the possibility of infringement of privacy, due to changes over the years. For example, among programs related to the medical field, there were some in the past where the patient's name and disease name could be deciphered in scenes where there is a close-up of a medical record. However, there are now requests from the patient's family and involved physicians to not publicize this scene in secondary use of the program. Such requests would be unknown unless permission was sought after for secondary use of the program.

- Parody (moral right of author)

Finally, parodies, variations of a song, etc., are often used in various shows and are difficult to make judgments regarding in copyright clearance. Even among moral rights of authors, they are particularly related to the right to indicate the name and right to maintain integrity (Saito 2007).

In centralized management by copyright management organizations, moral rights of authors are not included in trust contents. In other words, permission must be obtained individually from lyricists and composers.

However, in terms of their properties, parodies and variations of songs are not used upon obtaining permission from the copyright holder of the original copyrighted work, and there are also no copyright holders who agree beforehand to altering their song to make it more amusing. Therefore, it is difficult to judge whether permission should be obtained in distributing the parody or song variation.

In the first place, what are parodies anyway? According to the Agency for Cultural Affairs (2013), there is no definition of parody in the Copyright Act, nor are there any individual restricted rights provisions that explicitly target use as a parody of a copyrighted work. Even among judicial precedents, there are none that explicitly hold the definition of a parody. When there is use as a parody, it is difficult to clarify the scope of conditions that can be generally considered.

It is difficult to anticipate beforehand whether there will be risks in the secondary use of a program containing a parody.

- Pseudocopyright

As an issue encountered frequently in copyright clearance of broadcast programs, there is "pseudocopyrights" (Fukui 2010). They are considered as "cases that are, in reality, handled (inevitably) in a close manner to copyrights, even though they are theoretically not copyrights." The following are examples.

- Portrait rights of pets (no rights to begin with)
- "Prohibited photography" of buildings and artwork (rights extinguished) owned by shrines and temples
- Conducting as if a character has rights even after extinguishment of rights.

Discussions are being conducted regarding the abovementioned portrait rights, privacy, and parodies as to a clear definition of rights and specifying individual restricted rights provisions. As of the current point in time, these have not been decided on, and our only choice is for broadcasting organizations to obtain permission individually from copyright holders and make judgments.

For pseudocopyrights, it is dependent on users increasing their literacy and being able to conduct negotiations appropriate with other parties. If users are not used to negotiation, this may lead to rejection of use, which leads in turn to calling off secondary use of programs or paying an unnecessary usage fee.

Compared with a state where risks cannot be predicted, for cases in which copyright clearance costs have increased enormously, or where the deadline could not be met because of the number of days it takes for clearance, a judgment to not distribute that program is often made. These are cases that hinder smooth use in terms of actual work.

4 The "wall" of Copyright Clearance and the Digital Network Era

As we saw in the preceding Section 11.3, despite revisions to laws and development of systems, such solutions do not keep up with the speed of occurrence of issues, and cases where copyright clearance itself hinders smooth use definitely exist. In particular, the difficult cases that makeup approximately 10–20% of all copyright clearance in secondary use overall are thought to cause impacts on overall use.

Does this signify that there are obstructive factors to smooth use that are unique to the digital network era (Fukui 2018)?

Although there are thought to be hints to solving this question, the state is as explained by Takahiro Kojima (Associate Professor, Chukyo University Faculty of Law) (2014) in "2-2 Legal Nature of Extended Collective Licensing: Relationship with Rights Restrictions, etc." in *Report on Investigative Research Concerning Extended Collective Licensing* (FY2015 Agency for Cultural Affairs Commissioned Projects) (Software Information Center 2017).

> Under the market's failure theory, in reality, failures arise in the market, and even in cases where recognizing use of copyrighted works, etc. is socially desirable, it is not justified to restrict exclusive rights across the board if the incentive of the copyright holder to create is excessively impaired due to recognition of use.
>
> However, when digitizing a large number of copyrighted works, such as building and publishing digital archives, or when conducting a business of presenting a large number of copyrighted works to users through the internet, copyright clearance of a massive number of copyrighted works, etc. is necessary, resulting in a large possibility of increased transaction costs. In addition, when the percentage of copyrighted works, etc. with unknown right holders increases, there is the risk of copyright clearance fees increasing drastically. In such conditions, there is the possibility that the problem of anticommons will arise that will prohibit the use of works, due to many rights being duplicated and set for specific works. In addition, in cases where relationship-specific investments are made regarding use of copyrighted works, etc. and it is forecast that these will become sunk costs during the breakdown of negotiations, the position of users of copyrighted works, etc. in negotiations may fall and licensing fees may become excessive (hold-up).
>
> Furthermore, as many rights are involved, even if individual licensing fees are low, there may be the problem of licensing fees becoming expensive as a whole due to an accumulation of such individual fees (royalty stacking).

Mass digitization differs from the scale of multiuse of broadcast programs, since it refers to digitization of a large number of copyrighted works at libraries, etc. The conditions explained here are well known in the intellectual property industry, which revolves mainly around patents. However, similar kinds of difficulties are anticipated when distributing many copyrighted works and performers that are contained in broadcast programs and copyright clearance such as records, as well as in simultaneous broadcast and distribution, which may occur in the future.

As a result, obstructive factors associated with the expansion and digitization of video distribution services are examined even in *Report by Review Committee on Promoting the Production and Distribution of Broadcast Contents* (July 2018, Information and Communications Policy sectional meeting of the Information and Communications Council) (MIC 2018) and through restricted rights provisions or some kind of a system, such as mandatory permission or centralized management of rights, a reduction in costs related to copyright clearance is requested.

Thus, let's now organize the trends and proposed measures in terms of actual copyright clearance work for broadcast programs.

4.1 Trends in Contents in Actual Copyright Clearance Work

When considering multiuse of broadcast programs, there is the program itself as well as distribution in the form of clips of a program after being edited by the broadcasting station. Since it is necessary to carry out massive amounts of copyright clearance in the simultaneous (regular) broadcast and distribution era in the future, we will compare the extent of difficulties in making judgments, surveying, and clearance in the current state, with a focus on distribution cases.

When the distribution timing is immediately after broadcast, such as to catch up on a missed show, the clearance period is extremely short. In the case of archive distribution, it is possible to spare a certain period of time for clearance. Also, depending on whether a program is old or new, there are also differences in difficult issues. As such, a matrix on distributed program contents is created below. If we anticipate that simultaneous (and regular) broadcast and distribution will be offered in the future, there is the possibility that all of the multiple program types will be included. By combining characteristic measures for each of the content types, it is possible to overcome the "wall."

As indicated in the matrix in Fig. 4, in "simultaneous (and regular) broadcast and distribution" that is anticipated in the future, it is likely that contents that include all of the types in (1)–(6) will be broadcast and distributed. Unless we have a method for resolving the many challenges that are apparent in each of the contents, "copyright

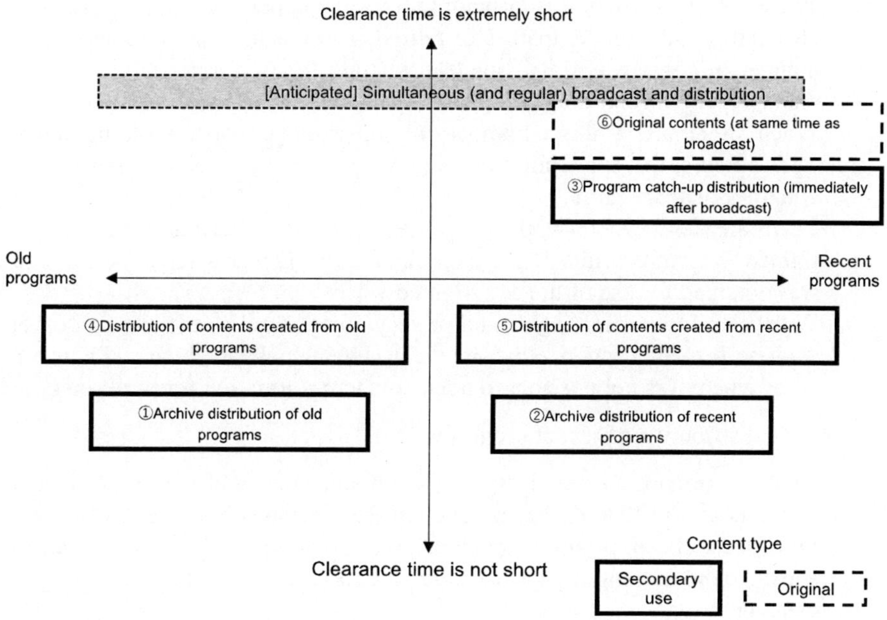

Fig. 4 Matrix based on distributed content type and clearance time

Legend ◎ : Extremely difficult ○ : Difficult

Type of distributed contents			Not managed (Performances)	Not managed (Records)	Copyrighted works, etc. with unknown right holders	Accompanying	Portrait rights	Privacy	Parodies
Secondary use	Broadcast programs	①Archives (old programs)	◎	◎	◎	◎	◎	◎	○
		②Archives (recent programs)	◎	◎	○	○	○	○	○
		③Catch-up (immediately after broadcast)	◎	◎	○	○	◎	◎	◎
	Contents	④Created from old programs	◎	◎	◎	◎	◎	◎	◎
		⑤Created from recent programs	◎	◎	◎	◎	○	○	○
Original		⑥Same time as broadcast	◎	◎	○	○	◎	◎	◎

Fig. 5 Reason and level of difficulty of "wall" for each distributed content type

clearance of undefined copyrighted works, etc. in comprehensive use of a large number of contents" will not be realized.

Figure 5 shows the wall for each type of distributed content.

The following is an explanation of obstructive factors, such as clearance difficulties, for each type of "wall."

(1) Archive distribution of old programs

- There are cases where it is difficult to track down performers, as he/she has changed production companies or retired. There is also an extremely large number of cases where it is unclear whether the performer is outside the management of recording companies, as there is no song information.
- When there are a large number of copyrighted works with unknown right holders, the application costs (work burden, fee) for a ruling by the commissioner are large.
- There are cases where work was judged as being an accompanying copyrighted work at the time of production, but it is unclear whether permission was obtained for use of the copyrighted work.
- With regard to portrait rights and privacy, there may be people who do not want performance video, etc. from the past being published today. There are cases where it is not possible to track contact information for performers.

(2) Archive distribution of recent programs

- Rights information is relatively easy to obtain, and it is also easy to conduct hearings on the state during production from persons in charge of production. Since the program is archived, a clearance period is established to some extent, making it possible to reduce risks through attentive copyright clearance.
- Even so, since there are many songs that cannot be distributed as they were within the scope of a blanket agreement at the time of broadcast as well as

performances and records that are outside management, close investigations are necessary. If there is no budget to pay expensive usage fees, etc. for music that is not under management, it is muted or replaced with other music, but this also incurs editing costs.

(3) Catch-up distribution of programs (immediately after broadcast)

- Rights information is accurate, due to the fact that the timing is immediately after broadcast, and there are also cases where close information regarding the persons in charge of program production and persons in charge of rights are shared, depending on the station, making it possible to preliminarily avoid copyrighted works for which distribution is difficult.
- Even so, individual clearance of works not under management is necessary.
- If it is discovered that it is not possible to acquire permission for distribution due to portrait rights, privacy, etc. at a point in time when the full package media for broadcast has been completed, there may be no time for copyright clearance or editing (cutting, mosaic, muting). In such cases, measures such as using a black screen to cover the corresponding scene at the time of distribution are carried out.
- In variety of programs, there are cases where parodies and song variations are broadcast based on judgments made at the time of production but are edited for distribution.

(4) Distribution of contents created from old programs

- Fundamentally, obstructive factors are the same as for the distribution of archives of old programs.
- There may be cases where, even in scenes where minimal accompanying copyrighted works can be seen, even after shortening and editing the program, such works appear clearly in the original program, or the copyrighted work was used upon obtaining permission. If adopted differently from the original program, it is necessary to pay attention to rights.
- Due to secular change, such as different social landscapes since the time of broadcast, judgments regarding parodies and song variations may change as well.

(5) Distribution of contents created from recent programs

- Fundamentally, obstructive factors are the same as for the distribution of archives of recent programs.
- It is necessary to pay attention to differences with the original program that is unique to cases where the program was shortened or edited.

(6) Original contents that are broadest at the same time as broadcasting

- In the past 6 months, the number of cases that are completely different from past secondary use of programs has been increasing. Although related to broadcast, they are not secondary use; rather, they are original contents for distribution. For example, say that the same contents as a live broadcast are distributed. In many cases, when distributing, the period during which commercials appear on TV turns into a dark screen. However, on new platforms, there are cases where original contents are distributed even during the commercial periods. When this happens, viewers are not able to leave. At the same time, various original contents have been on the rise, such as spinoffs and skits that could not be broadcast. For these, it is important to check the rights from an early stage, such as during the manuscript stage, before production of broadcast and distributed contents. This is because it will be too late even if rights are ascertained immediately before distribution. To put it another way, risks are minimal if proper attention is given beforehand.

4.2 Measures for Issues of Each Content Type

As mentioned above, we know that there are trends in obstructive factors for each distribution content type. What kinds of solutions then are suited for each issue?

Let's rely on the commentary "Ideals for Rights in the Copyright Act: Menu of Systems" by Associate Professor Tatsuhiro Ueno in the Faculty of Law, Waseda University in order to organize the state of troubling issues in actual work (Ueno 2015). Here, Associate Professor Ueno analyzes and advocates that because there are too many all-or-nothing-type restricted rights provisions in Japanese laws, the use of "restricted rights & right to demand compensation" should be examined (Ueno 2015, p. 17 and others).

To begin with, rights in the Copyright Act are based on the right to exclude. This means that first, if there is an infringement of rights, the right holder can demand an injunction. Second, in order for a person other than the right holder to carry out the corresponding action, it is necessary to obtain permission from the right holder.

Associate Professor Ueno wants to conduct an examination based on the three models below.

- Able to demand an injunction (Type I)
- Able to demand only monetary payment (Type II)
- Able to opt out (Type III)

- Able to demand an injunction (Type I)

According to Ueno (2015), although this is the principle of the Copyright Act, there are also issues with the ability to demand an injunction (p. 11).

First, although demanding an injunction in response to an infringement of rights is acknowledged in Type I, such a consequence may be extreme as a means of relief. Second, in Type I, the user must receive permission from the right holder regarding all use of the copyrighted work, etc., but such a conclusion may not be appropriate.

In such cases, it is necessary to restrict the exclusivity of copyrighted works, etc. However, when restricted rights regulations are then established and the copyrighted work is made completely free, the right holder is not only unable to demand an injunction in relation to this but he/she is also unable to receive compensation or profit sharing. In such a way, the conditions become such that when there are rights, there is an exclusive right, and when there are no exclusive rights, then the copyrighted work becomes completely free.

- Able to demand only monetary payment (Type II)

Next, according to Ueno (2015), as Type II, there are situations where the right holder cannot demand an injunction, but is able to demand certain monetary payment. Although this is realized in various forms, here we will discuss three (p. 12–19).

(a) Exclusive right + Restrictive rights & Right to demand compensation

Although an exclusive right is granted, this is restricted under certain requirements, and in addition, the right to demand certain monetary payment in the form of the right to demand compensation or the right to remuneration is granted (also referred to as "statutory license").

Even in Japan, the right to demand compensation associated with restricted rights for the copyright is specific within an extremely limited scope, such as a copyright levy for private audiovisual recordings, reproduction in textbooks, etc., reproduction to prepare textbooks, etc. in large print, broadcast in school education programs, etc., reproduction, etc. as a test question to be conducted for profit, etc.

On the other hand, in copyright laws that are common European laws, the right to remuneration is established broadly in place of broad restricted rights provisions. Compared to Japan, it can be said that the rights in Japan are extremely limited. Restricted rights provisions other than those mentioned above simply limit rights and do not establish the right to demand compensation, making copyrighted works completely free, without requiring permission or anything in return. As a result, this signifies that there are many "all-or-nothing" provisions in the Japanese Copyright Act.

(b) Right to remuneration

A method of granting the right to demand monetary payment in the form of the right to remuneration. The right to remuneration as mentioned here is also referred to as "legal right to remuneration," as it is not a claim that is based on an agreement.

In Japan, the right to remuneration is in the neighboring rights system; for example, the right to demand a secondary usage fee for a broadcast, etc. of a commercial recording is granted to the performer and record producer and can be considered a right to remuneration.

(c) Exclusive right + Compulsory license

Method where a compulsory license is carried out while granting an exclusive right. A compulsory license refers to the national government, etc. granting permission instead of the right holder in response to a request by a user in certain cases. It is classified as a "statutory license" when the submission of an application by the user is required. When a compulsory license is carried out, the right holder can demand compensation from the user, and since an injunction cannot be demanded, this falls under Type II. The Japanese ruling system for when the right holder is unknown, etc., is generally considered to correspond to the compulsory license system.

- Able to opt out (Type III)

According to Ueno (2015), in Type III cases, if the user of a copyrighted work, etc. carries out procedures for obtaining permission he/she becomes able to legally use copyrighted works, etc. without having to obtain permission individually from all right holders; at the same time, the right holder can obtain money from the user. Based on this alone, the conditions are the same as for [Exclusive right + Compulsory license] as above, but the characteristic of Type III is that the right holder is able to individually prohibit use. In other words, if there is a request from the right holder to prohibit use, the user must remove this work from applicability (p. 19–22).

Accordingly, Type III differs from Type III in that the right holder has the right to opt out; on the other hand, it differs from Type I in that the user can legally use a copyrighted work, etc. unless there is an individual request otherwise from the right holder.

(a) Exclusive right + Extended collective licensing

The main method to realize this is extended collective licensing (hereinafter referred to as ECL).

ECL is a system not only where permission is obtained for rights managed by a rights management organization if a user concludes an agreement with the said rights management organization but also where such an agreement has an effect on the rights of outsiders (nonconstituents) who do not belong to this organization. In ECL, it is common for the right holder to be able to individually opt out. Unless the opt-out right is recognized, this would be the same as compulsory license.

ECL is originally a system developed in North America. For example, if comprehensive use of an indeterminate mass volume of copyrighted works, etc. is carried out, such as for broadcasting or educational purposes, or for reproduction within an organization, ECL has been adopted as a part of restricted rights provisions, so that such use can be carried out smoothly.

4.3 Examinations from the Perspective of Actual Work

Based on the three types defined by Associate Professor Ueno, let's examine whether they can be realized in actual work. By rearranging the types so that they resemble types of contents, let's try and match the types of measures that can be broadly adopted (Fig. 6).

Legend ◎ : Extremely difficult ○ : Difficult

Type of distributed contents	Not managed (Performances)	Not managed (Records)	Copyrighted works, etc. with unknown right holders	Accompanying	Portrait rights	Privacy	Parodies
①Archive distribution (old programs)	◎	◎	◎	◎	◎	◎	○
④Contents distribution (created from old programs)	◎	◎	◎	◎	◎	◎	◎
⑤Contents distribution (created from recent programs)	◎	◎	◎	◎	○	○	○
②Archive distribution (old programs)	◎	◎	○	○	○	○	○
③Program catch-up distribution (immediately after broadcast)	◎	◎	○	○	◎	◎	◎
⑥Simultaneous distribution of original contents	◎	◎	○	○	◎	◎	◎
Copyright clearance type that can serve as a measure	Type II			Clarification of restriction provisions and rights, raising awareness at production sites			

Fig. 6 "Walls" and level of difficulty for each type of distributed contents and types of copyright clearance that can serve as measures. Created by author based on Ueno (2015)

- Which is on a path to being resolved—Type III or Type II?

According to Ueno (2015), Type III, which centers on ECL, has been gaining attention in recent years from rights management organizations and business operators (p. 21). In other words, for users of copyrighted works, etc., such as broadcasting organizations, there are advantages such as being able to obtain permission from rights management organizations in a single step and being able to legally use all copyrighted works, etc., related to certain services by paying usage fees.

On the other hand, right holders are not only to obtain compensation from users; but also at more of an advantage with Type III over Type II because they can individually opt out. Furthermore, in the case of ECL, if a copyright clearance organization is recognized as an ECL organization, it can manage not only the rights of its constituent members but also of outsiders; in reality, by licensing off of these rights, they are able to collect a usage fee for use of outsiders' copyrighted works as well.

A problem with Type III, however, is that managers who are strict about management of copyrighted works, for example, may opt out for all copyrighted works, etc., of his/her company. Another problem lies in whether it is acceptable to recognize the ECL system, in which it is possible to manage outsiders' rights without permission, in law. Accordingly, the state is one in which discussions will continue to be conducted in the future.

On the other hand, Type II is thought to be suited to copyright clearance of a massive amount of copyrighted works with unknown authors, such as for simultaneous broadcast and distribution.

Currently, in broadcasting commercial records, neither record producers nor performers have the right to demand secondary usage fees. For distribution, however, since it is positioned as automatic public transmission, the broadcasting organization must obtain permission from producers and performers, who have the right to make their works transmittable, which is an exclusive right. Thus, upon investigating whether this applies to works "not managed" by rights management organizations, it was found that it is not possible to distribute a program unless permission is obtained from all outsiders.

However, if committed to an agreement scheme while maintaining exclusive rights as such, it is pretty difficult to make overall distribution of services, such as of simultaneous broadcast and distribution of programs, run smoothly. If this is so, it may be worthwhile to examine the use of Type II's Restrictive rights & Right to demand compensation.

Associate Professor Ueno also explains that Type II has significance as an intermediate solution.

The Japanese Copyright Act has a strong tendency towards all-or-nothing, as its restrictive rights are narrow, and the scope of applicability of the right to demand compensation is also narrow.

As a result, services with social significance may not become implemented in actuality. Even in copyright clearance work, there are many case examples of being torn between two contradictory conditions that arise from this tendency. In addition, even if, for example, an action of a derivative work should be allowed in certain cases, if a rights infringement of such a work is negated due to a flexible interpretation of "citation," the work becomes completely free, without requiring permission or anything in return, and there is no economic distribution whatsoever to the copyright holder or author.

In such circumstances, Type II, which centers on "Restricted rights & Right to demand compensation," is examined as a more active method to achieve an appropriate balance between protection and use of copyrighted works, etc., in a form where only a claim to monetary payment is recognized.

What, then, are challenges with Type II? According to Ueno (2015), one of these is the issue of rationalization of restricting exclusive rights (pp. 27–28). Adopting Type II means that exclusive rights are restricted and injunctions will not be recognized; how this is to be rationalized becomes a problem. Various factors lie as the grounds for rationalization, and a great deal of discussion, such as on the adjustment of profits to right holders and users, will become necessary.

- Current discussions

In the July 2018, Review Committee on Promoting the Production and Distribution of Broadcast Contents by the MIC's Information and Communications Council, Information and Communications Policy Sectional Meeting (MIC 2018),

(a) Proposal to turn right to license into right to remuneration
(b) Proposal to change to extended collective management and enable opt-outs were discussed. However, a variety of issues became clear, and consultations are ongoing due to stakeholders not yet being able to come to terms.

In addition, according to *FY2016 Agency for Cultural Affairs Commissioned Project Report on Investigative Research Concerning Extended Collective Licensing* (Software Information Center 2017),

> In the copyright system, various things, including the extended collective licensing system, can be observed, such as restrictive rights associated with the right to demand compensation, right to remuneration, ruling system, license priority-type restricted rights, etc. It is necessary to examine in the future the kinds of cases in which implementation of extended collective licensing is appropriate.

- Other solutions

For accompanying copyrighted works, portrait rights, privacy, and parodies, it is difficult to judge whether those that are in a program and that are applicable require permission from the right holder. They are not suited to centralized management, since their applicability is unclear, regardless of whether they are Type II.

When summarizing the characteristics for each of these distribution contents, we can say that the issues are (1) how to solve the issue of extremely short clearance times as distribution is carried out at the same time or immediately after broadcast and (2) how to solve issues that are difficult to resolve, regardless of clearance time.

First, with regard to (2), clarification of "accompanying copyrighted works" restriction provisions, "portrait rights" and "privacy rights" is sought after. Although concepts that conform to the times have come to be discussed for each, including the fact that revision of laws related to "accompanying copyrighted works" restriction provisions has been moving forward little by little, each of these topics requires prudent discussions, making it difficult for change to occur rapidly.

With regard to (1), despite there being such issues, when one is forced to make a certain judgment, there is not enough time for copyright clearance as of the point in time of distribution.

Thus, during production, or even starting in the stage of scriptwriting, it is important to eliminate elements with rights risks. Also for this purpose, it is desirable for "consolidation of rights information" to move forward so that the state of rights can be comprehended accurately in a short period of time (Japan Music Data Co., Ltd. 2018). In addition, aim to not use copyrighted works in a way such that you do not know whether it would be an "accompanying copyrighted work"; and for performers' portraits and privacy, aim to acquire permission that includes future expansion, including broadcast and distribution. For parodies, consider whether to obtain permission from the copyright holder of the original copyrighted work or to emphasize freedom of expression, even if you have to bear some risks. It is necessary for production groups to be sufficiently education on these risks involving rights, and for sufficient measures to be adopted, such as establishing clear guidelines for broadcasting stations, receiving support from experts such as rights groups, etc.

5 Conclusion

Since archiving of broadcast programs started approximately 30 years ago, multiuse of programs has progressed together with media changes, and today, we are in a state where simultaneous (and regular) broadcasting and distribution are anticipated. Although revisions to laws and approaches toward systematic development have been carried out, the actual conditions are such that an optimal copyright clearance method for program content distribution has yet to be discovered in our digital network society.

Despite such circumstances, through discussions conducted in recent times, the orientation of several challenges and solutions has come to be indicated.

In the current state, even if committed to contract schemes, the "wall" cannot be resolved, and as a result, services with social significance cannot be implemented, and society as a whole cannot enjoy the benefits of such services. On the other hand, in all-or-nothing-type restricted rights, the right holder may not receive considerable profit distribution for use of their copyrighted works, etc.

Thus, discussions that take into consideration, the assertive use of Type II (Ueno 2015), which is centered on Restrictive rights & Right to demand compensation, is now actively being conducted.

At program production sites, it is desirable for progress to be made with anchoring and education of literacy related to securing of rights.

At copyright clearance sites, there are expectations to move toward a society where risks are identified and agreements concluded while getting rid of large transaction costs, where copyright clearance is a "wall," little by little.

Broadcast program contents and copyrighted works that are contained in programs are all considered copyrighted works, etc., and are both subjected to harmonization of protection and use. It is necessary for discussions to find a framework that incorporates this harmonization in an information explosion.

References

"Age of Regionalism" Video Festival Executive Committee (2011) Introduction to work list of past grand prix (in Japanese). From "Age of Regionalism" Video Festival: https://www.chihounojidai.jp/work/past.html. Accessed 24 Sept 2018

Agency for Cultural Affairs (2010) Outline of the act to partially amend the Copyoright Act (in Japanese). From https://www.bunka.go.jp/seisaku/chosakuken/hokaisei/h21_hokaisei/pdf/21_houkaisei_horitsu_gaiyou.pdf. Accessed 26 Sept 2018

Agency for Cultural Affairs (2012a) 2012 Ordinary session of the Diet revision of the Copyright Act (in Japanese). From https://www.bunka.go.jp/seisaku/chosakuken/hokaisei/h24_hokaisei/. Accessed 26 Sept 2018

Agency for Cultural Affairs (2012b) Development of provisions related to so-called "Accompanying Copyrighted Works" (in Japanese). From Agency for Cultural Affairs: https://www.bunka.go.jp/seisaku/chosakuken/hokaisei/utsurikomi.html. Accessed 26 Sept 2018

Agency for Cultural Affairs (2013) Parody Waorking Team report. https://www.bunka.go.jp/seisaku/bunkashingikai/chosakuken/hosei/parody/pdf/h25_03_parody_hokokusho.pdf. Accessed 4 Oct 2019

Agency for Cultural Affairs (2015) Outline of items related to development of the Copyright Act specified in the TPP Agreement (in Japanese). https://www.bunka.go.jp/seisaku/bunkashingikai/chosakuken/hoki/h27_06/pdf/shiryo_2.pdf. Accessed 28 Sept 2018

Agency for Cultural Affairs (2018a) Act to partially amend the Copyoright Act (Act No. 30 of 2018) (in Japanese). From Agency for Cultural Affairs: https://www.bunka.go.jp/seisaku/chosakuken/hokaisei/h30_hokaisei/. Accessed 26 Sept 2018

Agency for Cultural Affairs (2018b) Law to revise part of the Copyright Act general explanatory materials (in Japanese). https://www.bunka.go.jp/seisaku/chosakuken/hokaisei/h30_hokaisei/pdf/r1406693_02.pdf. Accessed 26 Sept 2018

Agency for Cultural Affairs (2018c) State of registration of copyright management business operators (in Japanese). https://www.bunka.go.jp/seisaku/chosakuken/seidokaisetsu/kanrijigyoho/toroku_jokyo/index.html. Accessed 26 Sept 2018

Agency for Cultural Affairs Chief Cabinet Secretary Copyright Section (2018) Copyright system and related measures: Regulatory Reform Promotion Council 25th Investment WG materials (in Japanese). https://www8.cao.go.jp/kisei-kaikaku/suishin/meeting/wg/toushi/20180424/180424toushi03.pdf. Accessed 26 Sept 2018

audiovisual Rights Management Association (2018) audiovisual Rights Management Association (in Japanese). https://www.arma.or.jp/. Accessed 29 Sept 2018

Broadcast Programming Center of Japan (2000) From Broadcast Library (in Japanese): https://www.bpcj.or.jp/. Accessed 24 Sept 2018

Copyright Data Clearinghouse (2018) From Copyright Data Clearinghouse (in Japanese): https://www.cdc.or.jp/. Accessed 29 Sept 2018

Copyright Research and Information Center (n.d.) List of attachments Attachment 1 Conceptual diagram of collective management of copyrights (in Japanese). https://www.cric.or.jp/db/report/h11_7/h11_7d_main.html. Accessed 26 Sept 2018

Fuji Television Network, Inc. (2018) TVer news release (in Japanese). https://www.fujitv.co.jp/company/news/180712.pdf

Fukui K (2010) Century of copyrights—the changing "monopoly system of information" (in Japanese). Shueisha, Inc.

Fukui K (2014) Infrastructure development of knowledge and challenge of digital copyrights (in Japanese). Inform Manag 56(10). https://doi.org/10.1241/johokanri.56.661

Fukui K (2018) Digital archives and the wall of copyrights/portrait rights (in Japanese). https://www.soumu.go.jp/main_content/000552609.pdf. Accessed 27 Sept 2018

Japan Broadcasting Corporation (2018a) From NHK On Demand (in Japanese): https://www.nhk-ondemand.jp/. Accessed 24 Sept 2018

Japan Broadcasting Corporation (2018b) Special article—backstage interview archives: conveying valuable video assets to the next generation (in Japanese). https://www.nhk.or.jp/archives/search/special/detail/?d=backstage010. Accessed 24 Sept 2018

Japan Broadcasting Corporation (2018c) Special article—backstage jnterview archives: opening up stored programs widely to the public (in Japanese). From NHK Archives: https://www.nhk.or.jp/archives/search/special/detail/?d=backstage012. Accessed 24 Sept 2018

Japan Broadcasting Corporation (2018d) Special article—backstage interview archives: backstage column (in Japanese). From NHK Archives: https://www.nhk.or.jp/archives/search/special/detail/?d=backstage009. Accessed 24 Sept 2018

Japan Music Data Co., Ltd. (2018) Report on "Verification project for consolidating rights information on contents" (in Japanese). Agency for Cultural Affairs. https://www.bunka.go.jp/tokei_hakusho_shuppan/tokeichosa/chosakuken/pdf/h30_kenrijohoshuyakuka_hokokusho.pdf. Accessed 28 Sept 2018

Japan Video Software Association (2018) Graph of shifts in sales amounts of video software (in Japanese). https://jva-net.or.jp/report/videomarket_1.pdf. Accessed 24 Sept 2018

Kanai S, Tatsumura Z (2011) Entertainment law (in Japanese). Gakuyo Shobo

Kawasaki City Museum (2013) From Kawasaki City Museum (in Japanese): https://www.kawasaki-museum.jp/. Accessed 24 Sept 2018

Kimizuka Y (2016) Special: digital networks and broadcasting (in Japanese). CPRA News, 80. https://cpra.jp/cpra_article/article/000352.html

Kojima T (2014) Interpretations of restricted rights provisions in the copyright and the 3-Step test (6/complete): from a strict interpretation to a flexible interpretation (in Japanese). Intellect Prop Law Policy J 45. https://hdl.handle.net/2115/57437. Accessed 28 Sept 2018

Ministry of Internal Affairs and Communications (2009) Protection of personal information by incorporated administrative agencies FAQs 1 Introduction (in Japanese). From Ministry of Internal Affairs and Communications. Accessed 26 Sept 2018

Ministry of Internal Affairs and Communications (2015) Current state of broadcasting (in Japanese). https://www.soumu.go.jp/main_content/000384300.pdf. Accessed 26 Sept 2018

Ministry of Internal Affairs and Communications (2016) Review committee on promoting the production and distribution of broadcast contents (in Japanese). https://www.soumu.go.jp/main_sosiki/joho_tsusin/policyreports/joho_tsusin/broadcas_content/index.html. Accessed 26 Sept 2018

Ministry of Internal Affairs and Communications (2018) Ideals for measures to promote the production and distribution of broadcast contents supporting changes in the viewing environment final report (proposal) Consultation No. 24 dated October 19, 2016 (in Japanese). Information and Communications Council Information and Communications Policy Sectional Meeting Review Committee on Promoting the Production and Distribution of Broadcast Contents. https://www.soumu.go.jp/main_content/000567188.pdf. Accessed 19 Sept 2018

Murakami K (2017) Discussion points surrounding TVs in the communications/broadcasting convergence era focusing on 4K/8K and simultaneous distribution (in Japanese). Inf Manag 59(11):721–731. https://doi.org/10.1241/johokanri.59.721

Nakayama N (2014) Copyright Act Ver. 2 (in Japanese). Yuhikaku Publishing

National Association of Commercial Broadcasters in Japan (2018) What is private broadcasting? (in Japanese). From National Association of Commercial Broadcasters in Japan: https://www.j-ba.or.jp/category/minpo/jba101970. Accessed 9 Oct 2018

Nomura Research Institute, Ltd. (2016) Report on investigative research on management and use of rights information contributing to smoother use of works, etc. (in Japanese). Agency for Cultural Affairs

Ootaka T (2018) "Copyrights in the 1970s" and use of broadcast archives (first volume) (in Japanese). Mon Rep Broadcast Res 68(8). https://www.nhk.or.jp/bunken/research/domestic/pdf/20180801_8.pdf

Saito H (2007) Copyright Act Ver. 3 (in Japanese). Yuhikaku Publishing Co., Ltd.

Software Information Center (2017) Report on investigative research concerning extended collective licensing (in Japanese). Agency for Cultural Affairs. https://www.bunka.go.jp/tokei_hakusho_shuppan/tokeichosa/chosakuken/pdf/h29_kakudai_kyodaku_hokokusho.pdf

Tokoro Y (2009) 3. Services based on IPTV 3-3. NHK On Demand (in Japanese). J Inst Image Inf Telev Eng 63(5), 600–603. https://www.jstage.jst.go.jp/article/itej/63/5/63_5_600/_pdf

TVer (2015) From TVer (in Japanese): https://tver.jp/. Accessed 26 Sept 2018

Ueno T (2015) Ideals for rights in the Copyright Act: menu of systems (in Japanese). Copyright 55(650)

Umeda Y, Nakagawa T (2016) 2nd edition easy-to-understand legal advice on TV program production (in Japanese). Nihon Kajo Publishing Co., Ltd

Globalization

Over-the-Top (OTT) Video Service

Yoko Nishioka

Abstract The Japanese Over-the-Top (OTT) video service market has been active since 2015, and the main OTT players in Japan are the US global players and a domestic mobile operator. The Japanese OTT market moves slower than that of the US and UK because key terrestrial television stations at the center of Japan's content business ecosystem have been reluctant to change existing business models. However, the internet is overtaking broadcasting as an advertising medium, and the initiation in 2020 of simulcasting on both the airwaves and the internet by NHK, a public broadcaster, may spur development of the Japanese OTT market.

1 Introduction

The Over-the-Top (OTT) video service is an important fruit of lengthy discussions and continuous attempts over the past 20 years regarding the convergence of telecommunications and broadcasting. Countries have altered regulatory environments for expected new markets and competed to deploy nationwide broadband networks. In the USA, the Telecommunications Act of 1966 allowed cross entry between cable television and telecommunications and the European Parliament and the Council adopted a new package of regulations for electronic communications in 2002. In Japan, substantial modification of the Broadcasting Act took place in 2010 (Nishioka and Sugaya 2014).

Through these legal and environmental changes, telecommunication carriers started to provide video services on their networks as Internet Protocol Television (IPTV) for their customers and cable television operators started telecommunication services such as telephone and internet access. Those service providers usually own or operate facilities and networks for their dedicated services.

Y. Nishioka (✉)
Faculty of Global Media Studies, Komazawa University, Tokyo, Japan
e-mail: nishioka@komazawa-u.ac.jp

M. Sugaya (ed.), *Perspectives on the Japanese Media and Content Policies*, Advances in Information and Communication Research 2,
https://doi.org/10.1007/978-981-15-4704-1_12

As broadband networks usage grew, streaming videos on the web became popular. Soon after this, we began to see the spread of OTT video service which can be provided on the web without dedicated facilities or strict regulations.

Within five years of the launch in 2007 of the streaming service, Netflix, the leading OTT provider obtained over 20 million subscribers (Marketing Charts 2017b). It thus became as big as the biggest multichannel operator in the USA, Comcast, which has seen its subscriber numbers decreasing. So, OTT has quickly become regarded as the most severe threat to cable companies who have suffered from accelerated cord-shaving or cord-cutting (Accenture 2016). Netflix has continued to grow and surpasses all the top cable companies combined (Marketing Charts 2017a). This dynamic growth of OTT has impacted content industries even overseas and is a clear signal of structural change.

This chapter analyzes the current status of the OTT market in Japan and discusses future policymaking by looking at the nature of OTT services, popular services, development history, and related content and the broadcasting market in Japan.

2 What is OTT?

Easy market entry, even from outside of broadcasting and telecommunications, is a critical characteristic of OTT, which explains well the current rapid global OTT market development. Anybody can start an OTT service site by utilizing cloud services and outside content delivery networks. There are also many solution companies to prepare service platforms. As for regulation, it depends on the country. However, countries such as Japan do not regard OTT using telecommunication networks as broadcasting which usually requires a license. The OTT regulatory environment is often less strict compared with that for existing broadcasting and telecommunications that are regulated as public services (Time Consulting 2017).

Accordingly, old and new players have been competing in the OTT market. As for the old kind, one of these is broadcasters who have an accumulation of know-how of program production and programming. The next is telecommunication carriers including mobile operators who have good networks and charging systems with a large customer base. These two kinds of players, typically cable operators and land-line telecommunications carriers, have been expanding their scopes into each other's business areas in the convergence era. Now mobile operators are also active in OTT.

Netflix and Amazon are examples of new players. Netflix was a Digital Video Disc (DVD) rental service through mail delivery, which has naturally accumulated large amounts of data on viewers. Amazon is the e-commerce giant and also has a huge amount of data on consumer behavior and huge customer bases across countries. They did not have program production functions initially, but now they are known for their award-winning quality original content, often supported by data about their customers' preferences. A well-known example is the original drama series, "House of Cards," which received many awards such as Golden Globes and Emmy Awards (IMDb n.d.).

OTT is one of the many video distribution business models. Video on demand (VOD) has a history starting in the 1990s. The typical business model of VOD has been Transactional VOD (TVOD), that is to say you pay some rental fee or purchase fee each time you view an archived movie or a TV program. At this stage, consumers were often asked to download programs because of slow and unstable networks.

OTT has developed as the next generation of VOD. A typical business model of OTT is Subscription VOD (SVOD). You usually pay a monthly fee for subscription to an on-demand video streaming service. Netflix is best known for bringing the SVOD model to the market. This flat-rate, all-you-can-eat-type pricing has been well accepted by consumers, which has further stimulated the development of the OTT market. Often the OTT market is regarded as an SVOD market.

Advertisement-supported VOD (AVOD) is virtually a free video service thanks to advertisement revenue. This is the traditional model for terrestrial broadcasting. As viewing habits have shifted from watching scheduled traditional television programs on TV sets to accessing archived ones on the net, traditional broadcasters have attempted to adapt to these viewing trends. However, they still want to maintain their existing business model. Also, as OTT develops, players other than broadcasters who might want to replace traditional broadcasters have started to provide internet TV following an AVOD business model.

As the first step for broadcasters entering the OTT market, they typically provide a catch-up service, through which customers can view TV programs for up to 1 week or so after the scheduled broadcasts. This is convenient for customers who miss the original schedule. In the next step, broadcasters start simultaneous broadcasting on both the airwaves and the net. Often later they start to produce original programs for the net.

Now Netflix provides services in more than 190 countries (Netflix 2018). Amazon and Hulu, a joint venture of US terrestrial broadcasters, have also entered the overseas markets. Although the explosion of OTT stands out in the USA, OTT has spread around the world very quickly.

Table 1 shows the five most prominent countries concerning TV revenue in 2016 (Ofcom 2017). TV revenue includes advertising, subscriptions, and public funds. Regarding SVOD, the US dwarfs other countries' penetration rates (84%). Although

Table 1 Key metrics of the five biggest TV markets

	USA	UK	Germany	Japan	China
OTT SVOD penetration (% TV household)	84	41	25	18	8
TV revenue ($ bn)	175	19	28	30	37
TV revenue per capita ($)	539	289	337	237	27
Online TV revenue ($ million)	18,447	2,610	1,233	1,328	6,267

Source Created based on data in "Fig. 46 Key Metrics" (Ofcom 2017)
Data is correct as of 2016. £ is converted to US $ at the rate of June 30, 2016 (1£ converted into 1.325324 US $)

the USA also has a far larger TV market compared with others in general, global players, in SVOD such as Netflix, Amazon, and Hulu, compete with each other, which quickly develop the SVOD market.

The UK has the second highest penetration (41%) and Germany has the third highest (25%). Japan has the fourth highest penetration of SVOD as well as TV revenue per capita. Considering TV revenue and online TV revenue are ranked third, there might be some room for SVOD penetration. The UK has much bigger online TV revenue compared with Germany and Japan, which have bigger national economies.

The UK developed a culture of online viewing of TV programs earlier than other countries. In the UK in 2007, the same year Netflix' s rollout of its streaming service, the BBC, the internationally known public broadcaster with a long history, launched BBC iPlayer. It was a catch-up service provided as a part of domestic public service television without either an additional fee or advertisements other than license fee. At that time, the BBC was the most viewed broadcasting station and website, so that their new service on the web was very well accepted. Accordingly, network usage surged and brought up discussion about network neutrality. BBC iPlayer had a platform-neutral policy and was provided on multiple platforms such as mobile phones and tablets, personal computers, and smart televisions. BBC iPlayer drew much attention overseas and stimulated the development of OTT in other countries.

3 Acceptance of OTT in Japan and the Main OTT Providers

This section looks at currently popular viewing content and popular services in Japan. Figure 1 shows popular video content types (Impress 2018). "Scheduled TV

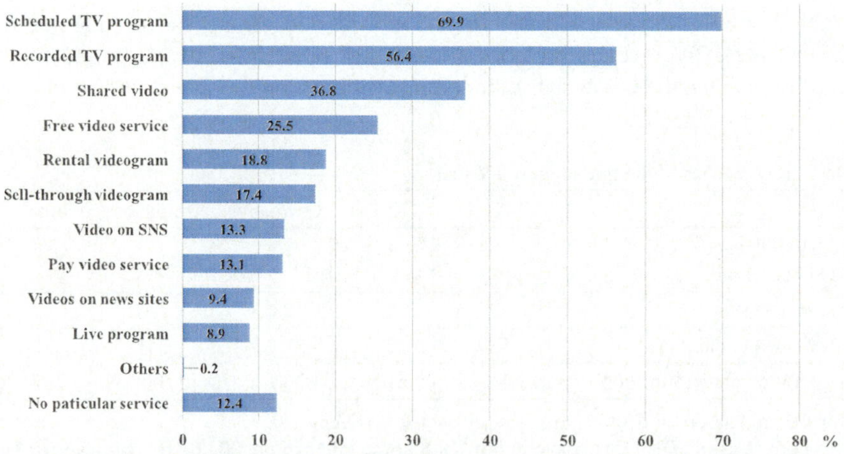

Fig. 1 Video content viewing share (2018). *Source* Created from Fig. 2 (Impress 2018)

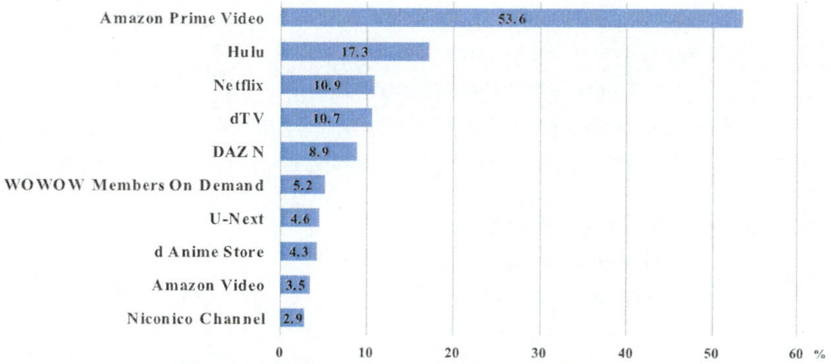

Fig. 2 Top 10 pay video streaming services (2018). *Source* Modified from Fig. 3 (Impress 2018)

programs" are the most frequent way to use audiovisual services (69.9%). The second is "recorded TV programs." Traditional TV programs are still the most popular. The third is "shared video services" such as YouTube. Regarding OTT services discussed in this chapter, "free video services" are ranked fourth (25.5%) and "pay video services" are ranked eighth (13.1%). This indicates that OTT is not yet a common way to watch video content in Japan.

Figure 2 shows the 10 most popular pay video services among people who have used pay video services within the last 3 months (Impress 2018). Among the top five, there is only one genuine Japanese service. The top three are the major US/international players: Amazon Prime Video, Hulu, and Netflix. Amazon Prime Video is the firm favorite. The second is Hulu with the longest history in Japan among foreign players and more terrestrial TV programs than Netflix, because Hulu in Japan is now operated by NTV, a major key terrestrial station. dTV, a Japanese service by Docomo, a mobile carrier with the top share (Ministry of Internal Affairs and Communications hereinafter referred to as MIC 2018c) follows the big three. The fifth is DAZN which specializes in sports content, which cooperates with Docomo for marketing. Japanese services follow DAZN in 5th, 6th, 7th, and 10th positions. Amazon Video, which is a video service outside of Amazon prime is ranked 9th, which shows Amazon's enormous popularity.

Figure 3 shows the top 10 free video services among people who used pay video services, free video services, and video provided by social network services (SNS) (Impress 2018). YouTube is clearly the most popular. The top four services are shared video services. AbemaTV, a linear channel service by a key terrestrial station and an IT venture is ranked 5th. TVer, a joint project of catch-up services by five key terrestrial stations is ranked 10th.

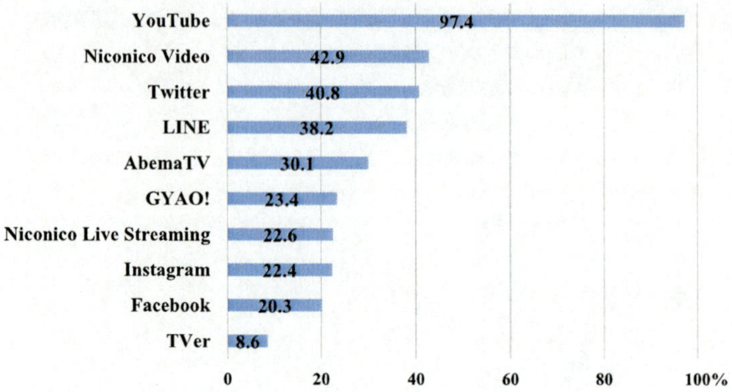

Fig. 3 Top 10 free video streaming services (2018). *Source* Modified from Fig. 4 (Impress 2018)

4 Development of OTT Services in Japan

This section shows how the Japanese OTT market has been developing with reference to the major overseas, mostly in the USA, developments (Table 2). We can observe a bourgeoning movement for future OTT in 2005. IPTV services such as Fios by Verizon and U-Verse by AT&T were rolled out in 2005 and 2006 consecutively. Although those IPTV projects attracted much attention as new competition against cable television, viewing programs on the web started at the same time. In 2005 YouTube started, and broadcasters such as CBS and CNN started to put content on the web.

Similar things happened in Japan. In 2005 and 2006, key terrestrial stations started to deliver TV programs by TVOD collaborating with telecommunication carriers for IPTV.

2007 saw the first OTT services when Netflix started a streaming service with an SVOD business model and BBC iPlayer launched its service (Nishioka 2010). In Japan, Japan Broadcasting Corporation (hereinafter referred to as NHK) followed the BBC after 1 year with a similar service, "NHK on Demand". However, it was a pay-service, because the delivery of TV programs through telecommunications networks was not regarded as a part of broadcasting. In contrast to the massive popularity of BBC iPlayer, "NHK on Demand" did not attract much attention from consumers and had a hard time making profits. In addition to insufficient revenue, time-consuming clearance of copyright transactions was a problem.

Commercial broadcasters did not follow this trend. While they kept their TVOD services, telecommunication operators started SVOD services for their customers and Hulu, one of the major US players, which is a consortium of commercial broadcasters, entered the Japanese market.

In the USA, a giant of e-commerce, Amazon, joined the OTT game. Thus, the OTT market became increasingly competitive. The Japanese commercial market created a consortium, "Mott TV," in order to experiment with a VOD service through the internet for TV sets.

Table 2 OTT service introduction in Japan and overseas

Year	Japan	Overseas
2005	GyaO by USEN Fuji TV on demand by Fuji Television Network Daini Nihon TV by Nippon TV (NTV) TBS Boobo Box by Tokyo Broadcasting System Television (TBS)	YouTube Fios by Verizon started to deliver NBC and PBS ABC and CNN put programs on Yahoo! CBS New Video (Website)
2006	Tele-Asa bb by TV Asahi	U-verse by AT&T CBS started free service through YouTube
2007	Niconico video	Netflix started streaming BBC iPlayer
2008	NHK on Demand by Japan Broadcasting Corporation (NHK)	Hulu by NBC, FOX, and ABC
2009	d market powered by BeeTV by Docomo and Avex (for Docomo users)	
2011	Hulu Japan	Amazon Prime Video
2012	Motto TV (for TV sets) by key stations Video Pass by au (for au users) U-NEXT (for PC) by USEN	
2013		Netflix released "House of Cards"
2014	Hulu Japan bought by NTV	CBS All Access
2015	Motto TV ended dTV (changed from d market) by Docomo Netflix Amazon prime video TVer by the consortium of terrestrial key stations	SlingTV Amazon "Transparent" received major awards
2016	AbemaTV by CyberAgent and TV Asahi DAZN by Perform Group	Fox started simulcasting DirecTV Now
2017		YouTube TV CBS All Access delivered original series Hulu with Live TV
2018	dTV Channel by Docomo Paravi by TBS, wowow, TV Tokyo, Nikkei Shimbun, Dentsu, Hakuhodos Amazon Prime Video Channel	

Source Created by the author

In 2013, *House of Cards* became a big hit and signaled a change in the global TV industry. However, the Japanese market remained still. Hulu in Japan had a hard time in a market dominated by terrestrial TV programs. NTV, one of the key terrestrial stations took over Hulu in Japan.

2015 was a significant year for OTT in Japan. dTV made their service open to consumers including non-Docomo users and aggressively marketed their service.

They recommend mobile customers at stores to subscribe to dTV as an option for a mobile contract for about 4 US dollars, which has been successful in boosting the number of subscribers. The two major US players, Netflix and Amazon, finally entered the Japanese market in 2015. These foreign players' entry seemingly stimulated Japanese broadcasters. Japanese key terrestrial stations finally started to consider PCs as terminals to watch TV programs instead of TV sets. They abandoned Mott TV and started TVer, which is primarily a catch-up service for PCs. The TVer project is supposed to provide better usability and to prevent illegal viewing, rather than to aggressively seek profits. However, the Japanese market became very active in 2015.

The following year, AbemaTV was started as a joint effort between an IT venture and a key terrestrial station. It has provided many original channels based on the traditional ad-supported terrestrial TV business model. It drew significant attention as a different business model from typical OTT services. Also, DAZN, a specialized sports OTT service, was started by Perform Group in the UK as a part of a world launch.

In 2018, more linear programming projects have been rolled out. dTV started dTV channels. Amazon started Amazon Prime Channel. The former sells a package of channels. The latter sells channels one by one. Both channels are mostly thematic satellite channels. Paravi by Premium Platform Japan was launched by six media companies across media industries, including two key terrestrial stations, one national newspaper, one major satellite movie channel, and two major advertising agencies. They say it is not only a mere OTT, but also incorporates text services.

Key terrestrial stations started the Japanese OTT market, but they had not been interested in providing TV programs on PCs, tablets, and smartphones, which would destroy existing business models. Meanwhile, mobile telecommunication operators became active in the OTT market. Then, major foreign players entered the Japanese market, which made the Japanese industry realize the global emergence of OTT and spurred terrestrial stations into action. Now there is a variety of OTT providers competing with each other.

5 OTT Market Scale and Growth in Japan

5.1 Overview of Video Content Market and Transitions in the Broadcasting Market in Japan

OTT services will affect and interact with the existing video content market. The following is an overview of the video content market and transitions in the broadcasting market in Japan based mainly on data from *White Paper Information and Communication in Japan* (MIC 2018a). In 2016, the Japanese content market earned 11.6986 trillion JPY, 55.7% of which was attributed to video content, 37.3% to text-based content, and 7.0% to audio-based content. The video content segment,

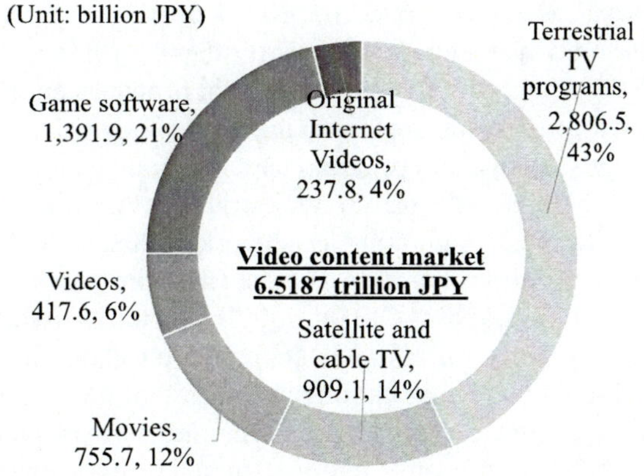

Fig. 4 Breakdown of Japan's video content market (2016). *Source* Modified from Fig. 5-1-7-1 (MIC 2018a)

worth 6.5187 trillion JPY, includes terrestrial TV programs, worth 2.8065 trillion JPY; games software, worth 1.3919 trillion JPY; satellite and cable TV broadcast programs, worth 909.1 billion JPY; movies, worth 755.7 billion JPY; videos, worth 417.6 billion JPY; and original internet videos, worth 237.8 billion JPY (Fig. 4).

TV programs in total were valued at 3.71 trillion JPY and they consist of 57% video content, while terrestrial TV programs constitute 43% of the video segment. Terrestrial TV programs are the core of the Japanese content market, with a market three times the size of the satellite and cable TV program markets. This seems to reflect the existence of five commercial terrestrial networks, and they have a much higher budget than satellite and cable TV program productions to attract a national audience. Besides, there is only a minimal ethnic market in Japan so far.

In Japan, broadcasting has a dual system of public broadcasting and commercial broadcasting. Broadcasters' total sales were 3.9312 trillion JPY in FY 2016 (Fig. 5) (MIC 2018b), and they have remained at about the same level since, while the share of terrestrial-based broadcasters has been increasing gradually. Terrestrial private

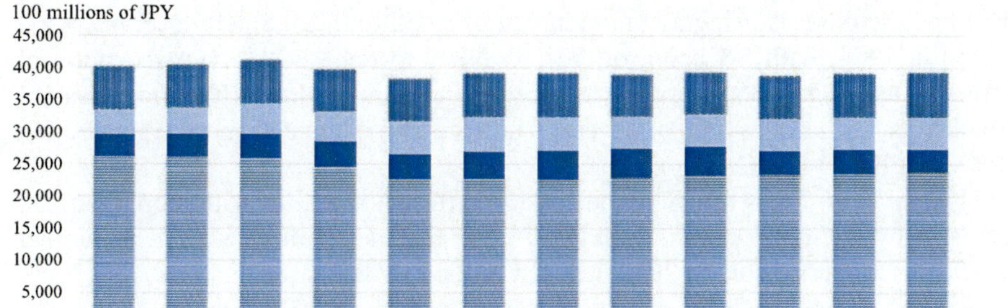

Fig. 5 Transitions in and breakdown of the broadcasting sector market size (total sales). *Source* Modified from Fig. 5-1-7-1 (MIC 2018b)

broadcasters accounted for 60.5% of the total broadcast market in 2016. However, the ratio of revenue from sources other than broadcasting has been growing, averaging 51% among the five key terrestrial broadcasters in 2015. Those broadcasters have tried to make up for shrinking advertising sales with other sales, such as movies, events, goods, and program exports (Yamaguchi 2017).

There are 141 private terrestrial television broadcasters in Japan in 2017 (MIC 2019), mostly operating as network affiliates divided into five national networks led by key stations based in Tokyo. These are Nippon TV (NTV), Tokyo Broadcasting System Television (TBS), Fuji Television Network (Fuji TV), TV Asahi, and TV Tokyo. Network affiliates cooperate on gathering news, producing programs, and selling advertising, although they are not necessarily financially related. These key stations play essential roles in running networks and are highly influential.

NHK is the only national broadcasting network with branch stations, which depends on license fee revenues and operates terrestrial, satellite, and radio channels. Its revenue constituted 17.9% of gross broadcasting revenue in 2016 (MIC 2018a). Thanks to this stable income, they can produce relatively big-budget programs and operate strong news teams.

The total multichannel market, comprising cable television multichannel services and satellite multichannel services, has been leveling out in recent years, as shown in Fig. 5, although it had a peak in 2010. In 2016, the share of cable television among private broadcasters was 16% and that of satellite was 11%; IPTV is included as part of cable television.

Those cable television stations had been mostly small and financially weak because they were initially formed in order to retransmit terrestrial signals with local capital. Cable television business models, though, have been changing. In the 1980s, cable television began providing multichannel services in urban areas and gradually expanded their service menus to include internet access and phone service. In 2016, the volume of internet access services finally exceeded that of multichannel services in addition to phone services (Japan Cable and Telecommunications Association 2017).

Satellite television has two types of platforms. One is using a broadcasting satellite (BS) and the other is using a communications satellite (CS). Satellite services first started in 1984, with BS being offered by NHK to remedy the poor reception of terrestrial television. BS offers viewers free channels, including NHK and terrestrial broadcaster affiliates as well as several paid thematic channels, and the penetration of BS is still growing (Nishioka 2017).

There are two types of CS services using different satellites with more than 250 thematic TV and radio channels. SkyPerfecTV provides both services. The number of CS subscribers peaked in 2012 at 3.725 million (MIC 2018b).

Figure 6 shows the Japanese advertisement market in 2018 (Dentsu 2019). The Internet share of the business was 1,759 billion JPY, which was outgrowing the terrestrial television segment of 1,785 billion JPY.

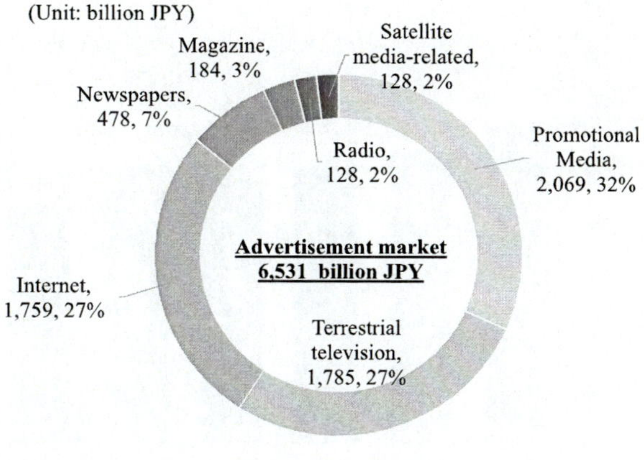

Fig. 6 Advertising market in Japan (2018). *Source* Created from the data of table of advertisement market by media category (Dentsu 2019)

6 OTT Market Sales and Forecast

This section discusses how the OTT market, including both pay services and ad-supported services, has been developing. According to IT Navigator 2018 (Nomura Research Institute 2018), the VOD market in Japan will continue to grow to reach 217.6 billion JPY in 2023 (Fig. 7). The growth is going to be slow, and the market will gradually become saturated, due to assumed reduced sales per capita.

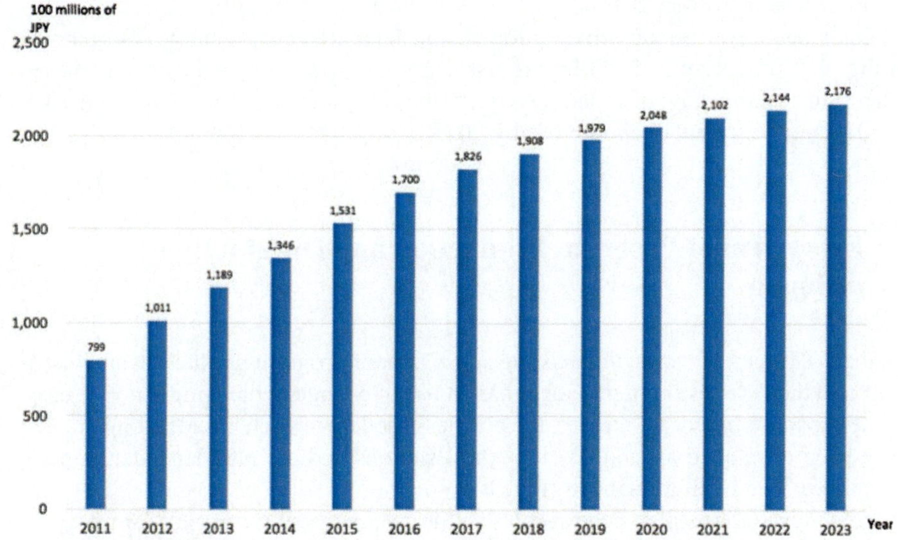

Fig. 7 Video on demand market forecast in Japan. *Source* Modified from Fig. 4.2-1 (Nomura Research Institute 2018)

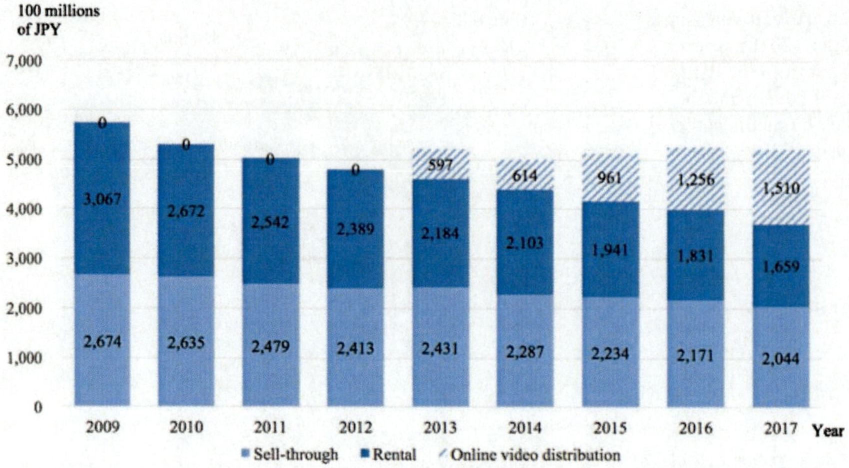

Fig. 8 Transition of video software market scale in Japan. *Source* Modified from Japan Video Software Association, Digital Entertainment Group Japan, & Institute for the Arts (2018)

The Japan Video Software Association, Digital Entertainment Group Japan & Institute for the Arts (2018) publicized survey results of sales of online video distribution, which are equivalent to SVOD services, over the years, as shown in Fig. 8. Sales have been gradually growing and substituting shrinking rental sales, which became close to 30% in 2017.

The video advertisement market forecast in Japan (Cyber Agent 2017) is shown in Fig. 9. The market in 2023 is forecast to be about four times the size as that in 2016. Smartphone advertisement occupied about 70% of the total video ad market in 2016 and will grow to about 90% by 2023.

7 Ecosystem of Program Production and Distribution in Japan

As the OTT market grows, the existing ecosystem of program production and distribution in the Japanese content video market has to change, which might not be easy. In the Japanese broadcast market, the business models of each broadcast media that have been developed around key terrestrial stations and are interdependent among them have been institutionalized (Fig. 10).

First, key stations play central roles in the five national terrestrial TV networks in many ways such as in program production, distribution, advertising sales, and newsgathering. In other words, local stations largely rely on key stations, regardless of financial relations. Network affiliation is very stable, and member stations work together closely and exclusively. Key stations, all of which are in Tokyo, collect advertising sales for the network and produce TV programs that are distributed

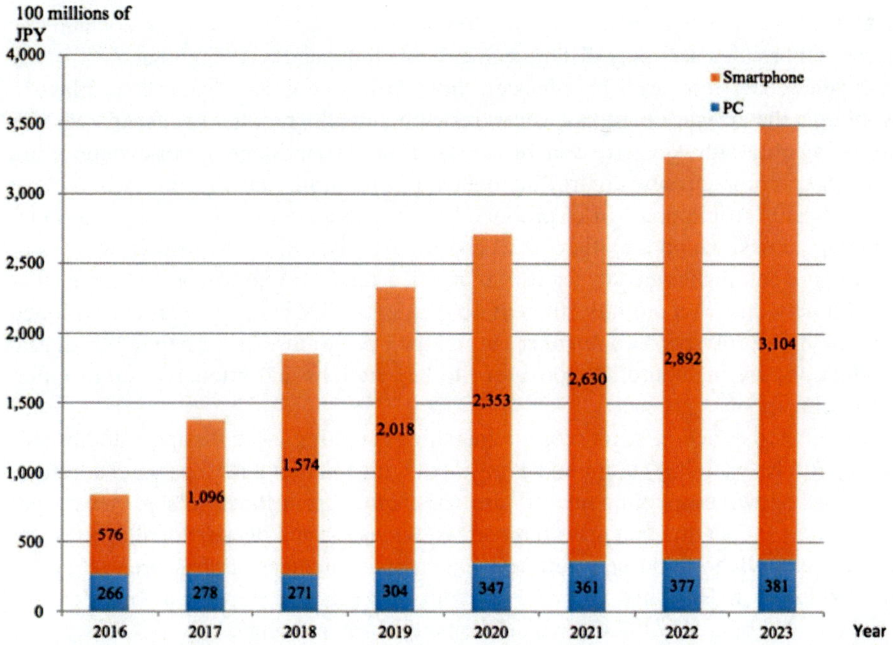

Fig. 9 Video advertisement market forecast in Japan (by devices). *Source* Modified from Cyber Agent (2017)

strictly within it. Local stations simply transmit those programs to local viewers and receive a percentage of the advertising fees earned by key stations.

Key stations produce more than 90% of the programs by themselves. In contrast, local stations produce only about 9% of their programs (Murakami 2015). In fact, most local stations not in the major city are typically understaffed, producing only short local news programs and taking part in programs produced by key stations.

Major BS channels are free channels affiliated with key terrestrial stations and those BS programs often complement key stations' terrestrial programs. Also, there are thematic subscription channels for both BS and CS; of course, they are watched through satellite dishes, but selected channels are sent through cable television systems, which are the main content for cable channels.

Cable television retransmits terrestrial and satellite channels and provides viewers with a few original channels, which are usually low-budget information programs about community news and events such as local festivals. For cable television, retransmission of the terrestrial channels and BS channels for free is vital for attracting potential subscribers.

From the viewpoint of terrestrial and BS broadcasters, cable television functions well as an outlet for their programs for viewers who are suffering from poor reception of terrestrial and/or satellite signals or who face difficulty in setting up antennas. Local terrestrial broadcasters, cable television broadcasters, satellite broadcasters, and key terrestrial broadcasters play different roles that all depend on each other.

Besides, key terrestrial broadcasters hold influence over other related players. Although the terrestrial broadcasters rely on outside production companies for preparing programs, key terrestrial broadcasters hold superior positions over program production companies by controlling the overall program market.

Television programs are often produced by or in cooperation with program production companies, which are often small and financially weak. The primary clients of production companies are key terrestrial broadcasters, who control program distribution for networks. Accordingly, there is no substantial TV program market developed for which the production companies can sell their programs. As a result, TV program productions are in subordinate positions to key stations and often give up program copyrights to key stations.

In Japan, the lack of strict cross-ownership regulation of newspapers and broadcasters allows each key station to be affiliated with a national newspaper. Therefore, TV news shows that commentators are most often from those related newspaper companies. In fact, the first private broadcaster was formed by a national newspaper. Since then collaboration between newspapers and broadcasters has been taken for granted in Japan. Recently, financial relations between newspapers and broadcasters have reduced but the collaborative relationships have remained.

Considering that program production companies actually have practical abilities in program production and that newspaper companies are supposedly better at gathering news than broadcasters, current business customs allow key terrestrial stations to control potential major competitors effectively.

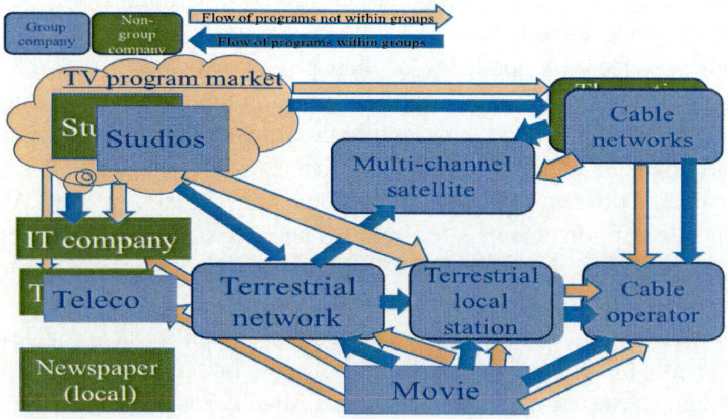

Fig. 10 The ecosystem of the Japanese broadcasting industry. *Source* Modified from Nishioka (2019)

8 Conclusion

OTT services have risen after a gradual convergence of telecommunications and broadcasting industries. The characteristics of OTT services, such as no need of specialized facilities to deliver programs and much looser regulatory environments compared with broadcasting, invite various new entrants, even from outside existing telecommunications and broadcasting industries, who have provided content services through networks and enabled rapid market expansion, even across countries, in addition to shifting from the airwaves to the net as the main delivery channel of TV programs.

The USA and the UK have the most significant penetrations of SVOD, and the major players in these countries have been stimulating other countries' markets. A variety of OTT services have been developing. Initially, SVOD and catch-up TV were typical but now more original content and internet TV with original channels are being offered. Regarding the penetration of SVOD, Japan is the fourth biggest in the world, which is not a small market. The Major OTT players in Japan are US global players and a domestic mobile operator. Broadcasters have been somewhat reluctant to promote OTT services in contrast to the USA where broadcasters have been aggressively introducing new services.

Terrestrial TV programs are the most significant segment of the content market in Japan. Key terrestrial broadcasters in Japan are in the central position in the broadcasting industry ecosystem including local terrestrial broadcasters, satellite television, cable television, program productions, and newspaper companies, which are different from the US situation. Key stations cannot advance themselves without taking care of local stations based on the existing business model. Introduction of OTT, which allows viewers access from anywhere, would largely undermine the role of local stations as local outlets of national advertising, the main revenue for terrestrial stations. The copyright issue is another obstacle for key stations who are interested in offering their programs for OTT. There is no TV program distribution system other than through networks, which makes a challenging environment for potential players interested in TV-like business. The scope of NHK's business is narrower than the BBC's as it only broadcasts on the airwaves; this is one of the reasons why NHK could not take the initiative to develop OTT services, unlike the BBC. In 2020, NHK was allowed to simulcast both on the airwaves and the net. This would urge private terrestrial broadcasters to start simulcasting and might change the climate of the broadcasting industry as a whole.

While the Japanese broadcasting industry moves gradually, the global competition is more developed. Already global players have entered and obtained substantial market share in Japan. Services can even be provided from outside Japan. We have to be aware of both the domestic and global OTT markets and related services and prepare policies for the future.

The research in this chapter is funded by Hoso Bunka Foundation in Japan.

Some description of the Japanese market is rewritten based on Nishioka (2017).

References

Accenture (2016) The rise of cord-shaving and cord-cutting. https://www.accenture.com/us-en/~/media/PDF-30/Accenture-The-Rise-Of-Cord-Shaving-And-Cord-Cutting.pdf. Accessed 14 Nov 2018

Cyber Agent (2017) Cyber Agent conducted video advertisement market survey in 2017 [Press Release] (in Japanese). https://www.cyberagent.co.jp/news/detail/id=20966. Accessed 14 Nov 2018

Dentsu (2019) Advertising market in Japan, 2018 [Press Release] (in Japanese). https://www.dentsu.co.jp/news/release/pdf-cms/2019023-0228.pdf. Accessed 14 Nov 2018

IMDb (n.d.) House of cards. https://www.imdb.com/title/tt1856010/awards. Accessed 14 Nov 2018

Impress (2018) Pay video business report will be released on June, 21 [Press Release] (in Japanese). https://www.impress.co.jp/newsrelease/2018/06/20180618-01.html. Accessed 14 Nov 2018

Japan Cable and Telecommunications Association (2017) Japan cable and telecommunications industry report 2017 (in Japanese). https://www.catv-jcta.jp/jcta/files/pdf/report/catv-report2017.pdf. Accessed 13 Apr 2020

Japan Video Software Association, Digital Entertainment Group Japan, & Institute for the Arts (2018) Video software market and user trend survey, 2017 (in Japanese). https://jva-net.or.jp/report/annual_2018_5-16.pdf. Accessed 14 Nov 2018

Marketing Charts (2017a) Netflix now has more paying subscribers in the US than all the top cable TV companies, combined. https://www.marketingcharts.com/television-78405. Accessed 14 Nov 2018

Marketing Charts (2017b) US subscriber count: Netflix vs. top cable companies Q1 2012-Q4 2016. https://www.marketingcharts.com/wp-content/uploads/2017/03/MC-Netflix-v-Cable-TV-Subscribers-Q42016-Apr2017.png. Accessed 14 Nov 2018

Ministry of Internal Affairs and Communications (MIC) (2018a) Information and communications in Japan—white paper 2018. https://www.soumu.go.jp/johotsusintokei/whitepaper/eng/WP2018/chapter-5.pdf#page=1. Accessed 14 Nov 2018

Ministry of Internal Affairs and Communications (MIC) (2018b) Information and communications in Japan—white paper 2018 (in Japanese). https://www.soumu.go.jp/johotsusintokei/whitepaper/ja/h30/pdf/n5100000.pdf. Accessed 14 Nov 2018

Ministry of Internal Affairs and Communications (MIC) (2018c) Publication of the quarter term data regarding telecommunications service contracts and marketing shares (The first quarter of the fiscal year of 2018 (the end of July)) (in Japanese). https://www.soumu.go.jp/menu_news/s-news/01kiban04_02000140.html. Accessed 14 Nov 2018

Ministry of Internal Affairs and Communications (MIC) (2019) Information and communications in Japan—white paper 2019 (in Japanese). https://www.soumu.go.jp/johotsusintokei/whitepaper/ja/h30/pdf/index.html. Accessed 6 Oct 2019

Murakami K (2015) Organizing future trends on TV Vol.6 2015 January-April (in Japanese). Hoso Kenkyuu to Chosa, June 2015, 39

Netflix (2018) Netflix releases third-quarter 2018 financial results [Press release]. https://www.netflixinvestor.com/investor-news-and-events/financial-releases/press-release-details/2018/Netflix-Releases-Third-Quarter-2018-Financial-Results/default.aspx. Accessed 14 Nov 2018

Nishioka (2010) Innovation and institutions around the BBC: a case study of the BBC IPTV service (in Japanese). J Public Util Econ 61(4):9–21

Nishioka Y, Sugaya M (2014) Japan's legislative framework for telecommunications: evolution toward convergence of communications and broadcasting. In: Liu Y, Picard RG (eds) Policy and marketing strategies for digital media. Routledge, New York, NY, pp 120–137

Nishioka (2017) Stability and possible change in the Japanese broadcast market: a comparative institutional analysis. In: 14th International Telecommunications Society (ITS) Asia-Pacific regional conference, Kyoto, Japan, 24–27 June, 2017

Nishioka (2019) How has the Japanese market responded to global OTT-TV development? In: PTC'19: Pacific Telecommunications Council, Honolulu, USA, 20–23, January 2019

Nomura Research Institute (2018) IT navigator, 2018 [Kindle]. Toyo Keizai
Ofcom (2017) International communications market report 2017. https://www.ofcom.org.uk/research-and-data/multi-sector-research/cmr/cmr-2017/international. Accessed 14 Nov 2018
Time Consulting Co. (2017) Final report: study of procedures for competition regulation for OTT TV. https://www.casbaa.com/regulatory/study-of-procedures-for-competition-regulation-for-ott-tv/. Accessed 14 Nov 2018
Yamaguchi T (2017) Broadcasting market (in Japanese). In: Nomura Research Institute (ed) IT navigator 2017. Toyo Keizai, Tokyo

Assistance for International Coproductions and Overseas Broadcasts of Japanese Broadcast Content

Masahiko Kamiya

1 Introduction

Japanese broadcast content exports were worth about 52 billion JPY in FY (Fiscal Year) 2018 (Ministry of Internal Affairs and Communications, hereinafter referred to as MIC 2020, p. 1). Broadcast content exports have continued to grow faster than projections made when the Japanese government first formulated export targets in 2013 (MIC 2019, p. 3). The government's plan went beyond simply expanding exports of broadcast content by seeking synergy from promoting Japan's various attractions to the world via broadcast content that would lead to increases in inbound tourism, greater sales of regional products, and revitalize regional economies. For these reasons, the government has assisted the expansion of broadcast content in overseas markets.

The main form of assistance is financial support by the MIC, which has jurisdiction over broadcasting. It provides assistance to initiatives of Japanese broadcasters, production studios, and other businesses coproducing broadcast content showcasing Japan's attractions with overseas broadcasters; and broadcasting that coproduced content in foreign markets. This assistance has received greater priority since the formation of the second Abe administration at the end of 2012. The value of exports has risen in tandem with this heightened priority focus.

This chapter traces the background leading up to MIC (formerly the Ministry of Posts and Telecommunications, hereinafter referred to as MPT, prior to the 2001 reorganization of central agencies and ministries) adopting this policy methodology. It also focuses on the policys' relationship with the central government's overall strategies and plans, along with consideration of future prospects.

M. Kamiya (✉)
National Strategy Office of Information and Communication Technology, Cabinet Secretariat, Tokyo, Japan
e-mail: masahiko.kamiya.e8t@cas.go.jp

M. Sugaya (ed.), *Perspectives on the Japanese Media and Content Policies*, Advances in Information and Communication Research 2,
https://doi.org/10.1007/978-981-15-4704-1_13

Section 2 provides an overview of MPT's content stimulus measures before 2000. Section 3 looks back at the policies pertaining to IT and intellectual property that the government as a whole has pushed since 2000 and examines the position of content stimulus measures within them. Section 4 provides an outline of the measures MIC has taken in the context of the central government's general policies given in Sect. 3, especially current measures connected to assistance with international coproductions and broadcasts of Japanese broadcast content in overseas markets. Section 5 investigates the results of the current assistance measures and their future prospects. Section 6 provides a conclusion.[1]

2 The Beginnings of Broadcast Content Stimulus as Industrial Policy

If we trace the mentions of policies focused on the use and export of broadcast programs in past white papers on communications, we find that until around 1990 or so, such policies were limited to measures of promoting the international community's understanding of Japan through international radio broadcasts, measures to collect and archive broadcast programs, and projects for international exchanges of broadcast programs. These were all conducted as cultural projects or promotion for the international understanding of Japan.

We first see the mention of stimulus for broadcast content as an industrial policy in around 1992. MPT recognized the lack of broadcast content (termed "software" at the time) as an issue, given the move toward a multimedia and multichannel broadcasting driven by the emergence of satellite broadcasting and other new broadcast media. MPT, in its 1992 White Paper (MPT 1992), proclaimed that it would launch full-scale measures to enhance broadcast content.

The following year's white paper (MPT 1993), recognizing the same general issue, listed concrete issues: a lack of personnel at broadcast program production studios, the overconcentration of broadcast program production studios in Tokyo, the necessity of local regions to having the capacity for creating and communicating their own content, the overwhelming amount of imported video content, and the necessity of bolstering functions to communicate video information to other counties. To address these issues, MPT indicated the need to study the assistance measures for the production of video content and the necessity to establish IP processing platforms to promote multiple use of video content. It is interesting to note that even in the early 1990s, due to predicted shortfall of content with the rise of a multimedia and

[1] It should be noted that MIC's broadcast content stimulus measures include important policies such as measures concerning IP rights processing and fair production dealings, that the administration should promote alongside budgetary measures. Because there is not sufficient space here to detail the path of these policies, this chapter concentrates on measures directly connected to assistance for broadcast content coproductions.

multichannel broadcasting world, there was already recognition of issues that still need to be addressed today through broadcast content stimulus measures.

Japan's first digital satellite broadcasts began in June 1996. This development spurred broadcasters' expectations for expanded markets with additional channels created by switching to digital broadcast formats, advanced broadcast services created through convergence with communications, and higher broadcast quality and functionality. These expectations were coupled with even greater recognition of the importance of broadcast content. Against the backdrop of social and economic globalization at the time, there were mounting hopes for broadcast content exports as well as early awareness of the related challenges. For example, the 1997 White Paper (MPT 1997) notes the need to promote the arrangement of distribution platforms that will enable the proactive international distribution of broadcast content and the creation of international rules governing the processing of copyrights and other rights in order to stimulate exports.

3 Content Stimulus Measures as Part of General Government Policy

Moving into the 2000s, the government placed content stimulus measures within comprehensive policies to be advanced by the government as a whole. The specific policies were IT (Information Technology) and IP (Intellectual Property) related. Furthermore, since the inauguration of the second Abe Cabinet in 2012, measures to promote broadcast content exports have been placed within national growth strategies. The following sections provide an overview of the transitions in the position of content stimulus measures within each of these policy domains.

3.1 IT Policies

The government as a whole pursued a comprehensive set of measures enhancing the transformations of industry and social structures brought about by information and communication technologies on a global scale that began in the latter half of the 1990s (the so-called IT revolution). The beginnings of this policy direction can be traced back to a point in 1994 when the Advanced Information and Telecommunications Society Promotion Headquarters, headed by the Prime Minister, were established in the cabinet. However, content stimulus measures took off in earnest with the e-Japan Strategy II, which the IT Strategic Headquarters[2] formulated as a general policy

[2]The Basic Act on the Formation of an Advanced Information and Telecommunications Network Society (the IT Basic Act) came into force in 2001. The Strategic Headquarters for the Promotion of an Advanced Information and Telecommunications Network Society (IT Strategic Headquarters), with the Prime Minister at the helm, was set up in the cabinet under the IT Basic Act. The IT

framework in 2003. The e-Japan Strategy II (Cabinet Secretariat 2003a, pp. 1–2, 16–8) emphasized the use and application of ICTs (information and communication technologies), as the establishment of IT infrastructure was well underway through a succession of earlier administrative measures; and stipulated policies aiming for improvement in the digital content industry's international competitiveness and the understanding of Japanese culture by people in other countries.

Later in 2006, the IT Strategic Headquarters established the New IT Reform Strategy as a general policy framework extending to FY 2010. As the country was dealing with the full effects of a declining and aging population, economic globalization, and the shift to an economy in which knowledge produces value, the New IT Reform Strategy (Cabinet Secretariat 2006b, p. 1) acknowledged the country's perilous position: "In order for us to continuously be in a position to act as a world leader, as well as to realize a high quality of life for our citizens in this era of dramatic social and economic change, it is necessary for Japan to implement ongoing reforms which aim to put in place a steady base that will serve to appropriately support a new society." The strategy (Cabinet Secretariat 2006b, pp. 38–39) made the "enhancement of Japan's presence in international competitive society" a priority and signaled a policy for "the strategic promotion of the creation of compelling content aimed at global markets to convey, over the Internet and by other means, Japan's cultural and historical attractions."

The previous year, the Cabinet had endorsed the Basic Policies for Economic and Fiscal Management and Structural Reform 2005 (the so-called Basic Policies 2005) in June 2005. The Basic Policies 2005 (Cabinet Office 2005, p. 1) stated in their introduction: "Whether we will be able to secure a basis for new growth by responding appropriately to the trends of the age, such as the emergence of a full-fledged population decline, a super-aging society and the advancement of globalization on a large scale, or follow a path of gradual decline depends solely on the progress of structural reform during the next year or two." From the Basic Policies 2005, the Council on Economic and Fiscal Policy established a Global Strategy in June 2006 that aimed to bolster the international competitiveness of Japan's labor force, its industry, and local regions. These policy positions demonstrate that the government at the time felt Japan was nearing a state of crisis, as the nation's population declined and aged even as the world was increasingly globalizing. This urgency fostered an attitude that Japan must look outward and spot growth opportunities in external markets. Policies to communicate Japanese content to the world, and to communicate Japan's attractions to the world through the export of Japanese content, fit neatly into this context.

The country has updated its IT policies numerous times since the New IT Reform Strategy. From this point forward, however, the government has generally dealt with measures involving content stimulus within intellectual property strategies.

Strategic Headquarters were tasked with creating and advancing the implementation of Priority Policy Programs connected to the formation of an advanced information and telecommunications network society.

3.2 *Policies Pertaining to the Strategic Protection and Use of Intellectual Property*

Then-Prime Minister Koizumi proclaimed in a February 2002 policy speech (Prime Minister's Office of Japan 2002): "One goal of our nation is to strategically protect and use the fruits of our research and creative activities as intellectual property in order to strengthen the international competitiveness of our industry." In July of that year, the Strategic Council on Intellectual Property—consisting of Cabinet ministers and experts in the field—formulated the Intellectual Property Policy Outline, a broad 3-year policy framework extending to FY 2005.[3] The Intellectual Property Policy Outline (Cabinet Secretariat 2002, p. 4) indicated a powerful awareness of the need to bolster the international competitiveness of the Japanese industry. The outline took a positive outlook on content as a competitive industry, stating:

> As a strategy to revitalize the economy and society of our nation, which suffers from a lack of natural resources and high labor costs,… it is essential to adopt the mindset of a nation built on intellectual property that produces wealth through the strategic creation, protection, and use of music, movies, broadcast programs, animation, game software, and other forms of content.

The Intellectual Property Strategic Program in 2003 (Cabinet Secretariat 2003b, pp. 1–5, Chap. 4) and its 2004 and 2005 versions, formulated under the policy outline, made the expansion of the content business one of the pillars of the programs. They also set as a goal the export of Japanese content and the communication of Japanese culture and the "Japanese brand" to overseas audiences.[4]

The Current State and Future Plan for the Intellectual Property Basic Act were a broad 3-year policy framework that ran from FY 2006 to FY 2008 endorsed by the Intellectual Property Strategy Headquarters in February 2006. The plan (Cabinet Secretariat 2006a, pp. 10, 14–5) placed additional importance on boosting the international competitiveness of the content industry and the communication of the "Japanese brand" overseas, by including as key priorities "content stimulus" and "Japanese brand stimulus." As mentioned in the section above on IT policies, the impetus was Japan's declining and aging population amid surging globalization worldwide and the fostering of an attitude within government that Japan must seek growth opportunities in external markets.

---

[3]In March 2003, The Basic Act on Intellectual Property came into force and the Intellectual Property Strategy Headquarters, led by the Prime Minister, were established. The Intellectual Property Strategy Headquarters were tasked with creating and advancing the implementation of the Strategic Program for the Creation, Protection and Exploitation of Intellectual Property (the Intellectual Property Strategic Program).

[4]The Act on the Promotion of Content Creation, Protection, and Usage, which was submitted as a private member's bill, was put into force in June 2004. Article 19 provides for assistance from the government for export of Japanese content: "The Japanese government... shall introduce attractive Japanese content to other countries, assist the holding of or the participation in international events intended to stimulate content transactions, collect and share information on overseas content markets, and put in place other necessary measures in order to enable promotion of understanding of Japan's culture through content dissemination abroad."

For example, Prime Minister Abe, in a September 2006 general policy speech at the National Diet (Prime Minister's Office of Japan 2006), spoke of establishing a "strategy for Japan's cultural industries" to strengthen international competitiveness and the capacity for communicating information to the world in the areas of anime, music, and other content as well as cuisine and traditional culture. In October of the same year, the Asian Gateway Strategy Council was formed, including the Prime Minister, experts, and other officials as members, to discuss the Asian Gateway Strategy, the aim of which was to convey the attractions of Japan to a broad number of countries. The initiative was conceived from the realization that a crucial issue for Japan's continued economic growth was to capture the growth and vitality present in Asia and other countries, as the country confronted a falling birthrate, an aging population, and other social issues. The Council for the Asian Gateway Strategy in May 2007 put together the Japanese Cultural Industry Strategy. The paper (Cabinet Secretariat 2007b, pp. 4, 6) included such strategies as expanding markets by means of communicating Japan's cultural attractions to other countries and strengthening the competitiveness of export-oriented cultural industries. In the same month, the Intellectual Property Strategy Headquarters established the Intellectual Property Strategic Program 2007, which (Cabinet Secretariat 2007a, pp. 4–5) included a higher degree of awareness than before of international expansion based on the Japanese Cultural Industry Strategy.

In September 2009, a transfer of power occurred from the Liberal Democratic Party to the Democratic Party. The Intellectual Property Strategic Program 2010 (established by the Intellectual Property Strategy Headquarters in May 2010), the first intellectual property strategic program after the change in government, was distinguished by its promotion of measures under the so-called "Cool Japan" banner. The program (Cabinet Secretariat 2010, p. 2) stated: "While Japan's advantageous cultural strength (expressive power), along with its technological prowess, is well regarded throughout the world as 'Cool Japan,' this potential has not been realized in terms of an industry and our soft power has not been fully utilized. Given the rising importance of digital content spurred by the development of digital and networked modalities, Japan must press forward with the international expansion of Cool Japan as a growth industry as well as realize synergistic effects in coordination with other industries." The program (Cabinet Secretariat 2010, pp. 10–22) placed the promotion of growth strategies at the core of enhancing content as a key strategy.

3.3 "Cool Japan" Strategy and Export of Broadcast Content as Part of the Third ABENOMICS Arrow (Growth Strategies)

The December 2012 House of Representatives election resulted in another change of government and the establishment of the second Abe Cabinet. This Cabinet set its primary focus on achieving sustainable economic growth (expansion of wealth) by means of the so-called "three arrows" of ABENOMICS: namely, aggressive monetary policy (the first arrow), flexible fiscal policy (the second arrow), and growth strategy including structural reform (the third arrow). The Cabinet has positioned the export of broadcast content as part of the Cool Japan strategy, which is itself part of the third arrow.

In June 2013, the Cabinet endorsed the Japan Revitalization Strategy—Japan is Back. This growth strategy paper (Cabinet Office 2013, p. 20) listed "promotion of Cool Japan" as a strategic initiative to capture overseas markets and set the numeric target of "Triple the sales of overseas broadcast content by 2018 from the current level (6.3 billion JPY)." The paper (Cabinet Office 2013, p. 20) also included measures for the establishment of a centralized office for more streamlined rights processing, full-fledged content localization assistance, the enlargement of assistance to international co-productions with overseas broadcasters, and securing of distribution channels for Japanese content, such as time slots of foreign broadcast channels.

The Intellectual Property Strategic Program 2013 took the same line regarding content policies. Since then, broadcast content exports have been incorporated in every annual growth strategy and intellectual property strategic program. This has led to the implementation of much larger fiscal measures than before.

4 Initiatives by MIC

In Sect. 3, we examined the policies pertaining to IT and the strategic protection and use of intellectual property undertaken since 2000 by the government as a whole; and formation of content stimulus measures as part of growth strategies in 2013. This section provides an overview of the broadcast content stimulus measures taken by MIC over this time.

4.1 MIC's Initiatives Until Around 2006 (Implementation of Measures Concerned with Rights Processing and Fair Program Production Dealings)

Measures related to broadcast content prior to around 2006 (the time when the government policy shifted from the e-Japan Strategy II to the New IT Reform Strategy) were mainly measures on rights management as it concerned the secondary use (multiple use) of broadcast content and measures on ensuring fair dealings in broadcast program production outsourcing, such as transactions between broadcasters and production studios. A number of research and study groups were held where experts and representatives from the broadcasting industry discussed issues in these spheres. These discussions would continue beyond 2006.

However, it is worth noting that, during this period at MIC, the Telecommunications Software Council (held from May to December 2003) conducted a thorough examination of the basic philosophy underlying content policy. The council recognized there was insufficient deployment of comprehensive policies in so-called software fields, even as IT infrastructure buildout progressed. Based on this recognition, the council (MIC 2003, pp. 1–10) worked out 10 provisions as guidelines for future content policy. Looking at these 10 provisions today, it is clear that as far back as 2003 discussions were held on policy foundations prior to the start of genuine content stimulus measures under the e-Japan Strategy II and intellectual property strategies and that there was a definite recognition of the issues that would become important for later content export measures—such as promotion of the Japan brand (Cool Japan), comprehensive cross-governmental initiatives, capturing overseas markets, and focusing on local regions.

4.2 MIC's Initiatives from Around 2007 to Around 2009 (Recognition of Global Content Deployment Importance with Expectation of Knock-On Benefits to Wide Industries)

As we saw in Sect. 3, around 2006 or so, the attitude that Japan must seek growth opportunities in external markets was fostered within government.

MIC also put priority on discussions from this perspective and launched, in October 2006, the ICT International Competitiveness Council, for the purpose of examining directions for basic strategies on boosting international competitiveness in the ICT field. The council recommended a plan for an ICT International Competitiveness Enhancement Program in its April 2007 final report.[5] The recommendation (MIC 2007, pp. 34–36) included proposals to study the construction of mechanisms to supply Japanese broadcast content regularly to overseas markets by securing time slots on local broadcasting channels as well as study models whereby Japanese companies and local subsidiaries would sponsor such broadcasts.[6]

In this way, examinations of fairly concrete measures promoting broadcast content exports were advanced as part of strengthening the international competitiveness

---

[5]MIC, in receipt of this plan, established the ICT International Competitiveness Enhancement Program in May 2007, and revised the program twice, in July 2008 and June 2009.

[6]The report (ICT International Competitiveness Council, 2007, pp. 34–6) contained many other recommendations concerning broadcast content exports besides obtaining time slots on channels in overseas markets. One key example was the recommendation for the government and the private sector to work together on promoting content exports to regions with special circumstances while monitoring the markets' future prospects. These include regions where the private sector on its own had failed to open up sales channels in the market and regions with import restrictions on foreign content. Examples of joint public–private initiatives include public–private missions on the exchange of broadcast programs and setting up meetings between broadcasting regulators from Japan and the partner country. The program plan noted that public–private collaboration and cooperation is essential, given the many powerful content industry players receive government support, notably in South Korea.

of the country's ICT industry. They also formed concepts connected to the MIC's present-day assistance for international coproductions and broadcasts in overseas markets, such as securing broadcast time slots in overseas markets in collaboration with other industries in the hope that broadcast content exports would bring knock-on benefits to other industries.

4.3 MIC's Initiatives from Around 2010 to Around 2012 (Deepening Examinations on Concrete Assistance Models for Global Content Deployment)

With the rising importance of the "Cool Japan" policy following 2009's change of government, MIC pushed ahead with discussions on content export measures aimed to strengthen international competitiveness and boost Japan's presence overseas. A final report of the Subcommittee Studying International Competitiveness Enhancement (MIC 2010, pp. 20–24), set its sights on bolstering the communication of Japanese content to other countries and thereby raising Japan's presence, strengthening international competitiveness, advancing Japan as a nation built on tourism, revitalizing regional economies, and enhancing the country's content production capacity. The report (MIC 2010, pp. 20–24) gave, as concrete initiatives, the acquisition of broadcast time slots in overseas markets as well as pilot projects for international coproductions. This was the first mention of the idea of assisting international coproductions.

In March 2012, in response to a recommendation issued by the Council for Enhancement of Digital Content Wealth-Creating Power (MIC 2011, pp. 15–27), the Overseas Content Expansion Conference was established as a venue comprising of experienced academics, experts in the field, broadcasters, content production studios, ad agencies, trading companies, related industry groups, for public and private sector representatives to coordinate and collaborate with a diverse membership. MIC and a number of other related ministries participated as observers. The purpose of this conference was to maintain and strengthen the international competitiveness of Japan's industry as a whole, centered on content, as well as to promote the production and distribution of content suitable for global export. The conference saw substantial examinations on the communication of information using broadcast time slots in overseas markets in cooperation with other industries.[7]

---

[7]The conference put together a report in August 2012 (Overseas Content Expansion Conference 2012, pp. 3–5) indicating public–private-led content exports would be significant for their contributions to Japan's economic growth, boosting Japan 's presence overseas, and revitalizing the content industry by removing its dependence on the domestic market. The report (Overseas Content Expansion Conference2012, pp.17–22) contained a wide range of recommendations, including communications via overseas broadcasting media, support for localization, boosting Japan's presence through the use of international events (such as broadcast program trade shows), comprehensive overseas expansion combining the content industry with related industries, further streamlining of rights processing, measures to combat pirated content, help with navigating other countries'

4.4 *Realization of Concrete Budgetary Measures*

As examinations proceeded into support for international coproductions and broadcasting content in overseas markets, MIC started implementing budgetary measures assisting broadcasting Japanese content in overseas broadcast time slots and for international coproductions of broadcast content showcasing Japan's attractions. Table 1 summarizes these early types of concrete budgetary measures. These would lead to supporting broadcast content exports on a much larger scale as part of the country's growth strategy from 2013, as mentioned in the section below.

Table 1 Major budgetary measures by MIC assisting the export of broadcast content (up to 2012)

Year	Summary
2009	• Pilot projects to create broadcast content promoting Japan's local regions and Japan's attractions in overseas markets and air Japanese content in time slots on overseas broadcasters • These projects were not executed due to the change in government in September 2009
2010	• Eleven councils across the country produced a total of 44 titles featuring the attractions of specific regions in Japan, which were broadcast on cable television in China, South Korea, and Taiwan, satellite broadcast networks in Asia, and international broadcasts to non-Japanese audiences by Japan International Broadcasting
2011–2012	• Projects to restore Japan's overseas image after the Great East Japan Earthquake and prevent damage through misinformation by means of communicating broadcast content to overseas audiences. This project consisted of programs in which Japanese broadcasters and production studios planned and produced broadcast content on the recovery from the earthquake disaster and broadcast the content via Japan International Broadcasting to non-Japanese audiences, and programs to coproduce the same type of broadcast content with overseas broadcasters and production studios and air the content in overseas markets • A total of 58 titles were produced and broadcast in regions around the world

foreign content regulations, and personnel training. With regard to comprehensive overseas expansion combining the content industry with related industries, the report (Overseas Content Expansion Conference 2012, p. 20) said: "If the content industry acts alone the potential revenues are limited. Therefore, to ensure revenue in a broad range of fields and the expansion of Japanese content becomes entrenched in other markets rather than being a transitory phenomenon, comprehensive overseas expansion should be undertaken, beginning with the combination of the content industry and the consumer goods industry."

4.5 MIC's Priority Measures Under Growth Strategies Since 2013 and the Establishment of the Broadcast Program Export Association of Japan

The FY 2012 supplementary budget (passed in February 2013) greatly stepped up the amount of assistance provided to international coproductions and to the broadcast of Japanese content in overseas markets after another change in government.[8] This marked the beginning of assistance to projects that MIC is still providing in the present day. The scale of assistance has remained consistent at this level ever since. From FY 2014 to FY 2019, it was given to approximately 250 projects. Assistance has primarily been focused on Asia (and particularly the six countries of Vietnam, Myanmar, Thailand, Malaysia, Indonesia, and the Philippines). Financial support has been provided to international coproductions of broadcast content, in cooperation with related industries, and to initiatives to regularly broadcast the coproduced content on prominent local media.[9] MIC recognizes that international coproduction with foreign broadcasters is an effective way of transmitting Japan's attractiveness to the aired country because partner broadcasters usually make strong effort to increase the quality of coproduced programs in order to utilize their broadcasting time slots effectively; and they have the know-how to obtain high ratings based on their deep understanding of the audience. This model enables the introduction of Japan's attractiveness via content that is highly acceptable in the aired country.

As assistance for broadcast content exports ratcheted up, the Broadcast Program Export Association of Japan (hereinafter referred to as BEAJ) was established in August 2013 as an organization to advance the export of broadcast content through support to a wide range of Japanese industries with broadcasting at their core, known as the "all-of-Japan" effort. BEAJ's broad range of participants include broadcasters, rights organizations, trading companies, ad agencies, and related industry groups. BEAJ was set up responding to a report from the MIC's Study Group on Methods for Promoting Broadcast Content Distribution (MIC 2012, pp. 9–10, 14), which examined exports of broadcast content and opening up new markets from November 2012

[8]During the same period, separate from international coproduction assistance, MIC, together with the Ministry of Economy, Trade and Industry, set up J-LOP, a fund for aiding localization and promotion related to content exports.

[9]Up to FY 2014, other assistance patterns were in existence, such as codevelopment of formats and anime promotion in North America and Europe, coproductions with the Discovery Channel, matching between local broadcast stations and overseas broadcasters, and broadcasts via WakuWaku Japan—a broadcasting platform dedicated to Japanese programs targeting Asian audiences. From this point on, however, the focus of assistance moved to international coproductions with Asian broadcasters and airing of the coproduced content in Asia. Furthermore, in FY 2015, assistance programs sought corporative and collaborative efforts with different industries, regional governments, and other players as well as initiatives that linked the dissemination of broadcast content to other projects, such as the development of sales channels for regional goods. In this way, more emphasis was placed on "all-of-Japan" overseas expansion, such as endorsing collaboration with projects run by other ministries and agencies encouraging global deployment of related industries.

to June 2013. BEAJ's prospectus (BEAJ 2013) states that the purpose of establishing the organization is to aid the implementation of national strategies. It says:

> As broadcast content is a highly influential type of media watched by people on a daily basis, delivering content produced by Japanese broadcasters in a concentrated fashion in Asia and other parts of the world is expected to foster greater understanding and a positive image of Japanese cuisine, culture, and products and to help strengthen the competitiveness of the full range of Japanese products in the global market.
>
> In parallel with this [the export of broadcast content], it is essential to advance the overseas expansion of Japanese products and to promote the international development and growth of Japan's industries as a whole.
>
> The purpose of founding BEAJ is to boost exports of broadcast programs and to leverage broadcast programs to expand overseas markets for Japanese goods and services and to contribute to Cool Japan, Visit Japan, and other national growth generation initiatives that cross industry and governmental agency boundaries. To this end, the participation of a broad range of players is essential.

In close collaboration with MIC,BEAJ assists broadcast content exports, for example, with the screening of proposals for assistance projects from a technical standpoint and the recommendations of plans expected to be highly effective when MIC selects projects eligible for assistance. The association also surveys media conditions in countries where Japanese content is broadcast, operates the Japan Program Catalog portal (BEAJ n.d.) that lists Japanese broadcast content for the convenience of overseas buyers, supports exhibits by local broadcast stations and others at overseas trade shows, and runs large broadcast content events overseas.[10] In this way, BEAJ has played a crucial role in aiding the export of Japanese broadcast content.

5 Results and Future Prospects

What have been the results of the assistance for broadcast content exports under growth strategies described in the Priority measures and the establishment of the BEAJ?

Looking at individual assistance projects, we find examples where regular program broadcasts have increased inbound tourism to local regions, sales channels for local products have been developed through projects coordinated with broadcast programs, and assistance projects were the first step in building a relationship with an overseas broadcaster, leading to an international coproduction without any government assistance. In this section, however, I want to look at the impact of assistance measures at a more macro level.

The first result to consider is the growth in the export value of broadcast content. The target set in 2013 of "achieving approximately 20 billion JPY in exports by FY

[10]Specific events include operating the secretariat of the Japan Country of Honor program at MIPCOM 2016 and cosponsoring the second ASEAN-Japan Television Festival held in September 2017.

2018" was met three years ahead of schedule in FY 2015. A new target was set in April 2017 "to reach 50 billion JPY by FY 2020" (MIC 2019, p. 3). Exports were worth 51.94 billion JPY in FY 2018, achieving the target again earlier than planned (MIC 2020, p. 1). The expansion in export value is, of course, subject to various external factors, such as increased demand for Japanese broadcast content from online video distributors in China. Nevertheless, it cannot be denied that assistance from MIC for the export of broadcast content has had the effect of shifting the attention of broadcasters and related businesses to expanding revenue by pushing their broadcast content in overseas markets.

The second result is greater participation in exports by local broadcast stations including regional cable television operators.[11] An example of this is the increase in BEAJ membership: the association had just 15 member companies and organizations at its launch, which jumped to 91 as of August 2020, many of which are local broadcast stations (BEAJ 2020). We have seen examples, through the implementation of MIC's assistance projects, where local broadcast stations and cable television operators have furthered collaborations with their local governments and industries and worked together to communicate the local region's attractions to overseas audiences.

The third result is the advancement of collaborations among multiple stakeholders, including broadcasters, through the implementation of MIC's assistance projects. There are numerous examples of a consortium being organized by multiple companies prior to implementing an assistance project, and in some cases the collaboration has continued for multiple years. Collaborations take several forms. Some are based on comparatively egalitarian relationships in which all local region stakeholders come together to push the region's presence overseas. Others partition roles like a consortium, with one company primarily in charge of overseas negotiations and another company primarily looking after liaising with local governments. Still others involve a broadcast network that has already delved into overseas expansion sharing its experience and knowledge with other stations forming relationships centered around the same key station in Tokyo. Partnering with multiple companies on initiatives and sharing in experience and knowledge from pioneering broadcast stations is seen as especially beneficial for local broadcast stations with smaller business scales and limited resources in pursuing exports effectively.

One issue that has been raised is the further expansion of export value by the major private broadcasters and NHK[12] subsidiaries, which occupy the lion's share of broadcast content exports.[13] One example of MIC's initiatives further encouraging key stations' global business is a public–private mission conducted in March 2018 to

[11] In Japan, over 120 terrestrial broadcasting companies exist in the private sector. Other than five major "key" stations based in Tokyo, they are located all over Japan. These broadcasting companies center their business around each of the five key stations in Tokyo, with whom they have cooperative relationships.

[12] NHK is the public broadcaster in Japan, called "Japan Broadcasting Company" in English. Its subsidiaries are charged with the international deployment of its content.

[13] According to MIC's analysis (MIC 2019a, p. 2) NHK subsidiaries, Tokyo-based "key" broadcasters, and anime productions accounted for over 95% of the export value of broadcast content.

promote remakes of Japanese TV drama series to Turkish broadcasters and production firms (MIC 2018a, p. 7). This move was taken because remakes of Japanese drama series have been big hits in Turkey and because the market was hot, with exports to multiple third-party countries. In situations like these, efforts by the public and private sectors working together to promote Japanese broadcast content are effective in promising markets and in markets where private broadcasters are reluctant to enter on their own. Furthermore, in places where the restrictions of other governments hinder the export of Japanese broadcast content, the Japanese government is expected to work with the other government.

Now that local broadcast stations are starting to look overseas, they are expected to make export efforts more effective, from the standpoint of broadening the base of exports and communicating Japan's diversity of attractions to the world. Regarding exports by local broadcast stations, the Promotion of Regulatory Reform Council, in its third report issued in June 2018 (Cabinet Office 2018b, p. 47), noted the following challenge: "While the trend towards population decline resulting from the country's declining birthrate and aging population is especially strong in rural Japan. It is a big challenge for community-based local stations to continue providing excellent local content by further increasing their performance in covering and transmitting local information." As one solution, the council stated that broadcasters will need to "operate globally by strengthening international competitiveness and developing new business models." Thus, examining assistance from this perspective is also important.[14] Taking into account the fact that local stations currently do not necessarily have enough experience in and resources for oversea business, appropriate assistance needs to be different than for key stations. The assistance would mainly be more basic, such as supporting the development of human resources for creating internationally oriented programs and deploying such content in international markets.

Needless to say, the recent rapid changes in content viewing must be taken into consideration. After the start of MIC's assistance to broadcasting content exports as the growth strategy implementation in 2013, internet distribution of high-bandwidth content including broadcasting programs has become quite common and more and more people are enjoying content through smart phones. Under these changes, broadcasters are required to find the best way to fully take advantage of their ability to create attractive content and communicate it globally.

---

[14]The Council for Promotion of Regulatory Reform's third report (Cabinet Office 2018b, p. 50) called for "the continuing and proactive implementation of programs assisting the export of broadcast content". In response to this report, the government formulated the Regulatory Reform Implementation Plan (Cabinet Office 2018a, p. 38), which followed the report in stating: "The government will continue the implementation of proactive programs assisting the export of broadcast content." MIC's Study Group on Issues Surrounding Broadcasting, which advanced discussions in parallel with the Promotion of Regulatory Reform Council, in its second interim report released in September 2018 (MIC 2018b, pp. 75–76), recommended multifaceted assistance in relation to broadcast content exports for personnel training and content production as well as assistance for expanding into global markets.

These steps, with the "all-of-Japan" push, are expected to further bolster the communication of Japan's attractions via broadcast content by enhancing and diversifying the country's capacity to export its broadcast content abroad.

6 Conclusion

The first direct step that led to the current assistance provided by MIC for international coproduction and overseas airing of broadcast content was Japan's situation with a declining and aging population coupled with worldwide globalization and the fostering of an attitude within government that Japan must seek growth opportunities in external markets. From this recognition, the government has aimed to promote the "Japanese brand" as part of the "Cool Japan" policy to strengthen the international competitiveness of Japan's industries. Broadcast content was selected as an eminent means to accomplish this because of its inherent communication power. Furthermore, even in situations where exports of broadcast content alone are unlikely to be profitable, broadcasters and production studios were expected to form business ventures with peripheral industries to enter overseas markets. Against this backdrop, assistance for broadcast content exports has proceeded as the all-of-Japan effort involving a broad range of stakeholders and government bodies.

The assistance has resulted in the growth of the export value of broadcast content and expansion of local broadcast stations who began participating in content exporting. Nevertheless, to achieve further growth and convey Japan's diverse attractions to the world, measures are needed to unlock markets and expand the export value contributions by major "key" broadcasters and other important players. In addition to that, pushing exports by local broadcast stations, which have only just started full-fledged foreign businesses, is essential. These steps, with the all-of-Japan push, are expected to further bolster the communication of Japan's attractions and revitalize the economy.

References

Broadcast Program Export Association of Japan. (n.d.). *Japan program catalog*. https://www.japan-programcatalog.com/en/forbuyers/ [Accessed on 31 May 2019]

Broadcast Program Export Association of Japan. (2013). *Prospectus for establishment of the Broadcast Program Export Association of Japan* (in Japanese). https://www.beaj.jp/pdf/charter.pdf [Accessed on 31 May 2019]

Broadcast Program Export Association of Japan. (2020). *List of members* (in Japanese). https://www.beaj.jp/members.html [Accessed on 31 August 2020]

Cabinet Office. (2005). *Basic policies for economic and fiscal management and structural reform 2005* (in Japanese).

Cabinet Office. (2013). *Japan revitalization strategy - Japan is Back* (in Japanese).

Cabinet Office. (2018a). *Regulatory reform implementation plan* (in Japanese).

Cabinet Office. (2018b). *Third report by the Council for Promotion of Regulatory Reform* (in Japanese).
Cabinet Secretariat. (2002). *Intellectual property policy outline* (in Japanese).
Cabinet Secretariat. (2003a). *e-Japan strategy II* (in Japanese).
Cabinet Secretariat. (2003b). *Intellectual property strategic program 2003* (in Japanese).
Cabinet Secretariat. (2006a). *Current state and future plan for the intellectual property basic act* (in Japanese).
Cabinet Secretariat. (2006b). *New IT reform strategy* (in Japanese).
Cabinet Secretariat. (2007a). *Intellectual property strategic program 2007* (in Japanese).
Cabinet Secretariat. (2007b). *Japanese Cultural Industry Strategy* (in Japanese).
Cabinet Secretariat. (2010). *Intellectual property strategic program 2010* (in Japanese).
Ministry of Internal Affairs and Communications. (2003). *Final report by the Telecommunications Software Council* (in Japanese).
Ministry of Internal Affairs and Communications. (2007). *Final report by the ICT International Competitiveness Council* (in Japanese).
Ministry of Internal Affairs and Communications. (2010). *Final report by the Subcommittee Studying International Competitiveness Enhancement* (in Japanese).
Ministry of Internal Affairs and Communications. (2011). *Interim report by the Council for Enhancement of Digital Content Wealth-Creating Power* (in Japanese). https://www.soumu.go.jp/main_content/000125825.pdf [Accessed on 22 March 2019]
Ministry of Internal Affairs and Communications. (2012). *Report on study results by the Study Group on Methods for Promoting Broadcast Content Distribution* (in Japanese). https://www.soumu.go.jp/main_content/000268698.pdf [Accessed on 22 March 2019]
Ministry of Internal Affairs and Communications. (2018a). *Overseas deployment of broadcast content* (in Japanese). https://www.kantei.go.jp/jp/singi/titeki2/tyousakai/kensho_hyoka_kikaku/2018/contents/dai4/siryou5.pdf [Accessed on 22 March 2019]
Ministry of Internal Affairs and Communications. (2018b). *Second interim report by the Study Group on Issues Surrounding Broadcasting* (in Japanese). https://www.soumu.go.jp/main_content/000616359.pdf [Accessed on 22 March 2019]
Ministry of Internal Affairs and Communications. (2019). *Overseas deployment of broadcast content* (in Japanese). https://www.kantei.go.jp/jp/singi/titeki2/tyousakai/kensho_hyoka_kikaku/2019/contents/dai3/siryou2.pdf [Accessed 22 March 2019]
Ministry of Internal Affairs and Communications. (2020). *Status analysis of overseas expansion of broadcast content (FY2018)* (in Japanese). https://www.soumu.go.jp/main_content/000691007.pdf [Accessed on 3 June 2020]
Ministry of Posts and Telecommunications. (1992). *Telecommunications white paper 1992* (in Japanese).
Ministry of Posts and Telecommunications. (1993). *Telecommunications white paper 1993* (in Japanese).
Ministry of Posts and Telecommunications. (1997). *Telecommunications white paper 1997* (in Japanese).
Overseas Content Expansion Conference. (2012). *Report by the Overseas Content Expansion Conference* (in Japanese). https://www.soumu.go.jp/main_content/000170772.pdf [Accessed on 22 March 2019]
Prime Minister's Office of Japan. (2002). *Remarks by the Prime Minister Junichiro Koizumi in the 154th Diet* (in Japanese). https://www.kantei.go.jp/jp//koizumispeech/2002/02/04sisei.html [Accessed on 22 March 2019]
Prime Minister's Office of Japan. (2006). *Remarks by the Prime Minister Shinzo Abe in the 165th Diet* (in Japanese). https://www.kantei.go.jp/jp//abespeech/2006/09/29syosin.html [Accessed on 22 March 2019]